The Secret of

The Discovery of the Holy Grail

Claire Nahmad and Margaret Bailey

www.capallbann.co.uk

The Secret of the Ages

ISBN   186163 309 2
ISBN 13   9781861633095

Cover design by HR Design - www.hr-design.co.uk
Cover photograph by the Los Angeles artist and photographer Claudia Kunin

Published by:

Capall Bann Publishing
Auton Farm
Milverton
Somerset
TA4 1NE

Claire Nahmad's dedication of this book is to
Mik Revill, the Grail Knight

Margaret Bailey's dedication is to her husband,
Pete Bailey ('Wayland')

Acknowledgements

We are greatly indebted to Laurence Gardner, who has opened numerous doors for us through his scholarly series on the subject of the Grail. Without the help of his clarification, particularly throughout his book *Genesis of the Grail Kings* (Bantam), we would have struggled in perplexity with much of the material that was given to us.

We would also like to thank our respective families for their help and support whilst we compiled this book.

Special thanks to all those who have contributed funds to make the writing of this book possible: May and Ivor Nahmad, Professional Classes Aid Council, Pete Bailey, Ann and Geoff Napier, Dianne and Toby Pegler (and thank you, Dianne, for your inspiring discussions regarding the 'crozier of light'), Olwen and Steve Ballantyne and Daphne Jones.

We will always be thankful to Lewis Carroll for his astounding *Alice* masterpieces, which form a beacon to guide humanity's tentative steps as it enters an entirely new perceptual dimension.

Thanks are due to the writers and researchers Anthony Roberts and Geoff Gilbertson for the illumination their work brought to our own.

"*Do you know, I've had such a quantity of poetry repeated to me today,*" *Alice began, a little frightened at finding that, the moment she opened her lips, there was dead silence, and all eyes were fixed upon her; "and it's a very curious thing, I think - every poem was about fishes in some way. Do you know why they're so fond of fishes, all about here?*"

Through the Looking-Glass, and What Alice Found There (Chap.1X, *Queen Alice*)   Lewis Carroll

Contents

5

Preface

This book is about the discovery of the exact location of the Holy Grail, about the mystery of its essence and the wonder of its virtues. The Grail has not yet been unearthed, but we are certain that, very soon, it will be retrieved from its current resting-place. We are confident that it will be given to the world at the appointed time. The current fortress of official refusal and denial that surrounds the Grail, as far as permission to excavate is concerned, is only in place to protect this most holy mystery until the time is right for humanity to receive it. In a sense, its advent among us is not only imminent but has already begun, as we hope our book will show.

Nevertheless, we are entirely convinced that the world will not have to wait for very long! Every outer indication, every heart-borne message from that deepest source out of which Margaret Bailey and I seek to draw, confirms and reaffirms this belief. The Grail *will* be given to each and every one of us who is willing to receive it. No barriers of religion or status of any kind can come between those who wish to partake of its blessing, and the inestimable and inconceivable gift of the Grail. It is a free gift from the heart of those who dwell within the mystery of Love. We call this mystery the Christ essence. You may call it by another name or term. It does not matter. The Grail is yours, it is for you if you want to receive it, and it will not be long in coming. We estimate the time in weeks and months, not years.

What is the Grail? What were the clues that led us to it? What are its properties, its secrets? What is its great gift to humankind?

How can we prepare for its coming? How will we receive its mystical attributes? What will its effect be on each one of us personally, and upon the world? What is its history? How did it come to be where it now lies, and who placed it there? We trust that this book will provide the answers to these questions. Our next book – a sequel to this volume – will focus in greater depth upon the clues which lead to the hidden Grail, and upon its more recent history (from the time of Jesus Christ until the present day). However, these clues, and the revealed architecture of its illustrious history, cannot be properly comprehended or perceived without an

7

understanding of all that is disclosed within the present volume.

Although the Grail will always remain an ineffable mystery, it can nonetheless be understood, because its very essence is enlightenment - light itself; light most hallowed, light divine, a light that will chase away the mists and the shadows from our collective consciousness. It is, in truth, a great chalice, a communion cup that will unite the world in brotherhood; but no cup lies buried in the tomb beneath the sacred ground which secretes the Grail. No physical treasure, no gleaming jewels, no fabulously precious chalice, is there. And yet, the most wondrous treasure ever to be given to this planet, and to its human occupants, lies hidden in the vault that contains the Grail.

What rests therein is a great Secret, a Secret that will transform everything, a Secret that will save the world. War-torn and chaotic, seething with grievous suffering as the world is now, indubitably we shall see things begin to change, and change dramatically, once the Grail is given to us. So this is a time for rejoicing, for thanksgiving, and for preparation, in consideration of which, we invite you to join us on our sacred Grail Quest. Put aside all hesitation, all self-limiting thought, because undoubtedly our combined Quest will be crowned with fulfilment.

This is the promise that was borne to us on the breath of the divine, and which we now dare to convey to you. Journey with us, and prepare to receive the Grail.

Introduction

When we predicted that, shortly after its publication, important archaeological evidence would come to light which would substantiate the storyline and theories belonging to our book, *The Secret Teachings of Mary Magdalene*, Margaret Bailey and I had no inkling that the location of the Holy Grail itself would soon be discovered. Yet such is the case, and together with the rest of the world we can only marvel, awestruck, at the magnitude of such a revelation, although our wonderment precedes the actual unearthing of the Grail, and that of the world must, necessarily, follow after its actual disentombment.

Nevertheless, we would like to make it clear from the outset that we ourselves did not discover the location of the Grail. We were given intimations of its coming, and we have received knowledge of its meaning and its mystery, but we did not pursue or solve the enigma of its whereabouts. The discoverer of the Grail is Callum Jensen, a resident of Lincoln who always remained a shadowy figure throughout my brief acquaintance with him. He was, almost undoubtedly, aided, directed and inspired in his search by a woman who has a unique aptitude for riddle-solving, cryptology and the esoteric aspect of language, but who shall remain nameless, in deference to her need for protection and privacy.

Unbeknown to us, as I was preparing our book for publication in the latter part of 2005, Callum Jensen had begun to receive tantalizing intuitions concerning the site of the buried Grail. The filming of *The Da Vinci Code* at Lincoln Cathedral had encouraged him to look more closely at certain clues he had long contemplated.

And, thanks to stroke after stroke of genius on his (and possibly another's) part, gradually all fell into place. Soon after the publication of our book (referred to above), of which Callum had no knowledge, he released his own, short and to the point, revealing the exact resting place of the Holy Grail.

Few people took him seriously. The general consensus was that it was all a bit of a joke, a money spinner generated by the filming of *The Da Vinci Code* and Lincoln's consequent newly found Hollywood status. We trust that this book will expose just how mistaken that view was. Our purpose in writing it is to reveal what the Holy Grail is, how it came to be secreted in Lincoln, and how each and every one of us can use it to heal and transfigure ourselves and the world. Our qualifications for writing it, we trust, will be vindicated in the fullness of time. Callum Jensen, always puckish and Merlinesque, has retreated into the enigmatic twilight from which he initially emerged to indicate where the Holy Grail lies. Margaret Bailey and I proceed from this point without him, but we salute him for his inestimable contribution to our quest, and we know the world will thank him, and offer him a place in history, for his part in the unfolding of this sacred story.

The Holy Grail contains within its essence four great wonders, called the Four Hallows of the Grail: the miracle of Nourishment, the miracle of Abundance, the miracle of Healing, and the miracle of Immortality. When we truly learn to imbibe these four divine gifts, and that fifth quality, the Grail's quintessence, which is the greatest gift of all and which delivers the other four gifts faithfully to us, we will no longer continue to make a madhouse out of our global civilization and our tenancy here on Earth. All our problems, even those that currently seem insoluble, will at last begin to loosen their grip and fade into the light which is the dawn of humanity's new day, blossoming in radiance over a new heaven and a new earth.

Authors' Note

We would like to offer this book as a conclusion to the first account of the
Grail, in the Arthurian tradition, ever to be written: *The Story of the Grail*,
by Chrétien de Troyes, a French writer and courtier of the twelfth century
who moved between the courts of north-east France and Flanders, and
who also seems to have visited the English court of Henry II. Chrétien's
account is unfinished. He introduces us to the concept of the Grail, and to
its symbolism; but Percival, the knight who pursues it, does not attain the
Grail. He fails to ask questions of the Grail Maidens, which would have
admitted its wonders into the realms of human consciousness. The
remainder of the romance veers away from the subject of the Grail,
leaving it as an intriguing, softly glimmering jewel, flashing in the
shadows of our half waking, half sleeping perception. Nevertheless, all the
esoteric lore is in place, ready for us to proceed, as we try down the
centuries to grasp an understanding of what the Grail *is*. What *is* it?

Many writers sought to give hints and intimations, and to finish
Chrétien's story; one even showed how Galahad, the son of Lancelot Du
Lac, did eventually attain the Grail. Margaret Bailey and I have
discovered that each of these stories contains some element of the many-
splendoured truth which is the Grail. Yet, in some respects, Chrétien's
story is the most compelling and the most mysterious of them all. We
believe he wrote the romance in the full knowledge that the time would
come for it to be concluded, and its promise fulfilled. That time is now.

We hope to show that the fact that the first of the Grail stories appeared
when it did was deeply significant, and that the romance in itself is neither
arbitrary nor fanciful, as has been claimed heretofore, although it is
couched in a fictional medium. The completion that we offer via our book
to Chrétien's *The Story of the Grail* differs in that respect to his - ours is
not presented as fiction, but as proclaimed fact.

These stories may be far from history, where one usually reads that such and such a king sent such and such a general to such and such a war, and that on such and such a day they made war or peace, and that this one defeated that one, or that this one, and then proceeded somewhere.

But I write what is worthy to be recorded.

Bayhaqi Tarikh
(6th century)

Chapter One

The Secret of the Ages

What lies there within, beneath the tomb in the ancient burial ground which houses the Holy Grail?

Imagine, if you will, that the excavation to disinter it has taken place. The vault that secretes the Grail has been opened, and steps lead down to a simple stone chest, waiting in the shadows. The excavators reach the chest, and prise it open with infinite care. What will meet their eyes?

Before we answer this question, I would like to relate a significant dream which came to Margaret Bailey during the time that we were contemplating the mystery of the Holy Grail. The dream offers us a teaching on the purity and power of its essence.

Margaret dreamed that she was leaning over the hole in the ground at the opened site, peering into the gloom of the vault below. A feeling of disappointment washed over her as she thought, 'Oh, after all this build-up and expectation, nothing's there!' Suddenly, from out of the vault there rushed a great plume of brilliant white light like a fire fountain that encircled and glorified all the world.

We must beware, then, of investing the idea of the Grail with physical splendour and riches, with visible spectacularity. The materialist will search in vain for any literal verification of the Grail legend, even though the songs and tales of the troubadours, each and every one, contain some glittering piece of the mirror in which, when once restored to its integrity, we shall behold the truth of the wondrous Grail.

Nevertheless, although the dream came as a teaching, it is not quite true to say that there is nothing there. Within the stone chest lies a book inscribed in Latin which is a copy of an original manuscript; some further documentation; and a little wizened thing, not much bigger than a large nut kernel.

The book is the lost Gospel of John, which vouchsafes a secret so precious, so stupendous, so liberating, that, down the centuries, adversarial forces hostile to humanity have done everything in their power (which is the power of the world, the power of materialism) to keep it hidden and prevent us from gaining any knowledge of it. And so it is that we have been denied our divinely granted legacy, that legacy of which the lost gospel tells, and, in part, dispenses.

The accompanying documentation reveals the true status and significance of Mary, the Magdalene, and of Tamar, the daughter and only child of Jesus and Mary. It verifies that Mary was the wife of Jesus, and was the feminine aspect of the Christ as Jesus was the male aspect, and that Tamar was in herself the Holy Grail. (How Tamar is the personification of the Grail, and yet the Grail lies hidden within the vault we describe, will be explained.)

The shrivelled nut kernel is in fact a dried human heart, whose identity we can disclose. It belonged to Dagobert, a French king of the seventh century, who was murdered by conspirators in AD 679. We will reveal his intriguing story in the second volume of our book, when we tell the history of the Grail.

For now, we draw attention to the fact that it is his *heart* which lies buried with the Grail, and that he met his death by being pierced straight through the eye by a lance, which impaled him to a tree. The heart, the pierced eye, and indeed the presence of the lance and the tree, are very important components in our understanding of the Grail.

You might well be inclined to ask: 'Is that all there is to the legendary Holy Grail? Just a mouldy old book, a few documents, and a wizened body part? Is that the sum total of what the world has been waiting, agog, to find down the centuries?'

The answer is, of course, no. Certainly the Grail is inconceivably more stupendous than the contents of the vault, at first sight, suggest; and all of it is not contained therein. The truth is that a part of the Grail already resides *within* each one of us, inside every human heart. Its greater essence is secreted in the higher worlds, in the spiritual spheres, ready to be given to us. The significant point is that within the book lies the vital key to how we shall receive it.

So, the Grail resides within our deeper being, upon the earth, and in the heavens. How can this be?

There is a mystical centre within the heart. Many ages ago, humanity turned away from the guidance given forth from the divine centre of the cosmos, and the entire planet experienced a shift that took it slightly out of alignment with its pole star (referred to today as the 'polar wobble'). Our physical hearts, likewise, began to shift a little off-centre throughout

14

our bodily incarnations, until the physical organ was established where it is today. Nevertheless, the mystical heart centre of humanity has not moved, and is located where our bodily heart used to be. So when we think of this divine heart centre, or chakra (see Chapter 4), we see it as encompassing our physical heart but yet in the perfect centre of the breast. The heart chakra is associated with three main symbols: the sign of a cross of light encompassed by a circle of light (the cross is equilateral and touches the perimeter of the circle at its four points), the exquisite form of a rose which dwells fragrantly at its centre – the 'heart of hearts' and the sign of the Holy Spirit which is linked with our breath, and the form of a six-pointed star, called the Star of Bethlehem but, unlike the Star of David, bearing no inner divisions. This star is the light of our spirit, and is our individual connection to, and our individual expression of, divine consciousness.

We can locate our subtle heart centre by gentle, focused breathing, as if we were drawing each breath through the heart; by visualizing one or more of its main symbols; and by allowing the mind to rest easily and softly within the heart, as if tenderly enfolded by it. Contact with this centre is so essential for our reception of the Grail that this little exercise is well worth carrying out for a few moments each day. This is the very best way to begin our Grail quest. Within a short time, it will become undeniably evident that a beautiful consciousness, a distilled perception, does indeed reside within the heart, and it will become easy to understand that it is within this spiritual centre of intelligence that the Grail, our own individual spark or drop of it, is secreted.

That part of the Grail which waits to be given to us from the higher worlds is so mysterious that we will need to accomplish many journeyings, many voyages into the interior of things, before we can bear away the trophy of realisation regarding its secrets. But it is promised to us all that we *will* be enabled to understand, and to make the trophy our own. Of this there can be no doubt. For now, we may perceive of that high essence of the Grail as embodied in and personified by a divine woman, a woman clothed with the sun, whom we know on earth as Tamar, the daughter of Jesus and Mary Magdalene.

The third part of the Grail (and we think there is a fourth which will be understood after the first three are given), that which exists on earth and is hidden in the grounds of Lincoln cathedral, is in every way as mystical and divine as its other components, although it is the only one (so far) to take physical, literal form. Even if in that mundane embodiment it is neither made of emerald nor a table, its true identity is known as The Emerald Table of Destinies, and it is precious indeed. Let our first journey into the interior be in pursuit of this mysterious Table!

Chapter Two

The Emerald Table

Before we begin, Margaret Bailey and I would like to make clear what kind of explorer's implements we will be using on our journey. As this is an interior passage, it equates to entry into Wonderland; and although we shall use recognised and respected tools such as verifiable research and intellectual deduction, we will make greater use of inner listening, spiritual guidance, visionary revelation and intuitional inspiration. Whilst these last four are nowhere near as well recognised and respected as the first two (which does not worry us in the least), they nevertheless command a measure of comprehension of their true worth in many quarters. What may be more difficult to understand for some is that we also intend to make full use of fairy stories, children's tales and children's games in our quest to unearth and unveil the truth.

It is said that initiates of the eternal verities teach that the world's deepest truths are concealed in myth and fairytale. They are given as nourishment to children before their intellect develops to the point where spiritual understanding is rejected, so that throughout their lives they may carry in their psyche some dim gleam, deeply buried, of the soul's mysteries. And it is not only to serve this purpose that fairytale, child's play and story are chosen vessels of the wisdom of the cosmos. A fact that humanity diligently likes to ignore is that the overriding spirit of the universe is one of *playfulness*.

Here is a way to test the veracity of this observation. The next time you find yourself wrestling with a problem because you need to find a solution to it quickly and none is forthcoming, let your fierce mental grip on the situation relax. If you listen to the quality of your approach whilst you wrestle, you will probably find that you are, at the inner level, shouting aggressively both at the problem and at your resources for solving it (*where* is it? *what is* the answer? *what* does it *mean*? etc., etc.). This is the stance of the intellect, which likes to dominate and frighten the child within. But if you let go of the regimented, sergeant-major approach generated by your intellect, step gently into your heart and, childlike, say to yourself: 'I wonder...I wonder where it can be, what the answer can be? I wonder...' then the universe will give you an answer much more easily and readily! The universe responds to us when we are *playful*. It loves to teach us through play. Wonder, like a dreaming child, like Alice, and you will be shown the way forward.

Margaret Bailey and I have been informed by those who guide us from the spiritual planes that the two *Alice* books by Lewis Carroll: *Alice in Wonderland* and *Alice through the Looking-Glass*,* contain the secrets of creation, and focus particularly on the mysteries of the Grail. We have already seen, in some measure, that indeed they do, via inspirations that we shall be pleased to share with you as we proceed. Those who wish to follow the Grail quest will need to come with us down the rabbit hole deep into the interior of the Earth mysteries, and eventually, to pass through the mirror. Like Alice, we have to be prepared to dream, to play, to puzzle and wonder.

Only by such means will we be enabled to step through the mirror and back again, and so attain the Grail; for that is where the Holy Grail lies: beyond the mirror of our perception.

We will come to see, as we progress, just how crucial the interior of the Earth is (equating to our own 'interior', the worlds within), and of what great import is the mirror. What a debt we owe to wise Lewis Carroll, the child-hearted Oxford don who was a gifted mathematician and who, through his masterly use of 'non-sense', showed us how to free ourselves from the aggressive, unbending, oppressive dogma of our blinkered perception of logic!

Remembering Alice, then, who fell down a rabbit hole and found herself in a Wonderland which was comically but also mystically structured on playing cards, let us first explore the enigma of the Emerald Table by contemplating the card deck of clubs, spades, hearts and diamonds. We will find that these first appeared in their present format, although with slightly different but correlative symbols, in the French and Italian courts during the time of the Renaissance. They emerged from the mystery schools of both the east and the west (their Druidic links are very

---

*These titles actually read as *Alice's Adventures in Wonderland* and *Through the Looking-Glass and What Alice Found There*, but for the sake of familiarity we prefer to use the popular references.

evident[1]), which had decided that the knowledge, the keys and the powers that the cards possessed, should be released into the mainstream of human consciousness at that time. The Tarot pack was formulated simultaneously.

Both decks of cards appeared to belong to the secular and the profane. That was their secret. In fact, the knowledge they embody is profoundly sacred. It is based on the secret of the four Cathar[2] treasures, which in turn is founded upon the secret treasures of four cities, inhabited by a hidden commonwealth, a mysterious clan of people whom we shall discuss in detail in the second volume of the Grail story.

We have met them before, in fairytale and in myth, but we have never been able, or, perhaps more accurately, we have never been allowed, to appreciate their reality, their actuality. We have never understood that we share a deep affinity, even a certain quality of racial kinship, with these secret people.

Suffice it to say for now that the four symbols depicted in the card deck are the four Grail treasures, and indicate the four sacred directions in the manner of the ancient Celtic medicine wheel – akin to the Native American medicine wheel but bearing a slightly different emphasis. So now we may perceive that Wonderland – which comprises both subtle and physical creation, incorporating the dimensions of the soul worlds and, beyond these, the ineffable essence of the spirit – is indeed structured truly upon the hallowed and ancient symbol of the cross. Its four arms indicate the four sacred directions, the mystical orientation of our soul. Wonderland, we see, is the greater reality, the all-encompassing reality, within which, by rights, we should always dwell. It has been stolen from us, purposefully and maliciously, and its polarity has been reversed; but we can regain it. We perceive also that the first thing Alice must do in order to make entry is to go within. We, too, must be prepared to 'go within' if we are to find the Grail.

Alice followed the white rabbit into the rabbit hole which led into the interior of consciousness. The white rabbit is a lunar symbol of Goddess which, on its appearance in the story, also manifests the balance of the male aspect of divinity, because the white rabbit is masculine.[3] He is an emblem of the soul and the white light, the spark of spirit secreted within the soul. Whilst on earth, he is attached to the great wheel of linear time, and he mutters: 'I'm late! I'm late!', as he hurries into the interior.

Yes, the soul of humanity *is* late in turning at last to the truth, to the reality of life, which lies within, beyond the boundaries of materialism and materialistic theory. But the good news is that we are not *too* late, and late is certainly better than never! The white rabbit will attain his destination.

This white rabbit, who is a symbol of the soul and who bears the white light, equates with the diamond of the card deck, the 'stone' among its four symbols (now we are drawing nearer to our quarry, the Emerald Table). In the mysteries of the hidden people who first bore to us news of the Grail in a time unaccountably far off, and whose wisdom the card deck depicts, the white light of the diamond was the symbol of the sacred north. As our quest proceeds, we will discover a great deal about the North or Pole star, about its link with Sirius, jewel of the northern constellations, and how its secrets are associated with this pure white light within the heart which we all bear. We might also mention here that Alice herself is this personified heart centre, following her own white light (the rabbit) within, and that she correlates to the sacred west, where the Grail, or the Chalice, lies hidden; for she is, of course, Alice-Ch-Alice, the chalice which is the sacred vessel, the heart. For now, though, we will return to our task of unlocking the door of wisdom symbolised by the diamond.

If we contemplate the white light that the diamond reflects, and think of the colour spectrum it creates when it divides itself into the seven great rays of creation, depicted by the rainbow, (and it will help us in our quest if we bear in mind that the rainbow creates a bridge, a span, or a stairway between heaven and earth), we will see that the green ray is the heart of the spectrum. Three rays occur before it (red, orange and yellow, the fiery colours, often associated with the masculine principle), and three rays come after it (blue, indigo and violet, the cool colours, often associated with the feminine principle). Uniting these principles is the beautiful green ray, the colour of our Earth, for Earth is known as the green planet (although astronomers call her the 'blue' planet), and of course the basis of life here is our green vegetation.

If we connect this heart-ray of sparkling green to its source, the white or diamond-bright light that gave it birth and which is the ineffable light of the divine that dwells in our hearts and in the heart of all creation, we can see how this green ray is its heart of hearts, its most mysterious essence.

Can we imagine that that green light, most hallowed and secret, is in fact living consciousness? (It would be rather foolish, after all, to think of such a glorious mystery as inert, lifeless and non-intelligent!)

Can we now imagine that that living consciousness could descend into a human vehicle and be born to our Earth as a child? The frail and mortal human vessel, drastic as it might be in its limitation and as less than a microbe within the entire scheme of creation itself, might still be able to contain a living drop of that consciousness, of that essence, which could yet connect with its greater source and so manifest through its circumscribed being the glory and the wonder of that source, so that the infinitesimal becomes the infinite.

That mortal vessel, that child, was Tamar, the daughter of Jesus and Mary Magdalene. The white light, the Christ essence embodied in Jesus and Mary, gave birth to its heart-of-hearts, and brought forth the mystical child Tamar. We will say much more about her, but for the present it will advance our quest to bear in mind that Tamar, the Divine Woman, is the green light, the clear and sparkling emerald light which was born from, and is the uttermost heart of, the white light, or the Christ light, which we all bear in equal measure within our mystical heart centre. Now we understand why this special table, of whose secrets we are in pursuit, is an *emerald* table!

A table or tablet, or a book, cannot be equated with a living being, of course; but if we think of the New Testament as containing the secrets of the Christ, of the Old Testament as an expression of the spiritual grandeur of the line of Abraham, the Koran as the enlightenment of Mohammad, the *Dhammapada* (the Eightfold path to Enlightenment) and the *Bardo Thodol* (Tibetan Book of the Dead) as conveying the wisdom of Buddha to the incarnate and to the departing soul, or the *Upanishads* as testifying to the light of Krishna, we will glean an inkling of how the Emerald Table was a representation in language and symbols of Tamar, the Divine Woman.

Do any of the Grail stories contain reference to the Green Stone (remembering always that the Green Stone is the heart of hearts of the white light which symbolises the diamond)? Indeed they do, and, in fact, the Grail is referred to in many of them as the 'Stone'. However, to reiterate, this reference is also to the diamond that dwells in the north of the card deck – the light in the north which is a symbol of the pure light of the spirit, that pure white light whose heart centre is the sacred emerald –

the two are synonymous. Esotericists inform us that the north is the positive polarity of the Earth from a spiritual perspective as well as a physical one. We are attuned in all ways to the north, to the light.

Strangely, it may seem, the hidden people who speak to us from the wisdom of the card deck refer to the diamond, or the Stone, as the 'Stone of Death'. We need to understand, however, that their reference was ambivalent. In one sense, they indeed recognised that the great Stone of Death kept every human soul entombed until the moment when the individual soul summoned the forces of light within itself by releasing the gift of the Grail within the heart. This Stone may be thought of as a mind-set: an attitude and a focus that embraces only materialism, which locks us into a dimension that can therefore express only death and degeneration. It is a mind-set peculiarly geared towards the denigration of the sacred feminine principle.

One of the disciples of Jesus embodied the essence of the Stone of Death; each of the disciples, in fact, represented one of the grand archetypes of the human condition.[4] Just as Jesus rolled away the Stone in order to rise again, so must we resurrect ourselves by overcoming the Stone that blocks the exit to our own tomb. We *will* do it, we will do it collectively, and it will be done by the grace of the Holy Grail.

In another sense, the bearers of the hidden knowledge did not mean 'death' as we conventionally conceive of it. 'Death' was the passage (the span, the bridge, the stairway) from the earth and the earth life to the everlasting realms beyond. It was the way through to freedom. An ancient term for the higher knowledge of the initiates of the mystery schools was *daäth,* and both the tomb and the womb were initiatory vessels which facilitated its absorption, the first being the portal to the stairway to heaven, the second the portal through which the soul descended the stairway to earth from the heaven worlds. So, as we see, the Stone itself is associated with this ladder between heaven and earth. Nevertheless, the hidden people sounded a vital warning about a certain aspect of the Stone by their nomenclature, as we shall see.

Another important point to remember about this wondrous Stone is that its earthly expression in the natural world manifests as gold, the precious incorruptible metal that withstands the death forces abroad on earth and gives forth its light undimmed. It is significant to note, in this respect, that, despite its incorruptibility, its mundane form does not prevent the lust for gold from overtaking some of those who seek it. The alchemists' true quest had nothing to do with this gold-lust. It was, on the contrary, dedicated to transforming the heavy, poisonous lead of the earthly, corruptible self into the light-bearing, realised Self whose essence was pure gold and whom the death forces could not vanquish. And so the Stone, one of the four qualities of the Grail (Abundance, Immortality, Healing, Nourishment), promises the gift of immortality. It is also known as the Philosopher's Stone, the 'Goldstone'. However, follow the false path to the Grail, and the quester assuredly will reap death. Do not worry, because we are confident that we are approaching the Grail via the true path! But we need to consider the false path, and learn from it.

A further depiction of the Grail as a stone proceeds from a Teutonic legend which tells how the Grail is an emerald that was the central jewel (note the heart reference) of the mightiest angel in heaven, and how, when the angel fell to earth, this most precious of all jewels in heaven fell with him. This truth-bearing myth is most interesting, because it tells the story of Lucifer ('light'), who became corrupt and fell from heaven. It may be fruitful to bring to mind again here that, however perfect a symbol gold is, corruption can come into the soul via gold-lust. Could a being, dwelling in light and knowing the mysteries, really enclose his light within the dangerous confines of his ego to the point where his whole perspective darkened, and he lost the route to heaven because he was denied access to the stairway to the higher worlds? And how was it that the precious emerald stone, or table, fell with him?

The story of the angel falling from heaven is profoundly esoteric, and of course it cannot be understood literally. Nonetheless, at the point when the plane of physical matter was conceived of by Divine Consciousness as an adventure, as a challenge, and as the sweetest, ultimate promise of unprecedented wonders once the spirit had triumphed within that physical plane and so performed its greatest act of alchemy ever achieved, something unique happened.

It was at that cosmic moment that the godly dream of the highest in heaven descending to the lowest of the low (for that, we are told, is the true identity of the earth plane and its many astral dimensions) sprang into being. Spirit began its long descent into densest matter, and the inconceivable mystery of the story of the falling angel began to be realised upon ever more concrete levels. Eventually, it occurred in a way that our human comprehension might now, in our own time, at last be able to grasp. Let us put this to the test; for there was a fall from grace, and the Emerald Table was lost.

The terrain that now faces us must be crossed, for it is the terrain that requires us to understand this fall from grace and its gravest of grave consequences, in both senses of the word. It is the next stage of our Grail quest.

Notes and References

1. The Druidic link to the card deck is evident from its Celtic medicine wheel structure, which occurs within Druidic teachings. Moreover, the earliest European suit bore acorns and leaves instead of clubs and spades, which were introduced in the sixteenth century. The Druids were known as 'oak men', and they worshipped trees, particularly the oak, as symbols of God-consciousness.

2. The Cathars were a Christian religious sect who arose in eleventh-century France, espousing ideals of purity and brotherly love. They were the guardians of the *consolamentum* (a limited form of the power of the Holy Grail), which allowed ordinary people to see vividly into, not just the astral spheres (which many individuals are able to perceive), but also the beauty and the magic of the higher spiritual worlds. At the dictate of the Catholic Church, a crusade was mounted against them, and they were brutally slaughtered during the thirteenth century in one of the earliest acts of European genocide. Their final stand was in the citadel at the top of Montségur. It is said that the night before they were forced to leave the citadel to be put to death, four Cathar priests were lowered down the mountain side on ropes, escaping with the four great Cathar treasures. One of the four secret treasures was a portion of the lost Gospel of John, which contains the secret of the Holy Grail.

3. Whilst the white rabbit, emblem of the feminine moon and the psyche, does indeed balance the presence of Alice by being portrayed as male for the sake of the esoteric element of the story, it is interesting to consider how Lewis Carroll layers his tale with mirror meanings. The symbolism also shows us how the soul within humankind has been taken over and come to be dominated by the masculine principle, which in its unbalanced or unharmonised state has developed an overbearing mechanised, clockwork mentality which sets great store by the superficial, or surface, meaning of life. When Alice next encounters the white rabbit, he mistakes her as his housemaid (the masculine principle forces the feminine principle into the role of menial and domestic servant).

Alice obediently hurries to his house in response to his imperious commands, but in the house she finds a little upstairs room (she ascends to the higher plane of consciousness within the house or seat of the soul) where a magic bottle stands on a table, (she has encountered this before, when it was labelled 'Drink Me').

She drinks from this magical container, and the sacred fluid within it immediately makes her grow to such a deity-like size that she bursts out of the house and out of her role within it as servant, scaring the white rabbit and his companions into comical attempts to oust her. It is interesting that Lewis Carroll introduces the dual symbols of

24

the ladder and lizard at this point. As we shall discover on our quest, the idea of the table, the divine fluid, the female deity breaking free of the tyranny of an unbalanced masculinised mind-set, the ladder and the lizard, are all highly pertinent to the theme of the Grail.

What is even more intriguing is the fact that the 'white stone' associated with the Grail was, as we shall show, artificially masculinised, and that, within the context of the Wonderland story, the divine fluid which Alice drank released her from the power of this 'white stone' (the white rabbit) and reinvested her with her feminine power.

Thus does Lewis Carroll signal to us that there is something wrong, something gravely off kilter, with this particular rendition of the 'white light'. It pretends to be the white diamond light, the light of the sacred north; but, somehow, something has got into it – what appears to be an unbalanced masculine influence that purposely mechanises and controls. This is worth bearing in mind as we proceed!

4. According to the gospels, Jesus stated that one of his disciples was a demon. This has commonly been understaood to refer to Judas Iscariot. We consider that to be a mistake, as we shall demonstrate.

Chapter Three

The God-Headed People

Every civilisation, including and preceding our present era, has had its gods. Those of more recent antiquity (the gods of ancient Greece and Rome, for instance) are imbued with a rich, fantastical history that reflects the foci, and the literary and dramatic cultural influences, of the time. Although many Roman and Greek citizens wholeheartedly believed in their gods, they perceived these deities largely from an imaginal perspective. There are historical accounts (in contradistinction to the stories of mythology) of direct encounters between mortals and members of the pantheon, but these are rare. In general, the gods, although central to the culture of the people, remained at the periphery of the everyday life of human affairs.

The strange thing is that the further back into history we go, the more we find, commensurately, that the reported activities of the gods begin to take on the nature of practical, and sometimes even pragmatic, assistance in human evolution. When we look at the gods of the earliest civilisation known to history, which are those of Sumer in ancient Mesopotamia, we discover that they perform all sorts of quite startling ministrations. These include the precise organization of advanced human society, the running of municipal affairs, the dispensation of academic, practical and technological education in every field, and, even more astonishing, genetic engineering and the science of embryonic manipulation and refinement.

Can this really be so? Are there really records in existence which verify such things? Indeed there are, although they were discovered relatively recently - in the first half of the nineteenth century - and there were certain factions at that time (the Church, for one), which ensured that these discoveries were overwhelmingly down-played. Their significance was simply too dangerous an influence for the fortifications of established opinion to withstand, should that significance begin to be truly understood, and, consequently, the scales begin to fall from the eyes of ordinary people. These discoveries threatened the bulwarks of science, religion, history, philosophy, social organization and the materialistic, patriarchal power of the state.

We have been given a collective name for these Sumerian 'gods', whose histories will stimulate all of us to stir in our sleep and, at last, to fully awaken. The reference revealed to us was 'the God-Headed people'.

We were taught that they were a human community, albeit with god-like attributes, who had settled on earth prior to the appearance of *Homo sapiens sapiens* humanity, for the distinct purpose of developing, nurturing and monitoring that humanity. We will explain why they were called the God-Headed people, but, for now, it will be as well to bear in mind the huge number of beheadings associated with the Knights Templar and the Grail stories, to say nothing of the French Revolution – and, of course, the monstrous queen in *Alice in Wonderland*, who strides around roaring: "Off with their heads!".

To return to the time of the God-Headed people, and to document that crucial fall from grace of which we have spoken in the preceding chapter, we must ask you, as once an elder of the Native American tribes said so beautifully, to walk with us 'back through the dawn-star cycles to a time long distant when the land was not as you see it'. We tell this story in the forthcoming chapters as we have been guided to tell it.

Much of it is verified via inscribed clay tablets from the aforementioned ancient Sumer, a civilisation which arose and flourished with a mysterious brilliancy in southern Mesopotamia from just after 4,000 BC until just after 2,000 BC. This corresponds with the Age of Taurus according to astrological cycles, which is interesting, because Taurus is associated with coming into physical being, and the element it celebrates is earth. As we shall see, the Sumerian tablets speak of Adam and Eve, or the *Adâma*, as emerging at the beginning of this time span.

The Sumerian clay tablets and cylinder-seals are numerous. Many tens of thousands have been unearthed from beneath the desert sands of ancient Mesopotamia (modern-day Iraq) since they were first discovered in 1843, although their strange cuneiform language, unlike any other on earth, was not deciphered until the twentieth century. They can be viewed today in collections at the British and Berlin Museums, the Louvre, and several other locations, and they comprise by far the most extensive record of any ancient civilisation ever discovered.

Although we are grateful in particular to the scholars Zechariah Sitchin and Laurence Gardner for their in-depth research pertaining to these artefacts, our account of the story told by the tablets differs from theirs quite dramatically in some respects. This is not because we are questioning their scholarship, but rather because, as there exist on the tablets varying accounts of the histories of the Sumerian 'gods', and as some of them are broken and indecipherable in places, more than one interpretation of what they report is feasible.

There are instances, however, where our story does not conform to what is written on the tablets.

We suggest that this is because the Sumerians, though a highly advanced people who clearly did not record their history from either an ignorant or superstitious stance, were, nevertheless, poised perceptually in a certain place and time, and their representation of chronology may have been vague or symbolic regarding the prehistory of their own civilisation. We agree that the tablets probably do record precise and actual history, but we think that the perspective of their scribes must necessarily have been limited, simply because it was impossible for them to obtain a bird's eye view of the last four thousand years of history in the way that we can today. Looking back from the overview of our own time, a sweeping, panoramic pattern emerges. It is precisely this design to which the history of the tablets attests, but which it was not possible for them to actually accommodate.

Again, we stress that inner listening, spiritual revelation and visionary intuition (whereby we are actually shown images), have guided us to our conclusions, as well as the more normal forms of deduction. Nevertheless, we ask you to judge our conclusions, not by their roots, but by their fruits! We have one terrible secret to reveal from the history of these tablets, as well as many wonderful ones. The discovery of this secret was so profoundly shocking that it has taken quite some time to summon the stoical wherewithal to write the following account of it. We regard it as an absolute necessity to do so, however; and as we will show, this deeply disturbing revelation pertains directly to the Grail, and our attainment of it.

The disclosure of this devastating secret will be given in the present volume. A discussion of certain aspects of it properly belongs to its sequel, but it is imperative that its import is clearly understood before we progress to the final exposure of what has been hidden for so long, with such catastrophic ramifications for humanity.

Chapter Four

The Dragon Queen and the Anunnaki

Let us begin with a much more beautiful emphasis. It is time to introduce the idea of the Dragon Queen (readers of the works of Laurence Gardner in particular will already be familiar with her). There were several Dragon Queens, but the one with whom we are concerned is Tiâmat, the original and almighty Dragon Queen: 'She who bore them all', according to the Sumerian records. She is not given particularly good press. Her sons are spoken of as 'overcoming' her, splitting her in two and 'slaying' her. In Iraq today (the site of ancient Sumer), she is still remembered in mythology as a composite of the forces of chaos, as a she-devil, as a night-hag – as Satan veritably personified!

What if Margaret and I were to say that that we have experienced the presence of this Queenly One, the Great Mother Tiâmat, and that she exuded a gentleness, a tenderness, a deep hushed peace and an enveloping and infinite love that was unforgettable and that has stayed with us like a healing benediction?

What if we were to say further that we are all dragons, each and every human being born to this earth, and that our dragon essence is our most holy inheritance? For we are indeed light-bearing beings, born of Divine Fire, utterly of the light and in the light, although we have forgotten it. We were shown that the true meaning of *Adâma* (translated as 'beings of the red earth or clay' and representing both Adam and Eve) is 'fire-beings descending into the clay/earth', 'red' indicating the holy fire whose essence we are, and 'clay' or 'earth' our destination.

It is no wonder, then, that according to the ancient clay tablets, the *Adâma* are spoken of as being created at this time, in ancient Mesopotamia in the age of Taurus, the great sign of earth and the labours of earth, signifying the season when all that is 'earthed' from heaven reaches a fullness, a completion, and all earthly labour bears fruit.

We have been given to understand that Adam and Eve, brought forth just after 4,000 BC, did indeed represent the penultimate stage of a mighty process that began millions of years ago (maybe even more remotely, because we believe that our planet is much older than the four and a half or five billion years attributed to it by modern scientists, and the universe itself is far more ancient than the current official calculation of $13^{1}/_{2}$ billion years). The aim of this original and ancient process was to bring humanity (which is divine) right down into the deepest point of earthly matter, where it would be contained entirely in an animal body composed of the physical atoms of earth.

Prior to this, men and women had not been wholly limited to containment within a casing of flesh, although the process had been all but complete for many ages prior to 4,000 BC. However, at this time there came the Great Flood (chronicled in Genesis and many other far more ancient texts, among them the Sumerian tablets). The problem was that after the Flood, the surviving remnant of humanity was found to have suffered a huge blow to its evolutionary impetus. Humankind, its numbers dramatically reduced and its biological programme of advancement via its diversity of genetic inheritance severely disrupted, needed help in order to continue along its evolutionary path. It was at this point that a new man and a new woman were brought forth, courtesy of the Sumerian 'gods', who would lead the way forward and create a new gene pool.

There was a mystical reason why Adam and Eve came into being at this time, and a mystical gift from the Godhead that was enshrined within their creation. We cannot comprehend the supreme significance of Adam and Eve until we understand the nature of this mystical reason and gift. If we try to grasp the great science of human creation in a purely pragmatic and positivist way, we shall surely find only an array of blind alleys leading to ultimate confusion. With the bringing into being of Adam and Eve through genetic engineering at the earthly, physical level of life, and spiritual infusion upon the more subtle planes of being, the omega stage of an alpha process that had begun millions of years previously was almost completed.

We say 'almost', but in fact we can be precise: 75% of the grand architectural design for the creation of humankind was brought to perfection at this time. We became three-quarters finished! In one sense, Adam and Eve did represent a final stage in human evolution, because the pair was given a genetic and soul structure which could successfully contain the precious human essence and allow it to flourish as it should, in full physicality upon the face of the Earth. Up to this point, no such genetic and soul structure had been created which would safely allow the human spirit its full expression of divinity whilst entirely contained within a physical body; but we have not yet achieved our full potential. The western arm of the cross which is our mystical soul-orientation has still to be won. In the coming years, we will become a fully human race; but we need think of no ceiling to our development. When we are fully human, true progress can begin.

To place this story in its proper framework and tell it as the Sumerians told it, we must return to their accounts as they appear in their unique cuneiform inscriptions upon the clay tablets; but first of all we need to establish clearly whose history they detail.

The answer is that they speak of a god-people called the Anunnaki (meaning 'heaven come down to earth') as existing contemporaneously with the Sumerian people. The tablets document the activities of the Anunnaki (our 'God-Headed people') as well as the ordinary people of Sumer, and, as previously cited, it is evident from the sober precision and meticulous quality of their reportage concerning the vicissitudes of the Anunnaki that in many instances they are recording history rather than story, albeit a history uncircumscribed by the humdrum parameters of everyday life.

The Anunnaki existed consciously upon another, higher, subtler dimension as well as existing upon earth in the normal way that we all do today. However, the 'higher' Anunnaki (for the overall community consisted of two ranks) did not incarnate, and remained within bodies whose more rarefied atoms spun at a higher rate of rotation than the slow, heavy, atoms of earth. We believe that these higher Anunnaki were the last human beings on earth to exist in full consciousness outside the constraints of an animal body as well as operating within it. After their departure, humanity as a whole was firmly contained within physical, animal vehicles, as we all are today. The higher Anunnaki referred to themselves as the 'God-Headed people'.

These two strains of Anunnaki, the 'higher' and the 'ordinary', both came from a mysterious globe, designated 'planet X' or 'Nibiru' by Zechariah Sitchin. The latter group finally did incarnate into entirely physical bodies, subject to all the limitations that hold us so densely in the shackles of matter today. Those who preceded them (fully evolved, divine human beings called the 'Nephilim', who were not from planet X) removed themselves to a subtle dimension beyond the Himalayas prior to the time of the last ice age, when, because of the increasing depravity of human society, it became impossible for them to associate with the physical Earth any longer.

As we have mentioned, not all of the Anunnaki descended into animal bodies in the outer world of matter. The higher Anunnaki, although they walked the Earth and, to some extent, lived earthly lives, remained on the finer planes attached to the Earth in order to continue to help their earthly brethren (originally the 'ordinary Anunnaki') eventually to return home to the higher dimensions they themselves occupied. We might think of the Earth as, in fact, many 'earths', all of the same essence and all the same entity, but spiralling higher and higher into ever more refined dimensions beyond the physical, until the material Earth and her lower planes are left behind, and the worlds of true spirit begin.

The home of the Anunnaki (therefore, our home) is not the Earth, but a much higher plane; even so, one day our beloved Earth will become a true 'home' planet, when we have done our work and our great task is at last fulfilled – the task of spiritualising the Earth until her vibrational wavelength becomes spiritual, not physical.

We can indeed confirm that we ourselves, the humanity of today, are the descendents of those Anunnaki who entered into material bodies. We *are* the Anunnaki, entirely enclosed in a physical body and living a mortal life on the outermost planes of creation. It is true to say that we have forgotten who we are. One reason for this is the length of time we have been deeply incarcerated in a physical body. As we shall see, we lost the Grail, and in losing it, fell soundly asleep in matter.

Another reason is that our means of remembering (literally, re-membering, or calling together all our scattered members or limbs so that we are fully functioning entities again and can wake up) has been purposely contaminated. Just who this contaminator is, we can make known; but we need to understand the length and breadth of the story first, because it is important that we do not miss any of its implications. Make no mistake, our deep sleep in matter is a dangerous and pathological state for us to be in – the true cause of all our planetary misery and conflagration. It cannot continue indefinitely without the direst consequences, both for ourselves and the Earth. This is no prophecy of doom, because, like Alice, we *will* awake. The process has already begun.

What, then, is the connection between the Anunnaki and the Dragon Queen? In fact, the Sumerian tablets begin their accounts of the Anunnaki with Tiâmat, the Dragon Queen, 'She who bore them all' (meaning everyone and everything). Tiâmat had a 'consort', but he came later, and there is a mystery to be revealed concerning him. The Anunnaki regarded Tiâmat as their cosmic mother, which indeed she was (and just who she was, we shall soon see), but she was in existence long, long before the Anunnaki came to this planet. Indeed, we can only conceive of her in terms of immortality, in terms of what we may perceive as the Divine. In the early days of their adventures on earth, the Anunnaki embraced their profound, umbilical connection to Tiâmat and lived in peace, beauty and creativity.

The history of the Anunnaki as it is given on the tablets implies that there were only one or two generations between Tiâmat and those Anunnaki who brought the new strain of human (Adam and Eve) into being, but we believe that the period which is represented between the manifestation of Tiâmat and the birth of the Anunnaki is truly an unconscionable one. This part of the story is symbolic, though not mythical in the ordinary sense of the word.

The pragmatic history of the Anunnaki begins with mention of what we have decided to refer to as the 'Nephilim'. The tablets refer to all the God-people as 'Anunnaki' ('Nephilim' is a later Hebrew reference). However, we make a distinction between the two, for purposes of clarity.

Reference is made to the Nephilim in Genesis, which states that in the early days of our planet's history, 'they were on the Earth', and that they 'found the daughters of men fair', and 'went into them'.[1] We believe that the Nephilim (meaning 'those who came down') were not angels, as has often been assumed. Genesis calls them 'sons of God', but later does refer to them specifically as 'angels'. We have been shown that this is actually an inaccuracy in interpretation, stemming partially from the fact that 'angel', as well as referring to a divine being, also means 'messenger'. The Nephilim brought the 'message' of God to Mother Earth, which was that she was to give birth to earthly humanity; but they were not angels, although angels accompanied them.

The Nephilim were human beings, but not human beings such as we are today. They were 'fully human', meaning that they were Godlike. They shone with the realisation of all the God qualities that were their birthright, and they were known as the 'shining ones'. Preceding the

Anunnaki, they came to our planet in its very beginnings, as soon as life had established itself here, and they chose a particular strain of that evolving life to modify and bring to a certain point of development whereby it might receive the precious human seed into itself, and so begin the great cycle of physical human life on earth.

As we know, they chose the simian strain as the most suitable and adaptable animal body according to the needs and demands of the evolutionary patterns of planet Earth, and according to the density of the earthly physical matter.

(For instance, on other planets, where conditions are different and matter vibrates at a quicker rate than that of dense physicality, other animal bodies, such as lions, might be suited to receive the human seed or light-essence. The more refined and quickened matter which constituted their bodies would ensure that the limitations of the lion form as we would experience them on earth, were we in lion bodies, would not apply and would not, therefore, hamper human progress.)

This does not mean that humans descended from apes. No ape ever became a human being via biological evolution, and no human being was ever an ape! (As Laurence Gardner points out, this was never Darwin's contention in any case.) A certain selected breed of simian was, through the scientific procedures and the spiritual and etheric manipulations of the Nephilim, gradually encouraged to stand upright, becoming *Homo erectus* and, crucially, developing frontal vision. When this strain was firmly established, a certain number of its members were selected, and work began again, this time with much more emphasis on the finer or psychic vehicles attached to the chakras, which had to be in place before humankind could take up residence within the physical body being so painstakingly prepared for it. (Chakras are energy points or vortices aligned along the spine to the crown of the head, which connect our physical body to the spiritual spheres. Each of our chakras has a subtle body attached to it. Animals have something akin to a chakra system, but it is different from, and simpler than, our own.)

Homo erectus, as a species, was left to gradually die out. The evolutionary dynamic was gently withdrawn from it, and it declined over many hundreds of thousands of years. The simian strain from which it was taken, of course, had its own evolutionary path, and continued to develop in line with its true animal nature, as is evident today.[2]

When the second creature (the one that, selected from its most

34

advanced members, followed on from *Homo erectus*), had, under the ministrations of the Nephilim, developed its chakra system sufficiently to be able to receive the essence of humanity and house its soul, once again a certain number were selected (those who had achieved the highest standards, as it were), all of them female. Very intensive processes were put in place in order to refine the wombs of these females so that the germ of humanity could be transferred to them, and the life forces necessary to build all the human vehicles, both subtle and physical, could operate unhindered within them.

Throughout this time of selection, and spiritual and biological procedure, a wonder occurred, to whose particular cosmic synchronicity the Nephilim project was specially attuned.

Notes and References

1. The information given in Genesis has led to some confusion over the Nephilim and the history of the beginning of human life on earth. The Hebraic texts were compiled long after the Sumerians had recorded the original version of it on their clay tablets (many tens of thousands of which were discovered in the nineteenth century, and finally deciphered in the twentieth). This new information has allowed us to see that the Genesis scribes borrowed heavily from what they learnt of ancient history in Babylon (formerly ancient Sumer, situated in southern Mesopotamia). The entire populace of Jerusalem (except the most severely ill-educated and unregenerate of its citizens, who of course would not include record-keepers and scribes) was captured and transplanted there from 586 – 536 BC by the Babylonian king, Nebuchadnezzar. Although the Israelites served the Babylonians as slaves, they were allowed to participate in Babylonian life and culture, an important part of which involved attendance at the New Year festivals.

During these eleven day celebrations, in which the Babylonian creation stories, based on the earlier Sumerian histories, were enacted through song, dance and ritual drama, and recited by the High Priest, the Israelite exiles absorbed information which they later began to compile into texts that served their own history.

From both these accounts – the Sumerian (later adapted by the Babylonians) and the Hebraic – emerged histories of the God people, whom the Sumerians called the Anunnaki and the Hebrews called the Nephilim. Therefore, the compilers of Genesis say that the Nephilim 'went into the daughters of men'. Although the Nephilim and the Anunnaki are essentially one, our own source makes it clear that there were actually three groups of humanity that first came to populate the Earth. These were the very highly evolved God people, who came first. We have retained the name of 'Nephilim' for this group. They were followed by the Anunnaki from the twelfth planet, which consisted of two further groups: the higher Anunnaki, and the ordinary Anunnaki. As the ordinary Anunnaki were the younger brethren (in evolutionary terms) of the higher Anunnaki, so the higher Anunnaki were the younger brethren of the Nephilim. All were human, all came to Earth, and all were Anunnaki (meaning 'Heaven come down to Earth').

Nevertheless, there were these three distinct groups or grades, which must be understood before a clear grasp can be gained of how Earth's humanity began. From our frame of reference, for instance, it was not the Nephilim who impregnated 'the daughters of men' (the daughters of the 'ordinary' Anunnaki), but rather certain selected male members of the higher Anunnaki. From these matings arose a fourth group of Anunnaki – the terrible godlike people or Naphidem, who terrorised the Earth.

2. The wonderful corollary to this is that, as the *Homo erectus* species died out, so that eventually it was impossible for its individual members to reincarnate into *Homo erectus* bodies (for we uphold the view that reincarnation is fundamental to every stage of evolution) their ensouled essence was given, by grace, a marvellous opportunity. It is true to say that the souls of this species were not truly individuated, and their thinking and overall consciousness was more group-orientated than independent. Nevertheless, each member was able to make a more or less conscious choice, once they had left their bodies and entered into the soul worlds. Would they, on their re-entry into the earth planes and into physical bodies, return to their simian ancestry, from which they had never truly emerged (and within the confines of which some of them certainly felt happiest), or would they accept the touch of the rod of initiation, and be elevated to the human line of evolution?

This was indeed a breathtaking choice, but it was not an easy one. The rod of initiation (which descends through the spiritual spheres) is difficult to bear, and even after its application, it meant a long wait for these simple souls, for they could only incarnate into human bodies that had been reduced to an entirely physical vehicle. These wholly physical bodies took quite some time to establish, and in fact the higher and the ordinary Anunnaki had made their arrival and had been present on earth for an extended span before any of the *Homo erectus* souls, newly humanised by the spiritual charge of the rod of initiation, could thus reincarnate. Nonetheless, some mustered the courage to take this glorious option, which was made available to them via spiritual law, which dictates that opportunity follows an act of service. And what greater service could these creatures have rendered, than to make their bodies the prototype for the first fully physical human beings?

Chapter Five

Planet X

The nature of this wonder was that a complete circle, the mystical 3600,[1] had been turned by Earth through the stars (it was not the precessional circuit [2]), and this event had opened a precisional portal or 'window' between the Earth and her twin or mirror-image planet (note again the huge significance of the twinned or mirror image). This twin planet is the strange and secret 'twelfth' planet of our solar system, referred to by Zechariah Sitchin as 'planet X' and called 'Nibiru' by the Sumerians. The work of the Nephilim had from the start been aligned in its chronology to a certain heavenly meeting between planet Earth and planet X as they travelled their majestic orbital pathway among the stars.

Some say planet X is the tenth planet, and equate this contention with X being the Roman numeral for ten. We say that it is actually the twelfth planet if you incorporate the moon and Chiron into the equation, but that it does indeed have a connection with the number ten, as we shall see. We would like to emphasise at this point that although our hands and feet – the extremities of our tactile consciousness – consist of ten digits, in fact they *mirror* one another in twinned sets of five, and that the human body has a pentagrammatical form. Earth has a magical identification with the number five (a number deeply associated with Mary Magdalene).

In its twin relationship with the Earth, planet X can be seen as the 'ten' planet, if not, according to us, the 'tenth' planet of the solar system.

When the moon is counted as a planet (and, even though technically she is a satellite, we think she most certainly ought to be regarded as a planet, as we discuss in our previous book [cited below]), we find that planet Earth, the 'five' planet, is actually the fourth planet of the solar system, as planet X is the twelfth.

Confirmation of planet X's existence occurred in 1982, and further news of it was brought to public attention in the spring of 2006, coinciding, we were interested to note, with the release of our book, The *Secret Teachings of Mary Magdalene* (which forms the basis of the ideas, concepts and discoveries of this book), and with the remarkable discovery in Egypt of an ancient tomb opposite the tomb of Tutankhamun. This Egyptian discovery, we feel, is a crucial one. Whilst its contents are being assessed and evaluated, we dare to predict that as well as offering further evidence that Moses and the pharaoh Akhenaten are one and the same (so firmly conjoining, Egyptian, Judaic, Christian and Islamic roots), this tomb will provide scholars with proof that the coming of Mary Magdalene as the great feminine Wise One and saviour of humankind was predicted down the ages, just as the coming of the Messiah was predicted in the ancient Hebraic texts.

To return to the subject of the mysterious planet X (it is worth noting that X, or the soltaire cross, is a mystical symbol for Mary Magdalene, the Soul of the World, and appears as an inscription, sometimes concealed, on paintings and artefacts of which she is the theme), let us imagine that we are on the top of the world looking out into the cosmos, across our solar system, to its furthest planet, planet X.

It is by no means always visible, even from our vantage point. Unlike the other members of our solar system, this sibling goes riding off into outer space, pursuing mysterious and heroic paths of its own, before returning for a flying visit and crossing Earth's orbital path once every 3,600 years.

3,600 is, of course, the measurement of a complete circle or circuit, and if we regard each unit of ten years of the twelfth planet's return journey as a single degree, we perceive that the signature of its relationship with its twin, the earth, is that of a circle, and that the circle has a compositional pattern of ten. If, from our imaginal station at the top of the world, we watch this planet hurtle towards us, we might sense that its essence bears a masculine aspect, just as the essence of our own Earth is undoubtedly feminine. Planet X is our twin, but it is also our opposite or mirror image.

We might think of it as indeed our twin, yet also our half-brother planet, because it was born of our system but, as it demonstrates by leaving it and returning to some far distant elsewhere, it has two sources of origin. And, wonderfully, it has just been discovered in the field of human biology that twins can have different fathers. Is this the cosmic dynamic that gives to the creative tides of our world its history of mated half-brothers and sisters, from Abraham through the pharaonic dynasties and the coming of Moses to King Arthur and his first wife? For planet X is the Earth's virile, outward-bound, celestial lover from beyond the stars.

We return now to that circuit of the stars which the Earth made in her early days, when life had flourished on her surface but she had not yet given birth to her own human children. This circle was not described around her outer body, but was made in the region of her centre, her heart. She received certain beautiful star emanations into her core which created the necessary conditions for a crystalline beam to pass through her heart, a beam which connected to planet X, homeward bound and due to cross her orbit. A portal or window was opened by the beam, and as the twelfth planet passed by, it released a fall of life, a miraculous rain of human beings (the Anunnaki) who descended into the finer or etheric spheres of the Earth.

They did not use space ships, but rather caught the current, as it were, and rode on the serpentine tide of energy that swept and coiled between the two planets.

What we were shown reminded us to some extent of the theory of panspermia, whereby life begins on planets by spore deposits propelled to them on beams of light from established ecosystems on other spheres. Margaret Bailey saw them in a vision as anti-matter sperm-like creatures swimming in a line across the skies along the path of the downward-spiralling celestial energy, bound for Earth. We presume that this journey was something akin to those across space described by ascended spiritual masters, whereby they relax and prepare mind and body as if for sleep, and are taken where their will directs in moments, the atoms of their bodies rearranging themselves according to the appropriate velocity of the matter environment they find themselves in as they awaken. If this is correct, then it is true to say that those human beings who came to Earth to initiate our species literally experienced the biblical 'fall'. However, something happened on a profound rather than prosaic level which dramatically characterised the 'fall' in terms of a spiritual darkening, as we shall see.

Notes and References

1. See the information under Notes and References, Chapter 16.

2. In order to distinguish between the 'circuit of stars' and the precessional circuit, it is necessary to have a clear grasp of the latter. The precession of the equinoxes may be understood as the progressively earlier occurrence of the equinoxes in each

consecutive sidereal year due to a gradual change in the direction of the Earth's axis. The planet's axis moves in the manner of the axis of a spinning top, so that the pole of the equator describes an approximate circle around the pole of the ecliptic once in about 26,000 years. This unit of earthly time is called an aeon. The completion of an aeon always opens a door between the Earth and the higher worlds, and in fact we passed through such a door in 2006. The 'circuit of stars' mentioned was related to the precessional circuit, but also involved an extraordinary cosmic phenomenon.

Chapter Six

The Wild Women

This ominous spiritual darkening came much later. In the beginning, the Anunnaki were joyfully welcomed by the Nephilim, their 'elder brethren', who were, though ever-young, much older and more evolutionally advanced than they were. These Nephilim had 'called' the Anunnaki to planet Earth, putting out the divine summons at the right time, when the Earth was ready to receive her lover's semen from beyond the stars.

There were among the Anunnaki mighty kings and queens, great lords of life (the 'higher' Anunnaki), who were given by the Nephilim divine tasks to fulfil on behalf of the earthly communities that would spring up once the female creatures with specially prepared wombs, descendants of the chosen line of *Homo erectus*, had received the Anunnaki essence into themselves and, after due gestation, brought forth human children. The Anunnaki who thus entered into physical bodies via the wombs of the designated 'wild women' were younger, less evolved human beings than these kingly and queenly overlords. These supreme Anunnaki ruled and held council beside the Nephilim, although the Nephilim continued to direct and monitor the development of Earth and her emergent humanity.

As we have explained, the Anunnaki kings and queens never undertook the strange, beautiful and miraculous journey into physical matter that the younger members of their clan ('ordinary' Anunnaki) embarked upon.

This consisted of receiving a call, given by divine grace once their decision to take on physical bodies had been made, and following it into a 'Creation Chamber', where they entered a state of perfect peace and transcendent bliss as their consciousness was absorbed into the all-pervading love of the great Mother-Father, that supernal containment in which we were all timelessly held until we were sent forth from the ineffable Source on our unique journeys as light-bearing, individual souls. When they emerged, they were in a body of light, of pure individuated spiritual essence, which could, marvellously, begin to interpenetrate the little body being specially built for it within one of the wombs of the 'wild women'. Into the wombs of this second creature, derived from perfected specimens of *Homo erectus*, the 'seed' of humanity (a fertilised egg) was introduced by means of what we can only call 'embryo implantation', although it must be stressed that we do not mean by this the clinical, purely physical procedure that pertains to the concept today. The word 'uterus' derives from 'utterer', because it utters the Divine Word from which life springs. By mystical means, by spiritual force, the Nephilim and the higher Anunnaki, working together, transferred the human essence of our distant ancestors into the wombs of these meek, noble, wild creatures, females of the race that were truly the 'wild men' of history and legend. What eventually came forth from those wombs were simian-related baby bodies containing the human essence of the Anunnaki from the twelfth planet, the planet of 'ten', called planet X, and they are we and we are they.

Sadly, some of them despised their sweet-natured, gentle surrogate mothers, although these hairy giantesses harboured a deep, loyal affection and reverence, even awe, for the children they had brought forth so mysteriously.

The Anunnaki children bore some characteristics of their host mothers in that they were strong, tall and generally hominoid, but they had serpentine features and their bodies were not as densely material as ours are today. To enter the furthest reaches of matter, as was our destiny, we had to penetrate its realms deeper and ever deeper. Work continued on this great project over an immense time-span. Gradually, we lost our serpentine facial characteristics and began to look as we do now, although the original 'black-headed people' whom the higher Anunnaki (those who did not enter the physical realm via birth) and the Nephilim created, and from whom we are directly descended, mirrored the original planet X Anunnaki.

The wombs of the 'wild women' were utilised once only, for a single generation, although there were rare cases when they had to be called on again. Generally speaking, however, the single generation plan was adhered to. Having almost human souls, and souls of great nobility and purity at that, the 'wild women' cleaved to their babies, bonding with them profoundly. They could not be allowed to rear these first human children, because they had no real grasp of their developmental needs. They were allowed to nurse them, however; and they grieved for their offspring when, eventually, they were removed from their care. These

42

gentle giantesses (for they were much bigger in stature than we are today) conceived a shyness and timidity towards human beings. They, and the males of their clan, remained sympathetic to the human race, perhaps in honour of the memory of those early days, when they acted as our surrogate mothers.

The Nephilim remained close to them in spirit, to comfort and sustain them, and to protect them from the varying races of humankind, who would have persecuted them.

Under the guidance of their divine protectors, these peaceful creatures became almost supernaturally adept at slipping away into invisibility whenever they were in danger of encountering human beings. They are still in existence today, called, variously, 'Yeti', 'the Abominable Snowmen', 'Bigfoot', 'Wild Men of the Woods'. Their numbers were never great, and have never increased. They remain on earth in secret and hidden clans. They have a modicum of language, and a depth of soul that resonates with the human family. One day soon, when we begin to appreciate the spiritual dimensions of our origins, these clandestine people will emerge from hiding, to allow us to learn how we came into physical being. They are not our ancestors, as their DNA will prove; our furthest ancestors are not of this earth. Yet they will teach us how the evolutional bridge was crossed. We will find that their DNA corresponds to patterns that are nearly simian and nearly human, yet are neither.

Human ova from the higher Anunnaki, subject to treatments and procedures and spiritually directed mutations, were fertilised with human (higher Anunnaki) sperm, both of which had to be slowed down in vibration in order to transmute into physical sperm and physical eggs before the resultant embryos could be implanted into the wombs of the 'wild women'. We stress that it was the etheric counterpart of the egg and the sperm that the Nephilim and the higher Anunnaki translated into biology. They took these substances from the higher Anunnaki themselves (we think that sperm and ova were donated particularly, and perhaps even exclusively, by the androgyne Kingu [see above]), and, after many processes, transported them medically into the prepared wombs of the surrogate mothers.

Some of the mothers' genetic material was mutated throughout this procedure and fused with the Anunnaki ova and sperm so that the little embryos could stabilise in their uterine environment, although in these initial stages of human creation, the resultant physical matter was far less dense than it is nowadays.

At a later point in the development of the foetus, the light body that was the essence of a member of the ordinary Anunnaki who had passed through the mysterious processes of the 'Creation Chamber' was introduced into the little foetal body, and fused with it by means of the available chakra system of the surrogate mother. Angelic presence and intelligence was involved in this great enterprise. Angels of high degree worked alongside the Nephilim and the elite Anunnaki to bring physical human life into creation, which no doubt added to the confusion of the Genesis chroniclers when, in their attempted exposition of tradition, orthodoxy and documentation, they failed to make the distinction between Nephilim and angels.

As we have seen, what came forth from those Nephilim-engineered, angel-tended wombs were the first of the earthly human strain. They were the Anunnaki sperm and ova slowed down in vibration so that they became physical, implanted into the wombs of the 'wild women' by wondrous process, and born to this earth as human babies.

As they grew, and mated and brought forth babies themselves, who grew in their turn, and became 'the sons and daughters of men', some members of the higher (undescended) Anunnaki hierarchy, in consultation with the Nephilim, decided to take certain of these daughters to be their wives.

The undescended Anunnaki had to limit themselves to relationships with earthly women only, because, if the daughters of the higher Anunnaki had mated with the sons of men, the resultant physical body would have taken an upward turn, so to speak, becoming less physical and more etheric. The wombs of the 'biologised' Anunnaki, now on earth in physical form, brought the ethereal Anunnaki essence on a downward course into matter, onto the descending staircase between heaven and earth. If physical men ('biologised' ordinary Anunnaki) had mated with higher female Anunnaki, the ethereal wombs of those females would have carried the body of the resulting child onto the ascending heavenly staircase, so that it was less physical and more etherealised. But of course the whole point of the project of planet Earth was to actually materialise human bodies at the level of dense, physical matter.

So it was that higher, undescended Anunnaki women were careful not to mate with physicalised or earthly (ordinary) Anunnaki men, but higher Anunnaki men purposely took earthly Anunnaki wives, as a special act of love and generosity towards the new creation. For when higher Anunnaki males impregnated earthly Anunnaki women, many of the godlike higher Anunnaki qualities now found a firm foothold in the processes of earthly biology, and successfully asserted themselves. Therefore, the children of ordinary Anunnaki mothers born to fathers of the higher Anunnaki exhibited godlike characteristics that had been granted to them as an act of grace, directly through the medium of biology. We will refer to this new race as the godlike people (as distinct from the God-Headed people who were the higher Anunnaki, and the God-realised people who were the Nephilim), although in the books of Enoch and Jubilees these godlike people are referred to as the Naphidem.

In telling this story, it tends to sound relatively straightforward, as if the procedure involved was smooth and uninterrupted and took immediate effect. But, of course, many difficulties and obstacles had to be surmounted, and the time-span which implemented it was vast, involving numerous civilisations which flourished and passed away.

Chapter Seven

The Coming of the Naphidem

It is important to understand that the higher, undescended Anunnaki, although an ethereal human race vibrating at a much higher rate than physical matter, could still be bodily present upon the physical earth. Their bodies were composed of atoms of light rather than dense, heavy, unspiritualised matter; but they could temporarily harmonise their vibrations with the wavelength of the material earth and walk upon it. Here they appeared as solid as earthly matter for a time, although their bodies gave off an electric energy which made the physical atoms of the ordinary Anunnaki tingle and quicken whenever they encountered a member of these higher Anunnaki, and the finer bodies attached to their chakra systems pulsate, as if stroked with divine fire.

It has to be said that the ordinary Anunnaki, those who had come through the earthly wombs of the 'wild women' mothers and who had eventually born children to one another in the normal way, did not approve of their heavenly overseers, the higher Anunnaki, taking earthly wives. They saw that it gave the resultant earthly sons and daughters of these heavenly parents an unfair advantage over ordinary Anunnaki, and they were resentful. Because of this, they spoke against the higher Anunnaki, accusing them of impure design and motivation in thus 'seducing' their daughters.

The Nephilim, and the higher Anunnaki themselves, had long contemplated this move before finally implementing it.

Some among them were never entirely reconciled to the idea, feeling that the element of earth now involved in Anunnaki evolution via the genetic material from what was essentially an animal uterine host, had to be carefully taken into account, and the risks were too severe to justify going ahead with the plan. Nevertheless, from their communion with Divine Spirit, some of the Nephilim and the higher Anunnaki felt that there was a beautiful *possibility* that this gift of God-realisation could be given safely (more or less) to the earthly Anunnaki. They could, whilst yet on earth, *still be in heaven.*

We believe that it was indeed divine inspiration which guided some of the Nephilim to lay this priceless possibility before the feet of the Anunnaki. The magical potential was there for humanity to experience its earth initiation (its cycle of lives on earth in a physical body) as an unfolding panorama of joy, radiance and beauty. This was Divine Will, which expressed itself through its summoning of the higher Anunnaki, under Nephilim tutelage, to give its own God-qualities as a free gift of love to the ordinary Anunnaki, the children of heaven who had descended into the material planes of Earth in physical bodies, and so become humanity; for it was Divine Will that Earth's children should be free and happy, untouched by death and suffering.

There did indeed reign a hallowed and exquisite golden age for a time, extending, we believe, into some thousands of years. During this golden morning of humanity's tenancy of the earth, no form of sentient life was abused or slain. Death did not exist, because when a human being's allotted span of earth-time was over, they happily ascended the stairway to heaven once their soul had heard the call, leaving their physical body behind.

Such was the perfect balance of the five elements within nature (earth, water, air, fire, ether) that corruption and decomposition was not the distressing horror that it is today. The Earth was filled with joy, and her delight knew no bounds or limitation in form. The younger brethren of the higher Anunnaki (humanity) walked with angels and spoke with gods, for in those days, even the illustrious Nephilim themselves could walk upon the earth in their light-bodies, whilst the higher Anunnaki walked among us in manifest bodies that we recognised as almost like our own. The God-Headed people, the higher Anunnaki, were our true ancestors, those who dwelt with the shining ones; together with and under the guidance of these exalted shining ones – the Nephilim – they taught the ancient mysteries from the stars to listening humanity. And then, gradually, we stopped listening.

Eventually, the human ego fell out of balance and its vision darkened. It began to know greed, and to want power and dominion. The roots of this malaise seemed to emerge from a misunderstanding of the male of the species, especially highlighted among the males of the Naphidem, of his role and origins. He knew that these lay in the feminine expression of life, and because of this he secretly and mistakenly felt that he must somehow be inferior to the female. He began to regard his penis as a sure sign that really it was the male who had originated life all along, and not the female. He persuaded himself that somehow, the female had stolen his true status and instigated a lie about the genesis of creation, putting him deliberately in the shade. He began to associate his penis with reclaiming his power and inaugurating a stance of aggression and dominion over the female. Here was proof in this regal rising of flesh, he thought, that he was king, and lord of all.

So began the terrible imbalance that led to a rigid covering of ice over the North Pole, which in the early days of the world had been as a lush Eden, the high place, sacred and mystical, where the Nephilim, the God-people, dwelt. They had to leave; they could bear the new, warring power-lust of humanity and its gross vibrations no longer. They retreated to an exalted dimension in the Himalayas, where the pure snow kept an inviolate boundary between their world (still associated with the North Pole and the Pole Star) and our own. It was at this time that the great polar shift came into effect, taking our planet out of alignment with the North Star and our perfect attunement to the light. Our hearts shifted slightly to the left of our bodies.

The Nephilim had gone, but, not so refined in vibration and therefore more able to tolerate the abhorrent pollution of the lower ethers that humanity had caused with its bloodshed, strife and cruelty, the higher Anunnaki were able to remain. We ought to explain that some of the descended or ordinary Anunnaki had not fallen prey to the prevailing imbalance among the peoples of earth at that time. These included members of both the Naphidem (the sons and daughters of earth who had been fathered directly by the higher Anunnaki, but whose mothers were ordinary or earthly Anunnaki), and the ordinary Anunnaki themselves (those who had come forth from the 'wild women' and who had married and bred with one another). Those godlike people or Naphidem who had fallen into disarray had slaughtered many of the ordinary Anunnaki, because the twin concepts of superiority and of treating others as worthless had overtaken them. It was indeed from the ranks of the Naphidem that the great imbalance had first arisen. They had cut themselves off from God when they began to despise the sacred feminine, and their ability to ascend to higher planes was severely compromised until it reached the point of annulment.

Once this had occurred, the godlike people used their mighty powers and titanic stature to indulge in pure savagery and black magic, or abuse of divine energy. They converted their god powers into animalistic and even demonic urges. By so doing, they brought destruction on themselves, and were 'purged from the Earth'. Their angelic and god powers were revoked (for they had also developed qualities akin to angelic forces), and they remained (and remain still) in a dimension removed from the Earth but not far from it, trying always to regain their status and dominion upon it.

Those of the godlike people who had refused to succumb to the prevailing spiritual darkness were not banished from the face of the Earth. They continued their existence with their god powers attenuated and curtailed; but their numbers diminished into terminal decline. Nevertheless, a few scattered cells of the aggressive godlike people managed to survive, often living a subterranean life. From their underground locations they sought to influence and overpower ordinary humanity, for they were determined to inherit the Earth, and reinstate their banished brethren.

The God-Headed people, the higher Anunnaki, remained behind and did their best to assume the mantle of the departed Nephilim. Most of them, at this point, were still pure of heart and of good intent, but they had by no means escaped the effects of the great imbalance which had devastated the Earth, as we shall see. They re-established Eden (originally located in what is now northernmost Britain) in the Fertile Crescent: the ancient lands of Mesopotamia, Canaan and Egypt. They shepherded the ordinary Anunnaki into newly-founded communities there, and began to instruct them again in the arts, crafts and sciences, as the Nephilim had done.

And they resumed their great task of advancing and adapting the bodies of the ordinary Anunnaki so that they could create fully physical vehicles for these younger brethren to incarnate into, because the mighty process of physicalisation, begun so long ago with the assistance of the 'wild women', remained incomplete, still in need of further refinement.

It is time to examine what is implied by the term 'God-Headed people', for, as we shall see, the Emerald Table, and, ultimately, the Grail, are associated with them.

Chapter Eight

Snakes and Ladders

As we have described, the Anunnaki were called to the Earth by the Nephilim, who, in readiness for their coming, prepared animal bodies from the simian line of evolution to receive the Anunnaki essence. They sent forth the divine call so that the Anunnaki would arrive at exactly the right cosmic moment to descend to the Earth from their home planet, planet X, the twelfth planet, when it crossed Earth's orbit (which happens once in every 3,600 years). The Nephilim were advanced God-people, highly evolved human beings who came to our planet in its earliest days to initiate the development of earthly humanity, which was, by supernal decree, to live in animal bodies at the outer level of physical matter, the plane furthest removed from the divine source, or God. A certain number of the human population (the Anunnaki) inhabiting the twelfth planet, planet X, which is Earth's twin planet and her cosmic lover, were chosen as those who would descend to Earth and enter the animal bodies previously prepared for the purpose by the Nephilim.

The Nephilim themselves could not begin the earthly human strain with their own essence, because their life-forces were too advanced in their evolution and too refined in their revolution to sustain the necessary heaviness and density that their slowing down into physicality would require. Besides, the creation of humanity, wherever it occurs throughout the universe, is never an arbitrary act.

Human life on planet Earth was planned, through divine geometrical and numerical design pertaining to all its relationships in every dimension, to emerge from an instigator belonging to her twin in the solar system.

The Nephilim directed and assisted the Anunnaki to enter the realm of physicality through the chosen 'wild women' strain, which had been developed from *Homo erectus*, a race of beings that the Nephilim had processed and nurtured from the specially selected simian family of creatures. Their physical bodies were adapted vehicles, not the ancestors, of human beings, whose essence is divine and who were originally brought to Earth as the Anunnaki by the Nephilim.

Among those people who came to Earth from planet X, there were both the ordinary Anunnaki, not as advanced in their spiritual evolution as the Anunnaki Lords of Life that accompanied them in their cosmically historic descent to Earth, and there were these Lords of Life themselves: Anunnaki kings and queens of such evolved essence that they could work alongside the Nephilim and, though not quite of their evolutionary order, could co-create with them. These great Anunnaki, like the Nephilim, were too quickened in essence to incarnate into animal bodies, as their lesser Anunnaki brethren had done, but, unlike the Nephilim, they had not crossed the final bridge into divine consciousness (that ineffable state which we can only dimly grasp in terms of 'standing before the throne of God'); and so, although they were exceptionally advanced and regal beings, they were not quite infallible.

At this juncture, it is pertinent (we assure you) to consider the game of Snakes and Ladders. With regard to this game, we might again perceive of that mystical bridge that spans heaven and earth, but this time we adjust our focus so that we see, not the version or dimension of it that carries souls down into and up out of earthly incarnation, but rather a spiralling ladder that, with great labour throughout many, many incarnations, the soul ascends, rung by rung (cycle by cycle) on its evolutionary journey towards heaven.

The beginning of the soul's journey is the first square, at the bottom left-hand corner of the board, where it is utterly imprisoned in earthliness, its consciousness struggling to reach beyond the darkness of matter. Its journey's end is at the top of the board, where it attains heaven and disappears into a celestial dimension. We can see that, as well as the actual ladders depicted on the board, the squares which comprise it make an approximation of a ladder in themselves, a grid-ladder with long horizontal pathways to be laboriously traversed before the soul reaches the end of each line and can at last make a slight vertical ascent to the line above.

Although it is set forth in ascending equal lines of squares, we might imagine that there is nevertheless a spiralling dimension within that ascending ladder. This spiralling dimension within the ladder manifests as the serpent of the lower self, travelling downwards by means of the snakes depicted on the board. (The upward-bound spiralling ladder is the serpent of the higher self, the 'serpent of light', replete with its little starbursts of energy, shown as ladders, that carry the soul upwards at a faster rate than that dispensed by the plodding squares.) The soul can, according to its karma (symbolised by the throw of the die, which provides the numbers [karma] that the soul has earned, or drawn to itself), transform opportunity into a direct ascent up a ladder of inspiration, or haplessly slide in a sickening plunge down one of the serpents of the lower self.

The most remarkable thing about the game of Snakes and Ladders is that there rises a great ladder from the bottom level of the board to the top, so that the soul can find a way to ascend directly to heaven, without the need to traverse the laborious horizontal path of each rung of the ascending ladder marked out by the squares.

But at the top level, the level of heaven, there dwells a huge serpent of the lower self, all too ready to cast the unwary soul hurtling downwards into the nethermost regions of consciousness, signified by the lowest level of the board. It is worth bearing in mind that the paths of ascent and descent are both serpentine. This game of Snakes and Ladders illustrates for us a great teaching of the ancient mystery schools – that there is a door at the mouth of hell which leads directly to heaven, and that there is a door at the gates of heaven which leads directly to hell. This is also an important secret to bear in mind as we study the history of the Anunnaki, and of what happened in particular to two of their members. An interesting feature of the game of Snakes and Ladders is that if we played it in Wonderland, we would go down the ladders and up the snakes. Although, for the purpose of what we wish to convey, we acknowledge the validity of the symbol of the serpent of the lower self, we nevertheless consider that Wonderland has it the right way round.

As well as the ordinary Anunnaki, who had initially passed through the wombs of the 'wild women' into a measure of physicality to become Earth's first humans and who afterwards bred with one another; and the higher Anunnaki, the great kings and queens who dwelt in an exalted dimension beyond that of the physical, and who guided and assisted the ordinary Anunnaki in their growing earthly communities, there existed a third group of Anunnaki: those who were born in the normal way to ordinary Anunnaki, but whose fathers were higher Anunnaki. Although the bodies of the higher Anunnaki belonged to a much more elevated vibrational wavelength than that of the physical, they could temporarily slow down their vibrations until they resonated with those of earth, thus enabling them to impregnate ordinary Anunnaki women.

52

The babies born from these unions (who became the Naphidem) possessed godlike qualities, but, even so, their evolutional state was less elevated than that of their fathers, the higher Anunnaki. It was these higher Anunnaki alone who were the true God-Headed people. The ordinary Anunnaki, we might say, possessed the *potential* to be God-Headed people, whilst the Naphidem were over halfway there.

What did it mean to be a God-Headed person? What was it like?

We can only conjecture, of course; but from the knowledge of them that Margaret Bailey and I have been given, we understand that they were not fully God-realised, as the Nephilim were, but that they were 'God-headed' – that is, they could attain a measure of exalted God-consciousness whilst living in an individuated state in a body that could walk the Earth, even though its atoms were not physical atoms. In a sense, we can even imagine, just as in *Alice*, that their heads left their earthbound bodies behind, although still firmly attached, of course, and shot off into the heavens! It is a description that makes us smile, but it is not so far removed from the true state of things! This is why we are quite sure that the game of Snakes and Ladders is organized according to a reversal of its truth, and that the Wonderland version is the proper one.

At this point we would draw attention to the many depictions of Mary Magdalene kneeling by a cross, sometimes in the form of a young tree or sapling, with a human skull at its base; and also to the fact that numerous beheadings were associated with those who upheld her honour and protected her mysteries. These symbols are in place to show us, when we are ready to see, that we are descended from and can share the secrets of the God-Headed people, those elevated ones who could attain God-consciousness whilst still on earth.

We can still do this today by means of individual striving through meditation and inner discipline, but the 'Path of Awe' between heaven and earth is not shining and grandly open as it used to be in the early Anunnaki days, so that ordinary people could see and sense and taste the radiant essence of the imperishable stars, and walk and talk with angels and receive the palpable blessing of the Holy Spirit.

The skull at the foot of the cross also teaches us into what decrepitude and degeneration we have allowed our inner vision, our heart-intelligence, to fall into throughout the ages, so that we are wearing our head on our earthbound feet.

It shows us that our consciousness has slipped down and become entrapped at the base of our spine, because the sapling cross is the Tree of the Knowledge of Good and Evil, with the sacred Book open before it, which Mary peruses. We shall see that the Book and the Tree of Knowledge of Good and Evil are actually one, and that Mary is the holy Shepherdess of this divine power.

The sapling also symbolises the Tree of Life, our spinal lightning rod which conducts heavenly fire or exalted wisdom right down into our physical and subtle bodies, and earths it there. But the holy light has become imprisoned in our base chakra at the bottom of the spine, and cannot rise to illumine the head-centres, because our head is at our feet, or at least stuck at the level of the base chakra! Something has beheaded us! 'Off with their heads!' roars the Queen in *Alice*.

There is a Grail story which tells of one particular form of the Dolorous Blow – an act of aggression that brings famine, pestilence, war and wasting (the four Grail qualities in reverse) to the land in the vicinity of its delivery. Interestingly, in this particular instance, the Dolorous Blow is a beheading, committed by a knight who, because of a rash promise, is coerced into slaying his sister. (Another form of the Dolorous Blow is one which permanently wounds the genitals of the Fisher King.)

We will see how these stories mirror a cosmic act of betrayal, a terrible deed perpetrated by the masculine principle against the sacred feminine. The association of the Dolorous Blow with decapitation is also a strong tradition within the Knights Templar, the warrior monks who came to prominence in the middle ages and who protected the secrets of Mary Magdalene and the Holy Grail. Their veneration of severed heads is central to their esoteric doctrine.

That the Dolorous Blow should fall as a beheading teaches us that something happened in the far distant past to confound and overwhelm the God-Headed people.

They were Lords of Life, kings and queens who had attained divinity, but who lived on earth and walked among humankind in a fully embodied, fully visible state, their feet fixed firmly on the terrestrial plane and their heads (their consciousness) in heaven, ascended, unaffected by the mighty gravitational pull of earthliness and the mists and obfuscations that gather at the level of matter. At any time, they could leave the material plane and return to their own dimension (called Eden) by quickening the rotation of their bodily atoms and harmonising their revolutions with those of their soul. This was an alchemical secret belonging to sacred science.

They were a living, practical example to the ordinary Anunnaki, teaching them to live by codes of justice, honour, mercy and all that comprised enlightenment. They showed them how to advance their culture by pursuing high aspirations in the fields of medicine, philosophy, astronomy, astrology, education, agriculture, the arts, sciences, history and literature, and, especially, the esoteric disciplines and mysteries that overarched all their lives.

In those days, the Path of Awe was indeed grandly open to the spiritual stars (meaning the divine mystery emanating from their essence), and we might pause and reflect here that this majestic, star strewn Open Way *was* and *is* the Holy Grail, for without it we slowly become moribund and fade away into death and darkness. This is the deeper, esoteric meaning behind the biblical quote: 'Without vision, the people perish.' The Holy Grail, the grand open pathway to the stars that links earth with heaven and heaven with earth, *is* vision – vision in all its dimensions and replete with all its aspects of meaning.

Vision is: knowing, understanding, seeing life not only in its limited, outer, mundane guise but in its eternal scope and spiritual magnitude. Vision is: dwelling at the heart of the dayspring of truth, being in the light and of the light. Vision is: living in heaven whilst still on earth. The body, the animal self, the lower earthly self walks the Earth and fulfils all its commissions there. Yet the greater self, the spirit exquisitely clothed in the translucent, shining garments of the soul, overlights all, sweeping away the darkness of the material planes, overcoming all their difficulties, miseries and limitations, supplanting them with joy, beauty and radiant life-energy.

The four great Horsemen of Doom, who ride from the four corners of the material Earth to its heart, to our hearts, and bring overwhelming Pestilence, Famine, War and Death, are transformed into their true guise by the glory of the Grail. They become its four Wise Knights, bearing to us on their solar steeds the inestimable Grail gifts of Healing (synonymous with Peace), Nourishment, Abundance and Immortality, and that fifth essence, the mystery of mysteries, the Quintessence, which rescues the overwhelmed heart and sets it once again on its rightful throne of supreme authority.

Is this the key? Is it by somehow overriding the heart centre that the God-Headed people lost the Grail, the divine ladder between heaven and earth? As we know, there can be no Grail without heart-centred consciousness, demonstrated so forcibly for us by the presence of the disembodied heart, King Dagobert's heart, as the Grail custodian. And the God-Headed people *did* lose the Grail, at some point just after 2,000 BC.[1] Something negative of tremendous import occurred which effectively closed down the Grail energies, so that it disappeared from the Earth. We can pinpoint this to the fall of the Tower of Babel, which occurred at that time, and which the Sumerians recorded on their clay tablets. Did this event, when the peoples of Mesopotamia fell into confusion and became incoherent to one another, mark some sort of override and obscuration of the heart centre? We have been shown that it did.

Certainly, the God-Headed people lost their ability to travel down to earth at this time. They had to return to their own dimension, and could find no way to return to earth anymore and walk among us with their feet on *terra firma* and their heads (their consciousness) firmly aloft in the heavens. The clay tablets tell us that they 'left like migrating birds'. The Sumerians no longer enjoyed the guidance and the example of the God-Headed people, and their awareness of the royal road between heaven and earth, that 'path of awe' which inspired them and made their life a marvel, so that they breathed the purest spiritual airs and beheld the light of the infinite, deserted them because the road had closed.

Invasion and warfare overtook Sumer, and it disintegrated. The imbalance between male and female became entrenched, and spread out over the whole world. There is evidence that the west held out longest against it, although it finally succumbed. The great patriarchies arose, that of Rome in particular, and in their train came endless wars. The world darkened. The Grail was lost.

Bloodshed and oppression held sway, and has never really loosened its grip. We think that the great imbalance which resulted in this dire state of affairs actually began much earlier in Earth's history, so that the Grail (the divine pathway) gradually lessened over a vast gulf of time until earthly conditions, purposely created by Earth's humanity, caused it to disappear altogether. The vital connection between earth and heaven was lost. This was the 'Dolorous Blow' that caused our 'beheading'.

It is interesting to consider that what had worked out so admirably on planet X had met with its final testing-ground on planet Earth, and had signally failed. This was because Earth represents the lowest, densest level of matter in existence, the point furthest away from God. Here, on Earth, the sword of the spirit is tested most stringently, to see whether it can match the exacting standard set for it. It must ring keen, true and invincible as it is wielded against the darkness of the lower planes. If it fails, it breaks, and must be re-forged.

When humanity was introduced to our solar system, it began with the Nephilim. They came from, or at least established themselves on, Venus, the only planet in the entire family to spin clockwise, so following the path of the sun. Because life on planet X is of a higher vibrational rate than that of Earth, the Nephilim (who are also the Anunnaki, but with certain qualifications) were able to use their own subtle life forces to produce a race of beings on planet X that were planetary, both individually and permanently embodied (subject to the law of eventual release from form), but which issued from the highly evolved divine essence of the Nephilim. The result was the 'ordinary' Anunnaki. Male Nephilim then mated with the daughters of these 'ordinary' planet X Anunnaki, and this time the result was the God-Headed people, the 'higher' Anunnaki. When the entire experiment and methodology was imported to Earth, a similar harmonious and progressive result was not attained.

What was achieved so splendidly on planet X could not after all be translated into earthly conditions. The spiritual tests inherent in earthly matter were too severe for the higher Anunnaki and the ordinary Anunnaki to hold the balance, although, of course, as fully evolved God people, the Nephilim themselves were not corrupted. However, as we have noted, Earth's humanity, led by the Naphidem, created such a discordant vibration with their behaviour that the Nephilim were forced to leave their ethereal settlements at the then temperate, Edenic North Pole. (It was 'Edenic' because it reflected, and was partially of, the Eden in which the Nephilim actually dwelt, which was a higher harmonic of the Eden in which the higher Anunnaki made their home – so we have three Edens, each one ascending in scale; firstly, that of earth, secondly, that of the higher Anunnaki, and thirdly, that of the Nephilim.) Hereafter, it was imperative for the Nephilim that they should reside at a level much further above that of the earthly dimension than had formerly been the case; and the Naphidem and their atrocities had to be forcibly banished from the Earth.

Gradually, the higher Anunnaki fell into confusion and dissonance, humanity (the ordinary Anunnaki) became chaotic, and at least two members of the higher Anunnaki (we think, in fact, that they each trailed a body of supporters in their wake) slid down the great snake waiting at the door of heaven to a realm that was not quite that of the physical sphere of matter, but was not far removed from it.

Let us now turn to the story as the Sumerians described it on their clay tablets, for by doing so we shall find that it connects directly with what we are seeking: the Emerald Table.

Notes and references

1. Whilst the Dolorous Blow which severed the Grail from the Earth was struck long before the fall of the Tower of Babel, the destruction of this mysterious Tower marked the final exhaustion of the Grail energies. These energies took many thousands of years to (almost) entirely close down.

Chapter Nine

The Dragon Queen

Any study of the Sumerian creation stories must take into account their highly politicised slant. The city states of Sumer each had their own allegiances and their own point of view, and their scribes recounted their history accordingly. Additionally, we believe, the great imbalance between the sacred masculine and the sacred feminine principles as they interrelate on earth had already occurred long before the Sumerians began to record their history. Again, we present this part of the story as we have been guided to tell it.

Tiâmat, the original Dragon Queen, brought our solar system, and indeed the entire universe, into manifestation. The wave form which is inherent in all life, all energy, is the essence of her serpentine emanations. This is the secret of her life and consciousness, of all life and consciousness. The most obvious and visually evident symbol of her mysteries upon the face of the Earth is the sea.

Tiâmat was and is a manifestation, or shall we say, a human understanding or ideation of the Godhead: an ineffable being of light that 'breathed fire' – the Holy Breath or Spirit that creates and infuses embodiment. She brought forth physical creation by mirroring herself, which manifested the sacred masculine principle. Father-God was of her and within her, and she externalised her deepest heart by giving birth to him.

Goddess brought forth God; but that profoundest point from which he emerged was Goddess and is Goddess; and that is why she seems to us to be the 'negative' polarity in the scheme of creation. Her deepest centre has been externalised, and yet that deepest centre remains Goddess, deep, deep within the heart of all that is.

Tiâmat, Goddess, her essence the bitter or salt waters of creation, brought forth, as her mirror image, God; his essence (which yet was and is hers) expressed itself materially in the formation of the fresh waters of life, and this fresh water, for the Sumerians, became symbolically, even magically, associated with semen. The wisdom that Goddess dwells deep in the heart of God, that she is to be found at the furthermost point of his profundity, is an indelible mystery that all the world expresses, for everywhere in myth, lake maidens and feminine spirits of pools and streams, fountains and rivers, rise from the profoundest depths of still water to greet members of humanity and bestow on them shining gifts of the soul.

Tiâmat's offspring were serpentine, (for the serpent is her emblem and her signature), but bore within them, as she did, the sacred pentagram, the fundamental human form. Tiâmat's sacred insignia, her magical sign and symbol, is an equilateral cross of light contained within a circle of light. The four arms of the cross connect with the four cardinal points of the circle. Its fifth point is its centre, its heart. This emblem, vast in its significance, for it denotes the heart, the Earth, and the creative principle, was also known as the Mark of Cain, to which we shall return later.

We believe that Tiâmat herself was God-in-Manifestation, the great act of 'putting forth into being' that the one God, the dynamic unity encircling creation and conjoining it at its root, perpetrated in order to initiate creation itself. We believe, and have been shown, that the divine creative principle – God, perceived as Tiâmat – is fundamentally feminine, not masculine, as almost all religions proclaim.

It is Divine Mother who is creative, and Divine Father who is reflective. The reason it seems to be the other way round is because our world, all creation, is mirrored. This does not mean, of course, that there is any imbalance between the two, for the two are one, and the one is the two. All is equal, is balanced, between Divine Mother and Divine Father.

Even so, when the third principle came into being, the divine Daughter-Son whom we may call Christ-Brigid (the Spirit and the Bride proclaimed at the end of Revelations in the New Testament), it was the divine feminine, the creative principle, that brought forth the divine child.

The dynamic of Divine Father was present too, of course; but as the second, not the first, principle. What this means for us is that, although male and female are entirely equal and, in fact, are the very living dynamic of equality itself, without which nothing can be balanced or remain in balance, the outer, active, intellectually orientated male principle must always bow its knee in reverence to the authority of the heart centre. He does not lose any status in doing so, of course, because the heart centre contains all, and unifies both principles. Moreover, women are not necessarily always more aware of the sacredness of the heart centre than men. It seems that both men and women must learn to make this chakra the centre of supreme command and authority in their lives and their expression of life; otherwise there will always be inequality, suffering and bloodshed upon the Earth, and, eventually and inevitably, as an act of mercy, Goddess-God will withdraw the life forces from our planet, and the entire project of earthly humanity will be aborted.

Of course, we do not need to worry about this scenario, because we will begin to listen to the heart, the soul of life – our inner guiding light.

The court scene at the end of *Alice in Wonderland* denotes this wonderful awakening of the whole of humanity – when as Alice-Chalice, or the heart-centred soul, we rise up in a great moment of realisation and scatter to the winds the absurd and distorted values active in the 'court' (our self-imposed societal and governmental systems that, with their blindness and inequities, bring so much suffering) and say decisively, 'They're nothing but a pack of cards!' In that moment the great power-source feeding our corrupt worldly structures and systems will be disconnected, and we will be free – free and awake, like Alice.

'Let the jury consider their verdict,' the King said, for about the twentieth time that day.

'No, no!' said the Queen. 'Sentence first – verdict afterwards!'

'Stuff and nonsense!' said Alice loudly. 'The idea of having the sentence first!'

'Hold your tongue!' said the Queen, turning purple.

'I won't!' said Alice.

'Off with her head!' the Queen shouted at the top of her voice. Nobody moved.

'Who cares for you?' said Alice (she had grown to her full size by this time). 'You're nothing but a pack of cards!'

At this the whole pack rose up into the air, and came flying down upon her; she gave a little scream, half of fright and half of anger, and tried to beat them off, and found herself lying on the bank, with her head in the lap of her sister, who was gently brushing away some dead leaves that had fluttered down from the trees upon her face.

'Wake up, Alice dear!' said her sister, 'Why, what a long sleep you've had!'

When Alice-Chalice, the universal soul of humanity which is also our individual soul, grows to her full size, and challenges the distorted mirror version of herself that has caused our beheading (represented by the false Queen), then the Divine Woman will gently wake her, and bless humanity in its moment of reawakening.

To return to the subject of Tiâmat: the ancient tablets tell us that Apsû was her 'consort'. He was representative of the 'First Father', the primordial male expression of life brought forth by the ineffable Dragon Queen as she 'moved over the face of the waters'. Mummu was the third principle (Tiâmat being the first and Apsû an expression of the second), the Divine Child, the hallowed fire-mist from which creation proceeded. As the Divine Child, Mummu bore within itself the first and the second principles, and from it came the Four Sacred Persons – issuing forth as two male and female pairings – Lahamu and her brother Lahmu, and Kishar and her brother Anshar. Although they 'came through' Mummu (Mummu had to precede them), all were children of Tiâmat and the First Father, whom the Sumerians called Apsû. In fact, Apsû was not the First Father – one much more ancient, godly and universally powerful than he undertook this role – but we may consider Apsû as one of the representatives of this supernal being, even though he was certainly not among the first.

This was the Sumerian idea of the first expression of the consecrated cross of life – the Sacred Four with Mummu at its centre – its divine heart. This figure gives us the mystery of five – of the quintessence – which is Tiâmat's mark or symbol, the fifth point being the heart, or Mummu. The figure is an ideograph of Christ, the Sacred Child, bearing both the male and female principles of Mother-Father God, which surround the cross and its centrepoint as an eternal circle.

So the circle of light is Mother-Father God, represented by Tiâmat and First Father, the centrepoint or heart is Christ or Mummu, expressing both of the principles which have brought it forth, and the cross (whose centre is Christ) is Creation issuing from these three ineffable principles, a perfect balance of the sacred feminine and the sacred masculine, supported and maintained by the mystery of the Christ essence. We need to understand this structure before we can grasp fully the meaning of the Grail. It is a structure or a symbol of Creation and the Creator in perfect harmony, the former suffering no separation from its source, no twisting away from the centre, the heart.

We see that when humanity was uttered forth, brought into being by the command of the Word, by the dynamics of love, it did not immediately sink into degradation. Humanity was indeed a bright and pure star within the scheme of creation, its highest point resonating in equilibrium with the highest angels – and, we may say, in a sense – even beyond the sphere of the angels. The greatest test came within our own solar system, when, under the aegis of Divine Spirit, the exalted human beings from Venus (they were originally from other star systems) cultivated humankind on the twelfth planet (and others), with the intention of bringing human life at last to the physical conditions prevalent on Earth, the twelfth planet's spiritual twin and cosmic lover.

When twelfth-planet humanity arrived here via the call of the Venus brethren (we have designated these Venus brethren 'the Nephilim', from the name given to them in Genesis) and descended into the furthest depths of matter – the outermost reaches of creation – the great imbalance occurred between the feminine and masculine principles that has been described in the previous two chapters. Let us see how this is related on the clay tablets.

Chapter Ten

The Mighty Anu

The problem seems to have begun with the sovereign lord of the higher Anunnaki, whose name was Anu. (For the sake of simplicity, we will refer to Anu as masculine in gender and as the favoured 'son', although from our perspective, which we will clarify later, neither term is satisfactory.)

Anu was the greatest of the God-Headed people in that 'he' bore within 'himself' the highest essence of the Nephilim. (To recapitulate, the God-Headed people were the sons and daughters born to Nephilim fathers and ordinary Anunnaki mothers after the Nephilim had established humanity [the Anunnaki] on the twelfth planet – planet X. This procedure of the initiating God-People mating with selected members of the humanity they had newly established on a planet worked perfectly on planet X, but resulted in disaster when applied under earthly conditions.)

So who was Anu? He was the chosen son of light, born from Anshar and Kishar, who were the two Persons of the Sacred Four designated to be the light-bearing vehicles for humanity. Lahamu and Lahmu were also beings of ineffable light, but they were the hidden, unmanifest ones, holding the spiritual balance of creation (indicated by the highly significant 'u' at the end of their names, the import of which is reflected in the *khu,* the ancient term given to menstrual blood, which was revered as the lunar manifestation of the power of Goddess), whilst Anshar and Kishar undertook the process of embodying and bringing forth.

We can equate this quartet of four sacred persons to some degree with the four universal forces of electromagnetism, gravity, and the two nuclear forces as they manifest in and support our universe, which gives us a limited understanding of them from a materialistic perspective. They are, of course, related to the Four Hallows of the Grail.

We might say that of the four-armed elemental Cross of Creation, Lahamu and Lahmu bore within themselves the essence of the subtle principles of fire and air, whilst Anshar and Kishar bore the essence of earth and water, the principles which bear the fruit and provide the composition of physical creation. One pair is the ideation, the other the fruit, of the processes of creation itself. All work in perfect harmony and equity, and, as we see, both pairs are supremely balanced between male and female. It is not a case of the feminine principle as exclusive embodier, and the masculine principle as exclusive seed-bearing spiritual and unmanifest essence, as almost all world religions teach us (i.e., the Mother is earthly and the Father is heavenly). Something sneaked into the bloodstream of the world religions to throw them off course, as we shall see.

Having established this, it is important to realise that Anu was not alone in his mission of light-bearer. He had a mate equal in status without whom his mission could neither have been initiated nor completed. This mate, Antu-Ki, was his sister. The tablets tell us that Anshar and Kishar, the son and daughter of Tiâmat (who were the 'earth' and 'water' of our Cross of Creation), 'produced' Anu as the designated vehicle of light, the 'son' (an inaccurate or insufficient designation from our point of view) who would be lord of all on the twelfth planet and lord of creation on planet Earth. They also tell us that he had 'two' wives, Antu and Ki.

Yet it is obvious that, as the great primordial trinity, in existence before the time, space and matter continuum began, was viewed by the Sumerians as consisting of Tiâmat, of the Father Principle she contained within her that the ancients knew as Apsû, and of Mummu, the Divine Child, the tablets cannot be discussing simple generational procession here. The time span involved is too awesomely, unimaginably vast to allow of any such interpretation.

Rather, we are surely being told that Anu and Antu-Ki were anointed as the 'divine couple' who would bear the light to developing humanity on planet X, just as Jesus and Mary Magdalene were anointed as the divine light-bearing couple for earthly humanity during the famous spikenard ceremony at the house in Bethany. Anu and Antu-Ki 'proceeded' from the mystical Anshar and Kishar (aspects of Mummu) because Anu and Antu-Ki were created beings, and Anshar and Kishar were the great initiating parents, the 'water' and the 'earth', who brought forth created beings. A special link of divine light to these holy two (Anshar and Kishar) went through the countless generations of created humanity on every planet where it took root, designating the divine couple again and again, in the rhythm that was needed to feed humanity with the light of the spirit.

Antu-Ki and Anu were an early rendition of this divine couple, but they were certainly not the first instance of it, as we know they were born of Nephilim fathers. The Nephilim themselves would have required a manifestation of the divine couple to dispense the light to them, as they trod the evolutionary path.

So, as we can see, the tablets are inscribed with accurate, but symbolic, history. Pragmatic, rather than symbolic, accuracy would no doubt have required more clay tablets to relate the tale than the Earth could hold!

Therefore, we have Antu-Ki and Anu as the designated divine couple, pride and joy of their parents, the Nephilim, reigning in perfect accord and harmony on planet X, and preparing to set out on their great adventure – the creation and establishment of, under the aegis of the Nephilim, the human strain on planet Earth, planet X's cosmic twin, sister, and lover (a pattern they themselves reflected, as we see, because Antu-Ki and Anu were brother and sister). Although in one sense they would leave planet X, in another it can be said that their dimension of rulership was so exalted that they never came down from on high. They came to Earth, but they never walked the Earth, as the other God-Headed people did. From their exalted dimension they could continue to provide a guiding light for planet X, just as it is perceived by many that Jesus and Mary Magdalene, although long departed from our planet, bathe the Earth in their light today.

The trouble was that this particular light-bearing couple (Antu-Ki and Anu) were not Jesus and Mary Magdalene. The latter were by far the most literally glorious of the divine couples ever to be sent forth from spirit, and they did not fail or falter in their mission, although that mission was the most adventurous, enterprising, treacherous, difficult and thankless travail ever to be undertaken. We hope that by the end of this book its full dimensions (inasmuch as we can ever hope to understand them) will lie revealed, for its supreme gift, in company with its teachings and example, was the Holy Grail. And within the ineffable dimensions of the Holy Grail exists the mystery of the Emerald Tablet.

Chapter Eleven

Dark Deeds

Something happened to Anu, or to the masculine aspect of him, when he came to Earth. Although never participating physically in earth life, he nonetheless was affected by, and finally partook of, the imbalance it generated. As the scribes who recorded the histories on the clay tablets also suffered from the effects of this imbalance, so rendering the story from their understanding and perspective, we ought to point out that according to them, Anu was always supposed to have married *two* wives – Antu and Ki. We feel, however, that these two spouses were really one, for the following reasons.

Firstly, there was no imbalance between the Sacred Four, the two pairs of offspring who, through Mummu, were generated by Tiâmat and First Father and were the fundamental structure of creation, the great Cross. The imbalance of two females to one male seems first to have occurred with Anu. Secondly, Antu and Ki were queens, one of the heavens, the other of the earth. We will see that Tiâmat, through collusion among her male offspring, was split in two – that she was heaven and she was earth (meaning that she was the spiritual dimension birthing or giving forth the material dimension, which proceeded from her), but through a mobilised and horrifically brutal attack planned and perpetrated by those male offspring, she was torn asunder into a separate heaven and a separate earth.

It is just too suspicious a situation for Anu, who was part of this shocking plot against the Great Mother of All, to suddenly have two wives who represent the split Tiâmat. Indeed, we see clearly that these wives, who were also the offspring of Tiâmat and who represented the feminine half of the divine couple, were originally one unified entity – as they must surely have been if they were once the feminine aspect of that divine, and divinely balanced, couple, whose entire original identity was that of an unsundered androgyne.

We must make one thing brilliantly clear – when Anu, with his other male conspirators, let fall the Dolorous Blow that 'beheaded' Tiâmat (so severing heaven and earth, or her consciousness [strictly speaking, our access to it] from her body) they put into operation an evil that actually separated consciousness, the inner worlds and the unifying principle itself, splitting asunder what could never be in balance again until healing and re-conjoinment took place.

From this great act of brutality arise the stories of the Lost Bride, roaming the Earth in mourning, awaiting the day when she will be admitted once more into the presence of her 'husband', God, in the heavens. (We recognise the validity of this story, but are rather exasperated by the (we believe erroneous) slant that the 'bride' is earthbound and awaiting the action or permission of her spouse before she can ascend to heaven. It is certainly a story bearing a true teaching, nevertheless, although it portrays attitudes, not esoteric truths.) From this cruel split, too, comes the story of the Fisher King, desperately wounded in his genitals where something has been torn away from him and which constantly weep blood, so that his whole life is one great supplication for the mercy of healing. It is this king's agony that the Arthurian knight Percival witnesses when he goes in search of the Grail.

By failing to ask questions of the Grail Maidens (who are the only two who can usher the Grail back into human consciousness so that a cure can be effected) the king's agony continues, the terrible curse of the wasteland prevails, and Percival, chastened and ashamed, fails to achieve the Grail.

We may well ask what happened after Anu and his co-conspirators split Tiâmat in two. Tiâmat was the very essence of all, her form the very emission, as it were, of the first divine principle giving birth to creation. She manifested as an all-enfolding being of light who, with her wave-form magic, summoned and integrated the act of embodiment. How did Anu and the others split her in two? By utilising their male power, via a reversed-spin magic, or what we would call 'black' magic today.

Zechariah Sitchin, in his analysis of the story, considers Tiâmat to be a planet into which the selected aggressor (Marduk, himself also a planet) purposely hurtled, thus splitting her in two. Laurence Gardner, on the other hand, draws on many valid sources to prove that Tiâmat was the original Dragon Queen, bearing a serpentine or wave-esque form. We believe that both these analyses are true. Tiâmat *was* the Dragon Queen, the great originator of life; and the battleground upon which she was rent in two was our own Mother Earth, a daughter or manifestation of Tiâmat in herself. The Earth as a goddess or an entity bore an expression of

Tiâmat's wounds after the Dolorous Blow. She was hit by a celestial body, there was a polar shift, and her heart centre was affected.

The tablets relate that Marduk, a grandson of Anu and Antu-Ki, made the final devastating blow. Apsû, the masculine principle faithfully reflecting (to a degree) the First Father, had already been 'killed' (we believe this means that he was rejected, ousted, denied and supplanted because he was the proclamation of equality between male and female, which the aggressors specifically wanted to overturn).

Even Apsû had been affected by the great imbalance, turning on his children, the younger male gods (the higher Anunnaki), and wanting to destroy them when he discovered their plot to slay him and split his 'consort' asunder, although we see that Apsû did not and could not regard Tiâmat as a consort, but rather recognised her sacred presence as his Divine Mother, as God (see Chapter 23). Tiâmat, the Great Mother, rebuked him in his heart (meaning that she strove to restore sanity and balance to his perspective), for she was willing to accept their worst violations rather than exterminate these wayward children. Apsû was (apparently) put to 'death' by one of the conspirators, and the final great battle to slaughter Tiâmat commenced.

Chapter Twelve

The Emerald Table

Anu himself had tried to slay Tiâmat, and had failed. The conspirators now summoned Marduk, Anu's grandson, to their aid.

Marduk seems to be an embodiment of the male as military aggressor and tyrant, having abandoned all concept of protector and server. He was the prototype of the new male, the rendition of the masculine principle that Anu and his companions wished to bring into being. Indeed, Marduk now demanded that the conditions of his assault on Tiâmat must be that he was given absolute authority over his fellow gods, and granted world dominion on earth. He insisted on claiming the first kingship of solely masculine rule, and advanced on Tiâmat, decorated with its insignia.

This, of course, was a direct outrage and usurpation. Tiâmat, omniscient and omnipresent, knowing the designs upon her 'life' (her vital presence within the conscious awareness of her beloved children), and seeing the horror that was to come, had already taken action. Prior to Marduk's action, she had instigated the kingly and queenly descent that for a certain period in Earth's history must, she decreed, necessarily manifest as a bloodline. This was the only way possible for the supreme divine couple (Mary Magdalene and Jesus), who would eventually arrive and re-establish healing, balance and harmony between the masculine and feminine principles and lead humanity out of its darkness and suffering, to actually reach the Earth.

Looking down the vistas of time, Tiâmat saw in futuristic vision that the Grail, which can be partially understood as the divine pathway between heaven and earth and all that such a passage entails, was closing, terminally wounded after the fall of the Dolorous Blow. Tiâmat knew that one day it would entirely disappear from the Earth, and be superseded by conditions that would engender mass ignorance and deception. She therefore gave into the keeping of her son-daughter, Kingu – an androgynous member of the higher Anunnaki (for all the higher Anunnaki were originally androgynous) who was constant in her-his loyalty to her and who remained at her side to protect her – an incomparable treasure:

the Tablet of Destinies (our Emerald Table).

This Emerald Table (also called the Anunnaki Table of Destiny) was the potent heart of the dynamic of wisdom or knowledge as it applied to the Earth and her peoples. It was, indeed, an objectification of Tiâmat's deepest heart, from which the wisdom ray emanated. (We have seen how the green ray, occurring in the middle of the seven great rays of creation, with three before it and three after it, is the 'heart of hearts' of the mystical white light of the Divine which separates into the seven rays.) So Tiâmat, in her final supreme act of love, mercy and forgiveness, left us a drop of her essence, of her heart, in entrusting to humanity this most sacred of all repositories of wisdom, of knowledge – the Emerald Table. We might say that it was the next-best thing to the Grail. In itself it was of the Grail essence.

It was said of the Emerald Table that it contained 'all that humankind had ever known, and all that would ever be known'. It enshrined the most ancient of alchemical formulae, arising from the purest source – the heart of the Divine, the heart of God.

This was not just about the overcoming of mortality or turning base metals into gold, but rather uttered the secret of how we transform material, earthly conditions into the flawless, incorruptible essence of pure spirit – in other words, how we transform suffering and darkness into unbounded joy and all-pervading light. It was the Secret of the Ages. It was one of the four sacred and shining aspects of the Holy Grail, which lies today at a designated spot beneath the grounds of Lincoln Cathedral, rescued for us by Jesus and Mary Magdalene via the greatest act of sacrifice ever made, and delivered to earth through the spiritual mystery of Tamar, their daughter (for the wondrous jewel that is the Grail must be carried down to the terrestrial sphere within the heart of the Divine Woman before it can actually manifest in all its four aspects on earth, remembering always that Tamar herself is the very quintessence, the very heart from which the Grail issues, and its greatest gift).

The Emerald Table or Tablet was entrusted to Kingu because it was imperative that she-he should restore order to the world once Tiâmat was 'slain' (banished from the consciousness of the peoples of earth). With it came the bestowing of the first divine 'kingship', a new dispensation different from former rulerships. It was vouchsafed in the first instance by Tiâmat to her beloved son-daughter Kingu, and bears the name of this androgynous being. (In fact, Laurence Gardner tells us that the titles of both 'king' and 'queen' derive from the all-important 'Cain' or 'Quayin' [meaning 'light' or 'the eye of God' – the divine *ayin*] – a conclusion we do not question – but we wonder whether the name 'Cain' itself linguistically echoes 'Kingu' [alternatively spelt 'Quingu']. 'Cain' is a titular name for supreme smithship, and kings and queens were properly the 'Divine Forgers', the chosen pair who brought forth gold or sacred light from the darkness of the earth experience.)

In their two aspects, they (King-u) were the designated divine couple whose duty it was to strive to restore the Emerald Table to earthly consciousness. They stood as protectors of the holy temple of Tiâmat, and guardians of the precious Emerald Table, in readiness to withstand the onslaught of the fearsome Marduk as he made his Satanic assault.

Chapter Thirteen

Marduk

We can imagine Marduk advancing on Tiâmat, or on the holy seat where her divine connection to the Earth was enshrined, showing her by his flaunting of the usurped kingly insignia (his false authority) that *his way,* his rule, his philosophy (a complete denial of the sacred feminine) was to supplant the Great Mother of All.

Interestingly, the tablets tell us that he had 'four eyes and four ears', and we may be certain that all his other senses were doubled as well. In other words, Marduk had suppressed the sacred feminine within himself – his other half – and had commandeered her senses, or intelligence, for his own use and his own purposes. We see in Marduk a Luciferic drive, a being obsessed with his own self-glorification and aggrandizement, a world dominator whose worst example in mundane human terms was Adolf Hitler.

How did Marduk 'kill' Tiâmat? First, he used the 'four winds' to disorientate and confuse Kingu. Then he reversed the winds, and blew them back through Tiâmat's 'mouth'. This is interesting, because we are also told that Anu had given the four winds to Marduk as toys for the young god to play with. It was the action of these winds upon her heart centre which so disturbed Tiâmat that she 'rose up' in remonstrance against Anu, the androgynous being who embodied the divine couple, designated to carry Tiâmat's light to the peoples of the Earth. Anu had been given the gift of the holy light of God, of Tiâmat, and Anu, through Marduk, had used it against her in an outrageous act of reversal. An unutterably sacred trust had been violated.

The entire body of Mother Earth shuddered through and through with the horror of this outrage. The waves of the sea, the powers of the air, the forces of the earth, the living dynamic within sunlight, arose in an act of cosmic admonishment. The sea boiled. The air cracked with strange lightning-strikes, as if the sanity of the planet – that which kept all its systems intact and in perfect perpetuation – were itself beginning to hallucinate. The winds howled like a macrocosmic beast in a

73

supernaturally vast cavern.

It is worth contemplating (although perhaps not for too long) this act of ultimate betrayal and unimaginable treachery. We might begin to glimpse thereby how Jesus, on his cross, had to endure the re-enactment of that unspeakable deed, willingly and lovingly accepting its brutal impact into himself, in order to cosmically reverse it. By so doing, Jesus reversed the reversal. And we might also understand why it was unnecessary for Mary Magdalene, in her representation of the feminine half of the divine couple whom once Anu had embodied, to undergo the same sacrificial crucifixion.

Why was it that Anu could not commit the atrocity of 'slaying' Tiâmat himself? We will explain the reason shortly, when we examine the human aspects at play in this dire history. First, we need to understand Marduk's central, yet puppet-role, in the drama.

We sense that Marduk was groomed from the start to 'kill' Tiâmat, that he was indeed the chosen assassin, and that the 'four winds' with which he toyed represent the Holy Spirit, the Holy Breath, which Jesus and Mary Magdalene shared and which is profoundly feminine in essence. This Holy Spirit breathes through the structure of creation, the Cross, manifesting physically as the four winds, the eight half winds, and the sixteen quarter winds.

Within the spiritual structure of our being, these winds (the Holy Breath) are an expression of the Divine Feminine essence moving through us, as they moved upon the face of the waters at the beginning of time. We see that, through participation in dark ceremony, Marduk reversed the giving-forth nature of the Holy Spirit or Breath. Marduk was taught how to 'toy' with these sacred winds, how to make them his playthings. He did this by first abusing the feminine essence within himself.

Marduk was not an androgynous being, as were all the higher Anunnaki, without exception, before the great imbalance struck. They came forth as androgynous beings, perfectly balanced between the feminine and masculine aspects of creation. These unified androgynes could separate to perform certain functions associated with earthly life at both the exalted and physical level, but they always remained conjoined at the heart. The inverted uterine-shaped 'u', indicating a receptive vessel, at the end of higher Anunnaki names indicates that the Anunnaki being was androgynous, united with its feminine essence and in a state of equilibrium. We note from this that even Apsû was birthed forth from

Tiâmat as a perfect androgyne – given the potential to create semen in order to continue the grand creational dynamic, but also united in equality with his feminine essence. Thus we see that Tiâmat was indeed not his 'consort', but rather the ineffable cause, the great initiating force behind him – at his root, as it were. This truth is substantiated in the Sumerian texts via references on the clay tablets to Apsû, not only as the primordial Father, but also as a feminine deity.

When Anu conceived the idea of destroying Tiâmat, he found, after first destroying Apsû, that he could not do it himself (he tried and failed on several occasions), because the feminine half of him always prevented this unconscionable outrage. He could not permanently cut himself off from his feminine essence.

Before he could be enabled to do this, Tiâmat herself would have to be split asunder. An adult, fully developed androgyne would never be able to achieve such a deed. What was required was a child, not an androgyne but a new-born male child of greater evolution than the ordinary Anunnaki, who could be instructed and influenced from the first to begin to suppress and oppress his feminine essence before it could either assert or protect itself. A member of the Naphidem would fit the requirement perfectly.

This plan was implemented as soon as Marduk was born. He was subjected to an abusive process that mutated his little soul into a potential tyrant. His was a conditioned and manipulated psyche which, through maiming and twisting, began to be purposely trained in the technique of suppressing his feminine essence.

Horrifically, Anu's scheme had its genesis in child abuse. This process was all part of the negative-spin magic that Anu used to pursue the new ideal of the penis as supreme originator of all life, and man as lord and master of woman, his sexual plaything. Air or wind, in esoteric terms, always denotes the mind, and mental images were used to teach men how to pornographise and prostitute women both visually and (as a natural corollary of the process) psychologically.[1]

This degradation (which men began to assume was their inalienable and 'natural' right) was brought about by powerful black magic, which corrupts images and symbols into oppression and imbalance through bypassing the heart – the chakra that always transforms and releases energy or force into higher consciousness – and proceeding instead to the base chakra, the 'foot' of the spine or tree of life. It is another of the beheading processes.

Anu chose Marduk, his own grandson, to instigate this perversion of the creational forces because he wanted to punish his own son, Marduk's father, for his insubordination as far as collusion in the plot to implement feminine subjugation was concerned. The son whom Anu wished to punish and bring into line by thus using Marduk, was named Enki; and it was upon Enki, and his noble female consorts, that the fate of humanity hung.

Notes and References

1 The corollary of this was that women won the 'consolation' prize of apparently being given power over men via their bodies. Thus were women tempted away from their own wisdom, which would have shown them what was going on and urged them to rise up against such a desecration. Although this power seemed to serve women, it actually contributed towards the perpetuation of the cycle of violation and oppression from which they suffered. The problem was not, of course, the free expression of female physical beauty, or men's appreciation of it, but rather the carnal objectification and dehumanizing of women, which descended not only over the vision of men, but of women as well. Today's expression of it can be seen in the endless array of magazines and other media which keep girls and women trapped in a mad hamster wheel of anxiety and obsession. Thus are both genders forced into a consciousness trapped at the level of the body, which of course is exactly where a certain ill-willed member of the higher Anunnaki wants us. When the Falling Knight, who represents a 'falling away' from the truth of Tiâmat, reawakens from his enchanted stupor, the True Knight will re-establish himself within the heart of humanity. Simultaneously, the Divine Woman will come forth in women and light her flame in the hearts of men, who in their turn will allow her to manifest. Thus Ascension can begin.

Chapter Fourteen

The Striking of the Dolorous Blow

Paradoxically, Tiâmat was not 'beheaded' by having her head cut off! It was her heart centre that was attacked and 'slain' (hidden from humanity's view and banished from humanity's perception in an act of purposeful and malicious intent). Marduk accomplished this horrendous deed by reversing or rejecting the Holy Spirit, so that it 'inflated' Tiâmat's heart or centre.

We feel this means that he somehow, by reverse-spin magic pertaining to the Holy Spirit, brought about a highly dangerous situation on earth that could be tipped into catastrophe by precipitation. This situation was not 'natural' in the true sense, but it did arise through the agency of the powers of nature, which of course are an expression of the Holy Spirit or Breath. Marduk then proceeded to his planned act of precipitation by shooting a 'red arrow' through Tiâmat's centre, or heart.

This 'red arrow' is the lance in the Grail stories that continually drips blood. It is a revered constituent of the Grail mysteries, and it manifests as the Rod of Justice (purloined by Marduk and wielded by him as a supreme token of his kingly insignia); as the lance which was thrust through the side of Jesus as he hung on the cross, delivering the death-blow and piercing, first his spleen (an important chakra, and deeply significant to the nature and meaning of the lance, as the spleen is anciently and esoterically associated with the forces of wrath) and then his heart; as Joseph of Arimathea's staff; as the lance which appears in the histories of the Grail; as the lance that pierces Dagobert's eye; and, finally (though that is an ill-advised word to use in relation to this mystic lance!), as the Spear of Longinus once again, this time in Hitler's possession and, interestingly, called the Spear of Destiny, so linking it with the hallowed knowledge engraved upon the Emerald Tablet of Destiny or Destinies.[1]

In this context of sacred knowledge, it has another, most interesting aspect in that it relates to what Dr Peter Coveney and Dr Roger Highfield refer to as 'the Arrow of Time' in their scientific best-seller of the same title. Here, they ask the question as to why time points from the past to the future with the precision and focus of an arrow, and compare ideas of linear and circular time. We feel that the unforgiving nature of time, where every nano-second slips fugitively into the unmanifest as we experience it, is somehow connected with a certain master and lord of karma and time, and is one of his distortions, in the perpetration of which he was aided by a mind whose scientific vision was cosmic in its proportions (we shall reveal more of this astonishingly gifted scientist in due course).

We remain convinced that the nature of this 'arrow of time' (a term originated in 1927 by the astrophysicist Arthur Eddington) has some connection with the misuse of the Red Arrow or sacred lance, especially as two earlier scientists who specifically dedicated their lives to the study of 'the arrow of time' died in sinister circumstances, by their own hand, as a culmination of progressive madness.

Hitler, the very embodiment of the False Path to the Grail, was obsessed with discovering the four Grail treasures, certain that when he had attained them, his dream of world domination would be granted realisation. He managed to obtain a lance which, he claimed, was once the treasured possession of certain ancient kings of Britain and France, and which was actually the Spear of Longinus, the centurion who had killed Jesus by plunging it into his side at the crucifixion.

This spear had, allegedly, assured victory after victory for the great king Charlemagne, but had eventually passed from his ownership into other hands, whereupon his triumphs promptly came to an end. In fact, on the same day that the American 7th Army seized the lance appropriated by Hitler as a trophy from Nuremberg Castle (30th of April 1945), Hitler conceded that his mission had failed and, within the confines of his bunker, whose walls were painted with sinister Nazi 'angels' which were actually depictions of the Naphidem, took his own life.

Eerily, Nuremberg was renowned as a centre of toymaking and playthings, echoing associations with Hitler's prototype, Marduk. The lance, rescued from Nuremberg, was eventually entrusted to the Hofburg museum in Austria. On its appearance in Wolfram von Eschenbach's *Parzival*, one of the earliest and most famous of the Grail stories, the lance engenders alarm among the knights of the Grail Castle.

They instruct Parzival concerning its malignity, explaining that it is an embodiment of the forces which corrupt and kill that which enables human beings to access their higher spirit. In other words, it represents what reversed the Holy Spirit, 'killing' Tiâmat and eventually banishing the sacred stairway from earth to heaven (one of the Four Hallows or aspects of the Grail, and in fact its unified essence). Although this is indeed so, the spear (or the lance or the arrow) bears within it the magnificent life-giving potential of what it truly is in its positive state. The 'red arrow' that is described in the Sumerian texts has a deep esoteric meaning. It was given to Marduk by one to whom in comparison he was but a callow youth.

The Red Arrows flying team who grace the skies above the ancient city of Lincoln today, creating endlessly significant symbols pertinent to the Grail story among the clouds, unknowingly commemorate this red arrow, this most holy lance, this Spear of Destiny.

The statue of the Falling Knight within the cathedral, who bears it in his back, through his spleen, and points via its agency towards the resting-place of the Holy Grail (from our turbulent past to the glory of our future), tells of the mystery of the Red Arrow, for he awaits the heart-piercing awakening that it will eventually bestow, and that in time, together with the rest of humanity, he will no longer be able to resist or deny. Its mystical properties were put into reverse-spin by Anu, Marduk and others, and it 'killed' Tiâmat, piercing her heart and splitting her open.

Marduk then tore her apart, separating earth from heaven and cutting off humankind from its higher self or heart-centred soul, so that it had to struggle onwards along the path of evolution as one blind, deaf and dumb to spiritual realities.

Behind Marduk's action there was one mighty figure, who colluded and conspired with him every step of the way, although the two always despised each other and worked against, as well as scheming with, one another. We shall come to this great lord presently, and reveal who he is in all his corrupt dimensions.

When Marduk had torn Tiâmat asunder, he seized the Emerald Tablet of Destinies from the overwhelmed Kingu – the two aspects of whom manifested as the divine couple assigned to their task of light-bearers by Tiâmat – and fastened it to his own breast. Their authority and their destiny had been stolen from them, and they sank into near-powerlessness. Later, Kingu fomented a rebellion, and was 'executed' for doing so. No doubt the divine couple attempted to reinstate their divinely granted influence, trying to usher in a dispensation of balance and enlightenment that had been lost when Marduk struck the Dolorous Blow. Well might she-he be executed for striving to overthrow Marduk's tyrannical reign! In fact, other members of the God-Headed people occasionally tried to steal the Emerald Table, with far less pure aspirations. The clay tablets state specifically that, in doing so, they sought universal domination.

Like the Grail (which in part it is), the Emerald Table could be approached by either the false or the true way. To those who were seduced by the false way, the Emerald Table promised a supreme alchemy that they could only interpret through their petty ego as a golden and glorious rule with themselves as sole and absolute ruler. The true 'supreme alchemy' is, of course, unconscionably different in kind. It is a divine alchemy, whereby we may personally change what is base in us to gold, to what is divine. We can be certain that this process, carried out sincerely by the majority of humanity, will change the world unutterably and eternally.

We may glean a whisper of this divine alchemy from some words which are said to be direct extracts from the Emerald Table itself (quoted in Laurence Gardner's *Genesis of the Grail Kings*): 'By this, thou wilt partake of the Honours of the Whole World...And darkness will fly from thee...With this thou wilt be able to overcome all things'.

Though torn, banished, violated and despised by them, Tiâmat the Great Mother, the Giver of All, did not abandon her children. The two aspects of the androgynous Kingu had not survived with regard to their influence on the earthly plane, but they had initiated a very special royal line of descent.

Prior to Kingu's appointment, the androgyne Anu, as we know, had been made supreme guardian of planet X's humanity, and also, eventually, of Earth's humanity. When the masculine aspect of Anu fell out of balance and sought both to split off and degrade his feminine aspect and to 'kill' Tiâmat, the status of Anu as supreme guardian was, naturally, withdrawn. The male aspect of Anu, however, was now living lawlessly by its own code of values and objectives, and cared nothing for the injunctions of Tiâmat. He became a false ruler.

Shortly before Tiâmat received the Dolorous Blow by Anu's

command, she transferred the status of Divine Couple from Anu and his denigrated female consort to Kingu, her faithful daughter-son, giving the androgyne the guardianship of the Emerald Tablet. When Kingu was overcome by Marduk and lost the Emerald Tablet to him, Tiâmat selected another Divine Couple to serve her and to uphold the true secrets of the Emerald Tablet in Kingu's stead. (There was a plan afoot to distort and partially hide its secrets once Marduk had stolen it.)

Consequently, Kingu, sometimes named Quingu (so we have the intimation of both 'king' and 'queen' in the two renditions of the name) began an entirely new line of descent. This royal line was headed by 'kings' and 'queens' from that point on, divinely elected guardians who would strive to restore the Emerald Tablet to humanity and reveal the secret teachings pertaining to the soul and the spirit, which Anu, and others after him, sought to hold in suppression and denial. Kingu marked the initiation of the line of Grail kings and Grail queens who challenged the authority of the false rulers, just as Jesus and Mary did in Palestine many thousands of years later.

Therefore, although there were appointed Divine Couples (more accurately, androgynes) prior to Kingu's promotion to this honour, there were no Grail kings and queens. These came into being, together with their title of 'king' or 'queen', as a direct result of the Dolorous Blow, the subsequent loss of the Emerald Tablet, and the thus inevitable withdrawal of the Grail from the Earth (see Chapter Fifteen). Nevertheless, the words 'king' and 'queen' were derived from the titular name of Cain, who was the first fully-anointed earthly human Grail king, but whose own title had its roots, as well as the sacred *ayin*, in the name Kingu or Quingu.

And so the assignment of 'Divine Couple' now passed to Anu's son and daughter – namely, Enki and Nin-khursag. By this time, the higher Anunnaki were no longer functioning as androgynes. In fact, Kingu was the first and the last of the Grail kings and queens to manifest as an androgyne. Enki and Nin-khursag were a light-attuned couple who had demonstrated the necessary spiritual qualities for Tiâmat to make them her chosen ones. Of course, as previously related, the hapless and purposely misled Marduk was Enki's son, and Enki it was whom Anu sought to punish, derogate and humiliate via the selection of Marduk as the trained and dedicated assassin of Tiâmat.

The Sumerian texts tell us that Marduk was the son of Enki by another of his higher Anunnaki wives, the noble lady Damkina, whose name might translate as 'blood-dweller', meaning that she brought higher Anunnaki genes to dwell in the blood of the ordinary Anunnaki. She was, in fact, an ally and a colleague of both Enki and Nin-khursag, helping them with their great project of bringing genetic facilitation to the expression of human consciousness on earth. In this respect, she selected the ordinary Anunnaki woman who was to receive Enki's sperm in a natural act of coitus, and nurtured her pregnancy. She herself did not conceive a child by Enki, nor was she his wife, but rather worked alongside him and Nin-khursag as a devoted disciple. This was in the early history of the Anunnaki, when the experiment which produced the Naphidem was first implemented (and afterwards very hastily abandoned!).

The resultant son, Marduk, was indeed of the Naphidem. He was seized brutally from Damkina's and his mother's care, and given over to Anu. Neither Damkina nor his mother, nor indeed Enki, had any idea of what Anu and his co-conspirators secretly plotted with respect to the fate of poor little Marduk, or the horrors to which he was subjected in private. He was, to all appearances, a fortunate child, chosen specially by Anu to receive gifts and privileges and a cultured upbringing. At this point, Enki had yet to learn just how shadowed Anu's intentions had become.

We have seen that Marduk, on accomplishing his supreme transgression, stole the Emerald Tablet from Tiâmat, the Great Mother of All, and pinned it in triumph to his own breast (his heart centre). However, this is by no means the end of the story of the Emerald Table. Its mysteries continue to unfold, and, as true Grail aspirants, we must follow them to their stupendous conclusion. Let the quest continue!

Notes and References

1. Hitler was determined to find the Holy Grail and the Ark of the Covenant to complete his collection of renowned magical implements. He sensed (or was informed by the hideous 'chiefs' who controlled him from the Naphidem dimension) that each was a repository of unimaginable power. He sent scouts and spies on various missions in an effort to locate these implements. Rennes-le Château, in the south of France, was specifically targeted. He never managed to procure anything, thank goodness, except for his previous discovery of the Spear of Destiny (which in itself was worrying enough); but of course he could never have 'found' the Holy Grail. He was actually looking for the Emerald Tablet, which is only a part of it. Naturally, Hitler and his associates would not have been able to grasp or follow its pure, spiritually-attuned teachings on ascension, but we feel that, nevertheless, he might have been able to

reverse some powerful and beautiful collective soul opportunity that the teachings would reveal.

The subsequent events of history prove that he did not find it, which is hardly surprising, as the mountain village of Rennes-le-Château with its fifth century church dedicated to Mary Magdalene and strongly associated with King Dagobert, sacred guardian of the Grail, is actually an ingenious mirror reflection of the Grail's true resting place. In fact, Hitler, with his inside knowledge, was just as anxious to lay hands on The Ark of the Covenant (only not literally, as he fully realised it would kill him were he to do so!). Mercifully for the world, this feat was also denied him. We have learned from our source that one of the Old Testament Tamars, King David's daughter, oversaw the operation of hiding away the Ark in Jerusalem, in order to further curtail its harmful influence. It is there still. The Syndicate (see Chapter 23), although it is not able to approach very close, has nevertheless managed to establish subtle contact with its forces (which are vastly diluted, thanks to Bezaleel's art and the efforts of Miriam and the Davidic Princess Tamar), and is currently using them to stoke unrest in the Middle East.

The Ark represents the seven rays of creation in sinister reverse mode, like a false, back-to-front reflection of the rainbow (the true reflection makes the circle of eternity – of everlasting life). Its energetic technology is connected in its symbolism to the backwards-dancing swastika of the Nazis, who enshrined the mystic military order (the SS – note the indication of two separated, rather than entwined [Enki and Nin-khursag's seal and sign] rearing snakes) that was the embodiment of the Knights Templars in reverse-spin – in other words, their very opposite. The Holy Grail is the divine antidote to the poisonous death-forces of the reversed or false Ark, and will sweepingly overcome their worst menace.

Chapter Fifteen

The Kings and Queens of the Grail

Whilst the plot to 'kill' Tiâmat was underway, what was happening in those higher dimensions, above, but still attached to, the Earth, as the God-Headed people met in council and discussed and cast democratic votes on their affairs? And what was happening on the surface of the Earth, where we live today and where once the angels and the God-Headed people, in those far-off times, walked with us?

At this point, a clear understanding of the story becomes even more vital, as we shall shortly reveal the terrible secret previously mentioned – a secret which must galvanise all of us to action if we are to save the day (which, of course, we will). We might think of the God-Headed people, once they had established humanity upon the Earth, as bathed in light but slowly beginning to respond to the strong pull of that darkness which emanates from the forces of physical matter – the final testing-ground of the spirit.

We have seen how, because the forces of matter on Earth are at their deepest and strongest, it was impossible for the perfectly evolved Nephilim to slow down their vibrations to the point where they themselves could initiate earthly humanity. That task had to be assigned to the God-Headed people (as was, in any case, always the plan), those sons and daughters of the Nephilim who were the result of male Nephilim matings with designated, exalted 'ordinary' Anunnaki women on planet X (the 'ordinary' Anunnaki of planet X having been created by the Nephilim, who used creatures of planetary matter on planet X to receive their vibrationally-slowed sperm and ova, just as the higher Anunnaki did on Earth; certain younger members [in evolutionary terms] of the Nephilim community then incarnated into the developing planet X embryos).

Therefore, there was within those higher Anunnaki, the God-Headed people, a less-evolved element than there existed within the supreme God-people, the Nephilim. It was this element that was their ultimate downfall.

However, we are certainly not saying that everything is a matter of genetics. Free will and the individual light in each soul can always refuse to respond to the darkness. That choice is eternally available, and we must never forget the ladder to heaven at the lowest point of earth, and the door to hell which dwells at the gate of heaven. Indeed, no response to higher genetic patterning can occur until the individual begins to make the right choices within his or her heart. The higher Anunnaki were not, by any necessity or inevitability, doomed to lose their balance. Unfortunately, the choices they made led them to do so.

As we have related, the problem began with Anu, the overall heavenly lord, or the greatest of the God-Headed people, who, united with his consort of equal status, ruled Earth's humanity and the higher Anunnaki from an exalted dimension beyond the mundane plane.

Although his people, the higher Anunnaki, walked the earth in high-vibrational bodies specially and temporarily adapted for the purpose, Anu and his consort never came down to earth. They were revered on high by earth's humanity under the tutelage of those God-Headed people who did descend to walk the earth from time to time. Again, we draw the distinction between these God-Headed people (the higher Anunnaki) and Earth's 'ordinary Anunnaki', who lived upon earth just as we do today, except that their bodies were less dense than ours, and, correspondingly, their perception and understanding of life and its many dimensions were quite a lot less dense too!

When certain disasters on earth (see Chapters 7& 8)) rocked the very heavens (those lofty dimensions above the physical Earth, yet still attached to it), Anu, affected by the resultant magnified imbalance, began to plot and scheme against Tiâmat, so that the male gender might win dominion, and call itself the originator of life. Although the soul life upon these higher dimensions is very different from mundane reality as we understand it on earth from our circumscribed perspective, we may understand that Anu led a conspiracy to slay Tiâmat, and had her split asunder by the agency of Marduk, so that the perfect communion between heaven and earth became afflicted and sullied. Anu's wife, Antu-Ki, who was the feminine essence of Anu's androgynous being that was in itself a microcosm of Tiâmat, was torn apart at the same time as Tiâmat. This was part of Anu's plot. Antu-Ki lost her power and influence with her integrity, and thereafter manifested as 'two' wives, who were given inferior status to Anu.

Nevertheless, Tiâmat's spirit breathed through these two wives, now called Antu, Lady of Heaven, and Ki, Lady of Earth. Anu, now in truth only half a being, as he was solely a male aspect, kept the name of his complete, androgynous self out of pure arrogance, refusing to recognise that in his separated state he was incomplete.

Prior to Anu's betrayal of her, Tiâmat had selected Antu-Ki and Anu (who were at this point still an androgynous being) as the Divine Couple, the sacred pair who were vehicles of light for the Earth and for Earth's twin planet, planet X. They were not king and queen as we understand the royal office today, but reigned from above, so to speak. There was no kingly or queenly office, with its accessibility to the people, on the actual earth, because until this point it had been deemed unnecessary.

The God-Headed people assumed a guiding authority, taking upon themselves the roles of healers, tutors, lawmakers, philosophers, technological innovators and agriculturalists, also leading the way in the arts and sciences. They instigated high moral codes of conduct, teaching earthly people that the light at the heart of their institutions was a gift from the divine couple represented by Anu, that beyond this light-bearing couple there was the Divine Serpent and her 'consort' (Tiâmat and Apsû) with their holy child Mummu, and that the sacred structure of all creation proceeded from them in the form of the Cross of Issue. This deiform family, for the Sumerians (we do not think they were accurate in their designation of Apsû), expressed God, the ineffable and unseen, the beloved Mother-Father, constantly bringing the Child of Light into unutterable being. These procedures held all in balance, and, whilst this was so, there was no need of hierarchy and kingship.

Such were the teachings of the God-Headed people before Anu's treachery. After it, Tiâmat was portrayed as the source of all evil, gloriously overcome by the Saviour – the mighty and conquering male principle. This concept spread abroad until it found its way into every major religion. At first, it declared that the Good Dragon (Anu, championed by Marduk) defeated the Evil Dragon (Tiâmat, the female Mother of Chaos, championed by the criminal Kingu).

The God-Headed people, who themselves bore serpentine characteristics, would never have introduced to the peoples of earth the notion that the dragon was intrinsically evil. Despite their fall from grace, they still worshipped the principle of the Heavenly Dragon of Light, although they became confused as to its origin and began to associate it with a male ancestor who had brought forth the all-male Anu.

Afterwards, when the Grail had closed down entirely and the wonder of the God-Headed people had been completely forgotten on the face of the earth, this perception metamorphosed into the idea that the dragon itself was evil personified, and that God was anthropomorphic, all-male and martially glorious, omnipotent by divine force of arms. Earthly communities everywhere emulated this conception of God, and their rendition of it as applied to their rulership was all too often aggressive, brutal, offensive and tyrannical.

After the Emerald Tablet was appropriated by Marduk, Tiâmat, behind the veil that humanity (including the higher Anunnaki) had drawn between her and the earthly dimension, saw that from now on something other than the status quo was desperately required. The divine couples could no longer rule only from on high. Their light, attenuated in its dispersal by the Dolorous Blow dealt to her, was no longer properly reaching those who dwelt on the material plane below. In future, representatives of the divine couples needed to be down on the Earth, available to ordinary men and women at the mundane level, dispensing order, justice, protection, and the spirit of the divine, which would shape and inspire communities.

Therefore, although she continued to appoint the crucial divine couples, who would bestow spiritual light and all that comprised divinity onto the mundane level from their exalted soul dimension, she also did something else.

She gave forth a new dispensation, unprecedented in this particular phase of humanity's earthly tenancy (we are suggesting here that civilisation, with lengthy interruptions, extends much further back in time than present-day scientific opinion recognises). Starting with Kingu, passing thereafter to Enki and Nin-khursag and then onwards via a bloodline which would descend to earth, Tiâmat initiated the mystical line of Grail kings and Grail Queens.

Such a monarchic bloodline had never come into existence before. The Grail kings and queens were brought into being specifically to nurture the memory and understanding of the Holy Grail, which entailed keeping alive our human awareness of the all-enfolding love and knowledge of Tiâmat, and the true Father God contained within her, in humanity's deepest heart. It must not be allowed to forget, Tiâmat decreed, that the root of all is love, our origin and our destiny – even if it were possible for only a small band of the faithful to keep this knowledge alive at any one time. This sacred and immeasurably precious knowledge, sourced in the Emerald Tablet, must be upheld and secretly passed on from age to age amidst the turmoil and darkness that had descended so barbarously upon humankind.

Tiâmat's true-hearted children would bear forth this knowledge as esoteric teachings, ever striving to reconnect the Grail and restore the Emerald Tablet to its rightful throne in humanity's heart and higher perception. These children – the Grail kings and queens and all who faithfully served them – would be in themselves the very essence of the 'ayin', the Divine Eye which contained the light, the sacred truth, the vision and the veritable reality of all things that humanity had lost amidst a sea of confusion and illusion.

Tiâmat 'lowered the kingship from heaven' so that members of the higher Anunnaki could actually assume kingship and queenship on earth, reflecting the highest of the high, the divine couple in heaven, just as they had done previously, but also for the sake of the reinstatement of the Grail and the Emerald Tablet. Throughout the course of history (and it is worth remembering the impaled Dagobert at this point), adversarial forces would collude and conspire to try to put out that Divine Eye forever.

Chapter Sixteen

The Sumerian King List

Tiâmat's instigation of the office of kingship is stated specifically in the Sumerian King List, a compilation inscribed on fifteen of the Mesopotamian clay tablets at some point before 2,000 BC. The list begins with the declaration, 'When the kingship was lowered from heaven, the kingship was in Eridu'. There follows a complete list of kings from around 29,500 BC until 1,800 BC (Laurence Gardner's calculations), together with their seats of dominion.

This enthralling King List marks the interruption of the Flood after recording the reign of eight kings (stating: 'The Flood swept thereover'). It then resumes with the words, 'After the Food had swept thereover, when the kingship was lowered from heaven, the kingship was in Kish'. The king who was in power when the great flood came is not named on this ancient list, but other Sumerian texts confirm his identity as King Zi-u-sudra, who equates with the biblical Noah. Therefore, there were nine antediluvian kings of Sumer. Their queens are not mentioned, except when one ruled alone, no doubt because after the Dolorous Blow had been struck, the status of women, among both the higher and the ordinary Anunnaki, began to diminish.

One fascinating point concerning the nine antediluvian kings and their queens (all members of the higher Anunnaki except for one) is that they reigned for a certain specified cycle of time measured in *shas*, meaning a 'passing' and written as a circle (360 degrees).[1] They therefore reflect planet X's 'passing' or crossing of the Earth's orbit, which takes place every 3,600 years.

However, a *sha* as a calculation of earthly time divides this figure by ten, which gives us the 360 degrees of the circle. A single degree of an Anunnaki *sha* equates to one solar orbit of the earth, making an entire *sha* 360 years in length. In fact, Anu, after splitting Tiâmat, had to recalculate the calendar, because, when the Earth began to reverse the direction of her spin from clockwise to anti-clockwise as she registered the sundering of the mighty Dragon Queen, there was a period when it seemed as if time stood still. Thereafter, our orbit round the sun was disrupted, a disruption which cooled the globe and caused the Ice Age to begin.

Anu's Akkadian name was Anum, and it is from this source that we derive the word *annum* (year), the measure in duration of our solar orbit, recalculated for us by the man who messed it up in the first place. It is also interesting to note that if we divide the original *sha*, which measures 3,600 years, by nine, we arrive at the figure 400, which emphasises Earth's sacred connection to the number 4 and the Cross of Issue, the Earth being the place of creation for the physical Anunnaki (ultimately ourselves) – their mother and their teacher. This figure is also connected with the moon, as the moon is exactly 400 times smaller than the sun, and 400 times closer to the Earth. It would seem as if the Anunnaki *sha* is an astronomical calculation relating to both solar and lunar influences as they relate to the Earth.

The eight initial higher Anunnaki kings were set in place to rule until the office of kingship could pass safely into the hands of the ordinary Anunnaki, the 'normal' human beings of earth, beginning with Noah (Zi-u-sudra). Counting back from the great Ice Age of 70,000 years ago, we can see that it took 35,000 years for human society to re-establish itself under the higher Anunnaki and reach the point where Tiâmat 'lowered the kingship from heaven'.

After the rule of the eight higher Anunnaki kings, the great experiment began. Tiâmat placed King Zi-u sudra (Noah), the first ordinary Anunnaki monarch, on the Sumerian throne. He had been specially prepared for office, and he was the ninth king to rule on earth. Nine is an interesting number, as it is the number of the Tower, denoting the Sacred Feminine, the number of the Dragon, and the ultimate expression of 3 (3x3=9), the trinity of Mother, Father and Divine Child that Tiâmat brought forth from her innermost in order to initiate creation itself. We have just noted how a *sha* (see above), when divided by nine, gives us the sum of 400, a calculation which, in astronomical terms of measurement, links the sun, the moon, and the earth. The Wisdom Keepers of the Australian aborigines tell of the 'ninth wave', the ultimate expression of spiritual dynamism and creative power, when by divine decree something is accomplished, is brought into being. So it was with Noah, for he and his queen were the foundation stone of Tiâmat's great plan, as we shall see. There existed a prodigious adversary to Tiâmat's plan, however. He instigated the Flood, which 'swept thereover'.

It is pertinent at this point to explain that Tiâmat, having been severed from her creation (severed from their heads, their direct cognizance and consciousness), could never, of course, be entirely cut off from human hearts. Were this so, then the Earth would very quickly have nosedived into terminal decline after the Dolorous Blow. Therefore, she had to work clandestinely, hidden in the depths of human hearts. From this sequestered, and sometimes tiny and flickering, sacred point, her great causal influences continued to hold sway. However, because of her inestimable gift of human freewill, which she would not revoke, she was reliant upon certain good-willed or God-willed people to implement her divine workings, both among the higher and the ordinary Anunnaki.

Some of these key figures simply acted upon the whispered intuitions that came to them from the deepest point of their heart. Others, like Enki and Nin-khursag, received these precious intuitions in a fuller consciousness of the divine and omnipotent spirit of Tiâmat. For them, although the Grail was not present on earth in the same fulsomeness of vivid expression as before, it was still beautifully operative in their hearts.

In just the same way, there were a significant number among the higher Anunnaki, and on earth, who decided to express enmity to these whispered intuitions. They reversed them, so that, themselves deaf to them, they yet recognised their presence in others. They then set themselves in direct opposition to such people, darkly inspired to block and shatter their initiatives and the application of their plans at every opportunity. Most of them did not know in full consciousness that they were resisting Tiâmat, as they had almost forgotten her; although some (Anu's group of conspirators) definitely did suspect that her influences were still abroad. To a degree, however, Tiâmat's workings were always hidden and veiled from them.

After the Flood, therefore, Tiâmat's great project, conceived of her towering love for humanity, continued unabated. (There was also a wonderful plan for all her children, concerning the connection of spirit and matter and, of course, linked to the Grail, which involved this mighty project of the bloodline that Tiâmat was working to establish. We will explain this, and all its stupendous implications, in a later chapter.)

Noah's kingship had been swept aside and destroyed, but Tiâmat's resolve, to introduce the first earthly (ordinary Anunnaki) king and queen in the physical dimension of our world who were yet linked through to the higher Anunnaki dimension, was again implemented. This kingship was a second attempt to establish a 'ninth' king.

Once more it was attacked and overcome, this time not by physical but rather by psychic and etheric inundation, from the same virulent adversarial force that had displaced Noah. The Sumerian tablets relate that it had to be 'destroyed' because of its misdemeanours; however, the flames of the ethical conflagration that consumed it were fanned deliberately, and had nothing whatsoever to do with its king, who was a true hero of history, as we shall see.

The resultant onslaught caused the threat of such terrible depredation on both the soul and material levels of earthly existence that Tiâmat, despite the prevailing patriarchal stance among the higher and the ordinary Anunnaki, had to install a queen as sole monarch after the second 'ninth' ordinary Anunnaki king (the first post-diluvian king) fell. There was no other way to remedy the precipitate situation. This queen (referred to on the Sumerian King List as the 'heavenly Nidaba') restored mundane and cosmic balance to the existing civilisation, although she was enthroned only after encountering great difficulties in executing Tiâmat's will, which Nidaba obeyed intuitively, led by an inner guidance of which her conscious self was only semi-aware now that Tiâmat had been 'killed'.

Later, we will examine exactly how, and by whose means, Tiâmat continued to implement her will within the higher and ordinary Anunnaki communities, both of which had forsaken and denied her sacred and supreme authority.

Notes and References

1. We have been most intrigued by the authors Christopher Knight and Alan Butler's work on the significance of the existence of the 'Megalithic Yard', which is a prehistoric unit of linear measurement, extending to precisely 82.966656 centimetres. It was used in the creation of a multiplicity of Megalithic structures throughout France and Britain, and was derived from calculating the rate of spin of the Earth, based on a geometric system which correlated 3660 with the 366 rotations of the Earth in a year.

In their book, *Civilisation One*, the authors show how this is part of an integrated system which is much more advanced and mathematically precise than any system in use today, and how our Imperial and Metric systems of measurement are in fact crude renditions of this original and immeasurably ancient system.

There is therefore a compelling body of evidence which indicates that highly advanced civilisations existed on earth even prior to the Sumerian culture, which of course is what our own source has demonstrated to us. Consequently, we are inclined to believe that, prior to Anu's interference, the measurement of a circle was indeed 3660 rather than 3600, and that perhaps the orbit of planet X around the sun is more likely to be 3,660 years rather than 3,600.

What was Anu's objective in thus distorting humanity's cyclical measurement of time? We believe that it partly relates to the home journey of planet X, so that as it passed Earth on each of its orbital cycles, some kind of force which this distortion helped to generate would make its successive encounters with the Earth progressively more destructive and disruptive to our planet at both the physical and psychical levels of life. Anu took the first steps in reversing the cosmic power of the rainbow (what it is in its true essence rather than its outer physical manifestation), which is Tiâmat's sign and the true 'Arc' of the Covenant. We think that Anu's plan also relates to what is biblically referred to as 'the Beast', which received a severe battering each time planet X passed us by. Anu's plot against the Beast links directly into his objective in distorting humanity's system of cyclical measurement. The number of the Beast is 666 (which we even find in literal existence in the figure of 82.966656 centimetres, the unit of measurement related to the 3660 circle or orbit). If we apply numerological reduction (see Chapter 52) to 366, we have a resolution of 6. If we apply numerological reduction to 360, we have a resolution of 9.

The Beast in Revelation in the New Testament is represented as evil, but in fact this is only because its energies have been reversed. There is a wholly good and positive aspect to this Beast when it functions as it should. The good Beast has been referred to as the Rainbow Serpent of the Skies by the Aborigines, and as a great serpent of light by many other ancient cultures, including the Mayans. We think that this Beast of the earth-energies is somehow connected to planetary ley lines (a grid of spiritual and electromagnetic energy that covers the surface of the Earth) and to ancient sacred sites, such as stone circles. We know, for instance, that the advanced science of pre-history demonstrated by the Megalithic Yard understood the complexities of the dimensions, motions, relationships and subtle interrelationships, of the Earth, the moon and the sun, that it had measured the solar system and encompassed the knowledge of how the speed of light was integrated into the rotational movements of our planet.

This is the key. How the speed of light is integrated into the rotational movements of the Earth, and how the great Serpent of Light weaves and coils its way around the planet via the Earth's ley lines and sacred sites are one and the same process.

The Mayans (who provided the renowned calendar with its 'end-date' for our present civilisation of 21st of December 2012) give us another matrix besides the rainbow and its manifestation of the seven rays of Creation. The rainbow is, of course, the spectrum of the perfect white light from which everything is created. The Mayans saw that brilliant white light as placed above the rainbow, and the sacred blackness as below it. Being, respectively, the total unified radiation of light, and the total absence of light, black and white cannot be considered as 'colours' in the same sense that the rays of the rainbow are colours.

Nevertheless, the matrix gives us the blue ray as the 'heart' ray, placed at the centre of the nine inclusive gradations between pure light and no light. This is interesting, because, as we shall see as we progress through our story of the Grail, the blue ray is the colour of the priceless 'Stone of Ascension' which resides within our heads (the reason that it is blue is explained fully in Chapter 65). When Margaret Bailey and I see Tamar, her presence is announced by either a beautiful, all-pervading emerald-green light, or by a field of blue and green light (very similar to the swathes of colour, particularly green, which manifest as the northern lights). We think that, although the emerald ray is indeed the true heart-ray, the blue light of the head or mind must be lifted up into that heart-ray, and merge wholly into attunement with it, before the individual can become 'fully human'. The mind keeps its identity as individuated mind, but yet is as one with the green ray. When this happens, the blue ray becomes as beautiful and mystically jewel-like as the green ray. If the mind ray chooses to function on its own, refusing to centre itself in the heart, its colour becomes a deathly, chilling, sinister blue, disturbing to behold. This, we believe, is the esoteric teaching behind the Mayan matrix.

We know that the number 6 represents the 'beheaded' consciousness ("Off with their heads!" screams the false queen in *Alice in Wonderland)*, its connection with God (the Grail) lying severed at its feet, whilst the fully human, God-Headed individual who embraces the Grail and whose 'Stone of Ascension' in the head is fully functional, is represented by the number 9. There is also another aspect to 6 in that it is the receptive half of a full circle with its completion in 9; and so we see that 6 in its true aspect has a beautiful and noble function as divine receptacle, and that it is only ignorant human interference which has given it its afflicted and negative connotation. In fact, when we join up the figures six and nine, we can imagine that it is a model of the Earth with her two aligned poles in emphasis.

We believe that the Serpent of Light, which is the Earth-Serpent (the Earth's very life-system of energies), is a good and beautiful force in that it is a perfect receptacle for dynamic cosmic energies which it translates into exactly what the Earth needs in order to keep her informed and functioning at every level of her cognition as an individuated entity, but that, by dint of the actions of Anu and Enlil, it has been reversed, and, due to the blind and abusive way we use it and attune to it because of our afflicted collective consciousness, it has degenerated into the 'Beast' described in Revelation.

As we shall explain, something tremendous will happen around the time of the 'end-date' to return everything that Anu and his conspirators have put into reverse-spin, to positive or forward-spin once more. Anu, foreseeing the danger of this (his great hope being that even this tremendous act of the forces of light would ultimately fail because of his ever-increasing hold on human consciousness) wants the great Earth-Serpent to be impacted in such a way that the baptism of the 'end-date' will be thwarted. Instead of this great baptismal force creating a 9 out of a 6 (a re-heading or resurrection from a be-heading) which is what should happen by divine decree, Anu wants to create a 6 out of a 9. Thus can he be sure that the planet, and humanity with it, will begin to die.

He has, therefore, done something to impose a completely false '9' state upon the Earth-Serpent, so that, when the great baptism comes, the healing, resurrecting forces that reach it will be thrown into confusion, and it will be unable to revert to its true '9' expression of wholeness, spiritual unity and power. Instead, the poor Beast will be turned on its head to become a '6' creature, an empty vessel incapable of receiving and uniting with its '9' essence because the timing for the descent of this essence, when the Beast should have been in its receptive state, has been thrown awry.

Anu has created this bogus '9' state for the Earth-Serpent by abusively using the forces of linear time and mathematical manipulation in relation to the process by which the speed of light is integrated into the rotational movement of the Earth. By means of such malicious manoeuvering, he thinks he will effectively bag us!

Then is all hope lost? Absolutely not. Although what we ourselves must do as a planetary community cannot be removed from the arena of our responsibility and must be done by a sufficient number of us in order to ensure the earthly survival of humanity and the planet and to secure our freedom, this particular aspect of Anu's cunning plan has already been masterfully dealt with by the ancient Mayans. This beautiful, spiritual and awe-inspiring culture of antiquity perennially fascinates our own, and we continue to pay tribute to its wonders. There is one flaw, however. Why, oh why, people ask, did the Mayans carry out such bloodthirsty and barbarically cruel human sacrifices? We think we can provide an answer to this question.

We believe that it was a particularly severe and painful form of 'lapwinging' (see Chapter 20), undertaken by the noble Mayan culture in order to save the planet in 2012, although we predict that the dramatic 'end-day' event will actually take place at the beginning of 2013. A certain member of the higher Anunnaki (Anu's son) became particularly enmeshed in the plot to wipe earthly humanity out of existence and actually became its ringleader (an apt title, as we shall discover).

As he became more terrible and cruel in his wrath and spite and more entirely given over to demonic possession, so did he tighten his control over human society wherever he had managed to gain a foothold, which was virtually everywhere, as he had once been a beneficent and reasonably benevolent custodian of the Earth and her humanity. As we shall show later on in our story, this higher Anunnaki man was recognised as a deity in Sumerian times, and the same deity is recognised by scholarship as equating with the later Mayan god who demanded blood sacrifices of a particularly horrifying nature. Whilst appearing to appease and propitiate this wrathful god, the Mayans were actually keeping him at bay and skilfully dodging the restless gaze of his roving vengeful eye as they dedicated their highest esoteric knowledge and craft to the sole purpose of foiling the evil schemes of Anu, his son, and their followers.

They created by wondrous craftsmanship thirteen crystal skulls, one for each centre of the advanced chakra system which, towards the 'end-date', would begin to become active in humanity (the chakra system relates to the rainbow and the totality of the rays of creation). These crystal skulls will prevent the Earth-Serpent from suffering the death-strike planned for it via Anu's scheme, and will allow it to ascend in glory, becoming the thrice nine (999) creature whose essence accords with its true divine nature. (For an explanation of the hugely significant meaning of this 'thrice' pattern, see Chapter 33). The crystal skulls will also help to break the power and purify the subtle crystals of a vast evil mirror created by Anu's son. However, we offer a word of warning – unless humanity responds to the wisdom and love of its own heart centre, which is connected to God, the crystal skulls will not be able to function efficiently at the appointed time. The beautiful green ray surging from our collective quickened heart centre will activate the blue ray in its fullest and highest measure, and this exalted blue ray (called the 'Stone of Ascension') is the key to activation of the skulls.

Chapter Seventeen

Changing the Structure of the Soul

After Queen Nidaba had restored Tiâmat's celestial order on earth and her reign came to its conclusion, further higher Anunnaki kingships were reinstated as before. Thereafter Tiâmat decided that new gifts must be given to humanity so that it would not keep missing the mark, gifts exceeding even those she had bestowed on Noah and the second 'ninth' king; for these two ordinary Anunnaki kings had been given special powers via her divine dispensation, even though such powers had ultimately failed to protect the earthly monarchs from the terrible might of their adversary.

She decided that humanity must be provided with an intellectual and soul capacity that would broaden and stabilise before it heightened, in order to establish a sound base that could not be toppled so easily by a too eager vertical ascent into mystical secrets for which the young souls of humanity were not ready, thereby managing to depose themselves by impure and egotistical design in attaining the treasures of occult knowledge. Tiâmat would bestow upon us the mundane intellect that we possess today, in order that we could advance much more safely along the grand spiritual highway. From now on, humanity would take three steps forward, and then one step back, to make sure that it paused, reflected, considered the lessons it had absorbed and pondered the wider picture before continuing on its way. This method would restore balance and sure-footedness to her poor, ailing human creation. It would become as the mountain goat, a nimble, deft and inspired climber, unharried by rocky, steep and arid terrain.

What this actually meant from an esoteric and creational basis was that, from a certain chosen point onwards, Tiâmat would dispense with the initial structure of the human soul, which in those far-off days was built upon the concept of a tower – tall, slender, and thrusting upwards with great vigour and speed upon a narrow base designed to accommodate this lightning growth upwards – and instigate for it instead the shape of a pyramid. According to this shape the human soul would in future be constructed – its base broad and square, its four pyramidal sides erecting themselves sturdily and steadily upon this safe and sound foundation, and its pinnacle rising only in accordance with the spiritual speed upon which its four strong pyramidal sides progressed.

Our new intellects, although by no means any kind of higher or superior vessel of intelligence than the present humanity already possessed, would provide balance and a steadying hand, even a certain pragmatic blindness concerning spiritual reality. We would no longer be able to snatch the realisation of it out of the air, like a child catching a butterfly in cupped hands. In future, we would have to dig and delve for it.

Nevertheless, although our new kind of intellect would ensure for us a sound, cuboid base upon which to build our awareness, Tiâmat saw that it could and would become a stumbling block. She therefore, in order to dispense perfect balance, revealed to humanity new secrets, new initiations, new esoteric truth – new yet unaccountably ancient. So far, only the Nephilim and the leaders among the higher Anunnaki had been given this revelation of divine truth. However, Tiâmat was determined that humanity should not be deprived of this ultimate blessing. And so it was given forth, perhaps around 3,900-800 BC, and the new humanity emerged.

The Capricornian goat, rising up from the sea and climbing the mountain, would be the sign of the new human strain. It would initially have two horns (two aspects of consciousness) as goats have; but, by stages, it would evolve into the one-horned, one-pointed unicorn, receiving emanations from the spiritual stars (the imperishable stars, shining behind the physical stars), its consciousness honed into a beautiful unity. Only by such measures would humanity survive, and, with it, the special bloodline that Tiâmat wished to initiate on earth, the one which would bear such marvellous, hallowed fruit that our eternal survival would be assured thereby, as we shall discuss.

Tiâmat knew that, as the Grail closed down, the higher Anunnaki would eventually leave the earth spheres. Humanity would be forsaken, having caused its abandonment by its own hand. The designated bloodline, carried forward by her new humanity – those with modified mental and soul processes founded upon a cuboid base – and destined to convey its qualities to the whole of humankind, was its only hope. And so, for the third time, she instigated a bloodline of earthly kingship and queenship from the new humanity which would replicate exactly, in earthly terms, the overlighting divine couple. This time, it worked. And we see from the Sumerian King List that there were nine kings prior to the flood, and nine kings after it.

The ninth post-diluvian king (the 'ninth wave', the wave from Tiâmat's heart, her very essence) was Atabba (Adapa, or the *Adâma*) – Adam himself, although we shall see that it would be Eve, his all-important queen, from whom the bloodline actually descended.

Tiâmat decreed that future ordinary Anunnaki kings and queens (initially Adam and Eve, who came after the two false starts represented by Zi-u-sudra [Noah]) and the second 'ninth' king, who was Ga- nadin –ur, Noah's great grandson), or the sole ruler, if circumstances dictated, would not only reflect the divine couple in the heavens, but would be specially linked to them by means of magical ceremony, namely the royal coronation, or sacred anointing ritual. And then what was truly stupendous occurred, by means of the Dragon Queen's further divine decree.

Chapter Eighteen
Tíamat's Call

Tiâmat, in touch with circular, all-pervading time as well as limited linear time, saw that the divine couples whom she appointed would be continually attacked and injured by the earthly powers of darkness that had been unleashed by the Anunnaki fall from grace (remembering, of course, that we are all Anunnaki, both the God-Headed people and the people of earth – the 'ordinary' Anunnaki). Human (Anunnaki) free will, the free will that had been so sadly misdirected by it recipients as to permit the wholesale refusal of the gift of spiritual light and life from the Godhead, was yet the most precious gift of Tiâmat to her beloved children, and could not be countermanded. Whilst Tiâmat continued to embrace this decision, and would never consider committing the supremely tragic reversal of overturning that free will, even though it had begun so earnestly to court the darkness, she had to swiftly apply the dynamic of her omniscient will in a measure to save the Earth, and possibly even the physical solar system, from the terrible destruction that humanity seemed hell-bent on wreaking upon itself.

It must be remembered that, at this point in history, the divine couples who were the light-bearers of Tiâmat had never walked the earth. Anu and Kingu (both androgynes) had never descended to the lower planes of physicality.

Many revered teachers came and went at the level of earthly life, bearing the light of the third principle of the Godhead (the 'Christ') to some degree. However, the designated light-bearing couples who dwelt in the higher dimensions, reflecting the light of the mystical Christ for both the higher and the ordinary Anunnaki and assuming the role of king and queen in those loftier dimensions (the 'Eden' of the higher Anunnaki), never descended. When Enki and Nin-khursag took up the role of divine couple, they did occasionally walk the earth in temporary physical bodies; but as the Grail energies gradually closed down, they were able to do so less and less, until finally it became an impossible feat.

Tiâmat saw that even her plan of lowering the divine kingship and queenship from heaven so that it would eventually pass into the hands of the ordinary Anunnaki on earth, and in so doing, create a mirror reflection, within the earthly king and queen, of the divine couple dwelling in heaven, would not save humankind now. It would help the situation, and prolong life on earth for a certain time, but beyond this brief extension she saw that we would still insist on destroying ourselves.

The only thing to do, now this terrible state of affairs had occurred (the severing of the Grail), was to put out a call to the highest of the high, to the lordly Nephilim, her pure and incorruptible children who 'stood within the presence of God'. Could there be a divine pair among them, whom she would choose and yet who would freely volunteer, to do, not only the utterly unprecedented (for we must remember that we are talking about the Nephilim and not the higher Anunnaki: the Nephilim whose exalted vibrations prevented them from walking the physical earth except in their light bodies, and even then only when conditions were not nearly so adverse as they had become), but what seemed the utterly impossible – to descend to earth, *in physical bodies*, and bring the spiritual dimensions in which only the soul could dwell *right down to the mundane level*?

Such a thing had never been dreamed of before. The whole point of colonisation of planet Earth was, of course, eventually to lift the planet and its dimension of gross matter into the freedom and beauty of the everlasting spiritual worlds. But *this* - this startling plan to put the very opposite into effect first, and bring heaven *right down to earth* - could it be done? It was absolutely vital that it should be done, for only by such means could the Emerald Tablet be rescued and restored to humanity, and the Grail re-opened so that the teachings of the Nephilim couple – the teachings of the Christ – might finally be understood. Yet it would entail unique dedication, devotion and self-sacrifice on an undreamt-of scale for the divine couple involved, if indeed such a 'couple' (actually an androgyne) existed, even amongst the most illustrious of the Nephilim. There could be no possible incentive, motivation or reward for the implementation of this Herculean task except that of pure, unparalleled love for humanity.

This love would have to faithfully reflect Tiâmat's own love for her creation, would have to be commensurate, albeit on a human scale, with the glory of the great Daughter-Son, the Christ (Mummu in Sumerian terms), pure spirit, whom she had birthed out of her own heart as the

Divine Fire driving all creation, of whom all immortals and mortals alike – Nephilim, higher and ordinary Anunnaki (the latter representing people like ourselves today) – possess an infinitely precious spark.

The Nephilim had walked their appointed path. They had evolved over incalculable aeons on planets other than Earth, and had left the travail and brutishness of the lower levels behind forever. They were immeasurably far above the Earth, and had no reason to taste of its sorrow and sordidness, or to participate in its violence and suffering, ever again.

And even if volunteers for this unspeakably daunting, harrowing and thankless mission could be found, how could *Nephilim* ever walk the earth? How could what was made of the highest of the high, of the purest spirit, fire and dew in all its mystical dimensions, be lowered, compacted and compressed into physical, animal bodies? The very experience of that alone would be inappeasable agony. And then to be brutally assaulted by the darkness continually, and continually keep on course until all was finished and perfected although it would cost ocean-depths of unending bitterness, ignominy, anguish, sorrow and tears, and might even then be rendered useless at the eleventh hour – how could this be asked of even the highest of the high? Miracles are miracles, but this was something else again.

And yet Tiâmat put out the call. The task of the divine couple would be unconscionable in its terrifying dimensions. They would have to find a way to descend to earth, *without the Grail*, for that would have disappeared by the time of their appointed coming. They would have to find a way to gently lead humankind, who would by now have mired itself in the deepest ignorance, superstition and confusion, back to the path of light. They would have to singlehandedly break the shackles of the mightiest of the lower forces of earth, forged by one of whom we will presently speak. They would have to find a way to reintroduce the teachings on the divine alchemy detailed on the Emerald Tablet, whereby humankind could perceive that the potential of that divine alchemy existed within each individual soul, independently of any controlling third party, and that the responsibility for igniting and activating it lies with each one of us.

They would have to drive back the worst shadow ever to have fallen on the Earth and her peoples, and be ridiculed and despised for doing so.

And they would have to bring back the Grail by rescuing the Emerald Tablet, and revealing its final secret, in the most daring bid for freedom ever made on behalf of humanity. Not only all this, but they would have to bring back to earth, *through the agency of themselves*, the infinitely precious drop of Tiâmat's essence, that of Divine Goddess herself, which the Earth had lost when the great imbalance was perpetrated and the Grail was severed. But even all that would not be enough.

A new heaven and a new earth were needed, and nothing else would do. Tiâmat's essence would have to be brought back to the Earth in greater measure than it had ever been given before. A Divine Woman would have to touch down, who, through heavenly cooperation with her sacred parents, would heal the Earth and set it spinning the right way again, its negative gyration overcome at last.

How likely was it that an answer would come to Tiâmat's call? Yet come it did. Through unimaginable millennia, the divine couple, Jesus and Mary Magdalene, advanced towards the Earth, always in training for that most arduous of all missions, the saving of humanity from itself. Because of circular time, Tiâmat was able to summon them and prepare them in a limitless dimension, in existence before the Earth began. They were the two members of the Nephilim, the highest of the high, who answered her call. And when they came to earth, they brought a light whose measure had never been encountered on these planes before, nor ever has since.

Tamar was their daughter – Tamar who was Tiâmat. The Dragon Queen – God – was able to take the Earth back into her full embrace through the agency of Tamar, the Divine Woman, the Holy Grail. When Anu commanded Marduk to 'kill' Tiâmat, he placed the power of the kingly descent into Marduk's hands. But it did not belong to him. It belonged to the new line of Grail kings and queens, which would culminate in Tamar.

Marduk the usurper overcame the rightful divine couple (the androgyne Kingu, the first Grail king-queen and the initiator of the royal line), after the authority of divine couple had been removed from Anu and his consort (now, after the striking of the Dolorous Blow, manifesting as two wives). Therefore, Kingu was the grand ancestor of the Grail bloodline.

Does this mean that all of us outside this bloodline are somehow excluded from its inheritance? By no means; not only does spiritual law forbid exclusivity, but the calibre of that law is expressed in the fact that it was Kingu's blood which the Anunnaki used to bring about the descent of the ordinary Anunnaki into physicality, via the wombs of the 'wild women'. Kingu's blood was, of itself, higher Anunnaki blood, of course; but Tiâmat gave Kingu's blood or essence a special virtue – she connected it with greater power than before to her own essence. Clearly, this was a spiritual procedure rather than a physical one, yet nevertheless it demonstrates how we are, veritably, all of one blood.

We have seen how Tiâmat, seeing the terrible need of erring humanity after the Grail had been disconnected, 'lowered the kingship from heaven'. As previously stated, this quote is derived from the tablets which give the famous Sumerian King List. The tablets go on to confirm: 'They had not yet set up a king for the beclouded people. No headband and crown had been fastened; no sceptre had been studded with lapis lazuli... Sceptre, crown, headband and staff were still placed before Anu in heaven...There was no counselling of its people; then kingship descended from heaven.'

These inscriptions mark the point at which Tiâmat instigated the royal bloodline here on earth, although, as we know, the sceptre had to pass from the higher Anunnaki to the ordinary Anunnaki before it was properly established.

It was put in place so that it would provide, initially, a means of reinstating the dynamics of organization into new communities, ensuring protection, security and the progress of civilisation for the confused mass of humanity, left broken and chaotic after the depredations caused by the coming of the great imbalance. As we have seen, its ultimate design, incalculably mightier in its grandeur of purpose and innovation, was to provide a biological stairway down to earth, which, at the mystically designated time, the divine couple of all divine couples, Jesus and Mary Magdalene, would descend in humility and simplicity, touching down in a stable, a cave in Bethlehem, under a star which would gather and merge from all four corners of the heavens until it shone like a full moon and, at the appointed hour, release a serpent tail of light that would point directly over their place of birth.

This bloodline enshrined a special DNA pattern which was crucial to the outworking of the great plan. It had to do with mitochondrial DNA, present only in the female strain, and an originating gift from Tiâmat. Whilst this special bloodline was absolutely necessary in that it preserved the DNA patterns essential to the survival in earthly matter of the full expression of the sacred feminine (the origin and the continuing dynamic of life), its instigation was of itself born of the great imbalance that afflicted earthly humanity. Therefore, an imbalance manifested within it, an imbalance pertaining to the forced reliance of the purposes of the spirit on racial blood. In due course, Tamar herself, through great personal and cosmic sacrifice, would end this bloodline – the biological stairway down to earth – banishing it, and the imbalance it carried, forever from our world. She would replace it, gloriously, with the wonder of the reinstated Grail – a process that she will complete in our time, very shortly, perhaps before 2013. (This seems a bit unlikely now. We were given to understand that the Grail would appear shortly after publication of this book, but no date was specified, except that the time wouldn'y be long.)

This was all to take place in the far distant future. Mary Magdalene and Jesus would secure that future; but for now, after the fall of Anu and his consort, who retained their corrupt power as rulers but who were divested of their authority as Tiâmat's divine couple, her newly-appointed divine couple, Enki and Nin-khursag (Anu's son and daughter), were in trouble, as the great Dragon Queen had foreseen.

To understand the nature of their difficulties and to see how their determination and their momentous decisions and actions, put into operation almost six thousand years ago, continue to impact our world today, we must first examine how darkness descended on Anu, and how he began to despise humanity and to plot its destruction.

Chapter Nineteen

Lord and Lady of the Mountain

We have said that Tiâmat's spirit breathed through Anu's two wives, who had previously manifested as an integrated entity - the conjoined feminine essence of the androgyne Anu - until Tiâmat herself had been split. This feminine essence was Antu, Lady of Heaven, who was not only cast off from her husband, but was also fragmented into two. She now manifested as Antu and Ki. Being the feminine member of the divine androgyne, she was directly linked to Tiâmat. What befell Tiâmat befell her.

It is important to realise that the corruption of Anu, and the degradation of his consort, took place over a protracted period of time. Throughout many generations of human history, Anu and Antu-Ki could still be regarded as light-bearing beings. Anu himself, however, eventually became very dark indeed, and retreated to a sinister dimension which may be understood as a location among the physical stars in the constellation of Orion. (We will say more of this, and of Anu's peculiar influence on humanity's perception of time, in the second volume of The *Secret of the Ages*.) Many esotericists confirm that there is a cosmic body, a planet or a star, associated with the name of Anu, which is ominously ill-willed towards humanity, and continues to plot its destruction. We need not be in the least concerned, however, as Jesus, his soul-twin John, and Mary Magdalene and Tamar, have shown us how to disempower him and his plans to see humanity fail.

Tiâmat oversaw the fertility of Anu's two wives (originally a single entity, but now occupying two bodies). Antu, Lady of Heaven, gave birth to Enki, Lord of the Earth and Waters. Ki, Lady of Earth, gave birth to Enlil, Lord of the Air. We can see how this situation contributed in some degree to restoring a little of the cosmic balance that Anu had destroyed. Heaven and earth are united again through the Lady of Heaven giving birth to the Lord of Earth, and the Lady of Earth giving birth to the Lord of Heaven, or Air. Nevertheless, the Dolorous Blow had been struck, and

Lady Ki represented the bereaved and sundered Earth. We ask you to take particular note of the son (Enlil) she bore, and to ponder the conditions under which he was born.

From now on, the necessary cosmic balance would be held in a limited and unsatisfactory way, by means of genetics and biology, albeit an exalted and non-physical 'biology' pertaining to the bodies of the higher Anunnaki and the organisational principles of their life-systems. In other words, it would be a material balance, not a true spiritual one.

As we shall see, now that Anu had fallen from grace (although he retained his royal power for a long time after his spiritual darkening began, until his own imploding vision removed him from office), this restoration of balance through materiality was also almost the only means by which an imperfect and temporary rendition of the Grail could be preserved - manifesting in physicality on the Earth via a special bloodline emanating from Tiâmat. It carried within it, through a fusion of physical and spiritual DNA which was kept fed and nourished by a unique and exceptional method, the divine *potential* of receiving a drop of Tiâmat's ineffably precious essence and grounding it into the Earth's energies or grid system, thereby connecting with the Earth's heart and correcting the misalignment that took place when Tiâmat had been split asunder by Marduk.

(We might think of the Earth herself as a microcosmic expression in form of the mighty infinity that is Tiâmat, joined to Tiâmat's heart via her own heart, which made the Earth a perfect ideation of Tiâmat, and ensured that before the brutal split, heaven and earth [Tiâmat's heart and the Earth's heart] were conjoined as one. In those days, heaven was not cut off from earth, and earth was not cut off from heaven.)

Although the special royal bloodline that preserved the Grail carried within it the divine potential to receive the unutterably sacred drop of Tiâmat's essence which had to return to earth and be stabilised here before the Grail itself could come into being once again (heaven and earth reunited), it is important to note that potential is a long way from actualisation. Actualisation would come, in the far distant future, when the supreme Nephilim couple, Jesus and Mary Magdalene (the human rendition of the Christ), travelled from heaven to earth down the stairway of the Grail bloodline, and brought forth the drop of the Divine Essence as Tamar, their daughter.

Between them all, the four sacred persons (Tamar, Mary, Jesus, and John the Beloved) rescued for us, the people of earth, the genuine Emerald Tablet that had been hidden away and purposely made inaccessible to us. On this Emerald Tablet (a living record of Tiâmat's priceless wisdom, the divine alchemy that alone will save us and allow us to create a paradise out of earthly conditions) is inscribed the Secret that will make a gift of the Holy Grail to everyone who wishes to receive it. Jesus and Mary taught the divine alchemy; they received it direct from the heart of Tiâmat, the Great Mother, who was symbolised by the dove which appeared when John the Baptist baptised Jesus and Mary in the waters of the Jordan. Their teachings brought to us everything we need to know for our all-encompassing spiritual evolution.

But the teachings are facilitated by the Grail, which is the necessary component to permit entry into their deepest heart. This is the Secret that will be given to us as a gift by Jesus, Mary, Tamar and John, the ultimate gift of Tamar, the Divine Woman who is Tiâmat, that distilled drop of Tiâmat's essence which returned to earth and took human form. And so we see that, indeed, Tamar is in herself the veritable Holy Grail.

We shall learn, as we progress with our story, how the Grail bloodline was denounced, denied and purposely obscured, and how its women (because the line from Tiâmat was of course matrilinear), willingly sacrificed themselves and overcame monstrous obstacles in order to ensure its safety and its perpetuation, until the glorious moment came when the serpent tail issued forth from the Star of Bethlehem and pointed to the stable or cave where Mary and Jesus were about to be born.

Until the time arrived when Mary and Jesus brought down Tamar from on high as their beloved and most sacred daughter, the drop of Tiâmat's essence that was the Holy Grail could only be a symbolic drop, her sacred book rather than herself, signified by the Emerald Stone or Tablet.

To return to Anu and his wives: his second wife, Ki, Lady of Earth, also gave birth to Nin-khursag, who took her mother's title of Lady Earth. Nin-khursag was known additionally as Lady of Life and Lady of the Mountain. She had a deep spiritual connection with the Earth, and would revolutionise our DNA after the carnage of the Flood had, paradoxically, almost drained the human gene pool dry. She married Enki, Lord of Earth and Waters (the two elements of physical creation represented on the Cross of Issue). He was her half-brother (Antu was his mother, Anu his father), and so they continued to mirror the sacred pattern that existed between the Earth herself and her own half-brother, planet X, the twelfth planet.

This planetary mirroring was a microcosm of the inconceivably macrocosmic mirroring of herself that took place when Tiâmat the Dragon Queen, she who bore them all, brought forth the male or mirrored aspect of herself in order to initiate creation.

Nin-khursag was the sister of Enlil, Lord of Air, and she married him as well as Enki, again in an attempt to establish, through human (higher Anunnaki) means, the lost connection between heaven and earth. Her title of Lady of the Mountain referred, we think, to Nin-khursag's association with the high places, the upper dimensions of the spirit, and ultimately with the Orbit of Sharon, the exalted sphere connected with the North Pole, the Northern Lights, the Star of Bethlehem and the Pole Star - the pure white diamond light in the north whose heart is expressed by the emerald ray, of which the playing-card suit tells, and which is associated with the mystical Stone, one of the Four Grail Hallows.

Enlil shared her title, calling himself Lord of the Mountain. To some extent, this was initially his rightful title, because the Grand Council of the Anunnaki, under guidance from the Nephilim, had appointed Enlil to the role of a lesser lord of karma (the greater lords of karma are beyond what we can conceive of as human beings, and encompass both human and angelic consciousness).

In the days before darkness consumed Anu, Enlil was also attuned to the light, and had an important task to fulfil for the peoples of the Earth. It was his God-appointed duty to balance the record-book of their karma. Karma might be explained via the old Hebrew dictum, 'An eye for an eye and a tooth for a tooth', or, 'What goes around, comes around'. This is certainly not a cruel or savage law that promotes maiming others in revenge for abuses perpetrated by them, but a simple and fundamental law of balance that ensures the harmonious functioning of creation.

It means only that balance must be restored and maintained by equalisation throughout every detail of creation as it manifests and expresses itself. Thus, if we, symbolically speaking, 'take' an 'eye' or a 'tooth', then we are called to account for what we have done. We must make recompense, and, by an act of healing, restore the balance of wholeness and harmony that we have undermined. This act of healing will require that we give of ourselves, our spirit, our light, in some way that will re-establish the lost equilibrium that we have created. Our act of healing will achieve three objectives: it will return to perfection the disturbed balance of creation; it will make recompense for the suffering, shock and disablement that our deed caused; and it will heal the imbalance or lack of holistic perspective (always generated by a lack of love, whether ignorant or wanton) in ourselves that caused us to commit the harmful deed in the first place.

Afterwards, when Enlil followed in the footsteps of his father Anu and his own soul also darkened, he entirely lost the plot as far as the law of karma was concerned, and began to express this creational energy through a deep imbalance within himself which caused him to interpret it in terms of punishment, blame, retribution and revenge fuelled by anger. Far from setting in motion the spiritual dynamic of balance through equalisation, the expression of anger, retribution, revenge and punishment actually causes the severity of the original imbalance to increase dramatically, creating more and more negative karma which will throw off disruption and chaos until it is resolved. When Enlil began to blank out his apperception of this truth, we believe that his title as Lord of the High Places or Lord of the Mountain, and his upholding of his status as a Lord of Karma, gradually became misappropriated, because his office was removed from him.

Nevertheless, Enlil continued to wield the powers with which he had been entrusted in direct contravention of the spiritual law he had once held in such honour. He became a spiritual outlaw. Eventually, among many other unfortunate consequences of this stance, he began to breathe forth a power throughout the thought spheres of the Earth and her peoples which caused human society to become addicted to law-making, and to express this addiction in an increasingly unbalanced and obsessional manner. These unnecessary and largely invidious laws enshrined Enlil's warped and virulent perception of the law of karma, a law whose true objective and outworking is the benign restoration of wholeness and peace through a perfect justice which in itself is an expression of Divine Love.

As a human being, even a human being belonging to the God-Headed people (whom we refer to as the 'higher Anunnaki'), how is it possible that Enlil dispensed the law of karma to the people of earth? How could a human being undertake such a godly task?

The Nephilim and the higher Anunnaki worked with the planets of our solar system to nurture the evolution of earth's humanity. It is evident from many of the clay tablets and cylinder seals of ancient Sumer that the ordinary Anunnaki possessed a wide-ranging knowledge of astronomy and the science of the stars, both esoterically and physically. If we can think of the planets as great transmitting and receiving stations tended and fostered by gods and angels, thus bringing the wisdom and the evolutionary forces of the stars to earth, and if we can think of them also as conscious beings weaving their unique patterns in the cosmological web of destiny in order to give their gifts to the people of earth, we will gain some idea of how the constellations and the planets influence our lives.

This influence is effected in particular through the agency of our chakras (see Chapter 4), those centres within us that are aligned with the stars and the planets.

As a designated lord of karma, the soul of Enlil possessed the qualities and the dynamics which would enable him to receive the powers and influences of the planet Saturn. This mighty planet is fuelled by the living essence of the spirit of Saturn. He sometimes manifests to our inner vision as Old Father Time or the Wise Old Man. Sometimes people see him as Death with his Scythe, but this is only because Saturn brings completion, the end of cycles in form and matter.

The spirit of Saturn is kindly and compassionate, fatherly and protective. He is the lawgiver, associated with Merlin and the magic of the night, of benign darkness. His are the secrets of nature and the Earth. It is his job to guide us through our lessons in time and matter, and to hold us in stability (so we can't run off and play truant!) until these lessons are truly learned. Sadness and sorrow seem to be his dispensations, but these are only a veil, finally drawn aside to reveal a deeper joy, a keener bliss, than we were able to experience before we passed through the gates of Saturn. He is the planet of karma, and we receive his influences particularly via our 'first' chakra, at the base of the spine.

Saturn is the base, the foundation, upon which we must build the temple of our soul, and he rules the precious gems, the jewels of great price, which are dug out of the Earth by penetrating her deepest fastnesses through trauma and dogged effort. He governs the skin and the procreative organs (it is Saturn's influence which 'locks' the foetus securely in the womb for the specified number of months during gestation, an imprisonment without whose term nothing could be given life). He also rules our skeletal structure, the firm foundation upon which our body depends. His colours are rich rubescent red and deep, velvet, midnight

111

black, that darkness out of which we must ascend to the highest height, spurred on by the sacred life-force: the blood divine.

Enlil became his spiritual son and received his wisdom and ordinances. Enlil's chakras were attuned to the celestial emanations, to the knowledge and edicts of the great Father Saturn. Enlil's task was to dispense, usher, modify, coordinate, apply, regulate, foster, monitor and generally facilitate the Saturnine forces. How this was actually done must remain a mystery to mere mortal, ordinary Anunnaki like ourselves; nevertheless, it was within the capacity of the leaders among the God-Headed people to fulfil such missions. Yet, although godlike, they were human beings; and within us, the humanity of today, lies the same potential, waiting to unfold. It is important to remember these points for future reference.

At first, all went well, and Enlil was celebrated as a goodly ambassador of Saturn and a true Lord of the Mountain, pouring influences from on high that were fecund and beneficent. Eulogies were sung, and inscribed in pictorial form and in verse on clay tablets, to the greatness, the magnificence, the goodness of Enlil. Agriculture, civil organisation, and the abundance and fertility of the land and of human communities came under his auspices and received his blessing. One song praises him thus:

> "You are the lord!
> You are a great lord, a lord of the granary!
> You are the lord who makes the barley sprout!
> You are the lord who causes the vines to sprout!"

Another hymn extols:

> "Without Enlil's warrant,
> no city could be built and settled;
> no cattle-pen or sheepfold could be constructed;
> no king or lord appointed;
> no high priest or high priestess
> picked out by a divine sign."

It is pertinent to say at this juncture that Enlil's sister, Nin-khursag, Lady of Life and Lady of the Mountain, was granted just as much power and

112

dominion from Saturn as her brother; but Enlil, from his earliest days as a ruler and leader, developed the habit of denying, ignoring, and upstaging his co-workers, particularly women, and imagining that his alone among the higher Anunnaki was the starring role. Later this attitude signalled its extremity by an act of rape which he committed against a female member of the higher Anunnaki (Ninlil, Lady of the Wind). Some sources declare him innocent, others denounce him. What remains clear is that he was branded a rapist by the fifty great gods and the seven decision makers (leaders in the Grand Council of the higher Anunnaki) and banished from the city of Nippur, where he was considered, or perhaps considered himself, as chief of the gods. This act of rape, or the accusation of it, marked his spiritual demise.

It is interesting to note that in his sexual exploits and his dominion over the abundance of nature, Enlil reflects the great god Pan, the epitome of the sacred goat who rules Capricorn, the zodiacal constellation governed by Saturn. Pan means 'the one god' or 'god of all', the benevolent god of nature. This goat, the Goat of Mendes, traditionally bears an emerald (Tiâmat's heart-consciousness) at the point of the particular crown chakra that we have designated the 'unicorn's horn' (the crown chakra is a double chakra), indicating that the energies of Saturn, which include the nature kingdom, are properly ruled and regulated by the Sacred Feminine Principle, the divine heart-wisdom. It is this that Enlil so completely overrode and denied, eventually casting the Goat of Mendes, because of its esoteric teaching concerning Tiâmat and the centre of consciousness of the Sacred Feminine, in the role of adversarial demon. The Goat of Mendes became the scapegoat of Judaism, banished into the wilderness as a symbol of the outcast Tiâmat (called a whore and a harlot - language in keeping with the mentality of a rapist and a male supremacist).We need to understand that these notions emanated from Enlil.

It is easy to imagine that if Enlil, as Saturn's agent, became unbalanced, the corrupted power of the Saturnine energies would be extremely virulent. They contain the pivotal point of the life and death forces, which, when properly balanced, never culminate in death, but generate the life force in ever greater measure ('I am come that ye may have life, and have it more abundantly', said the Christ, who came into the world through the sacred gates of Capricorn, or the heavenly Goat whose zodiacal tenancy spans the winter solstice, to restore this lost balance).

But when the current of the life forces is perverted, through human failings and wanton error of choice, towards death and degeneration, and Saturn's essence is misunderstood, misappropriated and misdirected, Saturn becomes Satan. Saturn's power of gravitation, his power to keep the foetus in the womb, truly becomes an oppressive power of imprisonment. It shackles us in irons.

Whilst Nin-khursag fostered and ushered the forces of Saturn in a mode befitting her beautiful and profound connection to Tiâmat's deepest heart, and was in truth the pure and exalted Lady of the Mountain, Enlil sunk further and further into a morass of his own making, and became a reversed Lord of the Mountain – a marshal of the infernal regions.

Chapter Twenty

Lapwinging

Enki and Nin-khursag were Tiâmat's newly-appointed divine couple now that Anu had become corrupt and his consort had been disempowered. They had very important work to do together, and they would bring inestimable gifts to the earthly human race. The problem was that they had to hide from Anu their true identity as the new divine couple, because of course he was entirely hostile to Tiâmat's plans and influence. (She had been banished beyond the veil that separates the higher spiritual consciousness from the earthly dimensions [in this case, even the exalted earthly dimensions where Anu and the higher Anunnaki dwelt were included in the separation], but of course she continued to exert her godly influence from her straitened position. Tiâmat holds the reins of creation in unfaltering hands, and always maintains supreme control; but it was her decision in the beginning to give us free will, and that is a gift she will not countermand or withdraw, because her creation could not achieve its goal without it. Therefore, she permitted her influence over Earth to be curtailed by Marduk's act.)

Enki and Nin-khursag had to operate by stealth and cunning. Enki is often seen as a trickster god (although he is referred to as Enki the Wise on many of the clay tablets). We believe that this title gives the key to his 'tricks'. They were part of his wisdom, by which he sought to fulfil his destiny for the sake of the future of the Earth without directly antagonising Anu, who was perfectly capable of 'executing' him for rebellion, just as he had executed the unfortunate Kingu.

Enki, in company with Nin-khursag, had to play his hand carefully. This situation was reflected in the life of Jesus and Mary Magdalene, who had to fulfil their mission under the hostile domination of the Roman Empire and the savage cultural doctrines of the Jewish Sanhedrin court, equating in Enki and Nin-khursag's case to the ever-darkening, increasingly threatening conditions of Anu's realm, and to the mounting savagery benighting Enlil's vision and mentality.

Enki had even taken his wise trickery to the point of pretending to make an attempt on Tiâmat's life. We will see how he heard and obeyed her commands after she was ousted, and that all his actions served Tiâmat loyally, with a dedication that risked his status and even his life. We can reasonably deduce from this unswerving devotion that his assassination attempt was indeed one of his tricks.

It is further said that Enki killed Apsû, Tiâmat's 'consort', an expression of the Primordial Father. In fact we believe Enki did not kill him, but rather assumed his role as the balanced sacred masculine principle after Apsû had been banished with Tiâmat. There is evidence for this in that he 'seized Apsû's crown and cloak of fiery rays' as the 'Primordial Father' perished, and that the control of the 'Apsû', the underground ocean of fresh water associated with semen and with the esoteric 'underground stream', passed to Enki after Apsû's demise. Therefore, Enki seems not so much to have killed Apsû at the point when the 'First Father' was thrown off balance (we remember that he was suddenly struck with the idea that he wanted to slay all his children, and Tiâmat had to restrain him) as to have replaced him. However, Enki's reign as the balanced masculine principle was a furtive one.

In the great tradition of the Welsh bards (who were closely associated with Grail wisdom), there are three magical creatures who guard the great truths of the Grail and the higher worlds.

One is the dog, who guards the secret; one is the roebuck, who hides the secret; and one is the lapwing, who disguises the secret. The great secret - a vital aspect of which is love and reverence for the sacred feminine - Enki kept concealed and guarded in his heart; but he was most of all the lapwing, bearing within himself its magical essence, disguising the secret as he moved within the courts of his father Anu and within the council of the higher Anunnaki so that its hidden potency might flourish and be carried into the future.

Chapter Twenty-one

The Darkening of Anu

The first action Anu took after the 'death' of Tiâmat was to declare his intention (subject to democratic approval in the higher Anunnaki parliament) that his reign would pass into the hands of Enlil, his other son. This was illegal according to the laws of the higher Anunnaki, as Enki was the rightful successor; but Enlil was the apple of his father's eye and the darling of his heart. Anu was confident that he and Enlil were of the same mind and passion, and saw eye to eye. With Enlil at the helm, Anu saw the great project of the higher Anunnaki - Earth's humanity - developing and thriving as it should, with the masculine principle firmly in control, the feminine principle firmly denied, obscured and behind the veil, and the whole of humankind obedient to every edict and dictate of the higher Anunnaki. Anu was confident that Enlil would lead the way as far as his plans for the higher Anunnaki dictatorship was concerned. If humanity proved insubordinate, Anu could rest assured that Enlil would make the right decision and obliterate it from the face of the Earth.

As for Enki, Anu sensed that something was wrong with this son, actually his rightful heir. For some indefinable reason, he made Anu feel uncomfortable, as though Enki was hiding something of chilling significance from him. All appeared to be uniform and as it should with Enki, but he and Nin-khursag were forever retreating to corners and clandestine places, entering deep into communion and keen to keep their own counsel, frequently arguing over obscure matters incoherent to him.

Anu had a horrible suspicion that Enki often listened to her and followed her lead - a highly undesirable if not downright unforgivable trait in a male, and incontrovertible proof that Enki was somehow corrupt and untrustworthy, clearly undeserving of his rightful role as heir and leader. No, Anu would break the ridiculous law that honoured the matrilinear descent - which, he thought, absolutely should be broken in any case, as it proceeded from that evil one whom it was better not to name and who was the source of all trouble and reversal as far as every righteous plan and intention was concerned - and deselect Enki, raising up Enlil in his place.

117

As the Grand Assembly of the Anunnaki comprised a democracy, this change of plan would have to go before the Anunnaki council or parliament, the governing body of the higher Anunnaki, before it could be approved; but Anu foresaw no problem in implementing his will. So he let it be known to the Grand Council of the Anunnaki, thereby incurring Enki's consternation and anger. Because Enki proceeded from Anu's 'first' wife Antu, and the matrilinear descent from the first or senior wife dictated that her first-born son would assume the role of overlordship on his father's death or retirement, Enlil had no right to usurp Enki's title and status. Anu remained adamant, however, the Grand Council raised no objections to his directive, and Enki was powerless to change his decision.

From this time on, Enlil, though not yet king in Anu's place, was given greater authority, and became one of the leading members of the Anunnaki Grand Assembly. Meanwhile, Tiâmat had begun to instruct Enki and Nin-khursag in the formation of her special bloodline - the Grail bloodline which would ensure that Jesus and Mary, and, ultimately, via Tamar, she herself - would be able to descend to earth.

It is true to say that, since the terrible slaughter of Tiâmat, Anu and other key members of the Grand Assembly of the Anunnaki, especially Enlil, had gradually begun to conceive a hatred for humankind, their lesser Anunnaki brethren. As we know, in very early times, as soon as humanity had attained a degree of physicality, designated higher Anunnaki men had impregnated ordinary Anunnaki women, and between them they had produced the godlike people (in contradistinction to the God-Headed people: the higher Anunnaki). These godlike people - the Naphidem - giants among their own kind (possibly not so much in size - although we do think that they were appreciably taller than their ordinary Anunnaki kin - but more in their powers and their capacities, and especially in a kind of intellectual 'gianthood' that actually affected the balance of their sanity and spirituality), had behaved so atrociously, revelling in the murder of the ordinary Anunnaki and eventually even turning their advanced warfare on themselves, that they had had to be banished from the Earth. The thought-pollution they created worsened the great imbalance, affecting Anu and leading him to plot to 'kill' Tiâmat. He believed she had made an error of the gravest kind in sanctioning the impregnation of earthbound, ordinary Anunnaki by the illustrious higher Anunnaki, and no longer trusted her. Did he have a point?

We must understand that Tiâmat is of the very essence of God, *is* God, who in Her wisdom commanded that humanity should be brought into being, to become co-creators. In order that we might fulfil that decree, we had to be tested on every level. Matter - the dominion of earthliness - *had* to be made to show its hand. The sword of the spirit must needs shatter, if matter proved too great a challenge, and be reforged anew.

We are not saying, of course, that matter is stronger than spirit. This would be tantamount to saying that matter is stronger than God, which is clearly a nonsense. Nevertheless, matter is indeed 'a force to contend with', as the Christ expressed it in Mary's gospel. Matter will set itself up as a false god every time, ethically speaking, our back is turned. Our failings are our challenges and our briefings, and ultimately our lessons of modification. Therefore, opportunities must always be given to humanity, even if it chooses to utilise them by making a pig's ear out of a symbolic silken purse. This is the way by means of which we advance towards our unimaginable goal - equality and co-creation with the Godhead itself. The way is hard - harder than for any other kind of created being. Each one of us must be tested to the very extremity of every limit. This is because the rewards are so unutterably stupendous. We are truly gods in the making, and it is our destiny to learn how to call forth the god within ourselves, no matter how great the pull towards earthliness that matter - the tempter, the un-doer, the force whose name is 'I Am Not' - can devise.

Therefore, we can see that Tiâmat's decision to allow higher Anunnaki matings with ordinary Anunnaki women, which led to such disaster upon the Earth but which need not and should not have done so, was not a failure of judgment on her part, but a divinely decreed act of wisdom. It is up to us to learn how to handle fire properly, so that it warms, quickens, illumines, and brings us the gift of greater and higher life. We have no justification in blaming a higher source if, when given the divine gift of fire, we decide to blow up the world with it and burn ourselves severely in the process. Again and again we have been given this marvellous opportunity of huge advancement, or, by the same token, massive reversal - snakes and ladders! The choice is ours, and if we were offered only play-safe and fail-safe games, we would never ultimately be able to avail ourselves of the inconceivable future that is ours, laid down for us in an act of supreme love and self-giving by the Great Spirit.

As we stand upon the threshold of this new age which is dawning across the world, we are again being given such an opportunity. Will we, as a planetary community, receive the sublime and glorious wonders of the Grail and its Four Hallows, or will we refuse the priceless gift of its grace, thereby putting it into negative spin, and elect instead to attract to us its mirror-reversal, the Four Horsemen of Doom - famine, pestilence, war and death? Spiritually speaking, the word on the street is that yes, we will choose the Grail; but we cannot afford to be complacent in any way. Each one of us must strive wholeheartedly to make the right choice, and not be misled into thinking we can leave it up to others to do the necessary groundwork. For, as shall be explained, choosing the Grail means to make real choices every day of our lives, and to agree to take personal responsibility for those choices.

To return to Anu and the Grand Assembly of the Anunnaki: after the advent of the Naphidem and their subsequent removal, Anu began to suspect that he himself was wiser than Tiâmat, and that the source of wisdom lay in the masculine principle, not the feminine. He decided that the feminine principle was clearly dangerous, subversive and foolish. Anu saw himself as obviously wiser than God, which had to mean that God, the Great Source and Originator, must therefore be male, and certainly not Tiâmat. False pride and the lust for dominion, expressed by the godlike people (the Naphidem) when they were overcome by the forces of matter and which affected Anu from below, constituted the worm at the heart of Anu's conclusion. We feel that the originating source of this worm of imbalance occurred when the first splitting of the androgynes took place.

This did not happen initially among the higher Anunnaki, who chaotically followed suit afterwards, but among the ordinary Anunnaki, who were originally androgynous, but who were split, according to the ordinances of God, into separate male and female aspects so that they could descend into animal bodies on earth and express their lives and their souls through the medium of physicality. This was another example of a divine snakes and ladders challenge. However, earthly humanity's weakness was not exposed until the coming of the Naphidem.

There was, perhaps, a deeper source for this imbalance, and for Anu's subsequent fall from grace. At the point when the first expression in Creation of the spiritual masculine was birthed from Tiâmat's heart, as an androgyne complete with a male essence, (Tiâmat's mirrored self), a potential imbalance asserted itself. This was inevitable (although a negative response to the potential thus created was not), because in order to create a mirror image, the creator cannot be joined to the mirror, but has to step away from it. In other words, a principle of separation has to come into play. And the mirror image is by necessity an opposite image. In Apsû's case, for instance, 'his' male essence responded to the imbalance by attempting to *oppose* Tiâmat and impose his will to kill his own children when he learned that they were plotting against him and his God. When this happened, Tiâmat had to divest Apsû of divine authority.

We do not say, however, that the first expression of the sacred masculine to occur in Creation, or indeed Apsû, was actually God the Father. God the Father dwelt within Tiâmat in perfection, as Tiâmat was perfect; and no imbalance existed, or could come into existence, between them.

Enki, her chosen son, took over as the balanced male essence once Apsû had been overcome, but the note of Apsû's imbalance had nevertheless brought itself through into the sphere of being, into manifestation, had been sounded forth throughout the thought spheres of the Earth. It was this imbalance of aggression and dominance that began to hold sway when the godlike people (the Naphidem) appeared on earth. They recognised, like Anu, that an almighty power had come forth from Tiâmat when she had been delivered of what we understand as the male principle. It was a power she had separated off from herself in order that creation could begin, given in equal measure to the feminine and the masculine principle. But when, within the human androgyne, the expression of First Father was born (for human life initially came forth in androgynous form), this expression of First Father wanted to rule, and to subjugate Divine Mother!

This conception, sent abroad by Apsû, appealed to the godlike people, whom, we must remember, had been born of higher Anunnaki *fathers* - in other words, according to Naphidem perspective, their godlike qualities had been bestowed on them by the male principle. Their ordinary Anunnaki mothers (so they believed) had nothing whatsoever to do with their intrinsically superior qualities. They came to despise their mothers, and a contempt for the idea of being nurtured by women came into being. (We remember that the reason for higher Anunnaki men mating with earthly women, rather than the other way around, was because the higher Anunnaki male essence conjoining with the ordinary Anunnaki female essence brought the energy-vibrations of the resultant child onto a descending curve, down into the vibrational field of physicality [the Anunnaki's whole objective].

However, if higher Anunnaki females had mated with earthly males, the children of their union would instead have ascended the heavenly stairway - in other words, such children would have become more etherealised, and would consequently have moved away from an expression of their essence in physicality. Therefore, the conclusions of the Naphidem, despite their godlike qualities, were ignorant and brutish – and it was just such an embracing of their lower, earthly selves that unhinged them.)

The male members of the godlike people, then, fathered by certain chosen members of the higher Anunnaki, decided that Tiâmat had been a fool to place such power under the nose of the masculine principle, and to expect him to share it equally with the feminine principle. Of course they were going to seize it, if it was there for the seizing. They had penises, rising serpents with a head that spouted forth the very life-force itself! They were obviously made to be lords and masters, and if some Divine Female, in her stupidity, had laid the chance of rule and overrule at their feet, well, naturally they were going to take it and refuse to relinquish it!

The male godlike people need not have made such outrageously unjust, foolish, arrogant and callous choices, of course. If they had responded to their true godlike nature, they would never have dreamed of committing such an abomination. But once such ugliness of vision had gained ascendancy within their hearts, it was vital that they were allowed free choice as to whether or not it should be given expression. If it had been repressed and forbidden by the withdrawal of freewill, creation could never have worked. It would have carried within its belly the seeds of its own certain destruction.

The only way forward for Tiâmat's great Humanity Project was to educate her children, through the insight and empathy born of self-imposed suffering, not to make such brutal and self-worshipping choices. The pure and beautiful Nephilim, when they had undergone their tests and challenges on planets other than Earth, had not responded as the savage earth-men had. We think that the fearful response of the latter happened only in the environs of Earth. It did not take place on any other of the planets in our solar system. And to blame Tiâmat for giving early humanity such an opportunity (the potential for a great step forward in their evolution) is to miss the point. As we have explained, each opportunity for a mighty step forward carries with it an equally measured risk of retrogradation. And again we stress - how determined we must be, and will be, that we, as a planetary society, do not miss the divinely-bestowed contemporary opportunity to embrace the Holy Grail!

Having decided that the higher Anunnaki (as represented by himself) were wiser than God, Anu started to conceptualise a God in the image of himself (an arrogant, misogynistic, martially-inspired God) that he could deign to worship, and began to influence the other members of the higher Anunnaki to join him in his mission. Once he had overseen the operation to have Tiâmat destroyed, we see that the inevitable happened - namely, what was left of the true source of love, wisdom and compassion in his heart began to fail with a frightening rapidity. Within a short time, he was beginning to despise humanity (ordinary Anunnaki), seeing in them an inferior 'breed' of Anunnaki that had been sullied and terminally contaminated by entering into animal bodies. Pure bloods such as the higher Anunnaki should not have to continue to suffer their brutish existence, thereby continuing the abominable scheme of the degenerate Tiâmat. They were a disgrace to the glorious Anunnaki race! Unless they submitted wholly to every edict of the higher Anunnaki, they should be eliminated from the Earth, the whole project abandoned, and never spoken of again!

Such was the sway of Anu's musings and conclusions. The higher Anunnaki, although democratic amongst themselves (except, perhaps, for Enlil, who always found the concept rather difficult to grasp!) were promising fair to become a dictatorship to the people of earth. What a long and sorrowful way they had all come from that point in cosmic history when they had set out from their own planet, balanced by love and a sense of fraternity and equality, higher and ordinary Anunnaki alike, at peace with themselves and each other, and eager to implement their beloved Tiâmat's edicts! The pull of earth on their innermost souls had proved too much for them.

Of course, in his musings, Anu conveniently forgot that he himself, and all the higher Anunnaki just as much as the ordinary Anunnaki before the latter entered earthly existence, had been nurtured into being from a chosen life form on his own planet. But, considering that he had also forgotten that a man (for he was a man) can hardly be wiser than the infinity and eternality of God, this is hardly surprising. The canker of revulsion and hatred ate away at his heart, and the other higher Anunnaki, although still struggling to uphold the ideals and principles they had been taught before the 'death' of Tiâmat, slowly began to be affected.

It was at this point that Tiâmat, from beyond the veil of 'death' that Anu, through Marduk, had imposed on humanity's consciousness of her, took a second unprecedented step. She had already, through her unrecognised influence, caused 'the kingship to be lowered from heaven', which had appeared to Anu to be his own decision within the context of the Anunnaki council, but which had actually been secretly motivated, with Enki and Nin-khursag's help, by her silent encouragement.

We shall now see how Enki and Nin-khursag were brought to the point, under Tiâmat's direction, where they were enabled to bring forth the New Woman and the New Man.

Chapter Twenty-two

Teardrops

Before we begin to describe Enki and Nin-khursag's perplexities and consternations, we must first reveal a deep secret concerning Enki himself. This is not the 'terrible secret' (which actually relates to Enlil) that gave us so much heart-searching when we first realised its full implications, and which in part our readers may already have guessed. It is, in contrast, a beautiful secret

We have discussed how Apsû came forth from Tiâmat after the point when she had mirrored her own essence in order to give birth to creation, Apsû the androgyne who contained the male essence of the Primordial Father. In understanding that Apsû was actually an androgyne (the balanced essence of both the feminine and masculine spiritual principles), we depart to some extent from the exposition of the histories given on the Sumerian tablets, which declare that Apsû was the 'First Father' and that Tiâmat was his 'consort'. We see, rather, that Tiâmat was not 'his' consort, but the ineffable creator of a being that reflected the three divine principles within her, the Holy Trinity of Mother, Father and Holy Child (the Christ, containing the Daughter-Son principles, to whom we refer as Christ-Brigid). Therefore, Tiâmat brought forth Apsû, among others - all a reflection of the Mother-Father - who in turn brought forth approximations of Mummu, a reflection of the Daughter-Son.

So were the 'Four Sacred Persons' of the Cross of Life brought into being (a grand universal scheme, as we see, rather than four limited personalities - nevertheless, an individuated cosmic intelligence does stand at the head of each of these four vast reflective streams of consciousness that mirror divinity - Mother, Father, Daughter, Son); and so human (Anunnaki) creation began, initially on planes and planets other than our Earth and our solar system.

The androgyne Apsû might be said to have been one among the first expression, the first waves, of the ideation of humanity that Tiâmat brought into being. The dynamic of Father God existed within Tiâmat, and, with her, had formed the cosmos. Now it was time for the great project, humanity, already in existence in a pure and ethereal form, to be birthed forth into it.

All life up to this point had been androgynous, reproducing as hermaphrodites. When the first human beings were evoked from spiritual form into the creational life-energy patterns of the universe, they too were androgynous; yet Tiâmat had to find a way to allow the sacred masculine and the sacred feminine to temporarily disengage from one another in order that men and women might gain conscious awareness of themselves and one another and evolve into apperceptive beings who could co-create with the Godhead.

In order to do this, Tiâmat had to give a separate vehicle to the ova and sperm of her androgyne, as well as many other bodies, all attached to the chakras, for the purposes of self expression and self knowledge. Initially, none of these bodies were physical. Nevertheless, a simulacrum of the womb and the penis were brought into form, and 'men' and 'women' were enabled to separate off from one another and bring forth children, even though the procreating pairs were still fundamentally and spiritually androgynous.

Sexual consummation was not only a unification of the mirrored male and female procreative organs, but an actual entering inside one another from a spiritual as well as a bodily (although non-physical) perspective. The androgynous state, from which men and women were only ever temporarily disengaged, was one of blissful, spiritually orgasmic unity and love.

Apsû, then, was one of the great initiators, among the first waves of human souls breathed forth from the Godhead. They were the first Nephilim, and many of them evolved until they had earned God status and had passed into incorruptibility, thus being enabled to co-create with Mother-Father God. The androgyne Apsû was virtually at this point when she-he received the divine command to initiate human life in our galaxy, under the direction of the supreme Nephilim (those who had become perfected), who, guided by the divine Daughter-Son of Light, were co-creating with Mother-Father God. Apsû was indeed the divine couple who reflected this purely spiritual Daughter-Son (an ineffable presence in the heavens) on behalf of planet X, and Apsû's work on planet X was well done indeed. Apsû it was who, via Tiâmat's injunction, elected the shining, magnificent and gracious Anu, golden and glorious in those far-off days, as the divine couple who would carry the creative light of the spirit - the ineffable fire of the Dragon Queen - to Earth, in order to colonise it with humanity. Anu was Apsû's son-daughter whom, long after her-his arrival on planet Earth, the Sumerians referred to as 'the Son of Light' on their tablets.

Apsû was at the very door of heaven whilst she-he engaged with this task, and would soon have 'entered into the presence of God'. Unfortunately, under the pressure and extremity of earthly conditions, after she-he had come to Earth, descending deeply into the sphere of matter and experiencing the temporary separation of his-her two aspects in a new, raw, coarser way, the male half of Apsû took unlawful command over his female half and fell out of balance.

As a consequence of this fall from grace, he wanted to express the power of his will through vengeance and destruction when eventually he learned that the very children his androgynous self had helped to generate on planet X (non-physical children of the human spiritual essence whom we know as the higher Anunnaki) were plotting to kill him, together with Tiâmat and, consequently, Father God and the Daughter-Son of Light, for all dwelt within Tiâmat (by 'kill' we mean to brutally cut them off from the earthly dimension, or the conscious human awareness within that earthly dimension, and to block their re-entry). Apsû blundered through the door to hell at the threshold of heaven, and slid down the monstrous snake of degradation, whereupon Tiâmat divested him of his authority.

There was a Lady Apsû, who was cruelly severed from the male aspect of Apsû at the point when he fell into imbalance, and who mourned his loss. She was heart-bound to Tiâmat, and is important to the human story, as we shall reveal.

If the dynamic of Father God was present within Tiâmat when she decided to create, then clearly the male essence, the Father and the Son, must have existed within Tiâmat's being before creation came into existence, and therefore prior to the bringing forth of Apsû and her-his fellow Nephilim. We understand that this is indeed the case, and that, when Tiâmat embraced her own need to create, what came forth from her contained the primordial sacred masculine essence as well as the sacred feminine essence.

Tiâmat let fall a mystical rain - we may say almost a shower of teardrops - for this most holy water emerged from her deepest heart, as we ourselves give forth water in a release of tears when we are moved in our profoundest depths. Within this divine water, among many other potentialities, was the potential to create the physical domain.

Charged with the ineffable fire of God which manifested in the material dimension as radiation, a fire-mist was produced which brought the universe into being as an ever-begetting, ever birthing entity, for, as we know, systems and stars are forever dying and being born. This stupendous life began in the divine waters, the 'living waters' that first transformed into suns and planets, and then became physical life, always accompanied by its ethereal counterpart. Its initial, fundamental expression was that of little, rapidly wriggling fish, effervescing the waters so that they bubbled with life. We might think of Alice in her Pool of Tears (Tiâmat releasing the divine waters), which soon became filled with a variety of living creatures. Indeed, when Margaret Bailey and I were working on our first book together (*The Secret Teachings of Mary Magdalene*), we were shown that all life proceeded from a teardrop (the name 'Tiâmat' means 'saltwater' or bitter water' as does the name 'Mary'), and that the renowned teardrops of Mary Magdalene, far from being expressions of 'remorse' for her 'sins', were rather a symbol of her direct connection to Tiâmat and to the origins of life itself. She was indeed 'the All', as Jesus reverently and adoringly named her.

Within 'the All' (Tiâmat) dwelt the masculine essence of Father God, and when he manifested on Earth, in physical life, his primordial expression in matter consisted of these little wriggling sperm or fish, ready to fertilise the fecundity of the Living Waters so that they might bring forth all life-forms present on earth today.

But we must not be one-dimensional in our perception of this great mystery, and think only in terms of biology. When Tiâmat gave forth the divine rain, she released the Father aspect of creation in a great outpouring of her will. This omnipotent movement of divine will was the nature and essence of Father God - will birthed from love and, in its proper balance and expression, ever giving forth and embracing love. This power of will emerged from Tiâmat, and was Tiâmat.

Father God is the principle of the divine will-to-good, part of Tiâmat and utterly faithful to Divine Mother and the creation they have brought forth together. There is no imbalance, no dominance, no wish to undermine, in Father God. He expresses the drive towards organisation, civilisation, the attainment of the heights in human development, achievement and endeavour. In his promptings to scale the heights he manifests as the Goat of Mendes, Tiâmat's chosen symbol (amongst others) for her greatest project - humanity. And the Goat of Mendes is the Goat of Capricorn - the Goat-Fish or Sea-Goat, who emerges from the sea to dwell upon the mountain-tops.

When we think of the essence of Father-God entering physical creation in the energy-pattern of a fish, should we become literalists and imagine that a fish was ever a God? Surely this would be far too narrow, naive and absurd a concept! It bears a symbolic truth, certainly, in that Father God clothed himself in fish-garb as a devoted acknowledgement, even a proclaimed statement, that he was born of and issued forth from Tiâmat, the Great Mother. It was an affirmation of his love for Tiâmat.

Nevertheless, there did seem to have come into earthly being a divine creature who took the form of a fish-man, certainly not the type of fearsome 'creature from the Black Lagoon' that we might first visualise, but a beautiful entity which expressed the godly characteristics of the Son of Light, the Son of the Father. His name was Oannes; but in ancient Mesopotamia, the Sumerians knew him as Uan, or Enki.

Chapter Twenty-three

The Fisher King

This mystery of Enki's two Sumerian names repays deep contemplation, because we see that 'Uan' is almost 'Anu' in reverse. The 'u', representative of the sacred feminine, is placed firmly at the beginning of the name, instead of at the end, where it had been split off by the depredations of the darkening Anu - a declaration within the sacredness of words that the divine feminine is the first principle, and not the sub-principle that Anu tried to make it. In other words, we see that Enki (Uan-Oannes) is the positive rendition of his father, that he is indeed the remedy, the antidote to the negative Anu who plotted with Enlil, Enki's brother, to 'kill' Tiâmat and, in so doing, reversed the sunwise spin of the Earth as her polar alignment was displaced.

When the shadow of imbalance first fell over Anu, Enki was called upon by Tiâmat to embody the light of the true Father God, because Anu was beginning to reject this sacred task. However, the commencement of the darkening of Anu was synonymous with the falling into imbalance of the male essence of Apsû, the 'First Father', whose wish to dominate (once he had entered deeply into matter) was the seed of darkness that was later cultivated with such horrific intensity by the godlike people (the Naphidem). So Enki's task of deliverer, of saviour, began with his divinely inspired act of seizing Apsû's authority (we remember that Apsû intended to use it to destroy all his offspring).

As we have noted, Tiâmat herself withdrew Apsû's godly authority in order to save us, her children, from destruction. Simultaneously, Anu became unworthy of 'his' office. Divine authority then passed to the androgyne Kingu. Yet Tiâmat, centred in timelessness, saw that the great imbalance would make conditions impossible for any of the balanced androgynes to continue to hold authoritative sway at the earthly level. Kingu, she saw, would be weakened by these hostile conditions, and ultimately overwhelmed by the shadowed Anu, who would make a blood sacrifice of Kingu.

The only way forward was to select a separated male entity, not an androgyne, to receive the divine essence of Oannes - the true and perfect Father God in whom there was no betrayal, no passion for dominance or slaying - to hold the balance until the supreme Nephilim couple, the Christ-infused couple (Jesus and Mary Magdalene), could descend the stairway to earth via the sacred bloodline to put all to rights. So it was that Enki, the first true Knight and the original 'Gentle Man', was chosen by Tiâmat to fulfil the Oannes (John) mission. Tiâmat saw that he of all the males of Earth, and of those other higher dimensions belonging to it, was the one who possessed the courage, integrity, loyalty, soundness of purpose, and the sufficient depth of unsullied love in his heart, to carry the torch of the true Oannes and never let it go out.

Enki was aided and guided in his great mission by his wife, Nin-khursag, who, it seems, had to argue with him quite a lot to keep him on course! Nin-khursag received within herself the blessing and the grace of Tiâmat, and was the feminine member of the Divine Couple, who now manifested not as an androgyne, as all previous Divine Couples had done, but as separate, individuated souls - Enki and Nin-khursag.

Nin-khursag devoted herself to Tiâmat in the same measure as did Enki her brother, and in herself became the first Dragon Queen associated with planet Earth, meaning that she carried within her the precious gift of Tiâmat's Grail lineage – composed of those who remained faithful to Tiâmat's essence, which was Divine Love, and who would, by means of self-sacrifice, step by step, link by link, help to restore the Grail and the true teachings of the Emerald Tablet to planet Earth. This lineage was called by the Hebrews the *malkhut* - the 'Kingdom' or 'the place of the Throne'. From another perspective it translates as 'the Blood of the Dragon' - the divine inheritance from Tiâmat delivered via the bloodline. Nin-khursag guided and nurtured Enki, and initiated him into the mysteries of Tiâmat and the Father Principle.

And so Enki became the Oannes-man, the Johannes-man, the John-man. In a beautiful ceremony of the deepest magic, Enki was 'swallowed' by the Oannes form, the mighty fish, and became the sacred fish-man. This essence of Father God was indeed, in itself, the Fisher King; and so Enki, the Son of Light, took on his title and became the veritable Fisher King, the Fisher King who eventually showed us, in the dimension in which we could perceive him, that he was wounded, ever bleeding, ever agonised, because his other half (Tiâmat, Goddess, Divine Mother, the sacred feminine) had been brutally torn away from him.

We think that the Old Testament story of Jonah (John, or the John-man) reflects, in inhibited measure, the story of Enki. However, Enki's wisdom and tradition were sourced in Tiâmat, because if we go to the source of Oannes, there we find the Dragon Queen. So, as well as the fish-man, Enki held the perfect balance by becoming the Serpent of Light (by whom he was also swallowed), or the Golden Serpent, called Poimandres by the Greeks.

Nin-khursag initiated him into this mystery, and from the heart of her Dragon Queen heritage, bestowed on him the garb of the Serpent of Light, her own miraculous, Tiâmat-endowed form which we all share and can all manifest. We must, indeed, express this inner dragon essence if we are to partake of the Holy Grail.

As for Apsû: he was not destroyed, of course; he lost his androgynous status and descended to a much lower dimension than the exalted one he had previously enjoyed. We think in his confusion and rage he joined forces with the Naphidem, who are collected on a plane where they, symbolically speaking, continue to foam at the mouth and psycho-pathically try to take over the hearts and minds of humanity so that they can create the 'New Man' (suitable human bodies for their personal occupation) and descend to earth once again to make it the stamping ground for their abominations. (The Nazi research into genetic manipulation, with all its unimaginable cruelty, was the result of the Naphidem attempting to initiate this process.) Apsû and his flawed brethren will one day be led gently by Tiâmat and Oannes out of the restricted dimension in which they are currently gathered, and down into physical incarnation, where they will become ordinary human beings like ourselves, who have to strive just as we do for our individual self-evolution, with all its hardship and frustrations!

Of course, the Naphidem don't have any such plans; they want their return to earth to be princely and glorious, and an act of total, crushing dominion. But they will not succeed; down they will come, in humble fleshly garb, through normal human incarnation, with a long, difficult road ahead of them. We think this will begin to happen in about a thousand years' time. It might be true to say that, as little as the Naphidem want this outcome, we ourselves want it less. No doubt we would rather they did not visit our Earth at all!

But it is no use complaining; Tiâmat will never rest until all her child-ren are called safely into her pure sheepfold, into the light. Her patience and forgiveness are infinite, and it is part of our evolution to learn to mirror these qualities of divine, unconditional love.

When Apsû joined forces with the Naphidem, we see that some sort of sinister liaison between him, Anu and Enlil, came into being. Apsû's part of the deal was that, with Anu and Enlil's help, he would regain his former status, and lead the Naphidem in a triumphant invasion of the Earth, where he would at last be granted the satisfaction of slaughtering his offspring: the earthlings and all those members of the higher Anunnaki not in league with the conspiracy. Anu and Enlil's prospective advantage lay in the fact that Apsû would do the work of destroying humanity for them, and of overcoming the members of the Grand Assembly of the Anunnaki who would oppose the slaughter.

Yet, although they were just as psychopathic in their intentions as the deranged Apsû, Anu and Enlil were much more cunning. They both hated the Naphidem as much as they hated humanity (the ordinary Anunnaki living in animal bodies on the face of the Earth). They were quite confident that the brutal behaviour of the Naphidem would bring total destruction upon their heads, attracted by the divine scales of justice. Enlil, an appointed lord of karma, was particularly aware of the inevitability of this outcome. The foolishness of Anu and Enlil lay in the fact that they now believed that they were somehow in charge of divine law, and perhaps its ultimate dispensers - or, if this stance was a little too extreme even for their inflated egos, they at least believed that the vague all-male God that they conceptualised was in league with them, and entirely approved of all the death and annihilation they sought to accomplish.

Why was it that Apsû, who was a more ancient, advanced being than either Anu or Enlil, seemed in this context to be less intelligent than they were? We think the answer is because Anu and Enlil, up to this point, were still spiritually connected to their respective wives, albeit in an unequal and oppressive relationship, and this connection gave them a more encompassing perception than that of poor Apsû, who had entirely lost touch with his feminine aspect. In fact, the feminine essence of the androgyne Apsû became a beautiful expression of spiritual radiance in her own right, presiding over the current of esoteric knowledge that became known as 'the underground stream', bubbling up to the surface now and again to sing an exquisite rendition of pure and noble truth, drawn from the highest heights and the deepest depths. (The songs of the troubadours arose from this source.) Whilst her unfortunate, benighted other half remains in the lower dimensions with the lunatic Naphidem, the Lady Apsû must remain 'underground', too. But, as we perceive in Alice's adventures underground (the original title for *Alice in Wonderland*), the 'world beneath' is sacred, and yields fabulous treasures of matchless beauty and meaning. The netherworld of negative darkness where the fallen Apsû languishes could not be more different, and although they must both remain 'underground' until they are reunited, the secret depths over which the Lady Apsû presides are full of grace.

It is also of interest to consider, at this point, that Anu and Enlil were the original conspirators who had sought to kill Apsû, precisely because Apsû's male essence, although off kilter concerning his relationship with Lady Apsû, refused to countenance a complete splitting away from her. Whilst she waited for his return to sanity, the Lady Apsû's influence protected Tiâmat's shrine on earth, and the shedding of her spiritual light ensured that the subjugation of women and the sacred feminine remained only partial.

We remember that Anu, in league with others, had tried to kill Tiâmat on several occasions, but that his hand had been stayed by the presence within him of his own feminine essence (Antu). It was only when Anu was separate from her that he could plot and scheme against Tiâmat and her divine decrees, but at this point in history, separation was temporary, and it was by no means Anu's choice alone which decided when the two aspects of the androgyne would unite. Anu's feminine self (later called Antu) firmly put in an appearance when she sensed that he might try to perpetrate his atrocities!

Anu required of the masculine Apsû, who held some kind of originating and initiatory energy pattern with regard to the Anunnaki and was, of course, Anu's own father, to either finish what he had started and split himself off entirely from his feminine self once and for all, or to be taken out of action so that he could no longer block the path of Anu's desire for the complete split. Until Apsû complied, or was killed, and the inheritance of the energy pattern he held passed to Anu, males could not split themselves off in entirety from females, females could not be degraded to the degree that Anu desired, and Tiâmat could not be sundered in two and slain.

In the event, as we know, Apsû *did* entirely lose touch with the Lady Apsû at the point when he finally decided to kill his children. But, however enthusiastic they were for the task, it was not Anu and Enlil who killed him, but Tiâmat herself who decreed his removal from the earth planes. Tiâmat had called to Enki as he slept, in his dreams, and had spoken her will to him. She revealed to him that Apsû, upon whom madness had descended, was about to turn murderously on the very human creation, including the higher Anunnaki, that he had helped to initiate, unconscionably long ago in the cosmic history of our galaxy, before he helped to bring forth the earthlings.

(We must remember that Apsû was invested with a much greater measure of the divine power than the higher Anunnaki. Although, like them, he had not yet 'entered into the presence of God', he was far more ancient and mighty than they, and the destruction of all who dwelt upon or within the earthly realms lay well within his capability. In her-his harmonised androgynous state, Apsû had accompanied her-his beloved child Anu, the androgyne chosen to represent the Divine Couple upon the earth spheres and who would initiate humanity there, on its vast journey from planet X to Earth, to lend support and aid to Anu.)

Tiâmat told Enki she would ensure that Apsû did not carry out his plan, but would be removed to a dimension where he could be safely sealed off from access to the Earth. First of all, Enki must seize Apsû's crown and cloak of fiery rays, the regalia that kept him in power, whereupon Apsû would be delivered to another sphere.

We know that Enki did this, and that he 'lapwinged' the situation to make it appear, as a means of allaying their suspicions, that he was in league with Anu and Enlil. Therefore, although Apsû was aware that Anu and Enlil had plotted to destroy him, he was persuaded that they had been misled by Enki. Thus Enki became the special enemy of the Apsû-led Naphidem, who both henceforth nurtured a lethal hatred for him. They pathologically despised the Fisher King and his teachings, and would pursue him with malignant intent throughout history.

Chapter Twenty-four

The Angel of the North

Although maligning Enki to deflect the blame for the attack against Apsû off themselves and onto him was simply a ploy to manipulate the fallen 'First Father' to trust them (we remember that Apsû actually came into being on one of the waves of First Souls which was breathed forth from Tiâmat's heart, so there never truly was any 'first' man or woman), it is true to say that both Anu and Enlil felt a certain degree of hostility towards Enki. They did not mistrust him, exactly; but we see that they were made uneasy by him. Enki's very soul-emanations, heightened and refined more than ever now that he had dedicated himself to the spirit of Oannes (Father-God) and to the service of Tiâmat to a degree never known before on any plane belonging to Earth, unnerved them, although they remained unconscious of Enki's true allegiance.

We can see from all this woeful history how vital the setting up of Tiâmat's special bloodline was, because it would convey to Earth the divine couple who would bring a true understanding of Mother Tiâmat and the Daughter of Light, and Father Oannes and the Son of Light, to our confused, chaotic world, correct its reverse spin, and soothe its desperate suffering into the peace of enlightenment. Many of the lower, and even the higher, Anunnaki had completely lost touch with any correct perception of Mother-Father God, and pursued instead horrible phantoms of their own making. Father God in particular was almost entirely misunderstood, and Mother God in her highest aspect was almost forgotten.

Only a few held the precious truth close to their hearts, and indeed they had to follow the Lady Apsû 'underground' (into concealment, containment and secrecy), for their own protection and the protection of their devoutly-borne truths. The situation was about to worsen considerably, as we shall see.

'Oannes' reflects the name of Johannes or John; both originate from the same measurelessly ancient source, and it is the Sphere of John (sometimes called the Orbit of Sharon) to which the Earth was perfectly aligned before the great imbalance, quickly followed by the destruction of the Grail, asserted itself. The Sphere of John is associated with the North Star (the Pole Star), and with the mighty star Sirius, which are physical foci for this exalted dimension - in fact one direct link connects them all. It comprises a connection point for the consciousness of Father God to our earthly plane; and in this context it is of note that the diamond in the card pack is associated with the north, as is the 'stone of death' in the Celtic medicine wheel and the stone of the north (the diamond and its heart of hearts, the emerald) which is one of the four Grail Hallows.

The north is associated with the divine masculine, and it is interesting that in Britain, the sacred isle, we have the northernmost symbol of Rosslyn Chapel as a celebration of the masculine principle (reflecting the divine feminine, just as the divine feminine always reflects the divine masculine), and also the sculpture of the Angel of the North, a distinctly masculine figure. In fact, the consciousness of Father God, from the Sphere of John, streams through a mighty angelic medium, and the metallic Angel of the North seems to celebrate this mystery, especially as the King (Father God) is always associated with sacred smithship and the Divine Forges; and Enki, Master Craftsmen supreme, also bears the same stamp.

The Sphere of John, then, is the Sphere of Oannes (Johannes), the divine and balanced Father God, and the Son of Light, who would never betray Tiâmat and her creation.

Within the Sphere of John is the Orbit of Sharon, (its heart), the consciousness of Mother God (Tiâmat) and the Daughter of Light, whom we know as the beloved Brigid ('bright'), smithwoman, healer and life-giver, Divine Daughter of Tiâmat, who also manifested on earth as the exalted, pure and queenly Mary Magdalene, the Number Nine, the Tower. It is intriguing to note that Mary actually gave birth to Tiâmat the Great Mother by bringing forth the majestic Tamar, the essence of Tiâmat; and so the daughter bore the mother, and the mother became the daughter, who was the originating source of All. At last the old Gnostic poems begin to make perfect sense!

We would like to share with you some evocative words concerning the literalness of Enki-Uan-Oannes' existence in our physical world, or at least the human ability to see him and experience his reality from the standpoint of the physical world. We think these words reflect the simple truth of what was perceived in those ancient days. The quotes are drawn from the work of Berossus, a Babylonian priest writing in the third century BC, who compiled a book of ancient lore bearing the evocative title *Babylonica*.

> *The whole body of [Oannes] was like that of a fish;*
> *and had under a fish's head another head, and also*
> *feet below, similar to those of a man, subjoined to*
> *the fish's tail.*

We remember that members of the higher Anunnaki could programme the ethereal atoms of their bodies so that they decreased in rate and produced temporary physical bodies in which they could walk the earth. Here Enki shows us a profound symbol in flesh - that of the human soul swallowed by the Fish, Oannes, the Father God. He also shows us his allegiance to the Mother God, Tiâmat; for she was of the essence of the salt waters that contained the mystical fish, the living waters of creation which she let fall as a rain of teardrops (water produced from a movement of compassion and love through her heart). Tiâmat was the All; and within the All was contained the Father.

Berossus goes on to tell us:

His voice too, was articulate and human; and a representation of him is preserved even to this day...When the sun set, it was the custom of this Being to plunge again into the sea, and abide all night in the deep; for he was amphibious...In the daytime he used to converse with men; but took no food at that season; and he gave them an insight into letters and sciences, and every kind of art. He taught them to construct houses, to found temples, to compile laws, and explained to them the principles of geometrical knowledge. He made them distinguish the seeds of the earth, and showed them how to collect fruits; in short, he instructed them in every thing which could tend to soften manners and to humanise mankind. From that time, so universal were his instructions, nothing has been added materially by way of improvement.

The 'representation' of Enki does indeed 'survive even unto this day' (with reference in this context to the 21st century). Babylonian and Assyrian reliefs depict the sacred fish-man, and he also occurs in the form of a great statue in Tiahuanacu in western South America, carrying in his right hand what appears to be a knife with a sinuous blade and in his left a

138

hinged, casebound book with what might be some kind of weapon or other contraption protruding from its top, as though the book were a sheath.

We believe that, even though this statue is in the 'wrong' geographical location, the knife is a representation of Tiâmat (we are intrigued, beyond the mundane linguistic meaning, by the occurrence of 'Tia' in 'Tiahuanacu'!), and the book is a representation of the Emerald Tablet, with a device plunged into it like the Arthurian sword in the stone, showing us that, even in those unaccountably far off days when the statue was first carved, the esoteric knowledge was in place and recognised which tells us that a male sacrifice would be necessary to restore the Emerald Tablet to its rightful inheritors - the human race.

All the Sumerian clay tablets affirm that it was indeed Enki who brought civilisation and graciousness of conduct to the Sumerian people, that strange and magnificent culture which arrived as if from nowhere and rose like a floodlit tower of progress and learning far above any other contemporary civilisation on earth. Enki was their wise knight, the original 'Gentle Man', protecting them and bringing them gifts from the deeps of his divine Mother and Father to help to make them 'fully human', as Mary Magdalene expresses it in her in stunning, Tiâmat-Oannes inspired gospel.

Perhaps we can understand now exactly why the statue of the Falling Knight points towards the site of the Holy Grail (the Emerald Tablet). The Falling Knight represents the whole of humanity, and in particular, men, who fell from the divine grace expressed, embodied and upheld as a guiding principle by Enki, the Wise Knight and the Gentle Man. The recovery of the Emerald Table is our supreme hope and promise.

Chapter Twenty-five

City-Under-Wave

It is interesting to note that Enki 'abode all night in the deep'. We have the sense that he entered into the sacred abyss of the waters, there to experience meditation and communion deeper than the abyss itself, where he would 'walk and talk' with his beloved parents, Tiâmat and Oannes, and receive the graces also of the divine Daughter-Son whose light he carried with him to the face of the earth each day, there to tutor, inspire, enlighten and instruct the people of Sumer.

However, the waters of the abyss also offered another route. Enki could, by using the deep path of the abyss, return to that dimension, attached to the Earth but not of a physical vibration, within which dwelt the Grand Assembly of the Anunnaki. As he trod (or swam) this path, his body would change the rotational speed of its atoms until their physicality became etherealised once again. Water has always been the magical substance which links the dimensional worlds; when we think of Tiâmat bringing forth the unity of creation from the living waters, we see that this must be so.

So Enki 'abode in the deep' for these two purposes: either to go home to the dwelling-place of the higher Anunnaki, or to pursue that profounder path and reach much further and deeper to conjoin with his true and eternal home, where dwelt his Mother and Father, his beloved Ancestors, in the blessed worlds within.

It was indeed vital that both Enki, and Nin-khursag, his consort, sought such deep communion. They were now Tiâmat's newly-appointed divine couple, meaning that they were of a higher soul-essence than the people of earth had so far attained, and that they faithfully reflected the light of Christ-Brigid emanating from the loftiest heavens, just as the androgyne Anu had done before them, until its male essence became corrupted. To be precise, we think that Enki and Nin-khursag had now advanced to the point where they had become initiated Nephilim, rather than continuing to belong to the lesser-evolved higher Anunnaki. They enjoyed a status similar to that of Apsû before the male half of that androgyne lost his balance - in other words they were Nephilim who were approaching, but had not yet crossed the threshold into, the presence of God. Although they could take on impermanent bodies other than their fish-garbs in order to walk the earth, and in fact often did so, they needed the baptismal waters of the ocean deeps for their profoundest communion.

We note that Jesus and Mary also used these baptismal waters, and the sanctity of mountain tops, to enter into communion with their divine parents. Enki and Nin-khursag, when they were not in fish garb, likewise used the heights for this sanctified communion - not the mountain tops of the north, for they belonged to a distant geographical location - but of the Sumerian ziggurats. As the Gospel of Mary makes clear, the ziggurat is a special edifice which encompasses the powers, mysteries and knowledge of the structure of the soul, which therefore immediately connects the ziggurat to the Grail.

In the days before the Grail closed down completely, all of the higher Anunnaki used the ziggurats to descend to and ascend from the physical dimension of the Earth, from and back to the particular dimension they all occupied. Enki and Nin-khursag were certainly no exception; but they also used the ziggurat structures and heights for this other, deeper communion with the highest spiritual spheres.

There was also another place that Nin-khursag and Enki would often visit when in fish-garb. To this place they were drawn, as if into a dreamtime of distant memory and tender starlit perception, shadowed yet softly radiant. It was to the sunken Atlantis they travelled, back to the City of Light which was its central jewel.

Hand in hand, they swam in balletic motion around its drowned turrets and obelisks and domes, throughout its mighty halls, its healing chambers and its colleges of instruction, its vast temples and cultural arenas, remembering in both sorrow and delight; for Enki and Nin-khursag had nurtured the civilisation of Atlantis from her beginnings until the coming of the great deluge, when it sank beneath the waves.

Because of the information on the Sumerian clay tablets, we associate Enki with the Sumerian civilisation that was founded between six and eight thousand years ago. But the fall of Apsû, the darkening of Anu, the 'murder' of Tiâmat and the later appointment of Enki and Nin-Khursag as the divine couple happened long, long before Sumer came into being. Apart from its cultural luminosity, its special significance is that it was the civilisation chosen to carry the torch of humanity forward once more after the terrible consequences of the great flood (earlier than the biblical fllod), which similarly almost wiped out our species.

Enki and Nin-khursag did not visit the drowned Atlantis purely for nostalgic reasons, however. They went to receive a special vibration from a monumental crystal which still survived, buried in the Atlantean mountain range that looked down on the City of Light. Here was a secret dimension wherein dwelt an ancient brotherhood who, with the help of the crystal, fortified them for their special mission. The depths of the ocean held many mysteries for Enki and Nin-khursag. They heard Tiâmat's voice in the surge and fall of the waves, and understood that they, together with all humanity, were the Children of Water.

We are confident that Nin-khursag manifested, taught and bestowed enlightenment just as Enki did; but, as would befall Mary Magdalene in later days, history ignored her. This was part of the occupational hazard of being a woman after the great imbalance had struck: women were demoted to the invisible content of concepts such as 'man'kind and the universal use of the pronoun 'he' to denote its members, and entirely disappeared into the context of an all-male God. This is, we believe, one of the profound meanings of the woman in the Song of Solomon who declares, 'I am black, but I am beautiful'. In other words, 'I am blacked out, made invisible by an imposed vision which does not want you to see me - but I remain undiminished by your black magic and just as present as I ever was in my spiritual beauty and the beauty of my mighty signifi-cance and power'. After the depredations of Marduk, the truth of the sacred feminine would become invisible, blacked-out as far as men (and very often women) were concerned. The impact of their visibility would thereafter be channelled in a new way - through the deliberate degradation of the lens of pornographic perception. This little trick could be relied upon to keep the whole system of denial of the sacred feminine in self-perpetuation.

So Enki and Nin-khursag shared this beautiful secret: that they were of Oannes and Tiâmat, they were of the deeps of the Living Waters, they were of the white blood and the red, the 'water' and the 'blood' that was semen and the menstruum-borne ova at the physical level, but that spiralled into boundless symbolic significance on ever higher and deeper levels of spiritual understanding.

They were the golden entwining serpents of the caduceus, and they were the Golden Dragon or Serpent that was later called Poimandres but was first associated with the wisdom of Thoth (linked with Hermes), of Cain (*Qayin*, from which name derives the titles of 'queen' and 'king' and the *ayin*, the sacred eye of God) and Cain's descendant, Ham, (Zoroaster) - through whom Tiâmat's special bloodline descended - and which was the 'underground stream' of secret knowledge, presided over by the Lady Apsû, originally dispensed by Tiâmat via her precious Emerald Tablet.

This special Golden Dragon or Serpent wisdom was later venerated by the Druids, the Knights Templar, the Rosicrucians, the alchemists and the Masons, but initially and particularly, of course, by the Church ('circle') of Jesus and Mary Magdalene (Christ-Brigid). This beautiful, simple, and supremely exalted Church was the very one that was so virulently despised and overthrown by the later Church of Rome, led by Simon-Peter's legacy, he who was filled with wrath, who hated women, who wanted (and we think on one or two occasions actually attempted) to kill Mary Magdalene herself - Mary Magdalene, the feminine Christ. It was this early establishment that harlotised our divine and beloved Mary, airbrushed the toweringly significant Tamar out of historical existence, stamped out the Cathars and the Templars, and condemned as heretical the stories of King Arthur and the Holy Grail.

There was a very clearly defined link and purpose behind all these manoeuvres and abominations - they were not random acts of barbarity committed by an entity that did not understand what it was doing. The unearthly entity that drove them understood the strategic value of perpetrating these obscenities only too well. As we shall see, Peter was its key agent on earth.

Meanwhile, we may reflect on this mysterious and shining truth: that Enki bore the title of the Fisher King, the Fisher King who was Oannes of the Sphere of John, the Fisher King who was Father God, grieving perpetually, perpetually in agony, because his feminine half had been brutally torn away from him.

Chapter Twenty-six
Guileful Wisdom

To understand the difficulties of the task that lay before Nin-khursag and Enki, and to appreciate their ingenuity, fidelity, bravery and determination, we need to return to an overview of the nine kingships which were established in Sumer prior to the great flood that was recorded on the Sumerian king list.

First of all, it is important to understand that this particular flood was not the great deluge which sank Atlantis, nor was it the flood that resulted from the rise of the melt-water as the last Ice Age came to an end between ten and thirteen thousand years ago. It was a very dramatic inundation, however, and in fact our source confirms that it was indeed universal. It is also important to understand that this flood of six thousand years ago was the Flood recorded in the Old Testament.

(We remember that the Hebrew scribes began to compile their own histories during their captivity in Babylon under the yoke of the Babylonian king Nebuchadnezzar, no doubt as an act of empowerment to counter the degradation of slavery, and were potently influenced by the rites and dramas depicting ancient history enacted in the temples and other arenas [drawn from the *Enûma elish*, the Babylonian creation story based on earlier Sumerian texts]. Because the *Enûma elish* was not translated and published until 1876 (having been discovered during excavations some years previously), and the earlier Sumerian texts were not deciphered until less than a century ago, this undeniable realisation and the astonishing scope of its implications has only just begun to dawn on western society.)

Over the next few chapters, let us look at exactly what happened, according to the story that Margaret Bailey and I perceive as hidden in the Sumerian and later Babylonian texts, and the final Hebraic rendition of both, which includes the story of Genesis and other accounts in the Old Testament.

To return to the time of the pre-biblical flood which struck Atlantis approximately seventy thousand years ago, our deeper source tells us that the trouble which arose on the doomed continent had been Naphidem-influenced. Working through the mental and emotional centres of certain of the priests in Atlantis – younger souls who were persuaded to turn away from wisdom or heart-intelligence – the Naphidem had again begun to establish dominance, until the renegade priests had seized control of some of the most ancient and powerful occult secrets belonging to earth. From this purloined knowledge, they developed malignant technologies, which they used with hostile force in a bid to take over the globe. Atlantis had to be destroyed, and terrible calamity was visited upon the peoples of the Earth. The moon was drawn towards our planet (it had fallen on three previous occasions, and had reformed each time from gaseous matter released from the Earth which solidified within a period of two years: a process which would be repeated again in this instance), the Earth toppled off her axis, and, after a period of flooding and species mutation, snow and ice overtook our world.

This global disaster correlated to the time when Marduk 'slew' Tiâmat and ripped heaven and earth asunder. He was, of course, operating in those higher dimensions, the soul worlds attached to Earth upon which conditions and events are not limited to mundane circumscription in the same way that they are in the physical domain. Marduk, although his higher Anunnaki father was none other than Enki (Oannes or John), was himself a member of the Naphidem.

Marduk was one of the later Naphidem, born on earth when the first of his kind had already begun to fall from grace, and Anu had begun to conceive his plot to destroy Tiâmat (upon which his eye had turned to Marduk with sinister intention). Eventually, as we know, the Naphidem had to be banished to an enclosed and sealed off dimension from where they could perpetrate the least harm to the peoples of earth. Marduk had been granted reprieve from permanent confinement within this dimension via an act of black magic (a reversal of the forces which create order in the cosmos) engendered by Apsû, Anu and Enlil in collaboration, and had eventually marched against Tiâmat, having been groomed from his birth to destroy that connective point which linked the Earth and her beings in full consciousness to her creator, the Dragon Queen. From the sentient Earth's point of view, he was slaying Tiâmat herself.

Marduk had demanded supreme rulership as his reward for this brutal and treacherous deed, but he was given no such authority within the Grand Assembly. It was imperative, though, that his demands (those of a monstrously petulant child) were satisfied in order to maintain control over him. Eventually his kingship was allowed to extend, not over the higher Anunnaki, but rather over certain ordinary Anunnaki on earth (it descended at a designated time and place, from which point it was supposed to take over the world). It was first established over the Naphidem on his own plane (their enclosed dimension), with the fallen Apsû as a kind of presidential figure in the background. The seat of Marduk's earthly kingship ultimately became Babylon, after the fall of Sumer, which was directly related to his shenanigans, as we shall see.

However, although Marduk had been granted a certain degree of freedom from confinement in the Naphidem dimension (a rather vague, inchoate astral world where they are generally unable, thank goodness, to effectively materialize their rabid desires or to experience sensation or fulfilment in anything but a disconnected, dreamlike way), he was still prevented from actually walking the earth. He and his clan could only influence it via their thought-manipulation of willing and susceptible human beings, although it has to be said that they made a good job of doing so within the limitations of their restricted capacity.

Although Marduk's authority was less than that of Apsû, his real overlord was Enlil. Again and again we perceive that these two, Enlil and Marduk, worked together to bring about the fruition of their own individual plans for the Earth and her humanity (which, we are thankful to say, they have never entirely succeeded in implementing).

Marduk was always under the sway and dominance of Enlil, and we may think of them in truth as, in Enlil's case, the ancient, mighty, all-knowing patriarch, and, in Marduk's, the callow youth, bombastic, imperious and power-hungry, but also unstable, gullible and easily manipulated. He could never really escape the damaging limitations of the abused child that Enlil and Anu had inflicted on him when they chose him from birth to be the instigator of their murderous plot. As an abused child, he fumed impotently against Enlil's power over him, but could never escape his manipulations. Enlil stood beyond the periphery, a towering, overshadowing authority figure, whilst Marduk operated from inside the circle of action, its buzzing centre, apparently its dynamo but in fact receiving his orders from Enlil.

An important point concerning this relationship was that Enlil and Marduk always hated one another, and indeed still do. Marduk's great aim was to take over the Earth and use it for his own purposes of glorious

146

tyranny, with the rest of the Naphidem paying him allegiance. Enlil (and Anu's) plan was always to utterly destroy humanity (including the Naphidem), and to leave the Earth in such a sickened state that she herself would die, and pass away from the physical realm with her great mission eternally unfulfilled. As we have mentioned, Enlil and Anu were entirely confident that, once the Naphidem were allowed to invade the Earth, the destruction of humanity, soon followed by the Naphidem's own inevitable annihilation (visited upon them by the law of karma), would conveniently occur, and so neatly realise Enlil and Anu's goal.

Anu, Enlil and Marduk had begun to think of themselves as supreme gods in their own right, or as so nearly reflecting their own concept of an all-powerful, all-male God that there was hardly any distinction between themselves and the Godhead. Consequently, each believed that his own plan could be put into action without the fear of karmic retribution. The difference was that Marduk had no idea about the ultimate aim of Enlil, whilst Enlil thoroughly realised and cynically encouraged Marduk's scheme in all its dimensions, laughing at the younger god-man up his sleeve, because he knew what its tragic outcome, for both humanity and the Naphidem themselves, would be.

In fact, Enlil's own wisdom, mighty though it was, had fallen into what Mary Magdalene calls in her gospel, 'foolish' or 'guileful' wisdom, which occurs when the heart centre is shut down and denied by the intellect, and the intellect thinks it rules supreme.

Thus all the wisdom of the soul becomes stupefied, and the foolish intellect becomes hell-bent on its own destruction, never realising until the last moment what a terrible path it pursues.

As we have said, this destruction, caused each time by just such a shutting down of the heart centre and an over-inflation of the head-centres (the latter, in these cases, fed not by the heart but from the lower centres, in particular the solar plexus chakra, which stokes up the fires of ego, self importance, and the resultant desire to dominate), occurred four times on our Earth. In each instance the Naphidem were involved, initially influencing events from where they were based in their communities when they were actually dwelling upon the Earth, and thereafter from their confined dimension which gives them no admission to the material plane except through the thought spheres. The thought-spheres are those subtle levels of life where our collective thoughts congregate, and, if not guarded and guided by the heart, can be confused, manipulated and poisoned by corruptive emanations which bombard and contaminate these spheres. They then rebound on us. Our aim should be to rise upwards *through* them in mastery, rather than being waylaid and captured by them. Mary gives us invaluable counsel about these seven thought-spheres, to which we are attached via our chakras, in her gospel, and shows us how to free ourselves from their tyranny.

At this point, a little foray into Wonderland is just what we need in order to understand more of the nature of this 'guileful wisdom'.

Chapter Twenty-seven
Humpty Dumpty

It is interesting to consider the chapter on Humpty Dumpty in *Alice Through the Looking Glass* in the context of the overloaded intellect, which leads to the affliction of foolish or guileful wisdom. This is what Humpty, with his massive egg head supported on minuscule legs, truly represents. He is the grossly inflated mind which has decided to do away with the centre of its being (the heart) altogether, and sits atop the materialistic heights of ego it has built for itself (the' brick wall' of spiritual incomprehension), all the while fearful that it will drop off and shatter, which, in time, must inevitably happen.

Humpty, of course, is very imperious and scornful towards the soul (Alice-Chalice). His attitude is aggressive and contentious, and all his questions and answers are delivered with pugilistic intent. He tells Alice that 'glory' means a 'nice knock-down argument', which is all he can grasp of the true light in the heart reflected by the soul: i.e., victory and dominance by means of the intellect demonstrating its superiority. Humpty also does his sums upside down, which is most telling, because it means all his intellect-driven calculations give him answers that cause him to see the world the wrong way up, or, interestingly, in reverse mode. As we shall see, the Grail does indeed relate to the head as well as to the heart, and in one sense, the Grail cup is the skull; but before the human skull can truly become the Grail cup, it has to be inverted, otherwise it remains a warlike helmet.

When we invert the skull, so that it becomes a cup, and allow the egotistical brain to be absorbed into the heart, we will find that the brain has been forged by our creator with precious metals that, with the heart-mind's dynamic blessing, will become activated and allow us to ascend to regions of which, at present, we can only dream and wonder. (It is pertinent at this point to remember the Divine Forges, and the idea of the guardians of the Grail bloodline in their smithship and artisan mode – even the great and godly Brigid was known as the 'Smithwoman'.)

The intellect, however, is a very precious, God-inspired facility when

149

the heart holds it in balance, and must be developed so that we can begin to grasp the true scope and mystery of God-created existence. Humpty is ready to help with Alice's mystification over the Jabberwocky poem (wherein the false masculine principle, espoused by Enlil, the lower saurian or the serpent of darkness who is the Jabberwocky itself, is slain by the gallant knight with his 'vorpal blade', upon which his father, the true masculine principle [Oannes] praises him, rejoicing) and makes a very good job of facilitating her enlightenment. Yet Humpty is still the egg-head, out of touch with the sacred masculine that the intellect ought to represent - the faithful knight kneeling in reverence before the true Queen, the mind in the heart. He shows us this by reciting a poem about his difficulties in contacting the sacred masculine essence (the balanced Oannes) within himself.

The poem is about Humpty sending a message to the 'little fishes' (the spirit of Oannes within him). He tells the little fishes what he wants them to do, but, as Humpty's (the intellect's) wishes are out of balance with heart wisdom, the fishes refuse, only laughing at his egotistical rage when he tries to force them to comply.

(We shall find out later how very important the potency of laughter is in overcoming the rage and attempted dominance of the death forces, which the unbalanced intellect courts.) Humpty rants at the fishes, deaf to their reasons for non-compliance, but gets nowhere. In its exasperation, Humpty's intellect summons his soul (by 'filling the kettle at the pump', or allowing himself to hold a 'new' container for 'water', the stuff of the soul, and further allowing the container to be filled from the source [the pump or heart]).

His soul is summoned, and explains to Humpty that his sacred masculine essence (the fishes) is asleep within him. Humpty orders his soul to go and wake the fishes, and convey his message to them. The soul finds his stentorian commands objectionable (it will not be treated as a servile inferior by the intellect), and attempts to further elucidate what Humpty would have to do (as far as his attitude is concerned) before he is going to be able to waken his indwelling sacred masculine essence.

Humpty does not wait for his soul to expound its wisdom, however. He is far too impatient, and scornful of his soul, to do that. Instead, he takes a corkscrew (symbol of the twisted or incorrect way of summoning the sacred essence within oneself) and rushes off to awaken the fishes himself by force. Of course, the door out of his all-consuming intellectual perception is firmly locked! Humpty uses his favoured option of force to attempt to make the door open, but fails. He then tries to turn the handle, and in doing so, he might just have caught a glimpse of how to free himself from his own self-imposed incarceration...but no; the self-protective intellect takes over again, and entirely wipes from his perception his struggle to get in touch with his own sacred essence, and how he might have gained liberty.

Lewis Carroll ends the poem humorously with the line:

I tried to turn the handle, but -

This kind of dead halt occurs three times in the poem. The first instance is when the fishes seek to explain to Humpty why they cannot carry out his wishes. The second is when Humpty's soul begins to delineate to him the stipulations by which he must abide before his soul will be enabled to 'go and wake the fishes', and the third is when, as we have just seen, he is given the opportunity to understand why the handle of the door of perception he desires to open will not turn. This is just what the self-worshipping intellect constantly does, of course - it stops short of wider and deeper illumination and dismisses the terrain beyond its own boundaries into which it is about to step by wiping it from its awareness, failing to appreciate how illogically it is behaving! And so, when Alice-Chalice politely enquires if there is more, Humpty peremptorily dismisses her!

I once listened to a materialist scientist who, on claiming that the cosmos was a sort of inanimate machine endlessly and purposelessly grinding out existence with no self-awareness whatsoever, was asked why, if this was indeed the case, there was such beautiful and supremely intelligent organisation constantly expressing and manifesting itself throughout its cycles. The scientist replied that the question did not exist! Truly a scientist who properly belongs to Wonderland, on the wall beside Humpty!

Just in case his readers did not fully comprehend his drift, Lewis Carroll ensures that his point is driven home by sending Alice straight from the company of Humpty Dumpty into the midst of the battle between the Lion and the Unicorn - the symbolic scenario of the sun (the lion) and the moon (the unicorn), or the masculine and feminine aspects of the soul - the intellect and the intuition - engaged in warfare instead of co-existing in mutual love, harmony and balance. We may note that, on the coat of arms for Britain, which depicts the lion and the unicorn, the crown of the unicorn (the crown of the soul) has slipped off its head, down to the base of its horn. We need to re-crown our unicorn, and allow its glory to shine undiminished throughout every region of our being.

Chapter Twenty-eight
Nine Kings To Rule Them

To return to our overview of the previous attempts by the Naphidem to invade the Earth (and especially the four great instances of this endeavour, which destroyed continents), we need to make clear at this point that Enlil and his father, the mighty Anu, had entered into their secret negotiations with the Naphidem shortly after the onset of their fall from grace, having decided at that point that humanity and the Naphidem must be brought entirely under higher Anunnaki control. As a corollary of this, we may perceive that the Naphidem's sinister influence, in its later stages, had not taken hold on earth without the secret co-operation and facilitation of Anu and Enlil.

Concerning the biblical flood of six thousand years ago, recorded in the Old Testament, the Sumerian texts tell us that King Zi-u-sudra reigned in Sumer at that time. He was the ninth Sumerian king, and different from his forebears, as the eight previous monarchs had all been of the higher Anunnaki. He was a very special king, as he was the first among the ordinary Anunnaki to rule Sumer.

It is not quite true to say, however, that he was 'ordinary' Anunnaki. He and his queen were the first 'Adam' (a generic term denoting both sexes), the new humanity intended to initiate Tiâmat's bloodline and introduce a new DNA patterning into human genes. Zi-u-sudra and his wife (his half-sister) were both generated by higher Anunnaki sperm, although their ordinary Anunnaki mothers had had no sexual union with Ubar-tutu, their father, the eighth and last higher Anunnaki king to rule before them.

Nin-khursag had brought their embryos into being within her 'Creation Chamber', and had transferred them to the wombs of the ordinary Anunnaki mothers from whom the necessary ova had been taken.

Within the confines of her Creation Chamber, Nin-khursag, under Tiâmat's instruction and inconceivable mastership, introduced into the new human pair a celestial energy or quickening that gave them, first through their heart-awareness and then through their chakra and nervous systems, through their brains and every organ of perception, a new

153

capacity which allowed them to receive one quarter of the supreme consciousness that the ever-loving Dragon Queen had always planned to bestow on her beloved children of earth. As we know, this gift of higher perception, leading to the development of godlike qualities, had been given to humanity in its earliest days through the method of direct biology, when higher Anunnaki fathers had impregnated ordinary Anunnaki mothers.

The result had been the godlike people, the Naphidem, who had so abused their privileges and scorned their highest duty of passing on their DNA to increased numbers of the ordinary Anunnaki and serving them via kingship and the guardianship of their communities, that it became necessary to eliminate them from the Earth. Yet the qualities and powers of consciousness of the higher Anunnaki had to be given to the ordinary Anunnaki somehow, just as, on planet X, a slow transference of higher Anunnaki genes to the ordinary Anunnaki was successfully taking place, and just as augmented numbers of the higher Anunnaki were gradually passing into the exalted ranks of the Nephilim.

We should remember, however, that evolution is a spiritual process within the outer expression of physicality, as is evident from the fate of the Naphidem, who were given the genetic potential to express godlike qualities, but who, through their deliberate spurning of spiritual progress, transformed themselves into creatures much more like demons than gods, and lost their access to physical expression altogether. Therefore, we can see clearly that, on the one hand, what Tiâmat gave to us through genetic grace was a number of vital facilitators for our perfect spiritual unfoldment and expression; and, on the other, the deeply mystical, secret grace of the spirit, upon which everything depended, according to our free will, as to whether or not we would fulfil that spiritual potential.

Somehow, then, Tiâmat had to find a way to give the full gift of the potential of divine consciousness to her earthlings. It could not be conferred all at once, through the processes of natural biology, as before, when the outcome had been so disastrous; but it could be given, piece by piece, via the exceptional powers of her daughter, Nin-khursag, a richly gifted scientist and genetic engineer. Into genetic consciousness itself, Nin-khursag implanted enhanced perceptual receptors, and also shock absorbers and screening processes to block the automatic invasion of the Naphidem at the mental level (although our freewill response to them was not blocked). So it was that, when the time was right for her earth children to begin to receive the new DNA, Zi-u-sudra and his queen were graced from conception with the advanced creational dynamic.

They received a perceptual capacity which enabled them to absorb one quarter of the exalted knowledge written in letters of light upon Tiâmat's Emerald Table - that manifested glory which was the heart within the heart of her very essence, and which would enable her created beings to become individually God-realised. This was the promise that Zi-u-sudra took into his soul. From the first, he and his queen dedicated themselves to Nin-khursag and Enki, becoming their staunch supporters and devotees. Zi-u-sudra is better known to us as the biblical Noah.

For many generations prior to this cosmic event, Enlil had been trying to eliminate humanity by means of various plagues and famines, but (as he would also do later on in Egypt) Enki had invariably stepped in, hidden from Enlil's view, and had whispered wisdom, often through dreams, to key community members of the ordinary Anunnaki, so that they found ways to counteract the worst of the evils visited upon them. Enlil did not know that Enki constantly blocked his every destructive move, but his intuition (ever becoming more and more akin to cunning) warned him to beware of the seemingly harmless and generally compliant Enki. Enlil, frankly, wanted to conclude his plan of total extermination of the ordinary Anunnaki as quickly as possible, and grew more and more furious as each attempt was thwarted. However, he soon turned the situation to his advantage.

Enlil, Anu and the Naphidem had entered into a pact which involved the two higher Anunnaki leaders surreptitiously enabling the Naphidem to extend their sphere of influence over the peoples of the Earth as widely and deeply as possible (we remember that the Naphidem were prevented from actually incarnating or walking the earth). This resulted in warfare, evil-doing and general mayhem on earth, which Enlil capitalised on by declaring to the Anunnaki Assembly that such behaviour must be checked and corrected, and then releasing his plagues and famines upon humanity, as if his true aim were simply to administer enlightenment through karma to errant humankind.

At this point, there was sharp and increasing division among the ranks of the higher Anunnaki. Some (a large minority) were entirely repelled by Enlil's style of acting presidency (Anu always remained in charge, but seems to have followed an 'in and out' style of leadership. We presume that by this time, he had already begun to establish himself in new

155

surroundings on another planet or dimension, and was therefore not always available to attend meetings of the higher Anunnaki Council). Some feared and resented Enlil, but were unable to assert their authority and effectually defy him. Others were definitely falling under his spell, and openly supported him even though factions were not supposed to arise within the Grand Assembly; they treated those who disapproved of him and his methods with disdain and hostility.

We believe that none of the higher Anunnaki, except one or two close ministers, had any real idea that Anu and Enlil were in league with the despised Naphidem, or of the hideous nature of their long-term plan. The Grand Assembly still constituted a democracy, and some of the ideals and vision of its members had, to a certain degree, survived the 'death' of Tiâmat; but the seeds of corruption had already sprouted, and were thriving. Nevertheless, everything that Anu and Enlil wished to implement had still to be passed by the Grand Assembly, and in order to win a majority vote, it was necessary for Enlil to deceive, manipulate and mislead.

It was by such means, and by bringing the considerable force of his will to bear, that he managed to persuade the Assembly to agree to a universal flood. Yet again he had been secretly opening orifices of influence for the Naphidem, through which they eagerly poured their seductive poisons, until certain core groups of the ordinary Anunnaki had become so disruptive and chaotic that human society began to disintegrate once more. Triumphantly pointing out that no disaster he had inflicted so far had had the desired effect, Enlil argued eloquently in favour of a mighty inundation.

To the horror of Enki and Nin-khursag, he won the day. Nin-khursag let the Council know how she felt, vociferating her disgust. Enki kept silent, not openly opposing Enlil, but furtively planning his next move. After the meeting had been formerly closed, Enki and Nin-khursag repaired to the secret temple where they communed with Tiâmat. Entering into the sacred Silence, they heard her voice. The mighty Dragon Queen instructed Enki, for his own safety and honour, not to directly break higher Anunnaki law, but yet to carry out her will. It was time for Enki to lapwing!

What could he and Nin-khursag do? The entire human family stood in danger of extinction. Those who managed to survive the flood would have to live post-diluvian lives of savagery and want, reduced to brutishness by scant resources. In the midst of the ensuing social calamity, Enki and Nin-khursag knew that Anu, Enlil and the corrupted higher Anunnaki intended to bend the remnant of humanity to their will, and to force its straitened and desperate survivors into slavery. These slaves and their descendants would prepare the Earth for the coming of the Naphidem, who, because of Tiâmat's injunction against their inhabitation of the planet, needed certain conditions to prevail, and certain adaptations of human anatomy to be processed, before they could again descend into human bodies and make the world their own.

After they had done so, Anu and Enlil would sit back and watch with approval as the Naphidem, under their king, Marduk, blasted themselves out of existence via the great spiritual law of cause and effect, which the higher Anunnaki lords had persuaded themselves was in harmony with their atrocious intentions. The fact that they had abused poor Marduk in order to carry out their schemes, and had literally promised him the Earth as a reward, all the while knowing the cataclysmic outcome of his projected sovereignty, to say nothing of previously deposing Tiâmat (or cutting off our direct route to her) and thereby eventually destroying her earthly human creation, conveniently escaped their attention.

The Sumerian texts, together with many other flood myths from around the world, seem to suggest that the reason for the deluge was not only the misdemeanours of humankind, but an overpopulation problem. The *Enûma elish* tells us that 'In those days the world teemed, the people multiplied, and the great god [Enlil] was aroused by the clamour.' Enlil went on to complain that humankind was making such a racket that he could not sleep, and wholesale reduction of numbers was required. We think, however, that this is an incorrect interpretation.

H. P. Lovecraft, the American writer of supernatural fiction, experienced strange encounters with otherworldly beings who he suspected of attempting to influence him through mind control. His insight into their chilling and unsettling dimension occurred just before and during his frequent subjection to severe migraine attacks. Through the eye of his imagination, he gained deep insight into the Naphidem, who, it seemed, were targeting him in the hope that he would fulfil their objectives on earth. Instead, he resisted them and wrote 'fables' about them which give us a clue as to how they operate, and how they link up their own dimension with ours.

They told him that they would teach humanity new ways of maiming, cruelty and slaughter, and that there would be excitement and shouting upon the earth. This idea of the Naphidem causing a huge stir of excitement, of brutal conflict, of shouting, seems to echo uncannily the words of the *Enûma elish*, and of other ancient myths which tell of the time just prior to the great deluge.

We think that the myths reveal how in fact Enlil, having purposely helped to unleash Naphidem influences upon the Earth, reported to the Anunnaki Grand Assembly on the objectionable behaviour of humankind, once the mass of it was infected, as the second part of his manipulative strategy. It was not that there were too many people on earth, but rather that far too many people had fallen under the sway of Naphidem domination, which 'teemed' with their followers. Enlil's lack of 'sleep', we believe, should be interpreted as lack of 'rest'; in other words, the great god of corrective karma was kept impossibly busy in his generation of it, and was never able to rest, as there was so much evil-doing on the Earth to attend to. The only way he could hope to keep up, and sweep the wicked influences away from the world of men, was to impose a 'last resort' so that humankind, severely reduced and chastened, could be given the opportunity of a 'fresh start' (we are fairly sure that this is how he presented his argument in the Anunnaki parliament!).

The idea of the gods imposing near-annihilation simply because the population was rising does not make sense. Why would they try to wipe out a creature they had taken aeons upon aeons to laboriously bring into being, whom they intended to 'go forth and multiply', and whom they had saved from calamity again and again? The whole purpose of their mission on earth was to oversee the creation of human beings until the new creature stood shoulder to shoulder, in terms of spiritual evolution, with themselves.

It is true that many of the higher Anunnaki lost the plot to some degree after Marduk's brutal repulsion of Tiâmat, but it is also true that only Anu, Enlil, and a few others among the higher Anunnaki, were psychopathic exterminators. The rest, and, at this time, still the great majority, were not. Our belief is supported by the fact that the other gods reacted by 'cowering and trembling' when the floodwaters inundated the world. They were deeply horrified and traumatised, and they clearly had not understood what Enlil planned to unleash on humanity when they voted to assent to his proposal (he had not intended them to understand it, of course).

158

Although very material in its manifestation, the flood bore supernatural elements, and was accompanied by a burning, poisonous rain (no doubt arising from volcanic eruptions). We see that this rain, and the waters which were released, were the very opposite, in fact the illusory death-image (even though it caused real devastation) of Tiâmat's waters of life, her creation of mystical rain falling as 'teardrops' into the abysmal sphere or cup that would hold the universe. The flood waters were the waters of death, sent by one who had become, in his own limited sphere of operation, the mirror-opposite of life, of God.

To save humankind, Nin-khursag and Enki had to act fast. Enki had been advised by Tiâmat (who often spoke through Nin-khursag) not to break Anunnaki law, which prohibited discussion of higher Anunnaki affairs of council with the ordinary Anunnaki. So Enki did not descend to earth and simply tell Zi-u-sudra all about the coming crisis. Instead, he whispered it to the reeds growing by the river close to the royal residence. In his dreams, in his meditations (for the king and his queen were deeply spiritual people, and spent much time in contemplation of the inner worlds), Zi-u-sudra heard Enki's words:

> Man of Shuruppak, son of Ubar-Tutu,
> Tear down [thy] house; build a ship.
> Abandon [thy] possessions, and seek [thou] life.
> Discard [thy] goods, and keep thee alive.
> Aboard the ship take the seed of living things.

We see from this quote, derived from the *Epic of Gilgamesh*, (Tablet X1), how a spiritual test comes to the king and queen. Will they listen? Will they take heed? Will they be prepared to abandon their great wealth of possessions, to put aside materialism and save themselves, humanity and the human world? The answer is affirmative on all counts, and we may thank this royal pair, a reflection of the divine couple Nin-khursag and Enki, and then shining beyond them Christ-Brigid, for their keen and true spirituality, for without it, we ourselves would not exist as we do today in our physical world, and would not have been given the inconceivable opportunity of accepting the Grail, and becoming one with Tiâmat. Even so, and sad to relate of so noble a soul, Zi-u-sudra did eventually stumble on his path, as we shall see.

We note (as Laurence Gardner points out in *Genesis of the Grail*

Kings) that Enki advised the king, not to take pairs of animals on board his ship, but the *seed* of living things. In other words, the king and queen were being asked to build a great storehouse of clinically preserved material for the sake of future generations - a veritable ship of life to counteract the poisonous death Enlil sought to inflict on Earth and her humanity. This was where Nin-khursag came into her own. It was her great pride and joy that Zi-u-sudra and his queen had followed in her footsteps, and were educated scientists and philosophers like her. This had been her special part in their nurture and culture, and now she rejoiced in helping the royal couple to assemble their submersible boat with its great storehouse of practical and scientific provisions. Enki, of course, played an equal part in this grand procedure.

It was indeed Enki and Nin-khursag who together had civilised humanity in its early days, bringing them knowledge of agriculture and the 'distinguishing of seeds, one from another' as part of the full scale of human knowledge. The ark also contained embryonic material which would be implanted in the uteruses of the female animals it carried when Zi-u-sudra and his queen re-established their community.

They were only just in the nick of time. As the last touches were being administered to the ark, the inundation began. Before his crew had laid down their tools, it was underway, and the ship was beginning to float. Whilst the poisonous, acid rain fell, humans and animals (for some domestic beasts were taken on board) had to shelter within the body of the ship, in lamplit darkness. They returned to the womb, as it were, until they could be born again into the sunlight.

It is interesting to pose the question as to why Enlil chose this specific time for his most lethal attempt on humanity's collective life. Did he know about Tiâmat's great plan, already initiated by Enki and Nin-khursag in their bringing forth of Zi-u-sudra and his queen? We believe that he certainly did not know anything about it at this juncture, but that he sensed something major was afoot.

All he really knew was that his maddening brother Enki was on the side of this low-bred creature, humankind, and whilst he himself sought surreptitiously to destroy it, Enki kept succeeding in passing all sorts of ridiculous, unnecessary initiatives through parliament which allowed him to organise the setting up of 'kingships' of higher Anunnaki on the actual earth to try to help it out, so necessitating his own precious kind to be directly in contact with the vile little things for protracted periods of time

160

(we can imagine him rolling his eyes heavenwards as he pondered these things, and becoming more and more explosively irritated). And now, wasn't there some kind of deranged scheme underway to *mix their genes again* with those of his own kind? He shuddered at the very thought. Well, he would soon show them what was what!

He had begun to merge with a virulent demonic entity, perhaps one of the worst, which sprang into being when Tiâmat created humanity in love, and commanded the life forces to flow between them in a supreme act of union which manifests as sexual consummation. This demon was its opposite mirror-image, gaining even more power when the androgynes split because of the materialistic force of earth. Its name is Asmodeus, and we shall discuss it later, although only briefly, as any focus on demons is most unhelpful to the evolutionary impetus within us! (Demons are merely the 'life' forces of the illusory opposite or mirror-image, which had to occur so that creation could come into being. They are waiting to be absorbed into the truth and light of Tiâmat, so that they can become real, not mirror-images anymore. In the moment that they become real, that Tiâmat's life surrounds and absorbs them, they will be emancipated into their proper angelic form and release a new dynamic into the beauty, wisdom and power of creation.

Oddly enough, until that time comes, they are actually helping to advance the process of Tiâmat's magical transformation of the mirror-image of creation into true reality, but, of course, only if we resist their magnetism, not if we allow it to overmaster us! Naturally, their helpfulness lies in opposition, as they are mirror-images.)

So Enlil knew nothing of Tiâmat's mighty scheme, but his demonic impulses, arising from his allegiance with Asmodeus, sharpened his intuitive wits to a murderous degree. It seemed imperative to him to send his lethal flood just at the moment, so to speak, that Tiâmat's plan came into proper operation and her first earthly royal couple, reflecting the divine couple at the level of the higher Anunnaki and at the profounder level of the divine, touched down.

Enlil could not bear that the conjoinment of higher and lower Anunnaki genes was taking place once more, although he suspected and intuited much more than he actually knew. But, yet again, through her great plan, through Enki and Nin-khursag, through Zi-u-sudra and his queen, Tiâmat snatched her beloved human creation from the jaws of death.

Chapter Twenty-nine

The Coming of the Grail

We now come to a part of the story that, rather than receiving alteration through distortions and omissions both contrived and ignorant, has been effectively airbrushed out of history. It involves the next king, Zi-u-sudra's descendant: Ga-nadin-ur, and his queen. This king and his consort brought the great city of Ur into being, and the mighty dynasties that later flourished within it were of their seed, although any record of a direct line has been lost because of the cataclysm that overtook them. We need to look into their history, because Ga-nadin-ur is one of the titanic heroes of all time, and Ur, as we shall see, was very important indeed.

When Zi-u-sudra, his queen and his family, together with those colleagues and members of the royal household who had accompanied them, left the ark and set their feet on terra firma once the flood waters had started to recede, Tiâmat sent them the sign of the rainbow. The rainbow, the sign of the heavenly bridge or ladder, is a symbol of the Grail. It reassured the little group of vulnerable human beings that a loving, all-powerful God reigned supreme, not the pretender god who had caused so much cruel devastation. Tiâmat promised her children that he would never be able to destroy the world, and that, by following her presence in our hearts through our freewill choice, we would be led out of his dark and terrible incarceration forever.

This was the shining promise, the sure and certain hope, that Tiâmat made to her children on the mountaintop that sublime morning, when the sun shone for the first time after many weeks of gloom in a burst of alchemical gold. She showed them the rainbow, the Grail, the resurrection. Afterwards, she told them to go forth and multiply, because it was vital that all the ordinary Anunnaki souls who had been driven forth from their bodies by the poisonous deluge should have their path of physical incarnation and reincarnation restored to them. This was the king and the queen's great mission. [1]

A vital part of this mission included the conveyance of their newly activated DNA to all the generations about to proceed from Zi-u-sudra and his queen. This DNA comprised the specially guarded receptacle within us which could safely receive the specified one quarter of the deepest knowledge of all time and all worlds relating to the Earth, and which equated to one quarter of the Emerald Tablet. That only they and their children contained it, and their counsellors, servants and colleagues did not, was unimportant, as the children from both strains were bound to intermarry.

Also, a purely physical transference was not always necessary. As soon as the new inherent qualities had been 'earthed', so to speak, by implantation within the consciousness and biological systems of heart-attuned individuals such as Zi-u-sudra and his queen, they could be passed on by both psychic and spiritual means to others. (There is scientific evidence for this in that studies have shown that, where one animal in a group is taught a skill which is alien to the usual habits and perceptions of a species, it is transferred 'automatically' to the other animals in the group, so that they all take a step forward in their evolution together. The scientist Rupert Sheldrake's studies with mice confirm this as fact.)

We would like to make clear at this point that those members of humanity who preceded Zi-u-sudra (people from Atlantis, for instance, and those prior to Atlantis) were not in any way 'inferior' to this new strain of humankind. Humanity had taken a beating after the destruction of Atlantis and the simultaneous planetary shift from alignment with our pole star, and evolution had appeared to travel 'backwards' for a time. (Interestingly, Noah or Zi-u-sudra, a redoubtable scientist, was the first to discover that the Earth had actually slipped off her axis [64,000 years prior to his time] as recorded in the Hebrew Book of Enoch.) Primitive races appeared, such as the Neanderthals.

This was the expression of the retrograde energies with which the Earth had to deal after Tiâmat was 'slain'; but, of course, evolution does not really retreat, but ever moves forward. What was happening was an effort to restore some kind of balance after the great imbalance had struck. This is how the life forces operate. We now know, for instance, that many babies were originally one of twins, but that, aware that the uterus would be unable to support the growth of two babies, the directing intelligence within the life forces commanded the womb in which they were contained to absorb one of the embryos. This happens step by step, as each cell of the tiny body is cast off and reabsorbed. From a limited perspective, it might erroneously appear that this process indicates that evolution is in reverse, is moving backwards, as the body is deconstructed. But, of course, the opposite is true. So that evolution can move forwards, so that one child can survive and carry forward its torch, the womb adjusts and balances itself to the needs of a single baby.

This microcosmic process was evident in its macrocosm when Neanderthals walked the earth. They were the result of a rebalancing and adjustment by the Earth for the sake of her children. This is one reason why the fossil record seems to be confusing. It indicates the presence of primitive human evolution within a certain timescale, and then completely disrupts all scientific theory by producing the skeletal remains of a much more advanced example of our species in existence long before that timescale.

That the evolutionary forces of the Earth have had to adjust to reversals and disasters caused by our ancient civilisations is the reason why.

Nevertheless, it does not alter the fact that humanity has always carried within it the divine potential of its creator, and that those who went before us were in no sense less equipped than ourselves with all the intelligence and stature of being necessary to develop it; with the qualification that the Neanderthals, after having rendered the service of expressing the balancing and adjusting 'reverse' evolutionary forces, then proceeded to completely die out as a physical race.

The problem was that the Naphidem (and we have to remember that the Naphidem are entirely human, just as we, the ordinary Anunnaki, and the higher Anunnaki, are entirely human, though none of us are yet *fully* human) had caused a distortion on the path of attainment of our fully-evolved selves. Tiâmat (whose plans always encompass every eventuality) had made adjustments to our perceptual and cognitive apparatus accordingly, beginning with Zi-u-sudra, so that ordinary Anunnaki were protected from the evil-intentioned influences of the Naphidem.

(As we have discussed, this involved allowing our intellect to develop by a more materialistic, mundane route, so that it could be stabilised and guarded from invasion. From a steep vertical cone, the structure of the soul was transformed into a pyramid with a wide, four-square base (to accommodate the four portions of the Emerald Tablet, as it were), firmly and stoically rooted in the security of the Earth. [The strange secret of this cuboid form is that it is actually a circle.] Of course, because of the God-given principle of our freewill, this new security does not mean that the

Naphidem cannot influence us if we actively choose to allow them to do so.)

After Zi-u-sudra and his queen had established their new community, many generations passed before Ga-nadin-Ur was born. He and his queen were treated and implanted embryos, as were his great-great-grandfather and mother (Noah and his wife). They were the chosen ones, the second stage of Tiâmat's four-part plan. This time, the two specially selected embryos (who would become Ga-nadin-ur and his queen) were given the capacity to receive one half of the divine Emerald Tablet. However, to fully facilitate this process, the Divine Woman, who bore within her some measure of the essence of Tiâmat, must also be given to the Earth in addition to the scientific procedures of Nin-khursag; for, as we have learned, no part of the Emerald Tablet can be restored to humanity without Her. (Tamar was the final, integral and most perfect incarnation of the Divine Woman; and Nin-khursag, known by her other name of Nin-mah, was the first, initiating, Divine Woman or Daughter of Tiâmat, who began the process with Zi-u-sudra and his queen.)

This second Divine Woman would descend to earth through the agency of Ga-nadin-ur and his queen, as their daughter. Nin-khursag took the embryos of Ga-nadin-ur and his queen through the processes of her Creation Chamber, and they were born to different mothers, just as Zi-u-sudra and his queen were before them (we remember that higher Anunnaki sperm had to be used for the physical bodies of the ordinary Anunnaki, rather than higher Anunnaki ova, because the developing human bodies needed to descend the heavenly stairway into matter, rather than ascend it into an increased etherealisation of the human vehicle).

The midway point of Tiâmat's grand plan had been reached. Through Ga-nadin-ur and his queen, humanity now held the potential to realise the consciousness of one half of the mysteries of the Emerald Tablet. However, the work could not be accomplished without the coming of the Divine Woman. The midway point equates to the heart, and it was at this juncture that Tiâmat commanded the essence of her daughter to descend to earth into a human body, for this Divine Woman contained within herself the most holy Grail, the essence of Tiâmat, the essence of the Dragon.

The beloved daughter of Ga-nadin-ur was born two hundred years or more after the birth of Zi-u-sudra and his consort. The very early ancient Mesopotamian kings an queens lived an extraordinarily long time, particularly Zi-u-sudra, who was still taking an active part in history several hundred years after his descendant, Ga-nadin-ur, had died. In the beginning, the ordinary Anunnaki who were infused with higher Anunnaki blood via Nin-khursag's Creation Chamber were given Methuselah-esque life spans. These were withdrawn later, partly because the weight of suffering that humankind brought upon itself, and the need to speed up the frequency of incarnations, conspired to make such an extension of years too weighty a burden.

During his reign, at Tiâmat's injunction, Ga-nadin-ur established the ancient city of Ur, and built a magnificent temple ziggurat in its centre. This ziggurat was designed for a special reason. Ur contained the mystery of the Grail, and was a truly mighty power point of its containment. There were four gargantuan power points belonging to it in those days. The first, and also its original source, was in Glastonbury, England, its western arm. The second was in Mesopotamian (Sumerian) Ur, its eastern arm. The third was in Mexico, in Mayan country, its southern arm; and the fourth was located at a spot in the Arctic Circle, its northern arm.

Once the ziggurat had been constructed, Ga-nadin-ur and his queen were escorted via its power to the world of the higher Anunnaki. (Their sovereignty had begun in Kish, but a second palace was built for them in Ur when the city was complete.) Enki and Nin-khursag always accompanied them on these occasions. First, they were taken before Anu (if he was resident), and then to hold court with Enlil. These meetings were merely formalities, in which the two corrupt gods gave the king and the queen somewhat harsh directives concerning their rule and the activity of their subjects - oppressive commandments, the severity of which was intended to maintain strict higher Anunnaki control.

The king and the queen would then repair with Enki and Nin-khursag to their secret temple in the woods - the real purpose of their visit to the exalted dimension of the higher Anunnaki. This world was similar to the once lush and beautiful land which is now the `arctic region, in the time when it was an exquisite Eden of burgeoning loveliness. Within its supernaturally beautiful expanses there were hills and high peaks, and a strange indigo sea. The presence of the Nephilim and the angels could be felt here, and the handiwork of the nature spirits was wrought in a filigree delicacy of infinite wonder. It was indeed paradise, and it was called Eden, as its reflection on earth had been. The gods (the higher Anunnaki) had mirrored it on earth once again, after the demise of the North Pole

Eden, by nurturing the Fertile Crescent into being (comprising the land of Mesopotamia and the surrounding countries, which once flourished like a garden but nowadays contain huge tracts of arid desert.)

In the secret temple, Enki, Nin-khursag, Ga-nadin-ur and his queen entered the holy silence and communed with Tiâmat, who, on the particular occasion we now home into, was to give them momentous tidings.

Notes and References

1. According to one ancient text, the *Atra-hasis Epic*, Nin-khursag was also on hand at this time to help out with her Creation Chamber, named so beautifully in the Sumerian texts as the House of Shimtî (derived from the Sumerian sh-im-tî, which translates as 'breath-wind-life' and equates to the Holy Breath). According to this story, seven girls and seven boys were brought forth as treated embryos, fertilised with higher Anunnaki sperm, to be implanted in the wombs of ordinary Anunnaki mothers. This would have aided the great mission of Zi-u-sudra and his wife in carrying the new humanity forward to the point of the crucial emergence of Ga-nadin-ur. We have not tested this story via our 'source', but it has a ring of authenticity, especially as Zi-u-sudra and his queen (the biblical Noah and his wife) were shown the rainbow with its seven rays at the end of their long ordeal. We think that these seven girls and seven boys incarnated at this time to be of help to humanity, and that they represented, in the two aspects of gender, the seven rays of creation demonstrated in the form of the rainbow, the divine bridge linking heaven and earth which is properly recognised as the Holy Grail.

Chapter Thirty

Princess Gra-al

There it was, within the precincts of the secret temple, that Tiâmat told them a wondrous gift would be entrusted to them: a daughter of great beauty and spiritual power who would contain the pure essence of the Dragon Queen, and who would thereby, via her very incarnation, conduct one half-measure of the Holy Grail back to the Earth, to be kept there in secrecy and protection until its second half could unite with her and return it to humanity in fullness of measure. Tiâmat explained that although the four great power points of the Grail were still in partial operation, they would soon close, except for the veiled and hidden power in what we know today as Glastonbury (which has always born a name suggesting 'mirror' or 'glass'), where the Grail must reside in deep concealment. At this stage, the king and queen merely listened in delight, failing to register what Tiâmat's conveyed intelligence might truly mean.

In time, the promised daughter was born to the royal couple. She was named Gra-al, which means 'of the essence of the Dragon Queen'. In later times, the Hebraic rendition became *Grael* - the 'essence' or 'blood' of the Shining One (God)'. 'El' was appropriated by the male gods to denote themselves, but in fact it originally meant 'shining' or 'fiery one', synonymous with 'dragon' or 'serpent', and the principle it indicated was feminine. The European version of the spelling ('Grail') was an erroneous, phonetic one, although it bears connotations of a vessel containing nourishment, which is befitting in its symbolism; for nothing accidental can occur in the sacred history of the Grail.As the beautiful and exquisitely spiritual Gra-al grew up in her palace surroundings, she too travelled with her parents and their guardians, Nin-khursag and Enki, up the ziggurat to the lovely dimension of the higher Anunnaki. And so it was that one day she was summoned into the presence of Anu, who informed her that he had a suitor for her, and that she was to marry before the end of the year. The suitor was of higher Anunnaki blood, Anu informed the poised and gracious young woman, and it was an honour for her to contract an alliance with him. He was one of the gods.

Ga-nadin-ur and his queen were initially pleased for their daughter, but their happiness did not last for long. When they entered the secret temple in the forest, Tiâmat told them that the suitor whom Anu planned to be Gra-al's husband was of the dreaded Naphidem - Marduk himself! The marriage had three hideous objectives: to eliminate Gra-al's special connection with Tiâmat, to enslave the young princess and her God-granted power, and to bring the swarming Naphidem down the ziggurat of Ur from their own dimension to invade and colonise the Earth. Gra-al would be their key.

In ever-rising horror, the king and queen listened to Tiâmat's directions. They must send a secret messenger to the country we now know as Britain, to the clandestine brotherhood (of the Sphere of John, directly connected to the later Druids and Essenes) which held power there. Here dwelt a great king, who was the true heart-partner and love of Gra-al. They had met in dreams, and each knew the essence of the other, for they were one, even though they had no conscious knowledge of one another. This great king was the only person on earth who could guard the precious Gra-al. He was her true consort, the one who bore the flame of the Son within himself as she bore the flame of the Daughter, for of course she had not incarnated without her other half.

They must marry, and remain in that far distant, wild, holy and remote island in the west. Gra-al could never come home again; and all the royal household must be sworn to absolute secrecy as to her whereabouts. The gods *could* be fooled (we know this from many instances in the Sumerian texts), and Tiâmat herself would protect the incarnation of her divine daughter. This plan was urgent, Tiâmat advised them, and must be put into operation immediately. The slightest delay could mean death, not only to their beloved Gra-al, but to the entire human race, to the very Earth itself.

Tiâmat's instructions were acted upon instantly, and an emissary was dispatched the same day. Gra-al, on the advice of Tiâmat, feigned illness, so that she had an excuse for not ascending the ziggurat into Anu's dimension (where he intended to slowly bind her into the power of the Naphidem), and for staving off her forthcoming marriage for a few extra months. Meanwhile, in secret, the emissary returned with a small party of the 'British' king's men, disguised in Sumerian garb so that they would not arouse suspicion. Amidst terrible but silent grief and lamenting, the beautiful Gra-al bade her final farewells and went out into the night, under cover of the darkness and the soft starlight, and took swift flight, never to be seen again by any of her doting family.

She was borne to present-day England, to the isle of Avalon, where she married her king via deeply sacred rites. A daughter was born to Gra-al, who was named Brigid (Bri-ghid – 'Bright One' or 'Shining One'). There was something truly unusual about this child; she was more divine than earthly, more ethereal than she was flesh. Both mother and daughter were so precious to the king that he installed them for protection in his fort, an underground 'castle' consisting of a great cave system which was the interior of the hill that today we call Glastonbury Tor (the Grail Castle). This cave system has now crumbled and the caves have filled up with debris, but it was still partially in existence when Mary Magdalene and her daughter Tamar (fathered by Jesus) arrived in Glastonbury with Joseph of Arimathea in AD 36. Like their forebears, Gra-al and Brigid (for we must remember Abraham's distinct connection with the ruling family of Ur, and of course he was of the line that produced Jesus, Mary and Tamar), Mary and Tamar needed underground protection. The cave system at Glastonbury was used by Mary and Tamar for a few years, but it was steadily deteriorating, and finally the limestone network of caves in the south of France was deemed more suitable to provide shelter and protection. In the end, even these vast caves were not sufficiently safe for the illustrious Tamar, the 'full measure' of the Holy Grail, and she was forced into underground exile in Ireland, the only place where she could be kept safe from those who sought to kill her. The caves in Glastonbury continued to be used as tombs for the noble dead, and no doubt modern excavation methods would unearth some truly astonishing finds.

We also need to remember, as Europeans, our own connection to Ur. As confirmed by historians, the earliest Europeans were known as the *Ur*-people who came from an *Ur*-homeland and spoke an *Ur*-language. As we revealed in our book, *The Secret Teachings of Mary Magdalene*, the correct pronunciation of Ur is 'yore', not 'er', as most people pronounce it. The pronunciation corresponds exactly with that of 'Eur' in Europe, and indeed the connections between Ur, Sumer and the ancient Celtic world (the Celts were among the first Europeans) are numerous. The Sumerian deities, for instance, find exact echoes in both the Nordic and the Celtic pantheons.

The first Europeans were Indo-Europeans. It has lately been proven that old Sanskrit, the early language of India, was actually derived from a source outside the sub-continent, and corresponds to the language spoken and written by a group of Zoroastrians - and, as we shall see, Zoroaster, who is hugely significant to our story, originated from Sumer in southern Mesopotamia, where Ur is located. The 'marriage' of Ur and Europe came about through Gra-al and her English king (England did not exist by that name in those times, of course), and it was a cosmic event indeed.

Brigid, the third Divine Woman, held the sacred energies of the Grail in safekeeping for the eventual descent of Tamar, the Holy Grail. Both Brigid and her mother possessed supernatural qualities, and were revered as the sacred priestesses of Avalon. Brigid was worshipped as a snake goddess (meaning she carried the lineage or blood of Tiâmat, the Dragon Queen), and indeed the spiritual presence of the divine Brigid in the heavens (of whom the earthly Brigid was a bright flame or incarnation) was worshipped in these isles for a considerable time before Brigid was born in Avalon. Her name was pronounced 'Bri-ght' or 'bright'. She was the holy Shining One, the woman of the essence of the Dragon or Serpent. Her mother, Gra-al, was of course also considered deeply sacred and mystical, and we need not explain how her name has gone down in history! She was of the Blood Royal, not only of kingly and queenly lineage from Ur, but the 'heart daughter', the second Divine Woman, of the 'blood' of Tiâmat, of her direct spiritual essence. (It is worth bearing in mind that we are *all* of the Blood Royal, and that the Divine Women both guard and proclaim this most holy heritage for us.) Princess Gra-al was the mid-point, the heart-point, of Tiâmat's great plan to restore the Grail, the Emerald Tablet, to earth.

As we have mentioned, her name means 'of the essence of the Dragon Queen/Shining One/God'. Even her own mother, Brigid's grandmother, was considered sacred (her name bore within it the title 'Ann' ['of Anu', meaning that she was of the true Anu, the pure and undefiled androgyne who oversaw the plan to seed the Earth with humanity, before its male aspect fell from grace], which is how she is remembered today, for Ann, even in the John and Jesus story, is always the great Originator).

Nin-khursag and Enki taught Gra-al, and Gra-al taught Brigid, how to enter into the profound and holy dimension of mystical beauty whose doorway was contained in the sacred patterns of water, the creational tool of Tiâmat. Gra-al became the first Lady of the Lake, and her secret world within it carried the energy of the sacred feminine principle, a world of the essence of Tiâmat, and the daughter of Tiâmat. This was the true Avalon, the otherworldly Avalon shining like a fabulous jewel at the centre of its mundane expression on earth - the true heart of the Mother. Brigid was an expression of the heart of Gra-al and her king, and was worshipped as the triple goddess. Her spiritual partner was Ham, Cain's great-great-great (thrice greatest! [see reference below]) grandson. Cain was born to Eve but was not of Adam's lineage (Enki was his father). Brigid lived for a considerable time upon the Earth, and left a legacy which still endures today in the memories of the people of the Hebrides. She also gave her name to Britain, and is the essence of the light in its heart.

Ham (Hermes or Zoroaster) was also called Hermes Trismegistus ('thrice greatest') for the same reason as Brigid was called the triple goddess - they each bore within them the 'thrice' or 'triple' blessing of three-quarters of the Emerald Tablet. However, they bore its spiritual quickening, for they had come to prepare the souls of humankind for this gift. It would take further endeavour in the House of Shimtî before the physical and astral vehicles of humankind could be made ready to receive it. This great step was for the future.

When Brigid was born to Gra-al (Gra-al who represented the midway point of the Holy Grail, its very heart), she carried within her the sacrament of the entirety of the Grail, as did her mother. They both repaired to their mystical dimension within the lake of the Isle of Avalon (spoken of in legend as a sphere ruled and inhabited entirely by women, or the Sacred Feminine), and there found perfect unity with the Grail essence, Tiâmat's heart. There was no fragmentation or incompleteness in their expression of or communion - we might say their impregnation - with the Holy Grail. And yet the Grail mystery, although it shone through them, had not yet found full expression upon the Earth, nor could it until the Nephilim couple, Jesus and Mary Magdalene, touched down and eventually brought forth Tamar, the Divine Woman, for the highest essence of Tiâmat could only descend through them; this sacred Mother-Daughter expression was vital for the firm grounding of this essence. When Gra-al and Brigid returned from their female dimension within the sacred lake, when they were once again contained within their earthly bodies at the mundane level of consciousness, their expression of the Grail mysteries was confined to its midway point through Gra-al, and its three-quarters point through Brigid.

What was given to Brigid through the resonance and perfection of her soul was also given - indeed, conveyed via her - to Ham. He was more operative at the earthly level than the divine Brigid. She was the hallowed light within, whilst Ham was its outer practical resonance in human society, expressing its qualities in the day-to-day world. Ham, in old Sanscrit, means 'I Am', the ultimate declaration of God within us. Brigid, goddess of triple perfection, and Ham or Hermes Trismegistus, thrice greatest, were handmaiden and henchman to Nin-khursag and Enki, their ambassadors on earth.

Although Brigid and Ham, through the quality of the receptacle that was themselves, and through a special outpouring of highest benediction from Tiâmat, contained the spiritual essence of three of the four quarters of the Emerald Tablet, mundane humanity still required genetic infusion and manipulation in order to be able to receive in full the spiritual energy which would enable them to conceive of these three quarters at their lower level of resonance. Without this vital preparation, they would not be able to properly absorb Ham's teaching and Brigid's blessing, or the teachings of Jesus and Mary Magdalene when their time came to descend to earth; most certainly they would never be able to access that higher resonance which would eventually lift them into ascension via the Grail. And so it was that, back in Gra-al's beloved city of Ur, Tiâmat, through Enki and Nin-khursag, brought forth Adam and Eve.

Brigid's father, Gra-al's cherished husband, was a king who bore the Christ energies, as Gra-al bore the essence of the mystic Bride. This holy family preceded the Bethlehem family (including Mary Magdalene, who was one with it, as our book about her shows), and it is easy to see why, especially in the Hebridean islands (He-*bride*-s) where Brigid is still revered, she is known as the 'foster-mother' of the Christ. She did indeed foster the Christ essence before it came in human form to Britain; and Britain, as well as the beautiful Hebrides, with their tradition of the highest poetry and mysticism, comprise the 'western isles', those magical islands of godly promise which so many traditions, from the Celtic world to China and Japan, hold in highest esteem as a promise of paradise in their everlasting tales. It is evocative to remember, in this sense, that the Hebridean islands once comprised part of the land of Eden, the paradise which the Anunnaki established on earth as a reflection of the Eden within their own refined dimension.

It is interesting, too, on a lighter note, that Scotland also preserves a link with Brigid's divine partner, Ham, in the highland name 'Hamish'!

Chapter Thirty-one

The Forgotten Hero

Of the most mighty and noble Ga-nadin-ur and his queen, it is sad to relate that terrible tragedy overcame them. They were inconsolable after the loss of their adored daughter, whom they could never visit in case they were tracked to her far western sanctuary; but worse was yet to come. Gra-al's departure was hidden from the higher Anunnaki for a while, but all hell literally broke loose after her flight was discovered.

Enlil (who always did suffer from paroxysms of rage) and his father Anu were determined to punish the unbelievable presumption of the earthly royal couple, who had dared to disobey them. A cataclysmic battle ensued, not a battle such as we know today, where there is physical conflict and carnage, but a battle of mind and will. Truly, it was a battle of black and white magicians, for Ga-nadin-ur and his queen were masters of the mystic arts, as were their predecessor Zi-u-sudra and his consort, although the latter were also practical-minded scientists and natural philosophers.

Anu and Enlil, unbeknown to the rest of both the ordinary and the higher Anunnaki, unleashed the Naphidem from captivity in their ravaging, insane hordes, intending that their original plan should not be foiled by the loss of Gra-al and that the Naphidem should fulfil it by travelling down the special ziggurat of Ur (one of the four arms of the cross of the Grail) to completely overwhelm humankind.[1] Ga-nadin-ur, in one of the bravest, most crucial and most selfless feats that history has ever known, stood firm and fast as guardian of the ziggurat, barring and blocking their way.

Terrible eruptions followed in the physical world - traumatised energy-expressions such as whirlwinds, the spewing forth of volcanoes, and the rising of waters. This disastrous incident finally killed the lionhearted king and his valiant queen. We have seen him, in full regalia, brandishing a sceptre and dressed in serpent-skin, a noble soul indeed, guarding the entryway of Ur like some Gandalf the White protecting Middle Earth. He remained in place for long ages, until all danger, even the most remote, was past. If he had not, our world would not have survived; and so we can thank him and honour him at last, from our distant point in history. The memory and inspiration of his beloved daughter strengthened his resolve and put a supernatural steel into his core. His love for her taught him how to sacrifice all for the sake of spiritual love.

In the calamity, the ziggurat of Ur was completely destroyed, and the city fell. The Sumerian king list only tells us that this kingship 'failed' (in fact it most certainly did not!), and that the chaos and disruption was so bad that the 'heavenly Nidaba' had to be summoned so that her feminine essence, specially linked to Tiâmat, might set all to rights. The kingship (or queenship, in this case) returned to Kish. Again, all this comprised Tiâmat's directive, acted upon by Enki and Nin-khursag.

Queen Nidaba healed and made pure the poisonous leavings of the Naphidem, who had not been able to break through King Ga-nadin-ur's defences, but who had managed to infect humanity to some degree, as usual. (Their plan had been to use the Grail ziggurat of Ur as a their own connecting-point with the Earth, thereby to enslave humankind by psychic means until such time as the necessary conditions had been prepared for them to occupy physical bodies, and thereafter to take over the world in a final material invasion.) We note that only his queen and Ga-nadin-ur himself had possessed the power - and only then by dint of extreme self-sacrifice and exertion - to drive back the Naphidem foe, whom Anu and Enlil had released from their imprisoned dimension so that they could appropriate the Grail entryway to earth.

In the very early days of the Naphidem, Anu, Enlil and the higher Anunnaki had themselves banished the Naphidem from the Earth, as the great and powerful Anu and his son were not very far advanced in their corruption in those times. Sadly, it was immediately after this banishment that they lost faith in Tiâmat and decided to enter into collusion with them in order to forward their own plans for humanity's destruction. Later, when they themselves conspired to enable the Naphidem to poison humanity from the sphere in which they were incarcerated, it required a universal deluge, and the near-annihilation of humanity, for the Naphidem to be overcome.

At this stage of the game, Anu and Enlil had no intention whatsoever of banishing the Naphidem, should they succeed in once again occupying the Earth, and indeed, after the flood, they fully expected this to happen as soon as the Naphidem had gathered enough of the remnant of humanity to work as slaves for them in preparing their route back into physicality.

Thanks to the wonder of Tiâmat's ineffable omniscience and love (which are truly one and the same), we see that a member of the 'ordinary' Anunnaki, one of ourselves, had successfully stood firm against the Naphidem in company with his queen, due to the special gifts Tiâmat had unstintingly bestowed on us. What incontrovertible proof this is that we are all now safe from them! When the heroic king Ga-nadin-ur finally laid down his great task and service (which was not so very long ago) he gave to us all, by the 'Sheldrake method' [see Chapter Ten) an increased strength and insularity against them. They cannot encroach upon us - unless we, through our free will, choose to allow them to do so. We have no need to fear them.

The king and queen, bearing the new DNA, had died; but they had managed to convey it by spiritual means to others. This, of course, was also the particular task of Gra-al in Glastonbury. Nevertheless, in order to complete her grand scheme before Anu and Enlil became a huge source of trouble again, Tiâmat released a whirlwind force within the subtle spheres (as though she speeded up time) throughout the eight obligatory sovereignships of the higher Anunnaki. This enabled her to safely install her final 'ninth', ordinary Anunnaki king and queen on the throne, invested with the DNA which would provide them with three-quarters of the secrets of the Emerald Table, before events became too critical. She was aided in her response to the new chronological pressure via Enki and Nin-khursag, who, though ousted from their full investiture of power by Enlil, still held great sway in the Anunnaki Grand Assembly.

The necessary eight higher Anunnaki monarchies which occurred after Ga-nadin-ur and his queen fell, passed in the relative blink of an eye, enduring for only ten years each (somewhat different to the eight antediluvian higher Anunnaki kings, who ruled for ten *shas* [a total of 3,600 years!] apiece; this enormous difference in time span indicates the measure of Tiâmat's urgency to create the ninth 'wave' so that she might finish her handiwork before Anu, Enlil and Marduk became too obstructive). And so the time came, in about 3,800 BC, when Tiâmat was ready to create Adam and Eve.

Notes and References
1. It is important to note that Anu, Enlil and MArduk's knowledge of the Grail plan was at this time purely intentional. They knew nothing of it at the literal and pragmatic level.

Chapter Thirty-two
Star Fire

If Enki and Nin-khursag had been forced to 'lapwing' in order to establish and remove from office no fewer than eight higher Anunnaki monarchs in eighty years, their previous efforts were as nothing compared to what was now required of them in bringing forth the third level of the new humanity (the 'thrice greatest') and establishing it according to Tiâmat's directives.

Anu, Enlil and Marduk were still fuming with regard to what they saw as Ga-nadin-ur's terrible crime of disobedience towards them. Never again, they vowed, would they permit higher Anunnaki and ordinary Anunnaki genes to be fused, even for the purpose of creating slaves designed to prepare the Earth for the coming of the Naphidem. Of course, most of the Grand Assembly still had no idea about their ultimate scheme, and the conspirators were careful to maintain their colleagues' ignorance. They in turn did not realise that Enki and Nin-khursag's aim in creating the new DNA patterning in Zi-u-sudra, Ga-nadin-ur and their queens was actually to bolster and stabilise human beings against both the Naphidem and the depredations of Enlil.

Enlil himself had brought about Ga-nadin-ur's death, so he had as yet no fears that his own power could be overcome; but he and his conspirators were suspicious, as well as astonished and outraged, to note that Ga-nadin-ur had been able to hold back the Naphidem. They felt that Tiâmat was somehow involved with this new departure in the endurance and steadfastness of human beings, and they determined that, once and for all, they would disinherit the Earth, and themselves, from her power.

This was, naturally, an insane concept. How could God ever be entirely separated from her creation? Even if such a scheme could be realised, the Earth and the higher Anunnaki would cease to exist the moment that the God-forces were withdrawn. Yet Anu, Enlil and Marduk, already far down the road of megalomania, believed that they could achieve their objective. By now, God, for them, was a vague deity that they could only understand as equating almost entirely with themselves.

Together, Anu and Enlil had conceived a plan (which did not include

Marduk, whom they both despised as inferior, and who as far as they were concerned would in any case eventually go up in smoke with the rest of the Naphidem and be lost). According to this plan, Anu would ascend into the cosmos and extend his area of power over other worlds, whilst Enlil remained behind within the earthly spheres to ensure complete domination and an eventual realisation of their plot to seize the Earth planet for themselves, in the event that it could be saved from death once it was cleansed of the 'impure' races of the ordinary Anunnaki and the Naphidem. The problem still remained, however, as to how they would finally exterminate the earthlings and organise the invasion of the Earth by the Naphidem. Everything had been going so well until the rebel Ganadin-ur thwarted them so outrageously! Their rage and resentment continued to rumble and simmer.

Because of their suspicions regarding the continuing influence of Tiâmat, Anu and Enlil had agreed upon an unprecedented strategy. They decided to issue a decree making the precious Star Fire, provided for the higher Anunnaki community by the higher Anunnaki goddesses, a banned substance.

What exactly was Star Fire? The clue lies in the name. Laurence Gardner, in *Genesis of the Grail Kings*, tells us that it was the 'lunar essence' of the higher Anunnaki 'goddesses', which in its material translation was equivalent to high-vibrational menstrual blood. We think this conclusion is correct. Menstrual blood alone carries mitochondrial DNA (a spiritually active substance on the higher spheres), which gives the body cells their fiery centre. This is passed on to both males and females alike, of course; but its origin lies only within the female.

The lunar essence of the goddesses (the 'goddesses' being the most exalted of the higher Anunnaki women) was akin to physical menstrual blood in a certain sense, and it was received by them within an inner cup which objectified as the womb. It carried the divine sphere or egg of life itself, the divine spark of life at its centre engulfed or surrounded, like the white surrounds the yoke, by the individuated life of the dimension upon which that divine life sought to express itself. It enabled the goddesses to conceive and bring forth children in their uterus cups. It was the Star Fire, and it was a direct gift from Tiâmat of her very essence.

It is helpful to remember that humanity, including the higher Anunnaki, can only receive Tiâmat's godly essence via the means of water, of reflection. This is why the Star Fire - the fiery dynamic of the

178

imperishable stars, which convey and express Tiâmat's divine Dragon essence that is the magic of her sacred creational impetus, her very self translating into creation - has to be given to us through water, or the 'lunar' fluid which is menstrual blood, called the 'living waters' because it is the water that conveys the living God to humanity. It fills the uterus cup - another rendition of the Grail.

This uterus cup was something that the goddesses could actually manifest outside themselves. They did not give birth as we do, through the body. Their sexual experience was one of fusing together with their mate to form an androgyne, whereby they actually entered into one another completely. The sperm and ova would unite through the initiation rod of life, expressed through orgasm. The goddesses would then externalise their uterus cups and take them to the Creation Chamber, over which presided the supreme goddess of the womb (Nin-khursag), mystically linked to Tiâmat.

Within the Creation Chamber was the Holy Breath, the Holy Presence. Here the higher Anunnaki babies would develop, occupying an elevated dimension within Tiâmat's heart until they gave their first cry, thus indicating that they were ready to come forth. Whilst they were developing, the mother felt a strong link with the child through her restored uterus cup, which she carried within her throughout the Creation Chamber pregnancy, even though this precious cup also resided within the Creation Chamber itself as a body of light, expanding with the growing child. It occupied two dimensions simultaneously. (This beautiful experience of being in two dimensions at the same time is often experienced by pregnant earthly mothers. It echoes the mysteries of the Creation Chamber.)

So how could Anu and Enlil effectively ban Star Fire, if it was the substance of creation itself?

They could not ban the receipt of the Star Fire by the higher Anunnaki women, of course. What they could do was denigrate it, and refuse to recognise its sanctity and its source, which is certainly what they did. But, as well as producing babies, the Star Fire had a second sacred purpose. It was actually fed to higher Anunnaki men, so that they could fully enter into the mysteries of God, of Tiâmat, just as higher Anunnaki women could by their very nature. When all of Tiâmat's creation was androgynous, this Star Fire was shared in equal measure by each of the two aspects of the individual androgynes, but when they split off from one another, the male aspect was unable to receive it directly. Therefore, the higher Anunnaki women had to feed it to the higher Anunnaki men to keep them entirely connected to their source.

When the great imbalance struck, the higher Anunnaki men began to absorb this precious Star Fire in a different way. Instead of fully accepting it, they admitted into themselves only its power and its potential, rejecting the heart-opening it also offered which gave enlightenment into the mysteries of their own feminine or 'Tiâmat' aspect - that aspect which was so deep within them that it could never split off from them because it contained their greater soul, even though, at one level, they had indeed broken away from that same feminine aspect. Nevertheless, a certain measure of this enlightenment still held sway within them at a subconscious level whilst ever they were taking the Star Fire. This 'nectar of supreme excellence' was indeed Tiâmat's very essence, the deepest heart of her mysteries, and it was known as the Gra-al.

Some higher Anunnaki men, indeed, resisted the great imbalance altogether and consequently did not alter the way they absorbed the Star Fire. These were the Oannes or John men, the Wise and Gentle Knights of High Degree. Chief among them, of course, was Enki himself, who was their leader.

What was this Star Fire like? How was it taken? Why was it called a *lunar* essence?

The Star Fire was given by a kind of reversed libation. It was poured into the uterus cups of the higher Anunnaki women or goddesses in an act of grace by Tiâmat, the all-loving Dragon Queen. We can connect this mysterious Star Fire to the source of human consciousness via the teachings of Nin-khursag and Enki, which were espoused with such profundity and inspiration by Ham or Hermes in Mesopotamia (who had a special relationship to the divine couple, as we shall see), and by Brigid, the Sacred Priestess of Avalon.

They show us that the Capricornian Goat of Mendes, with whom Ham is associated, is symbolised by the sacred pentagram, which relates to Brigid (and, of course, to the Earth, to all of humanity, and to Tiâmat herself). This symbol, and the Goat itself, represent Tiâmat's new humanity, being led upwards to its quintessential realisation upon the holy mountaintop by its sacred guides, Hermes and Brigid: Son of Oannes, Daughter of Tiâmat.

When inverted, the pentagram represents the masculine aspect of humanity. It becomes a geometrical drawing of a goat's head, with the two upward-reaching points of the inverted pentagram as its horns, the points at each side sloping downwards as its ears, and the single downward-reaching point as the tip of its beard. According to this ancient esoteric diagram, Tiâmat's Emerald Tablet appears as a precious stone (an emerald) at the top of the goat's head, between its eyes, at the point of the 'unicorn horn' chakra which allows us to receive spiritual emanations from the stars. Although this 'unicorn horn' is one of the two chakras of the double crown chakra, it is closely allied with the pineal gland: the third eye. In other words, the Emerald Tablet shows us in this aspect that it facilitates the reception of the mystical starlight by human consciousness.

When turned the opposite way, the pentagram symbolises the feminine aspect of humanity. The precious emerald occurs in this feminine representation of the pentagram in exactly the same location as before, but now that it is the right way up its two formerly upward-reaching points (the horns of the goat) are transformed into 'legs'. So it is between these 'legs' that the Emerald Tablet appears in the pentagram's feminine mode, at the point of the womb and vagina, showing us that the uterus cup is the recipient of the Star Fire, deposited there by the feminine Tiâmat, God who contains all principles within Herself. It is the divine function of the female to pass on this Star Fire to the male - literally to feed him with it. When he receives her wisdom, human consciousness throws off its chains, and opens itself to the cosmos, to the divine starlight - to the fire of the stars, or the Star Fire.

The higher Anunnaki men received their gift of Star Fire from the uterus cup of the higher Anunnaki women. It appeared as a substance within the cup, manifesting as the 'living waters' of Tiâmat. It was therefore a lunar substance ('lunar' signifying the principle of reflection), since it was water; but it was red water, because it contained within its mysteries the divine fire of Tiâmat - purest spirit - given to her beloved children by means of reflection, as the moon reflects the sun's light.

Whilst we are in our present state, evolving towards becoming 'fully human' but not yet so, we can receive it in no other way. If we were given it directly, we would be blinded, burnt up in an instant by its inconceivable heat and the unconscionable immensity of its power.

The moon, the receptive body that contains and reflects the ecstatic sunlight, is the exquisite pearl of the heavens, the pearl of great price, which is the great symbol of the uterus cup. It is the white-silver chalice or bowl that receives the red fire of the divine - the spirit - and ushers it into mundane human consciousness. It is the Woman reflecting God – reflecting God because it is only the feminine essence that can do so, be it within a man or a woman (it is in both, just as the masculine essence dwells in both). It is the lunar essence, the Star Fire, and it is given by Tiâmat to her feminine children, and by them to her masculine children. It carries within it, in safe measure, the wonder of the sun, the Dragon.

To the higher Anunnaki men, the Star Fire appeared as fluid, but it carried no sense of wetness. It was a spiritual substance, not a physical one; we might say that it was spiritual wine. It had to be given and received in love, or its potency was harmed and diminished. Indeed, in its highest essence, it *was* love. It was taken into the heart by the breath via the mouth.[1] It was this fiery breath that was the kiss of the Dragon Queen. The giving of the Star Fire was a sacred ceremony, and the divine marriage that followed was a marriage of being, a marriage of consciousness. It brought about perfect balance, perfect harmony, throughout every aspect of creation.

The ancient Sumerian texts tell of Enki and Nin-khursag drinking a lot of wine and arguing together! This was the half-understood rendition by the scribes of the old tales of the divine couple partaking of the Star Fire and discussing the sacred wisdom and enlightenment that they received thereby. Enki was always a little slower to catch on than his conduit and his partner, entailing much animated conversation between the two!

Enlil was having none of all this. He did not want perfect balance, because perfect balance meant that men could not claim to be superior to women and 'inherit' the cosmos. Symbolically speaking (although there is an occult literalness to its truth) Enlil wanted to cut the moon off from the sun, from Tiâmat.

He had already succeeded in splitting off the Earth and the earthly spheres from Tiâmat, so that her creation upon those spheres became less and less aware of the perfect white light that is the spiritual essence of the sun: the Star Fire within its heart, which enables us to attain to our full humanity and which keeps open the 'path of awe' - the Grail. Now it was the moon's turn.

Enlil wanted the mind, the psyche, the intellect, to belong to the masculine principle alone. He wanted to split it off from wisdom, which he saw as the usurping power of Tiâmat, of the feminine principle. He considered wisdom to be stupid and ignorant!

He had it in mind that he himself could feed the higher Anunnaki with the white power of the moon, with wisdom, Enlil-style. They needed no more of this contaminating Star Fire filth! Was he not driven by the will of God, whose thoughts, whose desires, were his very own? And so the god of control, oppression and self-glory (what Jesus of Nazareth described as 'the prince of this world') took ultimate root in his heart.

How would he formulate his own version of the white power of the moon, the new woman-denying wisdom? Enlil knew that the Star Fire, in its lowest vibration or most basic form, correlated to gold. This gave him an idea. He hit upon a secret method, which we shall expound later.

Notes and References
1. It was this precious Star Fire that Jesus received from MAry Magdalene when, according to the Gnostic gospels, he often 'kissed her on the mouth'.

Chapter Thirty-three
Enlil and Enki

It was in this dire climate that Enki and Nin-khursag had to find a way to persuade Enlil (who, due to Anu's increased periods of absence, had been granted acting kingship over the higher Anunnaki) to allow their creation plans for humanity to be passed by the Assembly. Tiâmat, in their meditations, in their prayer-time within the secret temple dedicated to her, and in those spiritually lucid moments between their sleeping and waking, summoned Nin-khursag and Enki to do her will, as the Sumerian texts relate:

> O my son, rise from your bed...
> Work what is wise. Fashion 'servants' (our quotation marks)
> of the gods, [and] may they produce
> their doubles.

To which Enki replies in due course:

> O my mother, the creature whose name you uttered,
> it exists. Bind upon it the image of the gods... Nin-mah
> [Nin-khursag] will work above you...[she] will stand by
> you at your fashioning. O my mother, decree upon its fate;
> Nin-mah will bind upon it in the mould of the gods. It is Man.

Nin-khursag was adored throughout the land. She was called Lady of Life, Mother of All Children, Lady of Form-giving, Lady Fashioner, Lady of the Embryo, Midwife of the Country. Hymns were sung in her honour, such as:

Nin-khursag, being uniquely great,
Makes the womb contract.
Nin-khursag, being a great mother,
Sets the birth-giving going.

Enki, too, was deeply revered, called Image Fashioner, Master of Shaping and Charmer of Making, who delivered his 'repeated incantations' upon the physical substances Nin-khursag used to modify embryos.

It might have seemed to them as if all their skill and craft was at an end, despite Tiâmat's bidding. Enlil and his cronies were adamant that no further indulgence should be shown to the ordinary Anunnaki. They were not to benefit any more from higher Anunnaki genetic material. They could not be trusted. Ga-nadin-ur had amply demonstrated that fact, and there was no more to be said on the matter - except that Enlil now, quite suddenly, needed help from the ordinary Anunnaki in order to carry out his plan of replacing the Star Fire with another, 'purer' substance that he himself intended to concoct. He needed miners, to mine gold and other precious metals for him, so that this new substance could be manufactured.

After the relatively recent full scale inundation, the lands comprising the 'fertile crescent' (Egypt, Mesopotamia, and Caanan [Palestine]) were laid waste. They were still in the process of recovering, and the human population was low. The gods organised the reclamation of the land, but they needed an increased ordinary Anunnaki workforce to supply physical labour and to carry out their objectives of reclaiming, rebuilding and restructuring the ordinary Anunnaki communities. Most of the Assembly were in favour of allowing the earthlings to rule their own communities through kingship once again. They were still, in the main, basically good-willed towards humanity. They knew little of what had really taken place during the last years of Ga-nadin-ur's reign, when the Naphidem had tried to invade. All they understood (from their leaders, Enlil and Anu) was that Ga-nadin-ur had been 'rebellious'.

Enki thus saw a wonderful opportunity to lapwing to the best of his ability, and immediately took advantage of it. It was true, he conceded in parliament, that the last two kingships had not been a success. Zi-u-sudra had proved unable to keep control of his people, and Ga-nadin-ur had flouted the will of the higher Anunnaki (of course, we are privy to what really happened in each case!). What was required, he argued eloquently, was a modification of the genetic engineering that he and Nin-khursag had initiated with Zi-u-sudra and his queen. They believed they knew where their work required attention, and were ready to bring it to perfection. They would ensure that the problems which arose with Ganadin-ur would not arise again.

Enlil was under pressure from Marduk, who also needed more miners so that his own plans of preparing the Earth and her gravitational forces for invasion by the Naphidem could be realised. And of course he needed miners himself, for just as dark a purpose. Enki, lapwinging away heartily, 'agreed' with his brother as they sat in council that the new humans should be nothing more than servants, enslaved to higher Anunnaki will and purposes. He 'seconded' Enlil's view that to allow the earthlings any measure of freewill and higher Anunnaki education was asking for trouble. He assured Enlil that the new humanity which he and Nin-khursag planned to engender would be mere workers, bearing the yoke of the higher Anunnaki. By no means would they be granted liberty. In this way, the Grand Assembly could congratulate itself on their success in achieving their goal of populating the Earth, but yet would be free from worry that the new creature would wax strong, aggressive and uncontrollable, vying with the higher Anunnaki and prepared to destroy worlds in order to exercise its selfish and degenerate free will.

Enlil was ready to accede to this plan. As we have noted, he needed workers for his own schemes, Marduk was pressurising him, and he had to appear to those members of the higher Anunnaki not under his domination as if he were reasonably good-willed towards the earthlings. Had he come to trust Enki any more than before? Not at all! But Enlil, as we know, had a brand new plan (his own version of the Star Fire) which would neatly nip in the bud any veering towards Tiâmat's influence that Enki might be guilty of. He considered his a wonderful, revolutionary plan. Enlil was really not worried. In fact, at this point, it might be said that he relaxed into a degree of self-complacency.

Little did he realise that Tiâmat had long foreseen his implementation of his hideous strategy, and had responded by sending Gra-al to earth as a member of the ordinary Anunnaki, so that human beings could eventually have the Holy Grail restored to them. Until the Emerald Tablet could be given to us in its entirety, and the Divine Woman a living, human rendition of the Star Fire, (Tiâmat's essence in its completeness) could touch down once again on earth, we could not receive the Grail. But Gra-al, who contained one available half of its essence, procured its sure and certain promise, and was its heart, although half of her light was shrouded in shadow, and was invisible and inaccessible to us.

And so Enki was formally instructed by the Assembly to approach Nin-khursag, and request that, together, they bring forth the new humanity. Both Nin-khursag and Enki delighted in the performance of this task. It was their third great work in the creation of the new earthlings, and this time, their human creation would be given the noble capacity to receive three quarters of Tiâmat's Emerald Tablet - to become 'thrice greatest'. On this third occasion of their endeavours, therefore, it was necessary to do things a little differently.

Chapter Thirty-four

The Birth of Adam and Eve

In this instance of Nin-khursag's and Enki's divinely inspired and divinely guided genetic engineering, Enki's own sperm was used to create both babies (Adam and Eve). Ova was donated by two earthly mothers, as had been the case with the two previous kings and their queens; but this time, when Nin-khursag took her prepared materials into the Creation Chamber, she externalised her own uterus cup and placed the first embryo of the pair within it. Eve was created first, before Adam. When she sprang into life within the uterus cup, Nin-Khursag took her, by specially protected means, out of the Creation Chamber and down the newly-constructed ziggurat of Ur. Before she did so, she replaced the cup carrying the embryonic Eve into her own high-vibrational form. Lowering her vibrations as she descended, she physicalised her body until it consisted of material, fleshly atoms, vibrating on the same wavelength as those of the ordinary Anunnaki. She was received into the Temple of Ur, where six higher Anunnaki goddesses awaited her coming. There she was tended, and there she gave birth some months later.

Nin-khursag had obeyed the directions of the Dragon Queen by following this plan. She imbued the child with her own essence, and fed it with her own life-force. Through Nin-khursag's ministrations, Tiâmat was able to permeate the foetal Eve with her vital influences and essence to a greater degree than was normally possible, so that Eve carried within her some answering resonance of Gra-al, Brigid and Tamar, and of Nin-khursag, her surrogate mother.

Nin-khursag is deeply associated with Eve in every sense, and in both women, one from the sphere of the higher Anunnaki and the other from the sphere of the ordinary Anunnaki, the presence of the Primordial Mother - Tiâmat, 'She who bore them all' – played and shone throughout them like an eternal flame in a living shrine. Goddesses and angels attended Eve's birth, and the presence of Tiâmat was even more potent than was usual at ordinary Anunnaki deliveries. Both children were called the *Adam* or *Adâma*, meaning the divine act of the Star Fire, Tiâmat's essence or holy blood, descending into the 'clay' or the matter of Earth - the animal bodies into which the celestial essence of the ordinary Anunnaki had penetrated - by her holy decree.[1]

The male child of the pair was called Attaba, and he was brought forth in the same way as Eve. Enki had rebuilt the ziggurat of Ur especially for their coming. The flagging Grail energies were revived to a certain, temporary, degree, and once again the ziggurat was used as Zi-u-sudra, Ga-nadin-ur and their queens had used it in the past: to attain to the elevated dimension of the higher Anunnaki, and to hold counsel, ostensibly with Anu and Enlil, but really, of course, with Nin-khursag, Enki and ultimately with Tiâmat herself in her secret temple in Eden. Attaba became the first priest-king, and held lordly sway over his people.

Eve, too, was queenly and regal; but she spent more time in the Garden of Eden (which existed within the higher Anunnaki dimension) than her husband-to-be, listening to the wisdom of Nin-khursag and Enki, and entering profoundly into the silence within Tiâmat's temple in the woods. With Nin-khursag and Enki, she was admitted into the Orbit of Sharon or John (which translates as 'the wheeling circle of light'[2]), the holy sphere of radiance in the north (associated with the North Star) which connects us directly to God. She was in training, and withdrew into the inner life more than Attaba.

Nin-khursag and Enki surreptitiously oversaw their education, and instructed them to a high degree, thus overriding Enlil's dictate and therefore careful to evade their brother's resentful and unquiet eye, full of suspicion again, so that he was ready to erupt at the slightest provocation. Whether they were on earth or in the higher Anunnaki dimension, Enki and Nin-khursag had to deliver their knowledge to the pair in discreet whispers. Enki and Nin-khursag often took their sacred serpent form within the Garden of Eden. There was nothing unusual about this. All of the higher Anunnaki exhibited dragon or serpent-like characteristics, and, as we know, Enki also used the form of the sacred fish or sea-serpent. Throughout all this shape-shifting, they retained their inherent, pentagrammatical, human form, as the surviving statues of hominoid figures engulfed in fish-garb attest. Enlil and Anu were also serpentine in essence, but they pretended that its source (Tiâmat) was other than it was.

Eventually, Tiâmat began to instruct Eve in the imbibing of the Star Fire. In one sense, this was a natural, automatic process; in another, the heart centre had to open entirely to Tiâmat in order to properly receive it. Eve recognised that the Star Fire travelled down two 'trees' to reach her. Both 'trees' were family trees, lineage trees springing forth in joy from, and leading back in mystery to, the heart and the essence of Tiâmat. (The beauty and sanctity of earthly trees express this dynamic unfolding of genetic patterns, the stupendous ramification and fruition of the thrust of life itself, and its cosmic familial patterns. Trees map our source, and arterially conjoin our origin with our destination. They are manifestations of the Blood Royal (which is the rising sap in all of us) and of spiritual blessing and facilitation - of the wonderful gift of this mighty genetic process.)

The Trees that Eve experienced were, of course, the Tree of Life (origin – initiation – life – Tiâmat) and the Tree of the Knowledge of Good and Evil (wisdom – heart – Tiâmat). It was these Trees – and especially the Tree of the Knowledge of Good and Evil, or the Tree of Wisdom, proceeding from the feminine-inspired intuition - that Enlil hated and feared above all else. It whispered to him, and he agonised. On one or two occasions, his heart was so stricken that he almost gave up his dominion of terror. He resisted it to the point where the merest hint of its intimations drove him into a pathological rage. His one great aim was to silence its voice forever - for himself, his followers, and for the despised earthlings.

He had long since decided that any realisation of, or connection to, this outrageous Tree, and particularly any fostering or nurturing of its rising sap or dedication to the subtle tracery of the foliage of its influences, must be ruthlessly repressed and entirely forbidden (which meant elimanting the Star Fire). He remained confident that his special white powder would do the trick, as well as the application of new laws and chastisements.

The death of the Tree was Enlil's great strategy.

Notes and References

1. Several ancient texts report that angels bowed to 'Adam', and concluded that Adam, or humanity, must therefore be more exalted than the angels themselves. In fact, the angels were bowing before the presecence of Tiâmat within Eve, and it was to this female rendition of the '*Adâma*' that they made obeisance.
2. It is interesting to not that 'the wheeling circle of light' is the literal translation of the name 'Galilee'.

Chapter Thirty-five

Reconnecting to the Sacred Tree

To understand the pattern of consciousness of the Tree of Life and the Tree of the Knowledge of Good and Evil, we need to return to the esoteric diagram of spiritual reality which is the Goat of Mendes. ('Mendes' is very similar to 'menses' [menstrual blood]; the word is derived from 'month' which in turn has its root in 'moon'; and of course we know that the moon has a very special significance in that it embodies the principle of reflection and is that 'pearl of great price' which dispenses Tiâmat's wisdom to her children).

Mendes was a city in Egypt whose deity or celestial ruler was Thoth or Enki, further associated with his great-great-great-grandson Ham. Thoth's (Enki's) spirit permeated the city, and, the Grail by this time having virtually closed down, he governed it through the earthly presence of the bloodline of his 'ordinary' Anunnaki descendant Ham. (Like Zi-u-sudra, Ga-nadin-ur, Adam and Eve, and others, Ham was in fact not quite 'ordinary' Anunnaki, but was the result, under strictly controlled conditions, of higher Anunnaki sperm united with ordinary Anunnaki ova - a new (and thoroughly revised!) form of 'Naphidem'.) King Raneb, Ham's descendant, was the monarch who initiated the veneration of the Goat of Mendes; he bore within himself the essence of his forebears Ham and Enki, and his queen mirrored Brigid's hallowed Star Fire.

An important feature of both Enki and Ham was that they were both black. Enki was not racially black, of course, as he was higher Anunnaki, and therefore did not occupy a physical body; but Ham inherited African blood from his mother, Queen Nin-banda, the daughter of Queen Shub-ad, whose title was 'the Great Lady of Ur' and who was a Dragon Queen, being a direct descendant of Lilith. This inheritance from Shu-bad, the great matriarch, together with his ancestor's hallowed darkness, caused him to be referred to as the black ruler of Mendes. Ham emphasised the beautiful, positive aspect of darkness, its divine mysteriousness, the shining darkness which is too great a light for us to be able to perceive it as anything other than blackness.

Ham and his forefather, Enki, were the positive aspect of Capricorn (the sea-goat) as Enlil and his son, Ba'al, were its negative aspect. The great stellar influences from Capricorn (for everything comes to us via starlight, via Tiâmat's Star Fire, her very essence) are concerned with the dimension of embodiment, with our stability within that dimension, and with cosmic law, particularly the law of karma, or cause and effect. Capricornian starlight is the most mystical influence within our solar system, according to the nineteenth century esoteric writer and philosopher, Madame Blavatsky. It symbolises the beautiful spiritual presence of the unicorn, and sheds its pure radiance upon our human souls.

Capricorn nurtures our base chakra, at the bottom of our spine. Its ruler is Saturn, and indeed we see that Enlil became a negative rendition of Saturn. Enlil was the negative aspect of darkness, of Saturn, as Enki and Ham embodied the pulchritude of its positive aspect. It is interesting to consider that Saturn has rulership over the precious jewels and gemstones of the Earth. If we take Enlil's path, they remain buried and invisible; if we take Enki's, they are revealed and given to us and become one with the stars: bright, brilliant and pure aspects of ourselves.

If we think of the Grail - the magical pathway between earth and heaven which connects us to God - as having the first rung of its ladder actually set within the Saturnine base chakra (for the base chakra connects us - our spiritual force - to the Earth), we see that the ladder rises from here, the base of the spine, to the top of the spine. The spine is our own personal rendition of the Grail. Each one of us has this microcosm of the wondrous Grail macrocosm. When it is in correct spiritual balance, it is our own lance or mighty broadsword that connects our spiritual force to the Earth (Tiâmat's *Adam*, 'divine fire entering earth') but which is, of itself, utterly and entirely of heaven. Whilst it is utterly and entirely of heaven, it yet embraces and wholly connects with the Earth. In doing so, it infuses the Earth herself with its life and light and lifts the heavy dimension of matter - in which death dwells - into its own eternal, spiritual dimension. This is our lance in right mode, functioning as it should, according to divine decree.

Unfortunately, because of the foolishness of Enlil, and our own foolishness in following him (for we follow him because we choose to

192

admire and embrace the illusions of the negative darkness which disguise so much pain and suffering), we have of our own free will elected to corrupt our lance into an implement which connects us to the Earth and then imprisons us there, so that we are its hapless captives.

This lance wounds. It delivers a death blow - the Dolorous Blow - and beheads us. It should be our entry point into, our guarantee of, the freedom, glory and joy of the spiritual worlds - those worlds which are our rightful and natural habitation, and which allow everything within us, each of our divine spiritual and soul gifts from Tiâmat, to grow and flourish and come into full expression. Instead, it traps us in a world where oppression and suffering overwhelm us, and where death - often a fearful and traumatic death - is the only exit. This rendition of the lance is the reversed 'red arrow' which Enlil gave to Marduk to enable him to 'destroy' Tiâmat. But, of course, what he really destroyed was simply our own and the Earth's divine connection to her, which is the Holy Grail itself. And so we see that the true lance is part of the Grail.

If, in imagination, we look up to the top of symbolic stairway of the spine, there we might see Marduk, sitting in state! Marduk is the false rendition of Mercury as Enlil is the false rendition of Saturn. The stellar influences of Virgo nourish this chakra at the top of the spine (actually the throat chakra).Virgo's true gift is the activation of the pure, virginal light within our soul, the true white light which is a magical, spiritual essence within the sun and within our own hearts. This is veritably the essence of the Grail, the essence of Tiâmat. It is virginal because it creates a tower of impregnable, incorruptible light into which each one of us may be securely locked (not imprisoned) once we have attained enlightenment, and it has absolutely nothing to do with whether or not we have experienced sex! Harm, evil influences, unbalancing forces, cannot touch us once we have entered into our invincible Grail Castle of virginal light. Another facet of its virginity is that it cannot be used for any other purpose than that purest and highest function for which it was designed. It emanates from our chakras and suffuses our spinal stairway, and then sweeps around our entire being in exquisite luminosity.

There is a second aspect to our tower of virginal light. If we think of the spine with its attached chakras as our rod or lance or sword of light (which it is), we will note that of course the chakras don't finish at the top of the spine, but rather extend upwards throughout the head. It is at this point that - although our lance of light remains sure and steadfast within our body of light, with its blade-tip connecting to the Earth and its hilt emanating from the site of our 'soul star' chakra in the heavens, located above the head - we see that there exists a second configuration within its dimensions.

If we think of the sword of light running up the back throughout the spine to reach our base-of-the-brain chakra, we will perceive that, as well as progressing straight upwards to connect with the soul star, it also loops over the head to the top of the forehead at the forehead's mid-point (our unicorn's horn chakra), and then descends to the brow chakra below that mid-point. This configuration forms the shape of the crozier, associated with the Shepherdess and the Shepherd (Mary Magdalene and Jesus), and particularly with Joseph of Arimathea, who carried his famous 'staff' or crozier as he disembarked in Glastonbury from the boat which had carried the disciples and the three Marys (Mary the mother of Jesus, Mary Jacob the mother of Mary Magdalene, and Mary Magdalene herself) from Alexandria in Egypt.

Shortly afterwards, Joseph and his party paused to rest on Wearyall Hill, and he drove his staff (the symbolic blade-tip) into the ground This was to connect his own sword of light, and the greater sword of light which was the spiritual dynamic of the great Christ mission, into the holy earth at Glastonbury, upon which, legend says, the wooden crozier or staff burst into blossom. We think that this actually happened, because in that cosmically blessed moment, the greater spiritual reality superseded the illusory material reality of Earth as she was lifted, for an instant at that special site, out of her imprisonment in the lower spheres. The Christ mission took root in Glastonbury, the place of the Mirror, at that moment.

We have been advised by the healers Renata and Steven Ash that Glastonbury corresponds to a central aspect of the heart chakra of Mother Earth which comes under the governance of Saturn. This entire concept of the principle of the mirror being a vital constituent of Tiâmat's act of creation, of Saturn providing the necessary dynamic to help her earthly creation step through the mirror and become eternally real or 'fully human', and of Enlil hijacking and corrupting these Saturnine energies and the power of the principle of reflection, or the mirror, to suit his own grandiose purposes and lead humanity to destruction instead of eternal life, is further validated by this poignant confirmation that the mystical Saturnine and Capricornian stellar influences are received by Mother Earth's heart chakra at the point of Glastonbury. This is where the Grail resides; not that part of it which is the Emerald Tablet, for that lies to the east, in Lincoln; but the Grail which is the very essence of Tiâmat, and which must be given to humanity at the appropriate time, after the unearthing of the treasure that lies in the grounds of Lincoln Cathedral. The Grail will be received and restored in Glastonbury.

All of this holy knowledge was held in Joseph of Arimathea's heart as he rooted his sacred crozier into the heart of Glastonbury, and watched in reverence as it burst into bloom. Joseph bears the spirit of Osiris, for it was this mighty soul that had reincarnated in him, and would reincarnate again as King Arthur – Osiris, who bore the first pharaonic crozier of Egypt, and was known by his worshipping subjects as the Shepherd of Brilliant Stars. Osiris is thus revealed as a leader who guides humanity towards the attainment of the true starlight – the light of God in the heart – the light which will guide us to step through the mirror and become 'fully human'.

It will benefit us hugely if we carry out a simple exercise, designed to do a great work. We have forgotten the divine crozier within us, which is part of our supreme legacy from Tiâmat and which connects us to the beautiful Tree of Wisdom (called in the Bible the 'tree of the knowledge of good and evil') in her heart. So that we might be led back into the pure sheep-fold of that ineffable heart, we need to properly reconnect our awareness, our consciousness, according to the shape and conductive power of our crozier. Only by so doing will we re-charge our unicorn's horn chakra, located at the top of the forehead at its mid-point, so that we might once again take our part in the grand symphony of the stars, and receive the grace of exalted, starlit consciousness, our link restored at last to the roots, the foliage and the fruits of the Tree of Divine Intelligence, the Tree of Wisdom.

We can do this work, either standing or sitting with the spine straight and relaxed, with a clear quartz crystal (a tumbled stone or a point), or by a simple act of visualization:

> Just see the brilliant white light of the spirit running up the spine to the base of the brain, progressing over the head to the first crown chakra (actually located at the point of the crown), to the second crown chakra, the unicorn's horn at the top of the forehead at its mid-point, and then dipping to the third eye chakra, which is situated inbetween, and a little above, the eyebrows. The light

comes up the spine, curves over the head, and dips to the brow, forming the shape of the divine crozier, or shepherd's crook. Hold this radiant form gently and firmly in your inner vision, and then see te light looping back over the head and down the spine. That is all there is to it. If you wish to use the clear quartz crystal, simply cleanse it by washing it swiftly under the cold tap each time you use it, and place it on the point of each chakra as you do the visualization exercise. Let the exercise flow, and your will and intention will do the work for you.

Practising this exercise once or twice a day will prepare us to receive the Grail and facilitate our enlightenment. If we also combine this daily exercise with the exercise involving the heart centre detailed in Chapter One, we will benefit from both to an even greater extent.

How do we thus seek enlightenment? Through living our ordinary, everyday lives here on earth in such a way that we purify and progress through the levels of the chakras (we remember that the chakras are all aligned with our spine, and that an ethereal spine continues from the base of the brain and connects with the heavens above the head), comprising seven steps by means of which we ascend the ethereal pyramid or ziggurat that is the structure of the soul. The Gospel of Mary gives us wonderful instruction regarding this sacred process.

The seven chakra-steps form a grand arched gateway with two fearsome guardians standing sentinel, one at each of its two posts - Enlil and Marduk, alpha and omega of the magnificent portal which leads through to everlasting life, but which, until we have passed its threshold, is a gateway of death. As this gateway is the connecting point between earth and the heavens, or death and everlasting life, it must necessarily bear the aspect of death from our point of view in our imprisonment here on earth, but actually it is the portal to the everlasting worlds. Whilst ever the great gate remains closed, whilst ever we cannot throw open its doors and cross its threshold, it keeps us incarcerated in death, in illusion; and it does so by courtesy of Enlil and Marduk, the first being the negative aspect of darkness, the 'false darkness', and the second the negative aspect of light, the 'false light'.

We can see how imperative it was for Tiâmat to give her beloved children this sacred opportunity to pass through the Gate of Death into Everlasting Life, of their own volition and by their free will. If she had made the entire process automatic, so that we had no choice or free will in the matter, we would have been saved immense suffering, but we would have been as puppets, as automatons.

To the Dragon Queen, our omnipotent, omniscient, omniloving mother, that would have been an incomplete gift, and Tiâmat is not in the habit of giving shabby gifts to her sons and daughters.

Tiâmat wanted to give us our individuality, our own veritable *beinghood*, if we may thus express it. Her plan was always that we should attain equality with the Godhead, and it was vital to the process of this objective that we should storm the gate of death and pass into life, into true being, via our own free will choice. Only by such means may we become self-realised beings; and so our great Earth initiation was put underway. Nevertheless, the unconscionable suffering involved in this majestic process, for humanity, animals, the world of nature and planet Earth herself, was never part of Tiâmat's intention or plan.

At every level of existence, suffering would have been greatly eased and quickly healed if only we had taken heed of Tiâmat's urgent messages of enlightenment to us, delivered through the agency of many great teachers, through nature herself, and through our own listening consciousness, the mind in the heart. Even the suffering we see today amongst wild animals, although minimised by the forces of nature, derives some of its distressing features from aspects of the polluted thought spheres which encircle the Earth. We are the creators of the contents of these spheres. When we change our thinking and behaviour, animal behaviour will change correspondingly. (We see this, to a certain extent, when we give correct care to, and interact lovingly with, our companion animals.)

Enlil and Marduk are commensurate with the two great forces that Rudolf Steiner identifies as the demons Ahriman and Lucifer. Ahriman is the great restrainer, his the cold and withering breath of limitation, of mortality and death, that dogs our progress and tempts us to believe in annihilation. He imprisons the spirit, shuts down its vision, and takes away its inheritance, locking us with iron shackles to the heaviness and bleakness of earth. The demon Asmodeus is allied with Ahriman, and indeed we see that Enlil has become their ambassador as far as our Earth is concerned. Moreover, in the Persian pantheon from which Ahriman hails, we find that Enlil himself *directly equates* to this entity, just as Enki directly relates to the Persian Mazda, God of Light and Truth. Ahriman and Enlil, and Mazda and Enki, are one and the same.

Lucifer, on the other hand, can hardly bear to be upon the Earth at all! He revels in the power of the mind, wanting always to exult in the ethereal dimensions of life. He uses the solar plexus chakra ('the bellows') to inflate the heart centre, so that we cannot properly recognise it, but begin instead to mistake the lunar fires from the sacral chakra, raging as a furnace now that they are being stoked up by the ego (whose fundamental power is the solar plexus), as the sacred heart-light. Imagining that these lower-chakra impulses in their unbalanced or unpurified state (meaning that they have not passed through the heart) are really the source of all wisdom and sanctity is utterly disastrous. We can see how this happened to Hitler and his followers in Nazi Germany, who became so engrossed by Lucifer that they almost gave full admission to the Naphidem via the horrors of their reign. Marduk, of course, stands in for Lucifer, and is his slave.

Creation does actually need these two great life-forces headed by Ahriman and Lucifer, but not in their unbalanced, undifferentiated form. If we accept them in this guise they bring cruelty, terror and annihilation.

When the heart, the point of balance, heals the negative darkness and the negative light of their respective imbalances, their hostility disappears and they revert to their true essence: the wise restrainer and lawgiver of Saturn, and the dancing, blithe, childlike energies of Mercury, who gives us wings at last and takes us up into the atmosphere of the spiritual worlds.

Here, Ham comes into his own, because although in one sense he is allied to the positive darkness of Enki and Saturn, he reveals his ultimate identity as Hermes (always associated with the god Mercury in mythology, the deity of the true light (Ham and Hermes are one). This must be so, as we know that the Grail enshrines the principle of reflection, and therefore it makes sense that Saturn and Mercury, the alpha and omega points of the spinal pathway up to heaven, should mirror one another, as indeed they do. When we study the zodiac, we clearly see that Virgo, the sign which nourishes the throat chakra at the top of the spine and whose ruling planet is Mercury, is located on the zodiacal circle exactly six months away from Capricorn, the sign which nourishes the first chakra at the base of the spine and whose ruler is Saturn. They are equi-distant from each other, and are one another's mirror reflection.

When Saturn and Mercury, or Enki and Ham, Nin-Khursag and Brigid, have given us their gifts of enlightenment and attainment, we surmount the eighth level on our chakra journey. This equates to the place we reach within our spirit when our head chakras become activated and we become one with the stars - with God. It lies beyond the chakras of the spine.

(The chakras in the head are seen as a continuation of the spine, with Mercury holding court in the fifth chakra, the pentagrammatical number which holds the key to the treasure we may claim within the head centres – namely, release into the starry heavens of the spirit, which manifest in our dimension as the cosmos itself.) When this happens, we are one with Tiâmat again, and the grand pathway to the stars is open within us. The life and the resurrection are ours. We have attained the Grail.

Chapter Thirty-six

The Secret of the Ring

Enlil, Anu and Marduk, despite their best efforts, could never take away this God-given dispensation of the Grail that exists deep within us, of course. Yet, for many thousands of years, we have only been able to express it at an individual, personal level; that is to say, only individuals have been able to open up the Grail highway within themselves and thus overcome the illusions of matter. When the Grail returns on a macrocosmic scale, not only individuals, but the entire world, the Earth herself, will be utterly transformed.

With this in mind, we may perceive that it is Saturn's job to ensure that the celestial light pierces downwards as a heavenly lance or sword, entering the body of the Earth. (We may also perceive just how Enlil has, within himself, corrupted Saturn's energies and consciousness, which in their true mode work to connect heaven with earth, to create a reverse-spin lance - the false red arrow - which actually destroys our point of connection with this celestial light.) Thus the spiritual electricity conducted by the true Saturnine energies is earthed or grounded. As this occurs, the buried light which dwells deep in the Earth - the essence of Tiâmat within her creation - rises and unites with the downcoming light. The two bodies of light meet to form a ring, a globe or a coiled serpent. The ideation of all three exists within these two conjoining rays of light that yet have one source - Tiâmat.

Saturn then locks the magical ring of light within his dominion - the base of the spine. There it remains as secret, buried treasure, until the heart-intelligence develops and radiates forth as a sun or a star. When we have thus become a star, when we have profoundly embraced our true dragon essence and achieved self-realisation as a being of purified fire, of most exalted and glorious light - then, and only then, will ancient Father Saturn release the unspeakably precious ring of light from his keeping. Within the ring or sphere or globe of light is contained the Divine Child (the coiled serpent), the essence of the one true light which will lift us back through the mirror, so to speak, and reunite us with Tiâmat, Tiâmat who is also Oannes, the Father God. In this way, Tiâmat lifts her children out of death and illusion (in one sense, her mirror-reflection creation) into everlasting life (her creation steps through the mirror and becomes one with her).

Via the balancing point of the heart, the uncoiling ring of light is drawn upwards to the third eye and crown chakras, where it becomes enlightenment. Herein we have a pictogram of the Grail itself, with its mirror reflection of male and female, its spinal pathway through the chakras, and its emphasis on the third eye and the crown chakra (the unicorn's horn) that reaches up into the stars to feed the vision of this third eye. The third eye, in ancient terminology, is called the Abode of Joy. This is the promise of the Grail.

Because we have fallen out of harmony with Saturn, and in doing so have elected, and for so long have followed, a false god - a god of materialism, greed, violence, cruelty, strife, chastisement and judgmentalism - we ourselves as a planetary community need to take charge of the situation and turn it around with our own hands. Enlil has planned a terrible death for us, but he can and will be rendered powerless by our refusal to continue to follow him to where he is leading us.

The Holy Grail itself will teach us how to overthrow his rule. However, the teachings of the Christ in the Gospel of Mary (the teachings of Jesus of Nazareth and Mary Magdalene, the divine Christ couple) specifically relate to the understanding we need in order to struggle free from Enlil's dominion. The comprehensive teachings of Christ as they appear in the four gospels of the New Testament comprise this gospel's firm foundation; they are the base upon which the sacred pyramid of Mary's gospel, with its seven ziggurat stairs and its eight levels of the soul, arises. These teachings, taken together as a whole, are the most perfect ever vouchsafed to humanity, but as yet they have not been properly understood in all the profundity of their spiralling dimensions both mighty and humble; for Jesus and Mary spoke to us simply, directly, timelessly, as their sisters and brothers toiling in our homes, our workplace, our relationships - and yet their words also encompassed universes, and mysteries deep as the ineffable love of God. The Emerald Tablet, which lies in Lincoln and which takes the form of a book, and the individual experience of the Holy Grail to which it is allied, will complete our understanding of the gospels, and will also reveal to us the secret of the ages.

We are aware that we have said little about the women involved in the grand parade of our story. During the times of which we speak, a dark veil of such heaviness and opacity had been drawn across the feminine expression of life that it is difficult to discern very clearly the lineaments and the impact of such distinguished women as the queens of Zi-u-sudra and Ga-nadin-ur.

Although the impetus to ignore the sacred feminine principle was coming to humanity from above, from the halls of the gods of the Grand Assembly of the higher Anunnaki, the queens of this far distant era were yet revered and cherished, as royal grave excavations at the archaeological site of ancient Ur confirm.

Anu and Enlil did not entirely bend the ordinary Anunnaki to their will. History attests to the fact that they did not wholly enslave humanity, despite their strenuous efforts. Ham of the divine blackness, son of the dark yet unutterably bright Enki, flourished in the east; and in the west, the daughter of the most Holy Gra-al, Brigid the White, as she has been known to the inhabitants of the western isles of Scotland for countless years, held exquisite spiritual sway in the consciousness of the people.

Nin-khursag presided over the white energies, and both Gra-al and Brigid were her spiritual sisters. Brigid, Gra-al, Nin-khursag and her sister or twin soul (see below), and later, Mary Magdalene, all embodied and expressed the bright white radiance that the beautiful darkness of the true Saturnine and Capricornian essence contains and secretes. Capricorn veritably is a microcosm of the inconceivably vast macrocosm that is Tiâmat - the mystery of the sacred darkness containing the wondrous Child of Light.

These beautiful black and white streams of divine consciousness that were nurtured and dispensed by the divine couple, Enki and Nin-khursag, were related to the Tree of the Knowledge of Good and Evil, and to the Tree of Life. Enki and Nin-khursag contained the teachings relating to these sacred Trees within themselves. The knowledge they imparted expressed the mysteries of the essence of Tiâmat, which was the Tree of Life, and the enlightenment which empowered discernment between the positive and the negative darkness, and the positive and the negative light, and all that encompasses wisdom, which comprised the Tree of the Knowledge of Good and Evil. The Trees were further connected to, respectively, the Star Fire of the higher Anunnaki goddesses, and the physical menstrual blood of women.

Anu and Enlil had already begun to denigrate the former and to inculcate associations with it of shame, stupidity and inferiority, and to utterly despise the latter and call it the Tree of Death, because they hated its teachings, and saw the truth it dispensed in exact reverse mode from that which it was. It was at this point that Nin-khursag began to find herself in trouble as she sought to nurture Adam and Eve, and to teach them these truths of the sacred and inviolate Trees in company with Enki, her eternal partner. We must remember that poor Nin-khursag was married to the domineering and wrathful Enlil, as well as to Enki the Wise!

Enlil had already banned the feeding of the lunar essence of the goddesses (the Star Fire, known as the 'tree' through which Tiâmat manifested: the Tree of Life) to the Anunnaki gods by the time Adam and Eve arrived upon the scene as babies, and Nin-khursag, although she maintained a certain degree of influence and manipulation over Enlil, began to find it increasingly difficult to bring them up and administer to their care and education as she knew she should.

The dispensing of her own Star Fire to Attaba (Eve did not need to ingest it, as she contained it within her own depths, but she was initiated into its mysteries, and its full expression was ritualistically activated within her) became well-nigh impossible under the obsessive watchfulness of Enlil, who knew when she was producing it and began to keep her in confinement, virtually under lock and key, at such times.

Nin-khursag and Enki, in private conference together, decided that the help of another goddess was needed. A very beautiful and powerful higher Anunnaki woman was subsequently approached by them, a goddess of great distinction and a natural high priestess of the feminine mysteries, deeply versed in occult lore of the loftiest order, who had not fallen prey to the confusion Enlil and Anu had spread abroad among most of the other higher Anunnaki.

Her name was Lilith.

Chapter Thirty-seven

The Offering of the Apple

Whilst Adam and Eve were growing up within the care of Nin-khursag and Enki (from now on we will give 'Adam' his proper name of Attaba), the divine couple deemed it necessary, for the reasons described above, to give Attaba into the care of Lilith. She was his nurse, his teacher, his authority and his inspiration, and she fed him tenderly with her own Star Fire. When Attaba attained manhood, he fell in love with her, as we shall see. Eve was his half-sister and his beloved companion, and Lilith also instructed her, although Eve was Nin-khursag's special charge. To make the close partnership of the three adults acceptable and less suspicious in the eyes of the other higher Anunnaki, especially Enlil and Anu, Enki and Lilith married. Lilith was Nin-khursag's twin soul, and there was a deep bond of love and power between the two higher Anunnaki women.

Lilith was Enlil's granddaughter, and although in a general sense he held females in contempt, he had a soft spot for this exceptional member of the higher Anunnaki community. He was not bothered much by what Nin-khursag seemed to be doing with Eve, as he regarded this sort of feminine bonding to be irrelevant to the affairs of all-important males and thus beneath his notice. He was extremely apprehensive regarding the ministrations of Lilith to Attaba, however. At first, Enlil accepted that she was merely his nurse, and was rearing him to be king of his own kind, according to the overall plan passed by parliament.

Attaba was to be the first priest-king, which, as far as Enlil was concerned, meant that he was to be indoctrinated according to the will and the purposes of the higher Anunnaki and to have no autonomy whatsoever. He would be the puppet ruler of the ordinary Anunnaki, and the ordinary Anunnaki were to be kept within the bounds of an entrenched slave mentality, by divine decree of the higher Anunnaki, which the priest-king would dispense. This was the designated programme which Enlil believed Lilith was following.

What was really going on, of course, was an entirely different scenario. In private, Enki, Nin-khursag and Lilith were busily educating the royal children to the highest degree and nourishing Attaba with the Star Fire - that spiritual substance which allowed them to fulfil the measure of their true humanity, with all its wondrous legacy gifted by Tiâmat. It was the Dragon Queen's supreme wish and command that the Star Fire fed to Attaba should gradually be replaced with Eve's menstrual blood, of which he should regularly partake.

This was because the Dragon Queen foresaw future events, and knew that very soon, Enlil would prevent Attaba from continuing to receive the precious Star Fire. Her plan was that the secretions within menstrual blood, which she intended to feed to Attaba and to the future ordinary Anunnaki kings of her designated lineage via specially selected priestesses ('Scarlet Women'), would not only esoterically nurture her chosen bloodline, but would introduce into the human gene pool a certain bolstering and fortification of ordinary Anunnaki DNA so that the full expression of the sacred feminine principle would always be able to manifest in and through the vehicle of physicality, and the living force of 'wo' or wisdom (conveyed by 'wo-man') would be powerfully protected.

Henceforth, this enriched buttressing, decreed by the Dragon Queen, would ensure that the pure waters of the godly 'wo' quality could no longer be so easily defiled and perverted by the Naphidem. From now on, only if a soul wholly gave itself over by virtue of its own free will to the control of the Naphidem could they fully put to use their wiles and powers of encroachment. Our new pyramidal soul-structure also greatly strengthened and secured our future safety and stability.

Unaware of Tiâmat's insurance scheme, Marduk, Anu and Enlil were indeed at this time involved in appalling experimentation, doing everything within their power to corrupt and pervert the life-forces in an attempt to bring about a chemical situation whereby, through interference with the fundamental structure of both ordinary and higher Anunnaki DNA, they could create a 'new man'. This plan, they thought, would rid Anunnaki blood of Tiâmat's influence forever. Their monstrous new creature, with its hideous, heretical female counterpart, would initiate a strain in which the wisdom, compassion and heart-enlightenment pouring into the human soul-vessel from Tiâmat could not manifest properly, but was subject to male dominance and distortion via an inherent pattern in the creature's DNA.

Enlil's investment in the experiments was to make the ordinary Anunnaki into guinea pigs so that, should there be a successful outcome, he might etherealise the process and translate its application to the higher Anunnaki. He still fiercely desired the obliteration of the ordinary Anunnaki, who disgusted him because they lived in physical, animal bodies. He saw them as degradations of the higher Anunnaki, his own noble and superior race, and he would never change his intentions even if the 'new man' experiments succeeded. Anu was of the same mind, although his conquering eye now ranged further than planet Earth.

Marduk pursued the plan with all his might and focus, because on its triumphant culmination depended the future of the ravening Naphidem, who craved release from the misty, dreamlike dimension into which Tiâmat had confined them. If the plan worked, the Naphidem would be able to descend to earth, eventually incarnate into physical bodies again, and enjoy wholesale carnal gratification. Both Anu and Enlil continued to despise Marduk, contaminated as he was in their eyes because of his semi-connection with the ordinary Anunnaki and his lust for material incarnation. Marduk suspected their true attitude (though not their intentions), and loathed them in return; but they served one another's purposes, and so continued to work together in apparently perfect collusion.

In order to block their menaces, Tiâmat dispensed the mercy of the Star Fire to Attaba, provided first by Nin-khursag, and later by Lilith. Eventually, when Eve herself began to menstruate, Tiâmat miraculously captured the full potency of the Star Fire essence in Eve's menstrual blood, translating its physicality into a new alchemy to ensure that she and Attaba could now both begin to benefit from it until the fortification process was complete, and there was no further need for Attaba to ingest it. The menstrual blood had come from Eve's heart, which was conjoined with Tiâmat's by means of special attunement, and which beat in unison with that of Attaba, her half-brother and lover.

This heart-blood stimulated the heart-chakra to release secretions which protected the perfect spiritual attunement of the pituitary, pineal and thymus glands, the head centres which Anu, Enlil and Marduk were specifically targeting. The facilitation of the secretions in the menses enabled a guard to come into being who stood sentinel before these chakras like an angel with a flaming, revolving sword.

206

Once this had taken place, Enlil lost the power to destroy human beings at will. The conspirators' plan failed. Even though certain overshadowed members of the higher Anunnaki did eventually manage to block the proper expression of the sacred feminine principle, this occurred through distortion, not through the dictates of DNA, and applied only to individuals who wilfully initiated themselves into the service of the forces of the negative darkness.

It is true to say that the great imbalance originally struck by the Naphidem in the early days of the world created a problem of polarity between the left and right sides of the brain, so that the left ventricle of the human brain (which controls the right side of the body) overpowered the right ventricle and still holds it in unlawful dominion, but this is a condition which can easily be set right, once we claim our power back from Enlil and Marduk. Perhaps then we can all look forward to becoming ambidextrous!

There came a time, at the point when Tiâmat, via Lilith, Nin-khursag and Enki, had initiated Eve into the mysteries of the Star fire, when Enlil was visited by a dream. The dream came to him through the evil auspices of the demon Asmodeus, who was one of the major powers behind Enlil's throne. In Enlil's dream, Asmodeus showed him, through a sequence of symbols, what was happening to Eve, and what was planned for her and Attaba. (We understand that Asmodeus, who occupied a very different dimension to that of the higher Anunnaki, could not speak directly to Enlil, but was able to contact him through dreams and thought-transference. He was, essentially, within Enlil.)

Because of his dream, Enlil realised that some 'unlawful' allegiance with Tiâmat was taking place under his very nose. He therefore summoned Attaba (not Eve, as he thought her unimportant, except in so far as she might 'mislead' Attaba), and formally prohibited him from 'eating of the fruit of the Tree of Knowledge of Good and Evil', on pain of death. (Prior to the interview, Enlil ensured that the banned Star Fire (the Tree of Life) would no longer be available for Attaba by placing strict prohibitions on Lilith as well as Nin-khursag.) This 'fruit' is symbolised in myth as an apple. In one sense, the apple is the fruit of the rose tree, because both trees belong to the same genus or family. If an apple is sliced in half, a representation of female genitalia can be clearly discerned, and in many types of apple, this depiction also takes the form of a perfect pentagram. The fruit that Enlil banned, therefore, was the fruit of the 'rose tree', or the rosy menstrual blood flowing from the 'tree': the menstruating woman or Anunnaki goddess representing the lineage that reached back to Tiâmat via the family 'tree' which Tiâmat initiated when she brought forth creation.

Poor Attaba left Enlil's mighty presence in fear and trembling. So far, he had not partaken of Eve's menstrual blood, but the ceremony in the temple of Ur in which this act would take place had already been arranged, and was scheduled to take place on the following Friday. (The names of the days were different, of course, but universally the days of the week have always been named after the gods; Friday has always been Goddess day, and has always been associated with fish [Oannes]; so it was the day of the week we would recognise as Friday upon which Attaba would, for the first time, ritually receive Eve's menstrual blood). He returned to the secret temple in the woods, where Enki, Nin-khursag, Lilith and Eve comforted and reassured him.

As we have mentioned, up until this point, Lilith (and occasionally Nin-khursag's) Star Fire had been fed to Attaba, but now Eve was about to start her first menstruation, and it was Tiâmat's express wish that Eve's blood, specially infused with the essence of the Dragon Queen, should be given to her half-brother. Eve must give of the fruit to Attaba. Perhaps we may be excused if we repeat the information we have just disclosed.

It was the express wish of God that Eve should give of the fruit of the Tree of Knowledge of Good and Evil to Adam so that he might 'eat thereof'.

Protesting, and still half out of his mind with terror (anyone who encountered Enlil immediately knew that he was not the kind of man to take prisoners!), Attaba told the company assembled in Tiâmat's secret temple that he could not partake of the fruit of the tree, because if he did, Enlil would kill him.

It was then that Enki escorted Attaba outside for a man-to-man talk. They entered into the sequestered depths of Eden, where the spirit of nature breathed forth its sweetest airs, and the essence of Goddess surrounded them. There, Attaba found calm, and reconnection to his source; and there, Enki, whispering, because Enlil's spies were everywhere, assured Attaba that, once he had undergone the ceremony in the temple of Ur and had partaken of the 'fruit of the tree', Enlil would no longer have the power to kill him.

Attaba objected half-heartedly that Enlil had intimated that, although

Enlil would certainly kill him for his disobedience if he dared to eat of the fruit, there probably would be no need for him to take the trouble, as the fruit would finish him off anyway. Again, Enki comforted Attaba, and reassured him that the fruit would save him, not kill him. It was not the fruit of death, as Enlil pretended, but the fruit of life.

At last Attaba rallied, and his courage returned. Guided further by his beloved Lilith, who escorted him into the Ur temple and presented him for initiation on the designated day, he accepted 'the fruit of the tree' from Eve, and 'ate of it'.

In that moment, the will of God was fulfilled; and from then on Attaba and Eve carried within themselves the divine mystery of three-quarters of Tiâmat's Emerald Tablet at the cellular level, and were protected from Enlil's hatred (Brigid, in far-off 'England', was an essential part of this supreme triumph). Enki and Nin-khursag, aided by Lilith, had achieved a glorious victory over the adversarial forces represented by Anu, Enlil and Marduk.

Against monumentally oppressive odds, they, the thrice greatest in the heaven worlds, had infused into Tiâmat's human creation all of the sacred potential that they themselves contained. Now Attaba and Eve were also the 'thrice-greatest', and their DNA would eventually bear Tiâmat's immeasurable gift to every human being born to the planet. There still remained the great issue of human self-will, which humanity itself must conquer, and the towering threat of Marduk and Enlil, who would manipulate it to their advantage. Nevertheless, the gargantuan task depending on the divine couple was done, and done admirably. They had acquitted themselves with the highest honour.

Chapter Thirty-eight

The Banishing of Adam and Eve

The important thing now was to keep Enlil in the dark so that Tiâmat's great plan for humanity could continue unhindered. Enki, Nin-khursag and Lilith trained Attaba and Eve in the basics of 'lapwinging', so that the next time they ascended the ziggurat, their state of enlightenment would be hidden from the mighty higher Anunnaki king. Yet although they were made ready with meticulous thoroughness before their next visit to Enlil's court, nothing could have prepared them for the shocking ordeal of what was to come.

Having partaken of the fruit of the rose tree, or the 'apple' of the Tree of the Knowledge of Good and Evil, the next time that Eve and Attaba ascended the ziggurat to enter the Garden of Eden (the higher Anunnaki dimension), they found that their inner vision was sharpened to the highest resolution of their 'thrice-greatest' capacity. Therefore, the enshrouding curtain woven by Anu, Enlil and Marduk's invasive encroachments fell away. Their vision cleared, their understanding was illumined, and they saw the unadorned reality that surrounded them in stark relief.

Eden was still a garden of surpassing beauty with a vastness beyond it which, as had always been the case, they were unable to penetrate. Yet, whereas before there was ever a sense of eternal space and freedom, as of a heavenly terrain where the spirit could sail aloft and travel on unhindered wings to a mystical horizon lit with a secret radiance, the young couple felt that now, looking into it with unclouded eyes, an oppression lurked there.

As if intent on keeping out of sight, a hidden menace slipped invisibly from point to point in a circuitous route to surround them. Their eyes could not see it, but their deeper soul registered its presence and felt its shadow. They had been summoned to appear before Enlil, but their courage entirely deserted them, and they begged Enki and Lilith to hide them from him. Enki, knowing only too well how severe Enlil's wrath would be once he discovered Attaba's disobedience to him, offered to shelter them in Tiâmat's secret temple. It was invisible to Enlil, and Enki and Lilith both hoped that the young couple could regain their strength there until they felt ready to confront Enlil, and perhaps even manage to continue to deceive him. If Enlil was not so deceived, Lilith and Enki knew that indeed the temple would be their only place of safe refuge; and, somehow, both of them sensed a storm brewing.

When Enlil ventured out in the cool of the evening, he came forth alone. He had, in fact, left the Hall of Justice in his palace especially to walk abroad and see where Attaba and Eve were. They had been called into his presence, but had failed to appear. Normally, his servants and ministers, junior members of the higher Anunnaki, would have sought out the royal ordinary Anunnaki couple on his behalf, but on this occasion Enlil dismissed their services. He knew that Attaba and Eve had entered the higher Anunnaki dimension - his own soul-awareness, through its links with his wife Nin-khursag's sensitive apperception, could not help but relay such information to him - so why were they daring to disobey him? Enlil was uneasy. This state of affairs was unprecedented. He needed to discover the reason why, and he needed to do so in secret. Most of the other higher Anunnaki were still unaware of his ultimate plan, and if it had been foiled in any way, it was better that he should amend the situation in secret, so that they should gather no inkling of his true intentions, nor witness the extremity of the remedies that he would be forced to put in place.

Sensing their nearness, Enlil called out to Attaba and Eve.

Enlil was still some distance from the secret temple in the woods. Lilith and Enki urged Attaba to leave its confines and go to meet the higher Anunnaki king, so that its existence would remain hidden. It was invisible to Enlil, because it expressed its existence on a higher vibrational wavelength than that upon which, since his coarsening and darkening, he now functioned; but Lilith and Enki preferred not to run any risk of its discovery. They explained to Attaba that they would rather Enlil was diverted away from its precincts than approach any closer.

Whilst Eve was able to stifle her fears, and was ready to appear before Enlil whilst he was still at a safe distance, she could not persuade Attaba to accompany her. Attaba had much more to fear from the irate king than Eve. The prohibition against eating of the fruit of the Tree had been laid upon Attaba, not Eve, who did not need to take it, because she produced it. The 'fruit' was within her, and it came forth from her. It was Attaba, rather than Eve, whom Enlil wished to interview (Eve sometimes attended these interviews with Attaba, unless she was scathingly ordered out of Enlil's presence, which was often the case; otherwise, her attendance was tolerated only if she kept completely silent and stood in the background with her eyes downcast), and therefore Attaba alone who was properly playing truant.

Eve, on the other hand, felt strangely elated. Her heart and crown centres sang and she was no longer afraid of Enlil. She was coming into her own as a woman, putting on her true womanhood, which meant that her spirit and her deepest soul hit the target of their highest aspiration and connected her consciously with Tiâmat. The Dragon Queen's fire streaked through her, and she became one with her exalted serpent essence. Lilith and Enki, aware of this transformation, instructed her to conceal her spiritual fire and to remain hidden in the temple with them.

Only Attaba must go to meet Enlil.

As the fruit of the Tree of Knowledge of Good and Evil released its full powers of protection within Eve, Attaba was lifted up in vision with her and by her. He saw even more clearly what utter slaves Enlil sought to make of them and all their kind. Now he understood how even he himself, as Enlil's 'priest' king, had been given his priestly role specifically in order to dupe and engulf his people into the debasement of complete bondage and servitude to a cruel and tyrannical ruler, all aspects of their God-given higher nature chained and confined within the dungeon of Enlil's hatred and denial, and mired in his wrath.

Attaba saw that he, himself, had been set on course to initiate a priesthood of damnation and abomination, and would have done so, if Enlil had had his way and Nin-khursag, Enki, Lilith, and, lastly, Eve, had not mercifully intervened. Eve saw with him. They looked through one another's eyes, and their vision was one. They were overwhelmed by Enlil's wickedness, his terrible rejection of God. Indeed, they now had the power of discrimination, the knowledge of good and evil, and Enlil, who saw things in exact reverse to them because he could not recognise what was mirrored and what was real, appeared to them at last in his true guise as an ireful monster. And the monster was approaching, closer and closer.

In vain, Enki sought to embolden Attaba to go out and meet Enlil before he advanced any further. Attaba was too desperately afraid to move, even to take his hands away from his face. Enlil, at their very door, stopped in his tracks and thundered his command that Attaba should appear before him. He *knew* Attaba was in the vicinity; he could sense it beyond any doubt. The fact that Enlil could not see where Attaba was infuriated him all the more.

Stumbling to the doorway of the temple, Attaba answered him at last, in timid and tremulous tones.

'Why are you hiding?' was the enraged rejoinder.

'Because I am naked,' Attaba responded.

All was lost now. By this statement, Attaba told Enlil that he realised that he was nothing more than a dupe and a slave, and that he knew he had been deceived. We think that Attaba was also saying in his fear that he had no defence against Enlil now that the veils had fallen away from Attaba's perception, although, of course, because of his decision to partake of the 'fruit of the tree', he certainly had.

Enlil's straightforward fury now turned ice-cold. The menace in his voice was a blight to Attaba's soul as the great king demanded, 'Who told you that you were naked?'

Something terrible began to happen. As Attaba's fear mounted, his vibrations began to resonate with those of Enlil. The king's tremendous fury and Attaba's tremendous fear entered into an antiphonal relationship and sounded forth the same note. Simultaneously, Attaba cut himself off from Tiâmat's temple, and yet revealed her temple. What Attaba saw and experienced, Enlil now saw and experienced. He saw faintly, as if in shadow-form or through a veil of antimatter, Lilith and Enki standing behind Attaba; and he saw Eve standing unashamed at Attaba's side, her eyes unafraid to meet his. From her crown a strange coiling fire scintillated, like a branching tree formed from tongues of brightest flame.

This, more than anything, revealed to Enlil that he was looking into the interior of a secret temple dedicated to Tiâmat. He listened as Attaba verified that indeed he had eaten of the forbidden fruit. His cataclysmic fury knew no bounds. He tried again and again to kill both Attaba and Eve on the spot by a process of blasting and withering of which he was master, but his psychic blows glanced off them as if he aimed at a mirror image instead of at the very core of their being, which is where he thought he was directing his lethal rays. His wrath made a split in the beautiful etheric matter of Eden, so that it was riven; but Eve and Attaba remained unharmed.

Henceforth, Enlil saw Enki as his sworn enemy (he was not interested in the fact that Enki refused to give any validity to the concept of enmity). Many distorted myths were born in that moment, whose conditioning power still holds sway within us today.

Chapter Thirty-nine

Enlil's Wrath

Having always admired and desired Lilith, Enlil now loathed her. Although hatred cannot approach love, and could not be further removed from it, there is indeed a thin line between desire and repudiation, or the polar opposites of passion. Enlil now repudiated Lilith, calling her (predictably) a whore, and instigating twisted rumours about her that were intended to arouse disgust and terror amongst the ignorant - namely, that she was a demon who drank blood (because she gave of her own Star Fire to the human Attaba), and that she ate children (because, following Tiâmat's divine decree, she taught Eve to give her menstrual blood to Attaba so that he might imbibe it for his own protection, which of course involved the ingestion of Eve's released but unfertilised ovum).

For Eve, Enlil reserved a similar blasting of the breath of odium. She would become the fallen, evil temptress who led Adam astray and scorned and betrayed the word of 'God '(Enlil). Following hot on the heels of Ganadin-ur's 'betrayal' as it did, Attaba and Eve's disobedience to the higher Anunnaki king seemed a terrible thing to him. He bemoaned and lamented it for century after century; and this was very odd, because there can be no doubt that almost from the start, he never intended anything for us but total and irretrievable annihilation.

This small detail, however, did not stop him from railing against Eve. He cursed her and all womankind, promising her and her descendants distress during menstruation and agonising pain during childbirth.

He certainly put abroad the idea, even prior to this event, that menstrual blood was 'filthy' and 'disgusting' (in fact it is absolutely pure, not having gone the rounds of the body and gathered impurities on the way, as ordinary blood has), and he introduced the disempowering idea that menstruation is a 'curse' (in fact it was a curse only to him and his schemes!), although it is a sacred phenomenon, and nothing is more venerable and holy than the 'living waters', as the ancients once knew.

He whispered rumours of virulently evil women, priestesses of a hideous cult, whose consciousness expressed itself in ravening tendrils of the brain that reared and struck like living vipers (his version of the spiritual consciousness of the feminine Tree of Life!), and so the Medusa myth was born, long before the ancient Greeks came into being. As Enlil, through wiles and terrorization, gained more and more followers on earth, he let it be known that the hair and crown centres of women in particular were offensive to him, reminding him as they did of the moment he beheld Eve in her Tiâmat-centred glory, growing the Tree of Life from her head, as if she were rooted into the highest heavens via that point of her anatomy, which, of course, she was.

It is interesting to note in this context that Lilith, and other members of the higher Anunnaki, were often depicted with horns in both later mythology surrounding them, and in the statues and images of the ancient Sumerian period. These horns were symbolic of the crown chakras, particularly the 'unicorn's horn' centre, which in those far off days was fully active and which received emanations from the stars - from Tiâmat's higher creation of the imperishable stars, for even the mighty higher Anunnaki were simplistic and almost primitive compared to some of the exalted spheres and civilisations that contacted them from on high via this special chakra.

We believe that the unicorn's horn chakra will again come into prominence during our own time, and develop to a capacity hitherto unknown even by our higher Anunnaki ancestors. Enlil also put a dividing sword of horror between woman and her blessed origins (Tiâmat) by seeking to cause her to fear and revile the serpent.

Attaba, of course, was not going to come off lightly either, even though Enlil reserved the worst of his wrath for Eve and womankind in general. Enlil pronounced eternal slavery upon him and his kin (the entire human world) and gave voice to his intention to steal away all the happiness, peace and joy that Tiâmat had planned for her earthly creation. (All of these things were part of his plan anyway, and measures had been set in place for their fulfilment long before he learnt of the 'treachery' of Attaba and Eve; it was just that, once he had discovered that they were not the pawns he thought they were, he took great pleasure in outlining his true intentions to them - intentions he had taken care to conceal heretofore.)

As for Enki, Enlil simply thought that all these schemes of his younger brother were merely a plot to oust him from authority in the Grand Assembly. He did not forget how outraged Enki had been to discover that their father Anu had given the royal inheritance to himself, Enlil, instead of to him, and how Enki believed that the matrilinear inheritance from Tiâmat which should have set him on the throne ought to have been honoured and obeyed, as indeed it ought, according to both spiritual and Anunnaki law.

Enlil set all this down to ego; in other words, he judged Enki according to his own standards. He thought that Enki looked upon Tiâmat as being on his side, as it were, in the matter of Anu's dismissal of his younger brother's claim to the kingly inheritance via the Dragon Queen. He did not realise that self-importance had no hold on Enki's heart, and that all that concerned Enki was centred on his realisation that Anu and Enlil were leading both the higher Anunnaki, and the earthly humanity which was their precious charge, into the jaws of evil and death. Enlil had no real conception at this point of what Enki really intended, which was to obey Tiâmat's injunction to rescue humanity in its entirety from the doom and destruction planned for it by his elder brother.

Believing as he did that Enki was merely planning to stage a take-over, that Lilith was his main co-conspirator and that this was why Enki had married her (no doubt, Enlil thought, offering her queenship by his side once he himself had been removed from power), Enlil drew the final conclusion that the whole affair amounted to nothing more than a planned political coup. He considered that the empowering of Attaba and Eve according to the old way - Tiâmat's way - was just a ruse of Enki's to gain favouritism, to bring them under his influence and tempt them over to his side.

Nevertheless, Enlil truly feared and despised the Dragon Queen because she reminded him, deny it as he might, that life did not conduct itself according to the principles he sought to force on it, and that the origin of all power, might and omniscience was not masculine, as he purported it to be.

When he discovered the secret temple in the woods which maintained a forbidden link with Tiâmat, he mustered all his forces of destruction and concentrated them on the temple and its mystical connection with his own sphere. We must remember that he was a past master at this art; it was he who gave the red arrow into Marduk's hands to 'destroy' Tiâmat, he who forged it himself in a perverted and deranged act of master craftsmanship into a reversed weapon of horror, blasphemy and destruction.

It was veritably a rod of initiation that in one of its aspects is expressed in the rod or sword of the spine and its inbuilt chakra system which is, at the subtle level of life, thrust into the Earth at each individual conception and birth to connect us with our divine nature, with heaven and with God.

Enlil wielded it because it was the staff of his office as a minor lord of karma. He purloined it and abused its power in an unconscionable act of betrayal. When he did so, in truth he destroyed, not Tiâmat, but our awareness of her, that silver umbilical cord which feeds the pure gold of the higher spheres into the bowl of consciousness. This lifeline could not be entirely destroyed, nor could it be entirely blocked; but it could be stifled, inhibited, choked to some degree, and it could be wrapped around with illusion, distortion and strange mirror-image reversals.

This is what Enlil did, this, the enormous challenge he set us (he did not mean it to be a challenge, of course, he intended it to entirely demolish us!). This was the highly dangerous lance that the knights of the Grail Castle cautioned Perceval against, warning him that it cut off from a man his higher nature, his perception of higher things, and that it bolted him through with a terrible urge to embrace what was vile in his lower nature. Enlil entrapped the sword (the spirit) in the stone (dense, slow-vibrational, earthly matter) and sought to persuade human beings that the stone was the sword and the sword was the stone. In other words, he reversed the truth.

We can see that, up to a point, he did what he should have done. It is Saturn's job (and Enlil was an emissary of Saturn) to lock the incoming light of the spirit at the base of the spine (the tip of the sword) until it conjoins with the light of the spirit within the Earth itself, which has to be called forth in full consciousness by the soul. When this happens, the sword conducts the light heavenwards again through the chakra system, until it rushes through the crown centres in a jewelled firework display like a fountainhead, becoming one and communing with the spiritual light of the stars. Thus are we infused with Star Fire in its ultimate mode of expression. We achieve enlightenment, and can ourselves, as individuals, at last wield the mighty sword of the spirit. We become queens, kings, invincible, godlike in our attainment of our true selves or our Christhood. We are virgins, safe in our crystal castle or tower of pure living light, and no darkness can assail us and bring us down.

The great mystery of this sword is that, although it is downward-pointing when it first enters into our being a few weeks prior to our physical birth, it has to be reversed in order that we may free it and wield it. It is its destiny, therefore, to be reversed. Its purpose in its act of reversal is to bolt us through with a baptism of ineffable light, not to lock us into our lower nature, although our struggle with our lower nature (the earthly dragon) is part of its initiatory process.

The problem, as far as Enlil's history, purpose and behaviour is concerned, is that although Saturn tests and challenges, he does so under the ordinances of Tiâmat, with benevolence, with love, wanting us and urging us always to achieve the highest within ourselves, whereas Enlil, on the other hand, does *not* want us to succeed. He is intent only on imprisoning and enslaving, debasing and destroying us. He is an affliction which intends never to be a blessing, and therefore he makes our initiatory path much harder, more beset with difficulties, than Tiâmat ever intended it to be. It is true that this desolate, stony path has been our choice for a great stretch of time. Yet we will learn how to overcome Enlil's influence and scare tactics, and throw off his yoke, for it seems that, at last, humanity is ready to deny him, and to move forward onto the spiritual road that Tiâmat has made ready for us.

When Enlil discovered the secret temple in the woods that day, he cast odium forever afterwards on Lilith and Enki, purposely to lessen their standing among the other higher Anunnaki. Yet again, using his 'red arrow', he cut off Tiâmat's link with his own sphere (Eden, the dimension of the higher Anunnaki) and laid waste to her temple. From now on, Enki, Nin-khursag, Lilith, and Tiâmat's other faithful followers among the higher Anunnaki, would have to find the Dragon Queen in the peace and silence of their own hearts. No dedicated communion point remained.

After unsuccessfully attempting to kill Attaba and Eve, Enlil banished them from the environs of Eden and closed down the Grail by removing the power of ascension from the ziggurat temple of Ur. This was a natural corollary of destroying Tiâmat's temple, or her conjoining point with the higher Anunnaki dimension. Enlil had been of the opinion that the power of the Grail (the power of ascension) was under his and Anu's control aftre the striking of the Dolorous Blow, and that this was why it still functioned to some degree. He soon found that he was mistaken.

Whilst it was true that he could 'slay' Tiâmat with his reversed red lance or arrow, and so close down the Grail energies, he could not re-engage them at will. The great king Ga-nadin-ur stood guard over the divine pathway between earth and heaven, and, by the grace of his sacrifice, only at Tiâmat's command could the Grail energies flow in either direction. Enlil discovered this fact once Attaba and Eve had been banished, and it was a huge problem for him. How could he now hope to open the flood-gates of the Naphidem dimension and allow them down onto the Earth, there to wreak their havoc until humanity and the Naphidem themselves were both utterly destroyed, and the Earth useless for anything but his own purposes? His great plan seemed foiled again.

Meanwhile, he 'gave coats of skin' to Attaba and Eve. In this regard, it is helpful to remember that, as well as being master of time, Saturn has dominion over the subterranean treasures of the earth - its precious stones and metals - over the skeletal structure of bodies, and over the skin. We infer from this that he has rulership over what crystallises and accretes, and over limitations and boundaries. The boundaries of the body are marked out by its skin.

When Enlil gave 'coats of skin' to Attaba and Eve, he bound them fast in their physical bodies. This means that he used his Saturnine powers to prevent them from etherealising their bodies to reach the higher Anunnaki dimension. (We remember that when the Grail energies were still present upon earth, members of the higher Anunnaki themselves would descend the ziggurats, gradually materialising their bodies on the downward journey to earth, and then, on ascending the ziggurat to return to their own dimension, would progressively etherealise themselves until their forms resonated with their own sphere once more; it seems that that this power was conferred on Attaba and Eve by Enki and Lilith, via the agency of the ever-receding Grail, until Enlil withdrew it.) When Enlil shut down the Grail, Attaba and Eve were circumscribed by their physical bodies and bound into their coats of skin. Except by meditation, no entry to the higher worlds was available to them, just as is the case for present-day humanity. Enki and Lilith, however, came to their rescue. Eve and Attaba had been humiliated by their experience with Enlil, and felt disgraced by the fact that they now knew they were nothing more than his slaves.

Laurence Gardner points out in *Genesis of the Grail Kings* that images of slaves of the period depict them as naked; and although Eve and Attaba no doubt possessed mundane clothing, they felt keenly that their position was one of thraldom, even though their status was that of king and queen. Lilith and Enki therefore provided them with royal robes, to remind them always of their true heritage and purpose upon the Earth. These royal robes were similar to the ones that the mighty and noble king, Ga-nadin-ur, had worn when he commanded matters of state, and when he repudiated the Naphidem. They were made up of scales, of intricate and beautiful design, and they were formed from serpent skin.

We would like to make clear that no serpent had suffered death in the obtaining of these skins. They were materialised through the power of magical thought and the manipulation of the etheric forces in matter. Enki and Lilith were eminent shape-shifters, and the fashioning and moulding of matter was Enki's special forte. He was the magnificent ancestor of all those who practised smithship in the world, the original grand master craftsman. Thousands of years later, the knights who still continued to honour Enki (Oannes) dressed in chain mail or 'shining' armour in reverent memory of these fish or serpent scales.

When Jesus of Nazareth plied his trade, first as a house carpenter, and then as ship's carpenter, he echoed the spirit of Enki. He was one of four sacred 'brothers' who were all craftsmen: Joseph, his father; Joseph (of 'Arimathea', or 'Mari-thea', literally, 'Mary-God' or the feminine God of the Sea, meaning Tiâmat)), his great-uncle; and Joseph, his illegitimate half brother, whom Jesus loved and cherished, even though he was an outcast from the family. All three Josephs were metal-workers, which as we shall see bears great relevance. Jesus alone worked with wood, with the Tree of Life, and this bears the greatest significance of all.

In later times, as the shadow of Enlil fell over the world, the kings of Tiâmat's bloodline, those of her direct dragon inheritance who would ensure the safe arrival of the ultimate king and queen (Jesus and Mary Magdalene), were anointed with the fat of the *Messeh,* the sacred dragon or crocodile. This was an Egyptian ritual of coronation, although the Hebraic word *Messiah,* the anointed one whose coming was awaited, derives from it (the Egyptian and Hebraic traditions are conjoined at their roots).

The custom of using animal fat for royal anointing or coronation ceremonies, rather than the original plant-oils, which the *Messeh* replaced, was initiated at the express command of Enlil. It is interesting to note that the 'dragon' fat for the anointing ritual was provided by either the crocodile or one of the great monitor lizards, such as the ancestors of the fearsome Komodo dragon, which forms communities today solely on a single Indonesian island and is extinct elsewhere. This highly aggressive animal is reported to have the most malodorous breath in the world, 'death-breath', because it often feasts on long dead carrion. The crocodile, too, is hostile to humanity. That these magnificent creatures should die an ignominious death for the purpose of anointing kings, especially those of the special bloodline, satisfied Enlil. He wanted kingship to express venomous, antagonistic and bloodletting qualities, the 'breath of death', which he admired, rather than the love and unity of Tiâmat's essence, which he despised.

The true dragon, he decided (for we must remember that he himself had serpentine aspects, and was of the Dragon or Serpent People, just as Enki and all the higher Anunnaki were) was exactly like the dangerous crocodile, or the Komodo dragon; and so the idea of the dragon of eternal venomous wrath was born. Their propensity to rend and to seek nourishment by eating death objectified a reflective truth about his inner nature which craved symbolic expression, and, by the sacred and incontestable law of truth, was bound to be granted such expression.

And so it was precisely these dangerous qualities of hostility, blood-lust and predation that Enlil wished to be psychically transferred to the kings of the special bloodline, not only for the reasons previously outlined, but also for a very specific purpose which shall be revealed. He eventually banned the ingestion of blood by his followers; Eve and Attaba's story tells us why he did so; but he was very careful to ensure that his followers should not confuse the killing and eating of animals with taboo activities such as the ingestion of blood. He had a vested interest in the suffering and cruel death of animals, which we shall discuss in a later chapter.

Enki and Lilith initiated the ancient anointing ritual, beginning with Zi-u-sudra and his queen. They used spikenard, the precious oil which is specifically reserved for rites that balance and conjoin the sacred masculine and feminine principles. It is applied to the head and the feet, signifying the royal and sacred Grail pathway between heaven and earth, and it is associated with ceremonies in which the Grail energies are invoked, and spiritual ascension attained. Its creation and application involve no abuse or slaying of animals, and it is indeed this original version of the royal ceremony that Jesus and Mary Magdalene chose, when Mary anointed Jesus, and herself, in her house in Bethany (she rubbed the oil she had applied to his feet onto her own hair). As we shall learn, there was also another very important tradition belonging to the kings of the special bloodline that Jesus entirely rejected.

Enki and Lilith anointed Attaba and Eve with oil of spikenard in the Ur temple on the designated Friday when Attaba received Eve's purified menstrual blood from her own hands, and thereby 'ate of the fruit' of the 'forbidden' Tree, shortly before they were banished from Eden forever. When Tiâmat's secret temple was destroyed by Enlil, the Ur temple was destroyed simultaneously. In later years it was rebuilt, and continued as a station of the Grail that contained great holding power, even though the Grail energy was no longer active within it. However, after their banishment from Eden and the destruction of the Ur temple, Enki and Lilith moved the young couple to Eridu, where they remained in kingly and queenly office. Eridu was, as Genesis relates, east of Eden (strictly speaking, south-east); that is to say, it lay east of the gate of Eden; and the gate of Eden, or the portal to the higher Anunnaki dimension, was of course located in Ur.

Once they had been banished from Eden, Lilith and Enki dressed their beloved charges in serpent skins, as we have related, and urged them to enlighten their people to Tiâmat's kindly and beautiful truths, even though they would have to do so indirectly and cautiously in order to avoid the wrath of Enlil. The higher Anunnaki king was indeed still very powerful in his dealings with earth, and was gathering greater strength and momentum with the passing of each day, despite the fact that he could no longer strike Eve and Attaba dead at a whim, which had been well within his capacity prior to the moment when Attaba ate of the 'forbidden' fruit.

Now that the secret temple had been destroyed, Lilith and Enki taught Eve and Attaba how to create a dedicated, sanctified altar to Tiâmat so that they could enter into heart-communion with her anywhere, at any time, even though they were no longer able to visit Eden. The altar could be either visible or invisible, but it was always an acknowledgement of, and a withdrawal to, their own heart centres.

This also provided the means for their future communication with Nin-khursag, Lilith and Enki themselves. Once the Grail had closed down, Enki, Nin-khursag and Lilith, as well as other members of the higher Anunnaki, could not walk the Earth in vibrationally-slowed, physicalised bodies any longer. This process was still possible, but only via great difficulty and highly specialised procedure. It was no longer what we might term automatic, as it had been. Nevertheless, provisions were made for the line of communication between Nin-khursag, Enki and Lilith and the royal couple on earth to be kept open.

There remained one problem that they could not solve, however. Attaba had fallen desperately in love with Lilith.

Chapter Forty

The Master Craftsman

Attaba's problem was that Enki was courting Eve. Love affairs in those days, unlike the early days of the world when all was in harmony, were not the one-pointed ideal that they are today, where generally the crown of a loving sexual relationship is complete devotion and fidelity to one's partner. Although this point of perfect balance between the masculine and feminine principles is usually our aspiration today, and was expressed with such beauty two thousand years ago by Jesus and Mary Magdalene, the prevailing situation between men and women of five or six thousand years ago was too unharmonised to allow for such attainment, except in rare cases. At this period in our history, sexual relationships were about securing and fortifying the four square base upon which they, and the structure of our own individual souls, rested. There was thus a certain amount of cross-over patterning to be put in place, as we saw with Anu, Enlil, Enki and their wives, particularly Nin-khursag and Lilith, whose own valiant examples of it ensured that Enlil never managed to obliterate the light of Enki. Enki's courtship of Eve – Eve who was Nin-khursag's spiritual and physical affinity - was part of Tiâmat's plan to strengthen and increase that light.

Nevertheless, Attaba felt that, if Eve, his own partner, were to enter into an alliance with Enki for a designated period of time, then Lilith, Enki's wife, should properly become his mate for a while! He had already formed a deep attachment to her, as she had been his nurse and mentor from his earliest days. He admired her beauty and nobility. There was a serious problem which obstructed the progress of his plan, however. Lilith did not desire Attaba, and had no intention whatsoever of becoming his sexual partner!

Her decision was not based merely on personal preference, but rather stemmed from her knowledge of the full sweep of the greater picture, which revealed the vital significance of Enki and Eve's union. When Attaba cleaved to his higher nature, he could appreciate the importance of what they sought to bring forth together, and the imperatives involved in the situation. Lilith revealed to him the necessity of balancing ethereality and physicality by only ever uniting higher Anunnaki sperm with ordinary Anunnaki ova; and how, if it were the other way around, the energies of the resulting child would be too etherealised for the purposes of earth.

Attaba therefore understood that Tiâmat's special bloodline would descend through Eve, and not him. His respect for Lilith's wisdom prevailed, and although he was tested by Eve's liaison with Enki and by Lilith's rejection of him as a lover, he was not found wanting. His sense of fairness and brotherliness towards Eve never failed, and his upright stance as a true man, an Oannes man, schooled and enlightened by Enki, helped to rectify to some extent the hold of the great imbalance on earth. His reign was known and celebrated as a wise era. Enlil took a blow from this noble Oannes or John man, and reeled. However, his determination to press ahead with his plan to annihilate humanity did not waver, and he waited in the wings, patient and wily, looking out for his next opportunity.

Enki certainly did not neglect Attaba in any way, and was full of praise for him, giving him many commissions and opportunities for greater and wider leadership within his kingly remit. He continued to educate him in all aspects of knowledge, and ensured that his priesthood was freed from the bondage of servility to Enlil and became the priesthood of a true devotee to Tiâmat (for he was the first priest-king, and the first king of the bloodline of the 'thrice greatest', or of those who had received three-quarters of Tiâmat's Emerald Tablet into themselves at the cellular level; he is described in the Sumerian texts as being of the Royal Seed [of Enki and Nin-khursag). The Sumerian texts report of Attaba, and of Enki, his overseer:

> [Oil] he commanded for him, and he was anointed.
> A garment he commanded for him, and he was clothed...
> His command was like the command of [Anu].
> With wide understanding, he had perfected
> him to expound the decrees of the land.
> He had given him wisdom (the 'apple' [our insertion]), but he had
> not given him eternal life.
> At that time, in those years of the wise son of Eridu,
> Enki had created him as a leader among mankind.
> Of the wise one, no one treated his command lightly.

'Eternal life' was not bequeathed to him because the kingly bloodline (esoterically linked to the Tree of Life, or the Star Fire) would not descend from him, but from Eve and Enki. Nevertheless, it seems that the reference in the texts also touched upon the fact that, although Attaba and Eve had been given the wisdom of the gods, or of three-quarters of Tiâmat's Emerald Tablet, they had not been granted the immortality the gods enjoyed. This was simply because, of course, they had to live out ordinary Anunnaki lives on earth in an animal body, which eventually, without the presence of the Grail, were each visited by an illusion which presented itself as physical death. After the severance of the Grail, immortal life, one of its Four Hallows or gifts, could not be given to any member of humanity.

In time, a son was born to Eve and Enki. He is known in biblical history as Cain, although according to Laurence Gardner's researches, this was a titular name denoting a master craftsman in the sacred, as well as the practical, sense of the word. We think in fact that it was a royal title, given to him by his father Enki. Enki himself taught smithship to humanity, and was the original craftsman and metallurgist 'par excellence'. This divine inheritance of smithship, of mastery within the Divine Forges, is a sacred state of consciousness, an aspiration of being, that we must particularly address today. Through divining its secret, another will be revealed which has been skilfully and deceptively hidden from us. It also has, of course, its practical application in the outer world, and bears both an occult and an extrinsic expression.

Cain derives from *Q'ayin*, which denotes the all-seeing eye (*ayin*), or the consciousness of God, in which we all partake, fronted by the Q, which has its root in the planetary symbol for Venus. This symbol represents the sacred feminine, Tiâmat herself; and the *ayin* (which we think is also echoed in 'Oannes') is associated with the lunar essence which flows through exalted females or goddesses: the ineffable Star Fire. The Star Fire, as we know from our study of the pentagram of the Goat of Mendes, is the divine conductor of Tiâmat's consciousness to her creation. It expresses itself in physical matter as menstrual blood, which was often referred to as 'red gold' or 'white (lunar) gold', because it combines and unites the red and the white life forces (as Lewis Carroll shows us via his red and white queens in *Alice Through the Looking Glass*).

Therefore, Cain (*Q'ayin*) does indeed stand revealed as the Grand Master Smith, the supreme goldsmith who works with the sacred Star

226

Fire, having been designated, and entrusted with it, by Tiâmat. It is said that angels attended Eve as she gave birth to Cain, and that these angels were the Virtues, ready to give Cain their inestimable soul-gifts. He is the beloved of the Dragon Queen, the true man (John or Oannes), born forth from her, whose spirit rings keen and true as the invincible heavenly sword, (our positive Saturnine lance) and will never betray Tiâmat or his sacred trust. We strenuously make the point at this juncture that the true Cain will only ever use the material of the sacred feminine in plying his divine craftsmanship. No manufactured substitute will ever do! We can deduce clearly now why it is Enki, Oannes's (the Father God in the heavens) true son, who is the original master goldsmith, and not his brother Enlil!

The reason why Enki courted Eve was that, of all ordinary Anunnaki women, Eve had been specially blessed by Tiâmat, who, through her surrogate mother Nin-khursag, had poured her royal essence into Eve to an unprecedented degree. It was Eve's sacred task to initiate earth's humanity into the state of being and consciousness that the absorption of three-quarters of the Emerald Tablet would give it. She herself contained this perfect heart-gift, and was thus 'thrice greatest', allied to Ham and to Brigid through Enki and Nin-khursag.

Via Tiâmat, Eve had conferred an equal status on Attaba by giving him 'the fruit of the Tree' to ingest, of course; this constituted the final stage of Tiâmat's plan to make them both 'thrice greatest'. Yet, as the receptacle of Tiâmat's consciousness, Eve needed to mate with Enki, the Master Craftsman, to bring forth, as an earthly son, Oannes in the flesh. He would not be in fish or sperm-garb, as Enki showed himself sometimes when he walked the Earth, but would be an ordinary human man.

It is true to say that Cain and his earlier descendants did not express the Oannes essence to the same supreme degree as Jesus of Nazareth, Master Carpenter, and his twin soul, John the Beloved Disciple; even Enki himself was a less advanced soul than these two; however, Enki, his son Cain, and Cain's descendants, especially Tubal-Cain and his son Ham, were vitally important to Tiâmat's special bloodline and to dispensing the light of Oannes to the peoples of earth.

Chapter Forty-one

Cain and Abel

After Cain was born, Eve gave birth to two further sons, Hevel (Abel) and Seth. These were Attaba's sons, and difficulties arose between both of them and Enki's son, Cain. The simple fact was that Enlil wanted to destroy Enki's lineage if he could, and, if not, at least denigrate and slander it. He took advantage of Abel and Seth's resentment that Attaba was not their brother's father, and stoked up their uncomfortable feelings about Cain and his entitlement to kingship. The perfect solution, according to Enlil, would be for Abel to kill both Cain and King Attaba, Enki's priests, and then for Abel, his own priest, to seize the throne and the lineage.

Their brother's actual name ('Cain' being a titular designation) was Ar-wi-um, meaning 'place of serpents' or 'throne of serpents'. In other words, Cain was entrusted with the sacred Grail energies, even though, since the Dolorous Blow, the Grail could not manifest in full expression on earth. He was Brigid's spiritual partner (as were his descendants, in particular Ham), and he married the daughter of Lilith, whose name was Luluwa-Lilith.

Lilith, like her twin soul Nin-khursag, gave physical birth to a daughter who had been generated from an ordinary Anunnaki ovum fertilised in the Creation Chamber by Enki's sperm. This daughter (Luluwa-Lilith) was of utmost significance in assisting her husband Cain to ground and stabilise the Grail energies. Without her, the task would have been impossible, because it is women - the feminine essence - alone that can contain the Grail energy; the male reflects rather than contains it.

Because of his connection to the Grail energies, Cain was associated with an area of land upon the Earth which provided the sanctified link with God, the ladder between heaven and earth, which the Grail enshrined. Here, the God-given forces he shepherded were grounded deep into the Earth, making it a holy place, a mighty power-point of the Grail, just as Ur had been before the banishment of Attaba and Eve, and indeed remained so, at an intrinsic rather than an extrinsic level. Via his link with

Eve and Enki, Cain carried forward the power to minister to the grandeur of the receding Grail energies, and earthed them anew through his wife Luluwa into an expanse of land that stretched between Ur and Egypt - Canaan, originally known as the Land of Cain (the Genesis account calls it the land of Nodh, its title prior to Cain's encampment there).

It was the chroniclers' confusion over Cain's monumental significance and his special connection with the land, as well as some discreet historical rewriting engendered by the influence of Enlil, which led to the misleading account of the story in Genesis. This tells how Abel was 'a keeper of sheep', and Cain a 'tiller of the land'. Both made offerings to God, but, whilst Abel's sacrifices were accepted, Cain's were repudiated. Cain then 'rose up' against his brother, and slew him. Cain was subsequently banished to the wilderness by God, yet to ensure that those who sought to kill him would be warned off, God put a mark on Cain, so protecting him from his would-be assassins. From this story, of course, arises the famous phrase: 'Am I my brother's keeper?'

This is a symbolic, but garbled, account of the story. Let us look at it again, and dig a little deeper.

First of all, it is clear that, as Cain and Abel were both royal princes, they were not, respectively, a shepherd and a ploughman.

As a symbolic keeper of 'sheep' (subjects), Abel seems to have held some office of governorship commensurate with his rank (rather as the princes of the British royal family today hold dukedoms). However, his office may have been merely a formality. It appears that Abel, as well as holding a title of privileged rank, was also a High Priest. It is established that the Serpent People (the higher Anunnaki) were protected by a legion of warrior priests, who eventually became, thousands of years later, the Children of Solomon, and, eventually, the Knights Templar.

These priests were generally answerable to Enki, but there were some among them who followed Enlil. Abel was such a priest. Cain, too, had been initiated into priesthood. Indeed, the post of High Priest awaited him, to which he would succeed on his father Attaba's death or retirement. However, Cain was most certainly a priest who was initiated and instructed by Enki. This is why Abel's sacrifices (which involved the spilling of animal blood) were acceptable to his lord, Enlil, but Cain's were not. The same situation obtained with Abel and Enki. Abel's sacrifices of burnt animals were anathema to Enki, and Cain used only honey, corn, herbs and fruits to make heart-offerings to Tiâmat via Enki.

Of course, Cain did not offer sacrifices to Enlil, and Abel did not offer sacrifices to Enki, so the question of rejection of any offerings never arose. What the scenario in Genesis tells us is that the princes offered sacrifices to two very different lords who had become adversaries, and who were entirely opposed in their stance, their system of values, their philosophy and their objectives.

Having made inroads into the royal family by means of Abel, Enlil encouraged his willing priest to instigate an uprising against his own father, Attaba, and attempt to slay him and his son and heir, Cain.

Enlil had never forgiven either Enki or Attaba (to say nothing of Lilith and Eve) for 'plotting' against him, as he saw it, and this coup was his revenge. He wanted to destroy the 'false priest' Attaba (false in his eyes because Attaba had become Enki's priest) and exterminate the bloodline which descended from Enki; firstly, because the direct blending of higher Anunnaki and ordinary Anunnaki genes which Cain represented affronted him deeply, and secondly, because he did not trust the plans Enki had for this bloodline. He wanted to see it eliminated, and the bondage and slavery to himself, as practiced by the sycophantic Abel (whose historical name, Hevel, means 'puff of vapour') restored. It is worth noting that, at this point, Enlil still remained in ignorance of Tiâmat's great plan for humanity.

Abel obeyed Enlil's command, and led an uprising against Attaba 'in the field', which was literally so, because Abel decided to strike at a time when Attaba was praying in his tent alone, and was relatively unprotected. (Tents were a means of erecting a sacred altar to Tiâmat out in the wilds, away from the hustle and bustle of the palace and the 'madding crowds' which milled around public buildings. It was a method of worship which Enki and Nin-khursag had instigated, teaching it to Eve and Attaba after the Grail energies of Ur had been closed down by Enlil. As a consequence of Enlil's action, the procedure of rising up ethereally into a higher dimension in a direct and immediate way, there to receive enlightenment and enter into communion with God in the perfect sanctuary of its atmosphere, was no longer an option for members of the ordinary Anunnaki; and so another way of communing with the Divine had to be devised.)

The problem for Abel (which, unaware of his own weakness, he actually saw as a splendid opportunity to fulfil his mission in one fell swoop) was that Cain had accompanied Attaba on his out-of-town spiritual excursion, and both men, father and son, were protected, as they prayed, by Cain's henchmen. These henchmen had been instructed by Cain, the master craftsman, in the fashioning of their weapons (only ever to be used in defensive mode); with these superior arms, they easily overcame Abel's rather ineffectual attempt at a coup, and Abel was slain 'in the field'.

We see from this that some of the features of the Genesis account have actually been reversed. Cain certainly did not kill Abel. Rather, Abel tried to slaughter Cain, but was prevented by the royal guard. This was the situation which provoked the angry response 'Am I my brother's keeper?' when Enlil later questioned Cain about Abel's disappearance. (The higher Anunnaki could not walk the Earth in temporary physical bodies anymore once the Grail had shut down, but, to high initiates such as Cain, Attaba and Eve, they could appear in ethereal form, such as Enlil now did to Cain). Cain, shocked and aggrieved at the culmination of events, expressed by this retort the scenario whereby Abel had his own keepers (his guards), and Cain in turn had his.

In other words, Enlil, who already knew that Abel had been killed, was accusingly demanding of Cain, 'Where is your brother?' (i.e., 'Why did you not prevent the slaying of your brother?') and Cain replied by pointing out that he, Cain, could hardly have been expected to spring to Abel's defence and become one of Abel's fighting men in order to safeguard Abel's life against the stalwart aggression of Cain's own soldiers, when these soldiers were only attempting to save, not only Cain's life, but also King Attaba's, from the murderous attack on them by Abel himself!

Nevertheless, despite the obvious injustice of the situation, some blame was laid at Cain's door (via the wiles of Enlil) for the death of Abel, even though he had had no personal part in it. Because of the pressure of public opinion, he was banished to the land of Nodh (later called Canaan), which became known as the land of Cain.

Chapter Forty-two

The Land of Nodh

Intriguingly, the name 'Nodh' is akin to 'John' in reverse. We will encounter this cosmic playfulness with names and language many times before we reach the end of our quest, just as Alice constantly meets with it in Lewis Carroll's two tales of her adventures. It is a delight to realise how dearly the spirit of the cosmos loves laughter!

Cain's banishment to the land of Nodh, however unfair its cause, was all perfectly in order as far as Tiâmat's greater plan was concerned, because it was here, in the land of Nodh, that Cain, the valiant, lordly and handsome Prince Ar-wi-um, married its queen: the illustrious Luluwa, daughter of Lilith; and it was here, in a very precise spot, that the straitened and reduced Grail energies were earthed anew. The location was what would later become Jerusalem.

Eventually, Cain returned to his homeland to take up the office of kingship on Attaba's retirement. He travelled back, not to Eridu, but to Kish, where his father had repaired in grief after his banishment. Cain and Luluwa's followers remained in Nodh to protect their sacred legacy. Their followers became their race, because children had been born to the wandering royal couple in Nodh, some of whom stayed behind when Cain and Luluwa left for Kish. They were integrated into the later Canaanites, who were also of Cain and Luluwa's descent.

Meanwhile, Enki stood guard over his beloved son (it was he who had alerted Cain to the offensive approach of Abel) as he established himself in the wilderness, and 'put a mark on him' to ward off the incursions of armed assassins, sent by Enlil to slaughter him. This sign was, of course, Tiâmat's sacred sign, the cross of light bound by a circle of light associated with the *ouroboros*, which we have previously examined. Together with the six-pointed star, this cross-within-the-circle is the most potent form of spiritual protection known on earth. It gave Cain 'sevenfold' or complete protection, for the number seven, as the Hebrew chroniclers recognised as well as their Sumerian forebears, was the number which denoted wholeness or completion. Later, we shall learn how to use it for personal protection, for, make no mistake, Enlil is still very much present in the ethereal dimensions of our planet, and still holds the Earth under his sway.

Cain, the 'tiller of the ground' or the 'ploughman', was thus called because the land that he 'ploughed' (in a spiritual sense) was the land that came to hold, via his efforts, the secret of the ages - the spiritual power on earth that was the most potent and the most precious - the site where God's link with our planet actually took root in the Earth; and it was rooted or ploughed right into the mysterious depths of the land by the sacred ploughman and craftsman, Q'ayin, or the noble king Ar-wi-um, whose name means, for reasons which we now understand all the more clearly, 'place (sacred site or throne) of serpents' - Tiâmat's seat. There is a reference within his title of 'ploughman' to the rites of the sacred marriage; for Cain 'ploughed' the fertile womb of his wife Luluwa, and 'seeded the furrow' (an esoteric erotic reference) to produce the tribe which would later become known as the Canaanites, the people who held the key to the holy land of Cain or Canaan.

Luluwa, Lilith's daughter, was the queen of Nodh, given this sacred site by Tiâmat's grace. She and Eve were the first two Grail maidens to walk the Earth as ordinary Anunnaki. There are always two, as Chrétien De Troyes knew, who contain the Grail; one to hold it, the other to reflect and disseminate its light or energies across the world via its secret essence and the Emerald Tablet.

They are invariably twin souls. Nin-khursag and her twin soul, Lilith, were the lunar goddesses who were first called to its service. Tiâmat poured their essence, via her own, into Eve and Luluwa, their daughters. Their names, Nin-khursag and Eve (or Khâwa, to give her her Sumerian name), Lilith and Luluwa, mean, respectively, 'pure light' and 'pearl' ('Eve' attunes to this theme by translating as 'pristine'). These references are always in the names of the Grail maidens, for the sacred essence is poured into them, and they come again from age to age to bear the promise of the Grail to the world.

When we examine the history of the Grail, we shall see that St Catherine of Alexandria and St Margaret of Antioch incarnated as Grail maidens, and their names lie within the clues leading to the Lincolnshire site of the Grail. The names and the language connected with the Grail link together like a mystical banner, reflecting and proclaiming its secrets, sometimes displaying a wonderfully childlike humour, as in the name

'Nodh'. As we shall see, in paintings and other depictions of the Grail, aspirants associated with it are often seen in a sleeping or delta consciousness state above the point where it lies - in the land of nod! The entire wonderland that Alice enters, both underground and through the mirror, is also the land of nod, because it is a land she enters whilst she sleeps. 'Wonderland' itself contains both 'land' and 'nod'!

The protective circle of the Mark of Cain signifies a serpent-dragon swallowing its own tail - *the ouroboros* - a symbol of wholeness, unity, completeness and eternity which portrays the mystical ring. This dragon ring is the way through to higher consciousness. It actually exists, and is not just a concept. Within the ring of light (the dragon or the serpent) dwells the Rosy Cross, representing Tiâmat's creation, properly both dwelling and held within the light of God's divine consciousness. This red cross symbolises the sacred chalice or Dew Cup, the 'cup of the living waters', akin to the sacred Star Fire, which is our gift of consciousness from the divine source. This cup of divine perception, which unites us all in brotherhood via the blood or wine of the spirit (the spiritual blood which flows forth from Tiâmat and which is the consciousness that created us all), is the Grail. We must drink of it to receive the Grail and thus pass through the ring of light.

Most people will be immensely relieved to hear that we will not be expected to drink menstrual blood! This was only necessary during the transitional phase when the structure of the human soul changed from a conical to a pyramidal design, during which process Tiâmat bequeathed three quarters of her Emerald Tablet - the essence of her wisdom - to us, and set a spiritual sword or firebrand in place within us which protected us, unless we otherwise willed it, from being overthrown by the destructive forces generated by Anu, Enlil, Marduk and the Naphidem. This Mark of Cain, therefore, protected Cain, Luluwa and their family and followers, and was the symbol of Enki, God of Light. It was this light which Enlil wished to put out, especially by destroying Cain and his Dragon Queen lineage, and the Mark of Cain which protected them from him.

The secret of the master smith (Enki, who passed on his inheritance to Cain and his descendants) is that he stands side by side with the cup-bearer, or the bearer of the Grail, the combined twin souls of the Grail Maiden. She gives him of her sacred essence to drink. The essence is from Tiâmat (formerly manifesting as the Star Fire), and is the consciousness of

God. From this essence, the red and the white gold, the master smith crafts his own consciousness. Nothing is wrought that is not wrought of the gold and the precious metals that the sacred blood contains. Any intrusive alloy is rejected outright.

The perfect consciousness of ascension - our own enlightened human consciousness - is to be crafted from the purest gold which streams to us from the God-source. The sacred feminine contains it and weaves it into an essence she can give forth, like the spider, from her own being; the sacred masculine, in reflecting it, crafts it in like measure which is yet different in kind. Together, they forge their own soul-vessels, which will ultimately become one. This soul-vessel, crafted so purely, from such precious, pristine, noble metals, receives into itself without reservation that spark of divine spirit which dwells in the heart of each one of us. The spiritual essence thus fills the unique, individually crafted soul-vessel, which is a fit receptacle, and the little spark becomes a star of measureless spiritual light and consciousness which, even so, retains its craft-forged individuality.

The sacred marriage thus takes place, the soul-vessel and the spirit become one, and the creature is no longer a creature. It steps through the mirror and finds itself of the veritable essence of the Divine.

Chapter Forty-three
The Stone of Death

In his book, *Genesis of the Grail Kings*, Laurence Gardner introduces a most interesting theory. He discusses the lost secrets of the 'highward fire stone', a shining metal or metallic compound which was revered in ancient Sumer. It was known as *shem-an-na*, meaning 'heavenly stone', 'shining stone', or 'stones that rise'. According to his research, it is associated with the tradition of the Master Craftsmen of the higher Anunnaki, an esoteric consortium headed by Enki, smith supreme, who passed on his sacred mastership to the earthly kings of his lineage through his son Cain. The tradition passed into the Egyptian line of pharaohs from this source. The pharaohs were fed with a special substance called *schefa* -food, which was fashioned into conical shaped 'bread' cakes. These cakes were baked from a fine white powder derived directly from gold and other highly prized shining metals, fragrant and sweet to the taste and produced by an alchemical method which was a guarded secret of the Egyptian priests.

As Laurence Gardner points out, the High Priest of Memphis was officially known as 'the Great Artificer', a title suggesting smithship (and, to us, something else; but we will come to that in due course).

The *schefa*-food of the pharaohs, he explains, was referred to in the Bible under the name of 'shewbread', which echoes the word *shem-an-na* or *she(w)-manna* in that a manifestation of sweet white food 'from heaven', appearing as if by a miracle to the children of Israel in the wilderness, was called by them 'manna' (meaning 'What is it?'), the name 'manna' afterwards denoting 'heavenly bread' or 'bread given by God'.

This manna was probably a product of the tamarisk plant, but it bore a remarkable resemblance to the substance fed to the pharaohs and to the kingly descendants of Cain (for they too received it) in that it was white, sweet, and powdery, and that it seemed to emerge from some magical dimension. The *shem-an-na* or *shew-manna* described in the Bible was not, like the actual manna that the children of Israel received, a herbal product, which was a symbolic reference or comparison to the miraculous, heavenly food, but the shewbread itself, the white powder of gold.

The book of Leviticus in the Old Testament (24:5-7), with reference to the shewbread, says of it, 'Thou shalt take fine flour, and bake twelve cakes thereof...' Laurence Gardner posits that an error in translation substituted the word 'flour' for 'powder', which would have been a more accurate definition of the substance. The shewbread appears within the context of the second Covenant, that which was made by Jehovah or Yahweh with Abraham. The Bible relates that it was present within the Tabernacle, laid out upon a table, next to a candelabra bearing seven candlesticks.[1]

At the time of the third Covenant, made with Moses, wherein the Covenant was codified by the stone tablets which Moses brought down from the mountain, the shewbread appears again. When the Israelites fashioned their golden calf 'idol' and apparently worshipped the bondage of the body thereby, Moses 'burnt it in the fire, and ground it to a powder, and strawed it upon the water, and made the children of Israel drink of it' (Exodus 32:20). From the time of Moses, consumption of the shewbread within the Judaic religion became the exclusive right of the priests, although, by their dispensation, it was still occasionally given to the kings. What had once been reserved for the kings of the special bloodline was later reserved for the priests alone. This is important in considering the shewbread, as is the fact that during the first Covenant, which took place with Noah, or Zi-u-sudra, his queen and their followers, the shewbread did *not* make an appearance. The significant sign in this case was the rainbow - the true arc or Ark - which is linked with the Grail, and with the seven-branched candelabra within the Tabernacle.

One of the reasons that the shewbread or the *shem-an-na* was not present at the time of the first Covenant was because it had not, as yet, come into existence. It seems to have first appeared shortly before the time of Abraham. The renowned priest-king of Salem, Melchizedek, is believed to have given the shewbread to Abraham in an important initiation ceremony (Genesis 14:18) at the time when Abraham, having settled in Canaan, gained victory over invaders. The invasion was led by four kings of the peoples of the surrounding area, who overcame five kings, among them the kings of Sodom and Gomorrah. Lot, Abraham's kinsman, was living in Sodom, which lay towards the plain of Jordan. Lot was carried off as a prisoner, until Abraham, hearing from an escapee of the warring kings concerning Lot's plight, mobilised an army and came to his rescue.

Because of this military victory, the king of Sodom and others, in particular Melchizedek, honoured Abraham, the kings presenting him with riches, whilst the priest-king Melchizedek, with offerings of 'bread and wine', initiated him as a spiritual leader, blessed by the 'most high God'. Although Abraham's act was undoubtedly both noble and brave, it is worth bearing in mind that it was a military achievement which earned Abraham his honour and standing, and conferred on him an equality of status with the priest-king, so that he himself was equated with this role. This is revealed by the fact that Melchizedek offered him tithes with the sacramental 'bread and wine', a privilege reserved exclusively for the priest-kings.

Intriguingly, the statue of Melchizedek in Chartres Cathedral (France) portrays the royal priest holding a chalice which contains a stone. This is a depiction of the communion or initiatory cup which King Melchizedek offered to Abraham after his victory. (Communion is a Christian ceremony, but the offering of the chalice of communion was certainly an established ritual prior to the commencement of Christianity. In the earlier ceremony, communion was with God, the ineffable and supreme, and it was directly associated with the precious Star Fire.)

Laurence Gardner suggests that the stone in the cup represents the shewbread, because it was during the lifetime of Abraham and Melchizedek that the higher Anunnaki Star Fire was lost to earth, and therefore to the kings of the Grail bloodline, necessitating its substitution with the venerated 'highward fire stone' or shewbread. We have discovered that, in addition to the white shewbread cakes, the Star Fire was symbolised and supplanted afterwards by a mysterious red powder dissolved in wine, as we shall see)

When the Tower of Babel fell, and Ur was destroyed, Abraham fled the stricken city with his father, and eventually led his followers into Canaan. It was precisely at this point (the fall of the Tower and the destruction of Ur) that the Sumerian texts report that the higher Anunnaki left the earth plane forever, abandoning it 'like migrating birds'. They took with them the facility of dispensing the Star Fire, but, Laurence Gardner states, 'the Master Craftsmen had been well prepared'. Although 'Scarlet Women' - members of the ordinary Anunnaki who were special priestesses or adepts of the mystery schools - provided the kings of

Tiâmat's chosen lineage with extracts of their menstrual blood for a short time afterwards (which we have seen was associated, as was the original Star Fire, with red and white gold), he explains that this process was soon thrown over in favour of the *shem-an-na*, the 'heavenly stone', which the Master Craftsmen produced by treating gold in such a way that it was transformed into a sweet white powder which could be baked into 'bread' cakes. This white powder of gold contained special properties which, when ingested, stimulated certain centres of consciousness within the recipient.

The statue of Melchizedek in Chartres Cathedral shows the priest-king holding the chalice with its stone or bread just below his heart. His eyes are closed, as if he has risen above the level of everyday consciousness. We might even say that he is in 'the land of Nod'. Considering the link between exalted consciousness and the Star Fire, which was later replaced with the mysterious shewbread or 'highward fire stone', could it be that the substance in Melchizedek's cup (the 'heavenly stone' crafted from the white [and the red] powder of gold) is a representation of the Grail? Is it possible that this miraculous 'highward fire stone' is the Philosophers' Stone spoken of in secret down the centuries, and that the Philosophers' Stone is in truth the Grail itself?

There is little doubt that Laurence Gardner considers this to be so. His research linking the white powder with the Star Fire certainly supports such a conclusion, as we know that the Star Fire provided for humanity a magical link with the consciousness of God, in that it manifested the very essence of God reflecting her ineffable, inconceivable fires of consciousness through the medium of water (creation) so that we might receive it without being obliterated by the sheer force of the Divine embrace. The ingestion of the Star Fire was akin to receiving God's light through our heart centre, which then rose to embrace and inundate our head centres. By being true to this sublime light of God, human beings could achieve the state of enlightenment. As the link with the heavenly worlds, with God, is the very substance of the Grail, does it not therefore make sense that the white powder of gold, the replacement for the Star Fire which can be made available to us today, must be the Holy Grail?

Laurence Gardner's research and findings are very exciting and compelling. They show us how an ancient temple was discovered at Mount Serabit in the Sinai range by Sir W. M. Flinders Petrie and his archaeological team in 1904. Mount Serabit was formerly known as

Mount Horeb, and is the 'Mount Sinai' of the book of Exodus in the Old Testament, the Holy Mountain itself, sometimes referred to as Mount Horeb (Sinai is actually a mountain range within which there are many peaks). Beneath this Egyptian temple (for the Sinai peninsula was actually an outlying part of Egypt) lay the Cave of Hathor; and it was within the area leading to it that a metallurgist's crucible, together with several tons of a mysterious white powder that the team were unable to satisfactorily identify, were discovered.

There can be no doubt, from the considerable evidence presented by Laurence Gardner, who himself is familiar with the process whereby the white powder is created, that W. M. Petrie had stumbled upon an important alchemical temple-laboratory, perhaps belonging to Akhenaten (Moses). The temple and the laboratory were sacred to the Egyptian goddess Hathor and appeared to have been used for the express purpose of creating the *shem-an-na* or highward fire stone.

The alchemical procedure which creates the stone is as mysterious as the *shem-an-na* itself. Only gold, silver, and the platinum group metals are utilised. Laurence Gardner discusses a highward or high-spin state, summarised below, to which the metals are taken that then converts them into the white powder.

An atom in its normal state is surrounded by a screening potential created by its nucleus. All the electrons belonging to the atom and moving round the nucleus are held within its screening potential, except for the electrons at the atom's outermost limit. When the nucleus is taken to a high-spin state, its screening potential increases to the point where all of the atom's electrons, even those at the furthest point from the nucleus, are brought under the control of the nucleus.

The atom's electrons normally dance around the nucleus in pairs: a forward-spin electron is coupled with a reverse-spin electron (we would say that these pairs are, in essence, male and female). Yet when the atom's nucleus is put into a high-spin state, simultaneously all its forward-spin electrons become correlated with all its reverse-spin electrons. As this consummation reaches a state of perfection, and absolute correlation occurs (we would say, the occurrence of the sacred marriage), the electrons release a burst of pure white light. Having done so, it is impossible for the individual atoms to return to their former condition (the actual metal that was treated so that its atoms would enter in to a high-spin state) because these atoms have, esoterically speaking, been released from the strictures of form. They have arisen and given out the pure white light. They can no longer link together to form dense, heavy-vibrational matter; all that is left, when the substance in the crucible finally cools, is a residue of fine white powder - gold (sometimes compounded with other noble metals) in its highward state. (There also exists a similar, soluble red powder, which we shall discuss in due course.) It is pure, sweet, fragrant and ingestible - the food of the gods - and, with its remarkable propensities for stimulating our head-chakras at the point of the pituitary (base of the brain) and pineal (third eye or mid-brow) glands, could it be a food which, in 'feeding our heads', would take us as a planetary society to 'unimaginable' heights of consciousness and evolutionary development, as Laurence Gardner posits?

The white powder certainly seems to bear within its essence the Four Hallows of the Grail. It nourishes, because it can be eaten and, as has been shown, it 'feeds our heads'. It secretes properties which are anti-aging in their application (which *Genesis of the Grail Kings* elucidates), thereby fulfilling the Grail's gift of immortality. It holds great healing potential, because, as Laurence Gardner explains, current research shows that the platinum group metals involved in the process of formulating the *shem-an-na* have qualities which cause them to act as a superconductor, which, when applied to human DNA afflicted with cancer, corrects the deformity of the diseased cells. It gives abundance, because one of the secret uses of the white powder relates directly to a scientific procedure by which base metals can be transmuted into gold.

Nourishment, Immortality, Healing and Abundance; all the requisite qualities are present within the stone; and many Grail stories refer straightforwardly to the Holy Grail as 'the Stone', all of them associating the Stone itself with a secret name (*shem-an-na*, shewbread, manna?).

There was every invitation within the impact of all this wonderful discovery for Margaret Bailey and I to feel elated at the revelation concerning the marvellous Stone which would lead to mass enlightenment, for the quintessential quality of the Grail is that it is for everyone who is willing to accept it; and, of course, the white powder could easily be made available *en masse*. The Stone therefore appeared to fulfil every criteria belonging to the Grail.

Yet we did not feel elated. We felt, on the contrary, very, very uneasy.

Laurence Gardner explains that the sealed burial chambers of the pharaohs were designed as superconductors so that the ancient Egyptian kings would, on death, be enabled effortlessly to enter into a higher dimension, aided by the mystical Stone.

(The earliest explorers of the Great Pyramid found only a coffin without a lid in the King's Chamber, empty save for a layer of white powder.) The Stone aids ascension because of its own ascended atoms, which translate into a higher dimension during the repeated heating and cooling sequences of the alchemical procedure. For instance, 44% of the weight of the metals is permanently lost when the compound is put into the high-spin state, and there is a point during the process when the entire weight of the metals, plus the crucible or pan in which they are being heated, are proven to weigh less than nothing. This provides evidence that, under the correct circumstances, the Stone actually conveys its weightlessness - or entry into a higher dimension - to its host, or that which contains it.

It was this mysterious quality which the Stone was intended to lend to the burial chamber and to the pharaoh within it, and it was within the confines of the burial chamber that the king's rite of passage to the Otherworld commenced, beginning, in accordance with the Egyptian Book of the Dead, with a question that he must ask. The question was answered, Laurence Gardner tells us, by the only clearly definable hieroglyph on the Giseh plateau, which appears as an inscription near the entrance to the King's Chamber. It depicts the conical loaf symbol for the sacred *schefa*-food, and reads simply and straightforwardly, 'bread'.

We will recognise the question, because it is the same as that which was asked by the children of Israel when they were wandering, starving and desolate, in the wilderness, and a mysterious white bread fell from heaven to nourish them: *Manna*? or, 'What is it?'

With regard to the white powder, we ask, *what is it indeed*?

Notes and References
1. The chapters in Exodus portraying the Ark of the Covenant describe a candlestick with six branches. In fact, the six branches radiate outwards, three on each side, from the central stem of the candlestick, making seven candle-holders in all. This is borne out by the later instruction that the 'seven lamps' of the Ark should be lit. *The Qabala*, the ancient mystical teaching of Judaism, always portrays the Tree of Life, the focal point of its teachings, as containing the seven-lamped candlestick pertaining to the Covenants of Abraham and Moses.

Chapter Forty-four

Rumpelstiltskin

We saw the kings)not only the pharaohs), being gathered into another dimension, a dimension higher, admittedly, than that of earth, but not nearly so high, nor so pure, as might be hoped. *Who was it who wanted the kings?*

As the perpetrator came into inner focus, we saw that he seemed to be a Nero or Herod-like figure, anything but benign, and he wanted - had, indeed, laid careful and highly intelligent, surreptitious plans - to capture them as one would triumphantly gather up kings from the chessboard in game after game of chess, the game of kings. And, curiouser and curiouser, another *Alice* figure came to mind: the Mad Hatter! We shall say more of this tutelary figure later.

For now, I may report that, as we silently contemplated all we knew of the white powder, we saw emerging into view a strange little man, a creature of the depths of the Earth, certainly, for he was of gnome or dwarf extraction. He had charge of the material riches of the Earth, and he was definitely Saturnine in essence, but of a distorted and unbalanced expression of Saturn's consciousness and energies. He was spinning, spinning, spinning - spinning gold, monatomic gold, or the shewbread. As he spun, (and he was helped by shadowy figures, like swastikas, or backwards-shaped spiders - the Negative Spinners) we saw that he spun backwards, so that all the gold was put into reverse-spin. With this reverse-spin gold, he was attempting to buy the first-born of the royal household, for he had managed to deceive the queen (the deceived queen equates to wisdom circumscribed and lamed by the arrogant dominion of the intellect) into promising the child to him.

Rumpelstiltsken!

We remembered that the evil little man did not, in the story, manage to attain his goal. According to the tale, he sat in an underground chamber (the Cave of Hathor?), 'brewing and baking' as in an alchemist's laboratory, and as he occultly created the means by which to produce the quantities of reverse-spin gold that would buy him the king, so that the royal child would fall under his influence from the day of his birth, he sang a song, giving a clue to those with ears to hear (for, karmically, he was bound by spiritual law to offer such a clue -the 'clew' that is the silken thread of the sacred spider, the positive spinner which is an aspect of Goddess and the law of Goddess, as in the tale of Ariadne leading Theseus safely out of the maze of the Minatour):

> Merrily the bread I'll make,
> Today I'll brew, tomorrow, bake;
> Merrily I'll dance and sing,
> For next day will bring the king!
> Little does my lady dream
> Rumpel-stilts-ken is my name!

The gnome's karmically generated promise is that, if the queen can guess his secret name (connected with the name secreted in the Stone, as the Grail legends tell), she may keep the gold, her life, and the child. She may have three guesses, and only three, after which, if she has still not named the gnome, the child will be forfeit to him.

The queen, who was, before her marriage to the king and the birth of their son, a rendition of 'everywoman', or a poor cotter's daughter, had been forced to comply with Rumpel-stilts-ken's terrible demand through force of circumstance. She had been picked up and placed onto the king's steed at her cottage door and borne away with him because he had heard her mother claim that she, her daughter, could spin gold out of common straw (base material). The 'mother' represents the link with the ancestral goddess within every woman, who faithfully bears and guards for her the gift of divine consciousness of the great Dragon Queen or God, and who can indeed give forth the 'red-gold' of the Star Fire, the 'positive-spin gold', if only she could free herself and be lifted into the true dimension of her unfettered soul.

The 'mother' assures her daughter that she can do it, but the daughter has forgotten how. The king promises marriage (the restoration of her rightful heritage as queen and equal ruler) to her, but his stipulation is that she must spin a cellar-full of straw into gold for three successive nights, or she will be beheaded (the Dolorous Blow will fall again, and divest her once more of her rights and her inheritance). So it is that the queen, forgetful of her own rightful royal heritage (the Star Fire), falls into

Rumpel-stilts-ken's power, for he comes to her secretly and offers to spin the gold for her, if only she will surrender to him her first-born son.

The queen's loyal handmaiden (the true wisdom or feminine spiritual principle banished into servitude) saves the day. She overhears the little man's boasts, and gives the secret name to the queen, who answers the gnome's question ('gnome' almost equates to 'name' in itself), set to her for the third and final time.

On hearing his name pronounced, the little gnome reveals himself in his true guise, which is as a dangerous and mighty power.

He is bound by spiritual law, however, and cannot hurt the queen or her child. Frothing at the mouth, he releases his wrath and retribution by stamping and 'splitting the earth in two' (he re-enacts the Dolorous Blow), disappearing into the infernal crack he has created, which heals over. The king pays proper court to his queen, the royal child is saved, and the story ends happily. The entire outcome, however, is dependent upon the discovery and uttering of the secret name of the little man.

The 'little man' (actually a considerably mighty man, as the story reveals at its close) was, to our mind, identifiable with none other than Enlil. It is interesting that, in the original Brothers Grimm text, his name is given in three separate syllables, just as the names of the kings often are in ancient Sumer. The meaning of the name is intriguing.

Rumpel is Middle Dutch, with a possible root in Old Frisian, and has given its meaning to the English 'rumple', which means to disorder or to make uneven. *Rumpel* translates as 'wrinkle', which in the mundane sense surely refers to the little man as being old and wrinkled, (simply denoting the ancientness of Saturn, who bears the originating energy of the universe); but we suspect that it also has an esoteric significance in that 'wrinkle' itself derives from Old English *gewrinclod*, which means twisting, crooked, skewed. Even more intriguingly, *wrencan*, to twist, seems to have been an alternative expression of *gewrinclod*, and it has a figurative meaning of a clever expedient or trick, a cunning innovation - which, as we shall see, exactly defines Enlil's timely introduction of the white powder. We have to admit that it was a masterpiece of deception, and of technological and occult brilliance, although it was by no means all, or even mostly, his own work, as we shall see.

We shall also see, as we examine the history of the Grail, just how important the Frisians (the ancient Netherland peoples, from whose language *Rumpel* derives) were to Lincolnshire, and how their most interesting religion may have contributed to the name of the county and therefore to the name of its capital city. 'Lin' (deriving from Old Norse) means serpent or dragon, but 'Lindume', the British Celtic name for Lincoln, means 'town by a lake', from which we may conclude that within the name of Lincoln resides the idea of a lake or water-serpent; and it was the water-serpent, belonging to lakes and rivers rather than the sea, that the Frisians worshipped.

The word 'stilts', from the Middle Dutch *stelte*, denotes a pair of crutches, or false legs worn to add artificial height to a person's stature. It gives us the idea of arrogance, false aspirations, a tendency to refuse to root the individual consciousness into the Earth, of ostentation and egotism, and all that the concept of crutches denotes from a non-therapeutic stance.

Ken means knowledge, awareness, perception. It derives from British Celtic, but actually has its furthest root in ancient Sumerian. If we put the three parts of Rumpel-stilts-ken's name together, we can deduce a meaning akin to 'knowledge that is a twisted, clever deception which disconnects its students from their source and inflames the ego'. This perfectly summarises the intentions, objectives and malevolent genius behind the creation and dispensing of the white powder.

The story is, we think, clearly a sacred text, as so many folk and fairy tales are. It deals with the matter of Enlil and his plot against Tiâmat's special lineage of kings and queens, which is to steal, via his interference with the consciousness of the kingly line, the inheritance the Dragon Queen has bestowed on every single member of humanity, and then destroy it. It revealed to us that the white powder, the Stone, was a false stone. It might masquerade as a marvel, carrying within its enticing potentiality divine secrets and gifts that promise to lift us up as a planetary society into heightened consciousness and spur us forward into an unprecedented evolutionary leap, but in reality it is malevolent. Its true purpose was and is to lead us into the jaws of death.

At this point, we may remind ourselves that the hidden people heretofore mentioned, whose wisdom reveals itself in the Tarot and the playing-card decks, referred to the Stone as 'the Stone of Death'. There is another Stone, spoken of in the book of Revelation by John the Beloved Disciple in the New Testament:

246

> To him that overcometh, I will give to eat of the hidden manna,
> and will give him a white stone, and in the stone a new name
> written which no man knoweth saving he that receiveth it.
> (Revelations 2:17)

This is properly the Stone of *Daäth*, bearing the secrets of ascension and the womb, which is associated with the Emerald Tablet. The other Stone, Enlil's Stone, which is 'taken' in a somewhat similar way to other nefarious white powdery substances, is the actual 'Stone of Death', which attracts with the beckoning of a false glamour. Later, we shall seek out the existence of the true Stone, for although there is a deep connection with the Emerald Tablet (the heart of hearts of the white light), the 'white stone' is distinct from it, and actually resides within the human head.

To trace the story of the false stone, we need to follow the counsel given in the fairytale of Rumpel-stilts-ken, and find out Enlil's power-name. This enterprise can be fulfilled without difficulty. Laurence Gardner, by means of many scholarly references, has already done the job for us. There can be no doubt whatever with regard to Enlil's later name.

Jehovah.

Chapter Forty-five

The False God

Considering our examination of the accurate Adam and Eve story, it hardly comes as a surprise to learn that Enlil reinvented himself as Jehovah. He is indeed the God of the Old Testament, who cursed the production of menstrual blood and child-bearing through Eve and who banished the couple from the higher Anunnaki dimension, pronouncing a sentence of slavery on them both. Of course, this judgment was not quite fulfilled in Attaba and Eve's case, as Enki, Lilith and Nin-khursag protected them and initiated them into the priesthood of the true God.

Both Attaba and Eve fully awoke to the fact that they had been yoked to the slavery imposed on them by Enlil and his precepts and plans once they had partaken of the Tree of the Knowledge of Good and Evil (thus they came to recognise their 'nakedness', simultaneously realising that Enlil himself very much embraced the evil spectrum of consciousness), and this realisation protected them from slavery. Nevertheless, the wider implications of Jehovah's pronouncement certainly came true, because, since that time, when the Grail finally shut down, humankind has indeed lived in slavery, chained to the illusion of material limitations and ever struggling and toiling to maintain its existence.

Enlil sought complete dominion over the Earth and over the higher Anunnaki dimension in those times, finally claiming to be the 'most high God' who rules heaven (the higher Anunnaki dimension) and earth. However, we have to say, with apologies to Monty Python, that he is not God, he's a very naughty boy, and it will be edifying to examine the history of his introduction of the invidious white powder (the False Communion bread, linking us with his consciousness instead of that of God), which has done so much damage over the centuries.

We know, of course, that once the great imbalance had struck, Enlil thereafter intended to destroy humanity, and with it, that strain of the creature known as Naphidem. Although he himself is human, as are all the higher Anunnaki, and indeed even the Nephilim, Enlil's objection to earthly humanity was that it had taken up residence in a fleshly, animal body, and was therefore degraded and disgusting, bringing shame by association on the pure, undefiled, higher-vibrational company of the higher Anunnaki. (He had not felt this way at first, of course, when the higher Anunnaki came in great love to the Earth planet, with only philanthropic, godly intent, carried here by planet X after being summoned by the Nephilim, who oversaw the entire, God-directed plan to establish humanity on Earth in a physical body.) These feelings of disgust were entangled with, and in truth arose from, Enlil's hatred of the sacred feminine and her all-embracing expression of life on every plane of creation.

The Nephilim made every attempt to bring Enlil and his conspirators back onto the path of the true light, but they would have none of it. Instead, they forged a link with the dark angels, Brothers of the Shadow, who are highly intelligent and organised, and who have dominion over what we might call the 'Black Lodges', which operate on earth and within many dimensions connected to earth. These dark angels (we might think of them as testing angels), who encouraged and applauded Enlil's darker self from the moment he began to fall, seemed at first, in Enlil's eyes, to comprise God - the all-male, all-commanding, all-conquering warrior God whom he constructed out of his own desires once he (and his associates) had rejected and 'slain' Tiâmat, the true God.

The aggressive warrior God, thriving on conflict, bloodshed, and the establishment of dictatorship, was always Enlil's highest ideal. Gradually, however, Enlil became so deranged that he identified himself entirely with this male supremacist, illusory 'God', forgetting even his father, Anu, whose presence might at least have reminded him, by scientific deduction, that he was hardly justified in calling himself the one and only 'God'! Anu and Enlil were permanently separated later in the story, as we shall show, so that even his dubious influence was no longer available to provide Enlil with a certain stability and sense of proportion.

At the point we have reached in our story, (the succession of Cain to his 'father' Attaba's kingship after his marriage to Queen Luluwa of Nodh), Enlil was gaining ever greater power and influence, both on earth and in the higher Anunnaki dimension of Eden. He was, though, by no means as yet the 'Almighty', as he would eventually become and which would be his favourite title. He continued to plot and to plan humanity's downfall, and he continued to be suspicious of his wife Nin-khursag and to engage in open rivalry with his brother Enki, who quietly went about his (Tiâmat and Oannes's) business, refusing to lock horns with Enlil unless it was absolutely unavoidable. Enlil also continued to castigate and generally rail against the many 'evils' of the regal Lilith, who steadfastly ignored him and his attempts to make her life as difficult and unpleasant as possible. He never quite managed to banish Lilith (her later reparation to the area of the Reed Sea was her own choice), although he proclaimed that this was his deliberateintention as punishment to her. Secretly, and against his will, however, he burned with desire for Lilith - a sinister, unsavoury desire, befitting the mentality of one who degraded the feminine into a chattel and a commodity.

So things progressed, with Enlil making a certain amount of headway, whilst Enki and his female associates strove to undo Enlil's mischief and to turn both earthly humanity's and the higher Anunnaki's footsteps on to the path to the true light of God. Unknown to Enlil, he was shortly to receive the biggest boost to his career since the slaying of Tiâmat and the triumph of his near-fatal flood. One of the most significant players in Enki's camp was about to play the turncoat and step over to his side.

It happened in this way. Ham, the son of King Tubal-Cain (descendant of Enki and famous as 'the Hero of the Good Land') and of Queen Ninbanda (who was in direct descent from Lilith), had been born and had come to manhood when this negatively momentous event occurred. He was, according to the research of Laurence Gardner, the Archon of the Tenth Age of Capricorn.[1] Capricorn is symbolised by the sea-goat which translates into the unicorn, and is ruled by Saturn. Capricorn is the tenth house of the zodiac, and its stellar influences are linked with the significance of planet X or the 'ten' planet, our own home planet (Earth herself is not a home planet). Therefore, we can see that Ham carried the essence within him of the harmonised, balanced energies and consciousness of Father Saturn, that magnificent and benign centre of stellar intelligence (even though Saturn manifests as a planet in our solar system) who gives to us our base, the fundamental aspects of our physical and soul being.

This sanctified base (codified by a cube) should have been brought forth into perfect spiritual and ethical manifestation on earth, but the Saturnine and Capricornian influences informing it were perverted and despoiled by the great imbalance expressed by the Naphidem, which then conveyed the distortion in ever-worsening mode to Anu and Enlil. Enki and his female associates maintained a correct course, however, because they never deserted Tiâmat. They delivered Ham to the Earth through their essence (we remember that Enki, Nin-Khursag and Lilith were his forebears) so that he could show poor enslaved, confused and deceived humanity the way home to the light of the true God, through which the dispensation of the perfect Saturnine and Capricornian influences functioned - the true starlight.

Enlil, leader and conveyor of the deranged Saturnine and Capricornian influences, was Ham's great adversary (as he was the adversary of Enki, and all of Enki's line). Ham is spoken of as Noah's son in the Old Testament, but in fact this information is confused, as is the idea that Noah was born after Adam and Eve. Noah, as we know, came first. He and his queen were the initial pair of Tiâmat's special bloodline, which was designated to produce future kings and queens who would rescue humanity from Enlil and his intention to destroy the human race, and whose destiny it was to carry the evolutionary dynamics of (eventually) three-quarters of the Emerald Tablet to all humankind, via both genetics and the Sheldrake method (see Chapter 29).

To briefly retrace our steps through the story so far, we remember that Ham is known to have emerged from the genetic line initiated by Enki and Nin-khursag, and continued by Enki and Lilith. Nin-khursag gave birth to Adam (Attaba) and Eve. They were genetically engineered from ordinary Anunnaki ova and Enki's sperm (yet by a process far removed from the material science of genetic engineering with which we are familiar today, because it also involved highly advanced physical, etheric and spiritual procedures), and delivered as human babies from the womb of Nin-khursag herself.

Eve was then specially blessed by Tiâmat, and, through feeding extracts of her menstrual blood to Adam (the substance known as the Tree of the Knowledge of Good and Evil, or the Tree of Wisdom), Eve initiated him into the 'thrice greatest' knowledge of the divine alchemy, and secured a change in the soul-structure of humanity (from a conical to a pyramidal shape, the latter being stable enough to overcome Enlil and the Naphidem's attacks and depredations). The base of this new pyramidal soul-shape had been laid by Zi-u-sudra and his queen. They founded it by being graced with the genetic and spiritual inheritance of the first quarter of the Emerald Table.

Eve, in her state of heightened spirituality, was able to conjoin with Enki and have a baby to him in the normal way, which was Cain, Enki's son and priest, whom Enlil did his best to kill via his own priest Abel

(Hevel). Cain was not Attaba's son, but he was greatly loved as such by Attaba, who mourned his departure when Cain was banished to the land of Nodh (later Canaan). Attaba understood, without quibble or resentment, that the rightful inheritance of king should pass to Enki and Eve's son Cain, rather than to either of his own sons, Abel and Seth, who instead were invested with the status of city governorship and priesthood.

In the land of Nodh, Cain re-established the remnant of the Grail energies (banished from Ur by Enlil) via his wife Luluwa, who was Lilith's daughter. Lilith gave birth to her in the same way as Nin-khursag had given birth to Eve. She was Enki's daughter, and, like Eve, had been specially blessed by Tiâmat so that Luluwa and Cain (daughter of Lilith and son of Eve, both children of Enki's seed[2]) could ground the Grail into the sacred earth of 'Nodh' ('John' or 'Oannes'), which became the land of Cain. Luluwa and Cain's followers established themselves here, remaining to guard the Grail when the royal couple moved to Kish to take up rulership of Sumer, and in later times became the Canaanites, having accepted Ham's son Canaan, descendant of Cain, as their leader.

When Ham came to manhood, long after the birth of Cain, Zi-u-sudra (Noah) was still alive. Because of their huge contribution to Tiâmat's plan, in that they were the founding parents of the Grail bloodline and had ensured humanity's survival via the scientific triumph of the Ark, Noah and his queen were granted an extraordinarily long lifespan (as were Adam and Eve, and all those of the Grail lineage, until Enlil's white powder was introduced). Noah or Zi-u-sudra was a deeply venerated patriarch. He understood the significance of the Grail (the true Ark of the Covenant, symbolised by the arc of the rainbow), and how its mysteries were connected with the Ark which had saved the day after Enlil's great inundation.

It has to be said, however, that his understanding of science veered a little too close to the purely materialistic, simply because this was where his greatest talent lay. Nevertheless, this too narrow and circumscribed focus constituted, in his armour of heightened perception, the tiniest chink. Enlil targeted him, keenly aware that he was on Enki's side and that his nobility of soul and his expertise had richly served Enki and Lilith's endeavours to foil his plans (he remained unaware, at this point, that Nin-khursag, his own wife as well as Enki's, was intricately involved in Enki's enterprises, and indeed often led the way).

At this point, Enlil had no idea of the extent of Tiâmat's involvement in the affairs of planet Earth. He did not acknowledge her as God, and

252

therefore failed to see how her hand steered everything, even though he and his cronies constantly worked against her laws. Nevertheless, although they created distress, darkness and confusion, they did not and do not have the power to change Tiâmat's course, or to thwart her ultimate objectives. Ignorant of this, Enlil believed that she only sneaked in her influences occasionally through the back door, so to speak, and that if he held to an unwavering course of ruthless determination, Enki and Tiâmat's other followers would soon lose ground and be overwhelmed entirely.

Enlil's mind, although brilliant, and of course from our standpoint akin to that of a god in a secular sense, functioned almost wholly at a materialistic level. It is true to say that, because of his lack of both spiritual vision and profundity of perception, he viewed the situation with Tiâmat as almost political. In spite of his insistence to himself that this was so, inevitably his soul-depths were touched by his contemplation of her and his awareness of her presence, however much he remained in denial. This secret call to his deepest soul, the entryway where the *nous* resides, was ever answered by him with revulsion, repudiation, wrath and hatred. Nevertheless, the call continued, and does so still, because one day, he will turn and sound the right note in his response.

So entirely is Tiâmat an expression of love, that love's will within her cannot be countered. This terrible son, in spite of his grievous crimes, is held within the heart of her omnipotent love and forgiveness, is indeed even blessed by her as one who undertakes a mighty mission, for he represents a polarity we must recognise, and, through freewill choice, ultimately reject. Via our choices, we step through the mirror and become real. They are what configure us in the Divine Forges, and with them we forge ourselves into divine womanhood, into divine manhood.

It is not that Tiâmat wants us to suffer, for at any time, at any juncture, the soul can turn from its mistakes to choose afresh, and the spell of the dark forces is thereby broken. But that the opportunity should arise for these dark forces to form themselves into a doorway, and attempt to trick and entice us through it, has to be so, otherwise we could not grasp the opposite or true opportunity to choose real beinghood and boundless and eternal spiritual freedom.

Notes and References

1. Archon, in its oldest sense expressed by the Gnostics, carries within it the idea of divine smithship, and means a king or ruler on earth whose power thereon is second only to God, and whose authority encompasses the actual moulding of the creational forces and the direction of planetary destiny, according to the highest inspiration of the Deity which the Archon receives from the stars as divine directives. Thus the Archonship was the highest state of office on earth.

2. Luluwa and Cain, another manifestation of the divine ouple, expressed yet again the age-old pattern of marriage between a brother and his half sister.

Chapter Forty-six

The Downfall of Noah

There came a day when Noah (Zi-u-sudra) was meditating alone in his tent. Enki and Lilith had descended to meet him, in their ethereal bodies now that the Grail had shut down and the preservation of its secrets had passed to the land of Nodh, known presently as the land of Cain. Lilith had offered her Star Fire to him, of which he duly partook. Entering into that higher state of consciousness which allowed him to be lifted up in spirit and taken by the higher Anunnaki couple to Tiâmat's temple in Eden (which to some extent, and subject to certain restrictions, had been resurrected by Nin-khursag, Enki and Lilith after Enlil had destroyed it), Noah, after offering worship to Tiâmat, put a question to Enki and his two wives, for Nin-khursag was waiting in the temple as they entered it. She was still wary of descending to the lower spheres, because the psychic link between her and her other partner, Enlil, enabled him to some extent to tune into what she was doing. It was imperative to keep him as unsuspicious as possible so that she, Enki and Lilith could continue to function on Tiâmat's behalf.

Noah asked when the three were planning to initiate his own son, Shem, into the ultimate mysteries of three-quarters of the knowledge of the Emerald Tablet (this always involved a ceremony for the purveyors of the special bloodline), so that Enki himself would become Shem's spiritual father, and Shem could be given the kingship of supreme honour within Tiâmat's special bloodline. Shem had been born in Noah's old age, and expected ultimately to assume the title of Archonship. Ham was currently king of Ur, but since the beginning of his rigorous esoteric and spiritual training for the Archonship, Shem was acting king on his behalf. Neither Noah nor Shem had understood that Shem's appointment would not eventually include the Archonship.

Because of his vast span of years, there had been several other kings of this lineage since Noah had retired from his throne, but, although he had given up his practical office, he was still greatly revered as a kingly patriarch. Noah was of Enki and Nin-khursag's genealogical creation, born to them (though not of their line) in the House of Shimtî, the Creation Chamber, and he had served Tiâmat, the Mother-God, with exceptional merit. He himself had not expected the distinction of becoming Enki's spiritual son and so being granted the status of Archon of Capricorn, but he did expect it for Shem. He was about to receive a terrible shock. Sad to relate, the old patriarch had another reason for preferring Shem. Shem, the 'shining one', was white, whilst Ham was black. Noah, once he had been thrown off balance by Enlil's gradual encroachment, began to suffer from the blight of racial dominance. We will see how Enlil manipulated this unfortunate tendency to his own advantage and ruthlessly encouraged aggressive racial patriarchy down the ages.

Gravely, the three higher Anunnaki looked at one another. They did not relish this moment, although they had known that it was bound to arrive. The time had come to explain to Noah that this special inheritance, the highest honour, was to pass permanently to Ham, not to Shem. The best way to lessen the trauma, the three higher Anunnaki had decided, was to actually show Noah why Ham had been chosen. He would understand then that the Archon had to proceed from the genetic line concocted by Nin-khursag and her twin-soul, Lilith, which was initiated when Nin-khursag brought forth Eve who was delivered of Cain, and Lilith brought forth Luluwa, who married Cain. Luluwa and Cain established the Grail in the land of Nodh, and their line eventually produced Ham. By special arrangement based on a sworn pact, Ham, king of Ur, had relinquished his kingship voluntarily to Shem (known as King Shulgi of Ur) so that he could dedicate himself to the Archonship and its mystical teachings.

As we know, Nin-khursag and Lilith were the two Grail maidens. Tiâmat had given them the sacred commission of returning the Grail to the Earth, and a particular concentration of her essence coursed through each of them. Ham had received his inheritance from the Grail maidens, and it was his great mission, together with his spiritual father Enki, to bring to the world the realisation of the true Father-God, Oannes, who bent his knee to the supremacy of the wisdom of the heart, and who honoured and revered Tiâmat in her expression as the sacred feminine. Until some headway had been made in this vital arena, the Grail, an entirely feminine energy, could not return to earth.

256

Therefore, Enki and Lilith escorted Noah, in his light-body, back down to the material world, and there, within his tent, they called to Ham to come to them. Ham, who was lodging as a guest in the nearby palace, came at once in answer to their summons. He stood obediently as Enki and Lilith 'stripped him naked', which means, not that they removed his actual garments, but that they showed Noah the image of his soul-force, with its links to Tiâmat and the Grail. They had not foreseen Noah's response, because Enlil's overtures to Noah had been hidden from them. Enlil had found a foothold in his soul, and had taken pains to carry the ancient king deeper and deeper into a narrowly materialistic view of life.

As far as Noah was concerned, *he* (and, he allowed begrudgingly - because male supremacism had already begun to root itself into his heart - to some extent his wife) had saved humanity, had ensured, through his floating laboratory, that the world could be made habitable again. It was his innovations in genetic engineering and embryonic science which had veritably *permitted* everything and everyone to continue, so that this wretched line from Eve and Lilith, that Tiâmat seemed to be making such an unnecessary fuss about, and which might not be as important as he had first thought, could come into existence in the first place. (Nin-khursag's considerable facilitation of the whole enterprise seemed to fade from his mind and become an erasable detail.) And now, what were his thanks for saving the world? Total and utter humiliation and dismissal of his own bloodline (from which Attaba [Adam]) had descended) in favour of Cain and Luluwa's lineage!

As Ham's soul qualifications to attain to the Archonship were revealed to him, Noah saw, not the mystery of the Grail contained in Ham's destiny, but only a guarantee that his own son would not inherit, and that the black man would. He gave a great shout of grief and anger, instantly cutting off the presence of his higher Anunnaki companions, and calling Shem, who was with Ham's older brother Japhet, to him. They came running, and turned Ham out of Noah's tent, believing that he had somehow dared to injure or insult the revered patriarch.

Later that night, Noah, his son Shem, and Japhet, Ham's brother, sat in conference. Noah explained what had happened, and confessed to them that he was now beginning to think that the visits he had received from Enlil's priest, which he had not welcomed, were at last beginning to make sense. The priest had foretold that his allegiance to the female deity Tiâmat and her supporter Enki could only do him harm, and lead to disaster for his entire family; and he had been proved right. The priest had gone on to say, that if only Noah would consider paying homage to Enlil, then Enlil would be sure to look after him. Noah, and Shem, who was even angrier about the news concerning Ham than his father, decided to put to the test the priest's alluring words, and see what Enlil could do for them. Japhet withdrew at this point, and went secretly to warn Ham, because, although he had been shocked by the incident in the tent, he could not countenance taking part in any plot against his brother. Ham, horrified by what he heard, set off immediately to warn his son Canaan of developing events, for he was bound to be adversely affected by them. Shem (King Shulgi), who a matter of hours ago had been a close friend and staunch ally of Canaan and those who worshipped Tiâmat, had now turned against him

Noah and Shem went to visit Enlil's high priest, who at once ushered them into the innermost chamber of Enlil's temple. Here, Enlil appeared, and listened to Noah and Shem's story. They revealed all - Tiâmat's plan, her special bloodline, how it was fed via Lilith's Star Fire, what it was being schooled to achieve. And they also informed him of something else.

Canaan, Ham's son, was called in Mesopotamia King Ur-baba. (We note with interest the Arabic-sounding name; the Arabic peoples as we know them today had yet to appear in the world, but they would proceed from Ishmael, Abraham's son, and the brothers Japhet and Canaan.) Due to his father Ham's alliance with Noah and Shem, the kingdom of Ur had been assigned to the latter, whose Mesopotamian name was Shulgi. This assignment was not necessarily permanent, but had been put in place to honour Noah's life of service to Tiâmat, and to accommodate Ham's need to retreat into private life in order to prepare himself for his life's mission as the great spiritual teacher and leader known to the ancient Greeks as Zoroaster.

Ham's son Ur-baba, who should have inherited the kingship of Ur from his father, was instead set up as king of nearby Lagesh (a city state). King Ur-baba, whose forebears had been mighty kings of Ur, shared a familial connection with the acting King Shulgi of Ur. With his kinsman's blessing and royal sanction, Ur-baba founded the city of Babylon just before 2,000 BC, building this new site of kingship close to the ancient city of Ur. The project had been instigated by Enki, Nin-khursag and Lilith, who directed Canaan to build a ziggurat temple at its centre, as was the custom in the cities of Sumer.

This temple was to be dedicated to the Father-God, Oannes or John, the gentle and kindly male deity who honoured the Great Mother (as she honoured him). The expression of noble manliness through the principles of the true John-man was a vital and fundamental lesson for men to learn so that the barbarity and conflict engendered by the influence of Enlil and the Naphidem might be countermanded. Tiâmat herself had promised to reawaken the remnant of the sleeping energies of the Grail secreted in Ur and, via King Ur-baba's wife, divert them into the new temple at Babylon as it was being built. Because of the act of denial and savagery perpetrated against her at the time of her 'slaying', it was impossible for Tiâmat to restore the Grail energies to the Earth in full measure without overriding her gift of free will to humanity.

This could not be done until the arrival of the great queen and king at the designated time in history, when, by an unprecedented act of sacrifice given wholeheartedly of their free will, they would deliver humankind from the conditions of its self-imposed bondage. Until that time, Tiâmat would avail herself of every opportunity to give life and hope to her children via the partial restoration of the Grail forces.

The construction of Babylon with its central ziggurat constituted such an opportunity. Enlil had blocked and barricaded the flow of the already constrained and dying Grail power in Ur; now Tiâmat would relocate it in Babylon. The name Babylon itself was given, not only as a derivative of King Ur-baba's name, but to honour the founding of this special temple dedicated to the authentic Father principle, the John-man whose first duty was always to bend his knee to the wisdom of the heart. It was to instigate the nurturing of an entirely new concept of manhood in the world - a glorious manhood replete with every manly quality, uncorrupted by the wish to slay, denigrate or dominate.

Up to this point, of course, King Shulgi had given every co-operation to King Ur-baba's plan, even helping to fund the enterprise, and lending craftsmen and workers to toil on Ur-baba's behalf. The city and its temple were by now well underway, and Ur Baba (a natural architect) was present in the metropolis, directing operations. The two kings had planned a gilded period of kindly and equitable rule in the manner of their venerable ancestor Attaba, side by side and, ethically, hand in hand, to set an example to the people of how the John-man should behave. They intended to demonstrate how harmonious and beautiful life would become when men turned for their inspiration on how to conduct themselves to the mighty Oannes, a concept which extended beyond Enki as an individual, even though he was known by his heavenly father's name Oannes or Dagon (intimating 'dragon'). Their intentions were to be kept secret until they could win a majority of Enlil's supporters over to their side, which promised to be an attainable goal.

The shock that Enlil received from Shem and Noah's information, especially concerning the restoration and diversion of the Grail energies to Canaan's new-fangled Babylon, struck him like a stunning blow. That this could all have been happening under his very nose, for such an appalling span of earthly time, without any proper realisation by him that such an outrageous plot was underway, shook him to his roots. He decided, there and then, that he would destroy Tiâmat's precious plans, and oust Enki, once and for all. He promised Noah, swearing to his word, that Noah's line *would* inherit the ultimate kingship. A kingdom would be built for Shem, a magnificent kingdom which would outshine any that the previous kings of Sumer had ruled. It would extend far and wide - it would encompass the whole world! Enlil would set to work immediately to bring his promise to fruition. All that Noah and Shem had to do was to vow loyalty to him and join his team.

It is sad to relate that the noble old king and his ambitious son were wholly seduced by Enlil's enticements. They agreed to his terms, a ceremony was undertaken, and Noah, with the blessing and facilitation of Enlil, pronounced a curse on Ham's line, embodied in the person of Canaan, Ham's son. At the same time, a promise and a benediction were granted to Shem by Enlil, formally pledging a mighty kingship to him. He wanted to outdo Enki and Nin-khursag's trifling gift of an 'acting' kingship in style. Genesis relates that only Shem was granted the privilege of access to Jehovah, whilst Ham was not, and cites Noah's curse (Genesis 9:25-26):

> Cursed be Canaan; a servant of servants shall he be to his
> brethren...Blessed be the Lord God of Shem, and Canaan
> shall be his servant.

Enlil thus brought down two birds with one stone. When Noah told him that the Grail had been secreted in the land of Cain (formerly the land of Nodh), Enlil immediately decided that that should be his first port of call as far as the gaining of insidious influence was concerned. He had not entertained any idea that the Grail had been concealed anew in the land of Cain, but in the light of the knowledge that Noah had revealed to him, his psychic senses informed him that Canaan, Ham's son, would be intimately involved with the land of Cain, and that it would eventually bear his name. They also sniffed out that the woman he both hated and desired with a ferocious, titanic obsession was involved - that the traitor Lilith was, in fact, a bearer, a holder, of the Grail. It perfectly suited Enlil's purposes, therefore, to have Noah curse the man Canaan, and, through him, curse the land also. Curses and blessings (the latter, from Enlil, always given for politically expedient reasons) were bestowed more effectively from the higher Anunnaki dimension if they were given vicariously, through the channel of an ordinary Anunnaki walking the material earth.

And so Enlil set the scene for today, the point at which he had always planned to ignite the destruction of humanity. He intended to light the touch-paper of its obliteration here, in the land of Canaan, the 'Land of Purple', the land of the royal purple which contained the most holy and royal energies of the Grail, albeit in its reduced, fragmented state, and the royal people of Cain and Luluwa's descent. He hated them in particular because they were the living proof of Tiâmat's plan to oust his own control and save what he found most loathsome - humanity. Plotting its destruction in this way was not only necessary because of the spiritual forces he would have to overcome to ensure doing so, it also provided a wonderful opportunity, first to get even with Tiâmat, and then to show her who was truly Lord of All.

The day that Noah forsook Enki and Tiâmat, and came over to his side, was a day of both horrific revelation and glorious triumph for the dark-hearted Enlil. A terrible axe fell, its blow delivered by a former hero and champion of the human race.

Enlil lost no time in calling a meeting back home in the higher Anunnaki dimension. In attendance were his most faithful ministers, as well as (unusually) his father Anu, and his nephew Marduk. Enlil revealed all he had learned from Noah, and it was universally agreed that their plan to exterminate humanity, and to render the Earth unfit for purpose as far as any chance of re-establishment of humanity's dominion was concerned, must be restructured, made fool-proof and water-tight, and put into effect immediately.

Chapter Forty-seven

The Desecration of the Emerald Table

Enlil's first priority was to perfect his own version of the highward firestone. It must replace the Star Fire, and be fed to the kings of Tiâmat's bloodline, so that they were thrown off course and confused. It would have to artificially increase their perception and intelligence, of course, or his deception would soon be discovered and overthrown; but it would stimulate the head centres and bypass the heart centre, so that no restraint or overriding commands should issue forth from that absurd feminine obstructer. Having absorbed it for a while, the kings would soon see that patriarchy was the only sane course, and in doing so, they would enter fully into the arena of his influence.

He would make sure that the accursed bloodline, far from producing a king at a certain allotted time who would deliver the nations from the grasp of Enlil's rule (there was even some talk from Noah of an accompanying queen, too, but he discounted such an impotent feminine irrelevance), would instead bring forth a king who, although perfectly equipped for the job he came to do (Enlil could do nothing about that), would be denigrated and spat upon, whose own people would betray him, degrade him and put him to death. Enlil would make an example of him, to show his brother Enki, the whole of humanity, and their filthy female champion, just what happened when anyone dared to challenge the authority of such a great ruler as himself.

He mused to himself that he should be able to perfect his technique regarding the white powder fairly soon. He had his own league of master craftsmen that he was training especially for this purpose. He had to supply the finished blueprint, of course, but they would initiate the process on earth, and in doing so, outmatch Enki's irritating smithship guild, which based its technique on all sorts of esoteric lies. Enlil would provide the genuine article.

Had he not come on in leaps and bounds since Noah had encompassed the project with his peerless genius, progressing the Naphidem's experiments with anti-gravity (executed for the sake of creating conditions on planet Earth which would comfortably contain and accommodate them once they had taken over) to the furthest point of advanced higher-dimensional technology in his grasp of the principles of production of the white powder? Of course he had! It would be Enlil's glorious, unanswerable, coup d'etat! Its subtle contortions of perception would permeate insidiously, invisibly, every belief-system on earth, even the most secret and esoteric, even those which believed they contained the deepest, hidden truths.

Enlil's master plan ran thus: firstly, he would manufacture his white powder (there was also a red powder involved) and feed it to the kings of Tiâmat's special bloodline so that it could begin to do its work; simultaneously, he would deepen his previously established genial influence in the land of Cain (the future Canaan), so that its people would continue to embrace him as a deity - gaining a firmer foothold there was absolutely essential to the successful outworking of his conspiracy, which depended on eracinating the deep-rooted spiritual tradition of Lilith; thirdly, he would increase his hold on Ur and its dynasties, because the mystical city of Ur was destined, as he had seen written in his perusal of the Emerald Tablet (which he held [protestingly] in joint guardianship with Enki), to bring forth a great father of nations and of planetary destiny, and this patriarch must be secured as his man; fourthly (his plan was four-square and four-fold), he would establish on the face of the physical Earth a company of ordinary Anunnaki who were susceptible to the worst influences of the Naphidem.

This secret syndicate, relatively small in number but lethally powerful, would clandestinely hold the reins of global political power and worldly wealth through the ages, and would work ineluctably, inexorably - ostensibly under Marduk's direction but really under his - towards the great culmination of his plan, which would extend over the next four thousand years, slowly, steadily, until humanity and the Earth were his to destroy (his calculations confirmed that he needed the four-square structure of two thousand years before the coming of Tiâmat's supreme king and queen, and two thousand years after the king's arranged demise, to be sure of his goal). He would integrate all these stages to overshadow every religion, every political system, every social structure on earth; they would look for God, or for some political ideal, or whatever took their collective fancy, and always, always, find him, Enlil, the one true God, the most high, the mightiest of all!

Already, the notion had begun to form in his mind that if he could instigate such a plan of total annihilation and bring it to fruition, then he must indeed be the one true God, for who else could undertake such a mission and be rewarded with success? The crowning glory of this articulated series of strategies concerned the Emerald Tablet itself. With Noah's wizardry, Enlil planned to cause a rumpus in the higher Anunnaki parliament between himself and Enki, whereby it would seem as if the Emerald Tablet had been seized by any one of a number of warring factions. In fact, it would not have been stolen at all, but hidden by Enlil in a secret dimension which Noah would open for him alone.

This dimension would be guarded by Enlil's dark angel brethren with a sinister, impassable sword of the death-forces (just as he had sealed off the higher Anunnaki dimension from penetration by the ordinary Anunnaki, via an inversion of Tiâmat's own protective forces, after he had banished Attaba and Eve - and hence all earthly humanity - from Eden), only in this instance the protection which secured it as forbidden territory would be invisible and inscrutable. No-one, either ordinary or higher Anunnaki, would even suspect it existed. And there the true Emerald Tablet would remain, stashed away in complete secrecy, in an impenetrable fortress hidden in the ethers.

No-one would know it was lost, no-one would ever stumble across it, because no-one would be able to breach the fastnesses of the locked sphere in which it was held. It would not be missed or searched for, because no-one would guess that it was actually missing. Why? Because, when he triumphantly brought forth what seemed to be the 'stolen' Emerald Tablet, pretending that he had wrested it back from the thief who took it and that it was restored to its rightful guardians (he and Enki) Enlil himself would release a false Emerald Tablet onto the world, an Emerald Tablet or an exalted energy package which would contain only partial truths, flickering with the evocative light of, now the glimmer of truth, now its fugitive shadow. It would have a hypnotic quality, the power to lull the soul into a sleep or stupor of progressive unrealisation or spiritual unconsciousness.

The false *shem*, the white powder, is how it would be done. The despotism of the white powder would replace Tiâmat's decrees as they were written upon her confounded Emerald Tablet, and Enlil would advance in influence and might and glory, century upon century, step by step. Many people would believe that they could access the Emerald Tablet; the most secret rites would whisper its name.

Those who despised what they saw and knew of Enlil's dominance in the outer world would turn to these rites in the hope that the 'truth' they read in the application of the Stone would at last set themselves and the stricken world free. And no-one, no-one would know that they did not behold the true Stone, but rather embraced the false one. Even the elect would be deceived. There was no hope of rescue, no hope that the inexorable course of destiny that he had instigated could be altered. The destiny of the despised human race would march to Enlil's tune. They would pass from the deepest degradation of slavery and suffering into irretrievable destruction!

Nevertheless, all this, however brilliant, constituted plan B. There was another, much quicker and more direct route to his dreams and desires, one that could be implemented without delay. If it failed (which he was confident it would not) the fall-out of its energies could be integrated into the slower but impregnable plan B. This plan, dearest to his heart, involved setting up Shem in the totalitarian kingship he had both envisaged and promised to the ambitious man, and making sure, as he did so, that Shem came under the influence and the tutelage of the Naphidem. Shem would be given Babylon; if possible, he would arrange to have Canaan slaughtered, and Canaan's new kingdom would be given a new name - a name fit for Enlil's plan, and a black joke against Tiâmat's.

Noah, with his wondrous scientific skill, could help Enlil to prepare the Earth for the Naphidem invasion (of course, the old king could be fobbed off with some story about Shem, via the Naphidem, holding the entire world in his power, which would certainly seem to be borne out during the early days of the Naphidem take-over). This cherished plan could be implemented throughout the short span of a mere half century, and, considering the secret headway that that treacherous wretch Enki had made, all the while keeping Enlil in ignorance until Noah had mercifully switched sides and come to his rescue, it was the sort of sudden strike that would best comfort Enlil's heart after his trauma of discovery. Certainly, beyond the merest fragment of doubt, Enlil would indeed show Tiâmat just who was Lord of All!

Chapter Forty-eight

The Sham Shem

Action was instigated, and Babylon was handed over to Shem. It ought to be explained that a *shem*, (after which Shem, whose former name was Shulgi, had been named by Enlil in preparation for, not only his royal status, but also his new mystical and spiritual inheritance as the Archon), was indeed, as Laurence Gardner cites, a highward firestone, revered in ancient Sumer. However, we believe that what this really indicates is not a shining stone *per se*, thus a metal (although it has a definite connection to certain precious metals), but the stone or brick conical towers which preceded the sacred stone ziggurats.

As we have seen, at one time, before Tiâmat's decision to change the structure of our souls because of the ruinous attacks on them by the Naphidem, the human soul was constructed in the form of a tall and slender conical obelisk or tower. These towers were given actual physical shape by the sacred craftsmen (and, at one time, women), the stone-masons and metalworkers (the builders were often in possession of both skills), who constructed them with steep steps progressing from their base to their topmost level. The steps were inside the *shem*, and formed an inner spiral. At the top was a chamber or temple, made of gold, crystal or some metal that shone. It was from this sacred chamber that ordinary Anunnaki initiates could ascend into Eden, and members of the higher Anunnaki could descend into physicality, as previously explained.

When an initiate left the temple to ascend, or a higher Anunnaki entered it in order to descend, the ethereal energy-release involved would glow throughout the temple, and the top level of the *shem* (the temple) would thus become the 'highward firestone', or an expression of the Grail.

It was this manifestation of the Grail dynamic that Enlil wished to capture in his own version of the *shem*, which he crafted from gold, or a compound of the noble metals from which the temple was always constructed. The white powder he formulated over four thousand years ago to deceptively feed the Grail kings on reverse-spin gold and other metals was not quite the same as the white powder produced today by the alchemical method that Laurence Gardner outlines in *Genesis of the Grail Kings*. This was actually brought into being by a contemporary scientist who clearly and definitively cites himself as 'Mr. Material', and, as ever, the clue is in the name. Today's formula for creating the white powder does offer some health and technological benefits, but it is only a blessing if its use is firmly restricted to the material plane. We can use it safely for purposes which belong to this mundane level, but it is highly dangerous to ingest it in an attempt directly to feed our soul-body or light-body with a material substance. This is tantamount to using drugs, which actually distort and derange the soul-body. If we choose to use today's white powder in this way, we will harm ourselves because we will damage our soul-perception. When taken as a drug, the white powder still succeeds, as it did in the past, to throw off balance the sacred masculine and the sacred feminine principles which reside within us, and to pitch us into confusion. Before long, this confusion starts to manifest as wisdom, and if we should fall for its masquerade, we lose our true vision and insight.

It serves us well to remember that it is our destiny to eventually take the physical dimension up with us into the spiritual worlds - to veritably spiritualise its atoms. But it is our soul-essence which will lift materiality into the transforming worlds of the spirit, not materiality which will bear our souls upward into the spiritual worlds, as if we could catch a plane to heaven - even a plane made of *shem* metals will not get us there! As ever, Enlil has put things into reverse-spin.

We saw him, waiting in his particular dimension (a dimension above that of physical matter, but certainly not of the spirit). As the monatomic (high-spin) gold became weightless, it entered this dimension. We watched Enlil seize it, alter it in some way, adding an ethereal influence which distorts and deranges, and then send it back into the material realm. In the old days, the gold was put into reverse-spin by a method, as far as we could see, of transforming all the electrons into positive or forward-spin mode. This, which actually threw the gold into a sinister, negative revolution that created etheric swastika-like patterns, was done at the etheric, not the physical, level. The gold was then returned to the physical dimension as white powder.

The sacred relationship or marriage between the sub-atomic particles, giving wholeness and truth of being to the atoms, had been destroyed - but not only destroyed. It was disfigured into a malevolent, mirror-image aspect of its once harmonious holistic self, and it carried the power to conduct its peculiar quality of disruptive malevolence (the masculine and feminine principles in conflict) to the third eye - the organ of perception. Thus wars and hatred, intolerance and abuse, flourished fulsomely, and the ideal of strident patriarchy perpetuated itself.

Even the Grail lineage of kings and queens was unable to prevent or transform this negative situation; when its supreme king and queen eventually did arrive, its king was slain, in line with the perceptual and cultural necessities imposed by Enlil, and its queen was denied and degraded, treated as a whore and an outcast. Their wondrous child, the Holy Grail herself, died of starvation in a Roman prison (the Roman Empire at its most extreme was an objectification in full of Enlil's soul dynamics - his most perfect and illustrious ideal), a symbolism which speaks for itself. Nevertheless, Jesus, John, Mary and Tamar's mission did not by any means fail. It was in fact a majestic triumph - only Enlil has not yet understood this to be so!

Noah's son Shem was the first to be fed with the white powder. He was its guinea pig (Noah saw this in the light of a royal and religious distinction - his son was the inaugural monarch to be honoured in this way), and its effects were an acclaimed success as far as Enlil and his co-conspirators were concerned. Noah, its main creator, was hailed a hero and warmly congratulated by them. He became the man of the moment, and was initiated into the ranks of the higher Anunnaki (we remember that his father was a higher Anunnaki sperm-donor, and Noah's own brilliance facilitated the rest of the procedure necessary to harmonise his atoms with those of the Eden dimension - notably a skill connected with the Grail, to which interesting fact we shall return).

Shem immediately fell into the power of the Naphidem upon taking Enlil's nefarious substance (the bread of the False Communion). He marks the point where the (sham) firestone - the white powder - was given to the Grail kings instead of the Star Fire or the menstrual blood. The menstrual blood, in fact, was given to the males of the line for an allotted time only. It needed to be administered just until our new pyramidal or zigguratesque soul shape had stabilised and become concrete in form. Once this had been achieved, Tiâmat ceased to prescribe it. The Star Fire essence from Lilith and Nin-khursag was always on hand, because they did not desert the Earth when Sumer fell, as the rest of the Anunnaki did. But in fact Tiâmat was already in the process of refining the Star Fire to the point where both men and women could avail themselves of it in a different way, a process which we can utilise today, and which will be explained in due course.

And so a parting of the ways opened up to humanity: each member could choose freely whether they would partake of the authentic white fire which was the starry essence of the true God, or feed instead upon the white powder, the exclusively intellectual and materialistic forces of consciousness aspiring to a robotic super-intelligence, promoted by the false God and his syndicate. We must not think that, because the Star Fire essence and, later, the malignant fire stone were given to the monarchs of Tiâmat's lineage, their properties were intended for the rulers alone. Whilst it is true that, as we have explained, a certain DNA patterning had to be preserved because of Enlil's conspiracy to destroy it, and that Mary Magdalene, Jesus, John the Beloved Disciple and Tamar, the Divine Woman who was the embodiment of the Holy Grail, would need to proceed from a specially designated and prepared bloodline, it is also true that the genuine, and eventually the false, fire or light was fed to the kings for another reason entirely.

A king or a queen has a mission of service in that they receive certain spiritual currents, benedictions and endowments from the Divine Source which they then distribute and diffuse at a subtle level among the populace. They are the vessel from which the spiritual wine is dispensed. We can see this esoteric truth amply demonstrated in the insect kingdom, whereby the queen ant or wasp, bee or termite, will disseminate her organisational commands and energies throughout the swarm by providing her saliva for the workers to ingest (we might call this a form of the Sheldrake method). From this high-powered 'Star Fire' cocktail, the members of the community are instructed how to function. In like manner, from the kings of the Grail bloodline there came forth this stream of consciousness, except that in their case it was a forked river, incorporating the false and the true light. The question remains with us today: which shall we choose?

Shem, thus marking the point where the sham *shem* came into being, conceived a raging disgust for anything to do with the menstrual blood or the Star Fire. Once Enki's man, he was Enlil's priest-king now, and no longer would he have anything to do with Enki, or his wives Nin-Khursag and Lilith. From being Ham's respectful deputy as acting King of Ur, and Canaan's good friend and co-devotee of Tiâmat and the Temple of Oannes, he became, because of his original weakness of self-importance and the later corruption of the white powder, a preening tyrant. A neurosis arose in him, brought to life by the white powder itself, which saw the sham *shem* as an essence born of purity, of wholesomeness, of qualities to aspire to. The *shem* became 'cool' and 'happening', the Star Fire anathema. Many, through his dissemination, fell under the influence of the white powder of the False Communion, thereby holding up the aggressive, all-conquering warrior in the act of dispensing death (an accurate image of the core of reality within the white powder) as a cherished ideal. The Naphidem breathed their influences through Shem to a greater and greater degree, and day by day he became more entrenched in his slavery to them.

Chapter Forty-nine

The Dark Tower

Meanwhile, the extended building programme which had been ordered for Shem's new city of Babylon, a gift from Enlil, came on apace. This half-constructed city was, by rights, the project and the property of Canaan, but he was ousted by Enlil's forces. Later, we shall examine the turbulent, but deeply blessed, history of Canaan. Everything was done to treat the recently-crowned King Shulgi, now Enlil's high priest, with right royal respect. Shulgi was now no longer only 'acting' king of Ur! Anu came back from his business on another sphere and poured flattering attentions and honours with velvet smoothness upon King Shulgi (Shem's royal name):

> Let Shulgi, king with a pleasant term of reign, perform
> correctly for me, Anu, the rites instituted of kingship.
> Let him direct the schedules of the gods for me.

The message was clear. Shem (Shulgi) was in favour with the highest of the high. He had arrived. Noah was filled with happiness, and he was pleased to cooperate with Enlil in every detail whilst such healing balm for his pride flowed forth from the higher Anunnaki king. What Enlil wanted particularly to do in Babylon (with Noah's help) was to construct, beside the half-finished temple ziggurat designated to dispense the sacred Oannes influences, a *shem* or a 'highward fire stone'. This was a tall, conical edifice as described in the previous chapter, topped by a temple of gold and formerly used to enable the ordinary Anunnaki to rise to the higher spheres, and the higher Anunnaki to descend and re-ascend to their own dimension. As we have explained, these *shem* structures preceded the ziggurats and the pyramids, and were the first structures to house the Grail energies. They were superseded by the pyramidal structures of later times; however, it was certainly not for the purposes of admitting the ordinary Anunnaki into Eden again that Enlil had ordered the Babylonian *shem* to be built.

After Enlil had banished Attaba and Eve from Eden, and had done his best to destroy the Grail forces in Ur, Tiâmat herself intervened, and earthed the Grail anew into the land of Nodh to prevent it from being annihilated entirely. (We may think of the Grail at this time as a seed, or an embryo of divine potential, kept alive after the fall of the Dolorous Blow for the sake of humanity's future rescue, and still containing some residual functioning power.) Ur remained a sanctified place, a deeply significant point upon the Earth's surface, and so, for safety's sake, Tiâmat had previously appointed Ga-nadin-ur to stand as guardian before the threshold of the Grail energies in Ur so that the Naphidem could be kept at bay. (We remember that Enlil and Marduk had attempted to bring the Naphidem down to earth via the Ur ziggurat in Ga-nadin-ur's time, and Enlil had in later days razed the newly-built ziggurat erected by Enki in his fury at discovering that Eve had given Attaba her menstrual blood [the Tree of the Knowledge of Good and Evil]. After Enlil's attempt to destroy the Grail, however, Tiâmat banned him from the use of the ziggurat form as a means of descent to the physical plane of the Earth (a judgment he had brought on himself).

Enlil had difficulties in using the ziggurat form anyway, as his own soul refused to respond to the promptings of Tiâmat's restructuring programme, and kept the earlier form of the *shem* out of sheer stubborn resistance to her injunctions. Enlil's problem was that if he tried to complete and utilise the half-finished temple ziggurat in Shem's new kingdom for his own purposes, Ga-nadin-ur was standing by with his increased capacity to protect the Earth, not only from the Naphidem, but now from Enlil himself.

The only thing to do, as far as Enlil could see, was to call upon the brilliant scientist Noah to block Ga-nadin-ur's obstruction, to seize the newly-awakened Grail forces in Ur which were currently being prepared by Tiâmat for diversion to the Babylonian ziggurat, and to redirect them to the site of the new *shem* which under Enlil's instructions was being built next to it on revised principles (we might call it a 'one way' *shem*, fit for Enlil's purpose). This custom-built *shem* would receive and activate the redirected Grail forces so that both Enlil and the Naphidem could actually descend to earth and take over. To this end Enlil had, via his priests now led by Shem, gathered together a great number of his supporters, and commanded them to build the new city with its central *shem* at breakneck speed, so that he could fulfil his plan before the Grail energies were confiscated and so wrestled from his grasp. (We remember that Babylon was within the vicinity of Ur, so that it was virtually contiguous with the old city and on the main artery or ley line sustained by the Grail energies.)

The twist in the tail to all this strategic brilliance was that Enlil's supporters had been instructed to take their orders from Marduk for the time being. This terrified them, because Marduk's influence was palpable and very, very sinister, more so than Enlil's, which was like that of a psychopathically authoritarian despot given to fits of rage, and was highly intimidating and unnerving rather than nightmarish. Enlil had by now, however, put into action his plan to cause distracting havoc in the Anunnaki parliament by secretly plotting that Marduk should 'illicitly' take control of Enlil's own followers whilst an almighty wrangle, specially contrived by Enlil, was going on between Enlil and Enki.

Whilst the Assembly, (for the greater part blissfully ignorant of all Enlil's machinations) tried to rectify this situation and reconcile the two brothers, Marduk duly took advantage of the strife (following direct orders from Enlil, whom he always obeyed slavishly, although he also hated him and privately spoke against him) to usurp the official ruling and gain his following among Enlil's supporters, who were themselves under strict orders by Enlil to obey Marduk from now on.

Marduk seized the Emerald Tablet, surreptitiously passing it over to Enlil, who, with the help of Noah, hid it in his secret dimension and sealed all entry to its place of concealment.

A little while later, Enlil announced to the Assembly that fortunately he had retrieved the Emerald Tablet, actually bringing forth the false one he and Noah had manufactured between them, which contained some fragmented parts of the living wisdom of Tiâmat, but now had a disguised negative energy-current running undetectably in reverse-spin throughout its dimensions. This was returned triumphantly to its official place of guardianship in Eden - a most holy shrine which constituted a barycentric cup of the divine forces within the higher Anunnaki dimension. Once installed in this centre of gravity (known as the Sacred Chalice), the false Emerald Tablet began to throw out harmful, subversive dynamics which coursed through the etheric structure of Eden, just as Enlil had planned it should.

Meanwhile, Enlil's poor followers on earth, now ruled by Marduk, had begun to extend King Shem's new city (purloined from Canaan) and construct its prominent *shem*. They were all in a state of terror, having been warned by Enlil that invaders were massing on all sides, particularly from the land of Cain, and that if they did not make haste in building the *shem* he had ordered, they would be cast out of Ur and Babylon by the marauders and scattered abroad. Only the *shem* they were building, Enlil's temple, could save them now. Enlil would protect them, but they must work in the sweat of their faces and complete the job swiftly. They were promised that if they succeeded, the temple would enable them to conquer the world; if not, Ur would fall. Enlil needed to get the Naphidem to earth before Ham and Canaan's many supporters in the land of Cain marched against him. They were indeed massing, and mobilising themselves to attack.

Chapter Fifty

Canaan

A wave of unease had broken out through all the lands surrounding Sumer once Enlil had ousted King Ur-baba (Canaan) from his throne in Babylon. Many understood that a terrible battle was about to commence, not only on earth, but in dimensions that they could no longer see or directly experience now that the Grail forces had all but gone, yet could still sense dimly, as of indistinct forms creeping from a mist. The aggressors were polarising, without fully understanding how or why. Those who would lay down life to defend the world against the brooding shadow that was about to descend pledged their allegiance to Enki. Those who sought glory in bloodshed and oppression prepared to join the ranks of Enlil.

Canaan was not, thanks to his brother Japhet, murdered in his sleep, as Enlil would have preferred. Japhet was staying in Shulgi's (Shem's) palace in Ur (actually Ham's and Canaan's ancestral home) with his father, Ham, at the time when Noah had been stricken in his tent. The tent had been erected in the gardens of the palace to provide Noah with a place of worship. Although Enki's temple still existed in Ur, Tiâmat had taught her worshippers, via Enki, Nin-khursag and Lilith, how to prepare a temporary altar within a tent out in nature, so that they might enter the Silence and commune with her away from the bustle of the world. Noah followed this practice, as did many of Tiâmat's followers. When Japhet and Shem had been called to the great patriarch's tent, and had afterwards entered the palace to confer, Japhet had excused himself, as if he needed to repair to his chambers to sleep. Instead, inspired by Enki's guidance, he had raced across the city limits, with a few trusted servants, to Babylon, only a few miles away, where his prestige as Canaan's brother admitted him into the royal palace. There, Japhet told Canaan his worst fears.

Intensifying the guard on his palace, Canaan (King Ur-baba) had prepared to leave. He would escape, with his wife who bore the remnant of the Ur Grail mysteries, into the land of Cain, where, many generations ago, the people of Nodh had embraced his famous ancestors Cain and Luluwa (Luluwa was their queen) and where today they honoured and revered him as the royal couple's descendant. There he would await Enki's further instructions. The Grail, after all, was secreted there, preserved and protected, and it may be that their efforts to spread the benign influence of the John-man could begin anew from this point.

Canaan left that night, and when daylight came, Enlil learned that he had escaped. His shrouded night-time strangler could not be despatched, after all, to solve the problem of King Ur-baba. He could not be followed into the land of Cain, because the influences there were adverse to Enlil. It was true that Enlil had a following in the country; this had arisen long, long ago, before the shadow had so completely fallen over him, when he was paid homage to in the land of Nodh as El Elyon, El Shaddai, with his seat at the head of the great rivers Tigris and Euphrates (actually in Sumerian Mesopotamia, where he was known, of course, as Enlil). In those days, he was a benign shepherd of the forces of nature, using his status as a lord of karma to bless and to encourage the people to attract greater and greater felicity to their lands and their lives.

It was this history that Enlil drew on to full advantage to gain a hold in the land of Cain, and indeed he continued to be worshipped there, which seems an enigma, as its people were allies of Enki and Cain, and particularly Lilith and Luluwa. This caused Canaan to be riven, as Eden had been riven by Enlil's depredations. Yet there is the expression of a beautiful truth here. The mystic land of Cain was destined to hold the memory, the imprint, the buried soul of what Enlil once was, so that the spiritual balance which the two brothers Enki and Enlil represented might be preserved and would not pass away from the Earth. However, Enki's followers also amassed there, and they rose up against Shulgi and Ur when Canaan was banished.

The hapless people of Ur and Babylon, with this threat to goad them, were only too eager to take on the yoke of slavery and work to build the required *shem* with its name (the name of the city) before Canaan's supporters struck. They worked at top speed, under the constant whiplash of Marduk, whose petrifying presence was breathed through the priests, especially the high priest, King Shem.

The name of the city was to be Shem, in Shem's honour, but to distinguish it from a too literal reference to its central *shem*, the name was translated into a different form. It meant the same, but it had an additional meaning. The truth had to be honoured, and by spiritual law, Enlil could not disguise the meaning and the teaching in the name. The name was in the stone *shem*, it proceeded from it and proclaimed its identity. The name was Babel.

Confusion.

This qualifying name of Enlil's false Emerald Tablet, the dynamic behind the creation of the white powder (for the white powder was created by distorting the truth of the real Emerald Tablet), gives us the defining clue as to its real essence and purpose. It was designed to confuse, to throw off track, to lead to a culmination of full-scale reversal and disintegration. Babel equals Confusion. And within the chosen name for his new city lurked, like a leering grin, Enlil's mockery of Babylon – Babylon that was to have been the home of the great temple to Tiâmat and Oannes – the birthplace of the new John-man.

Chapter Fifty-one

Horror in the Heavens

The unrivalled scientific genius Noah, now fuelled by a demonic inspiration, his nobility of soul completely scrambled and his wisdom in wild reverse-spin, was triumphantly successful in attaining all of Enlil's goals. The reawakened Ur Grail energies were diverted into the new *shem* (the Tower of Babel) and activated anew. The Naphidem gathered, forefronted by Enlil, who was to lead them exultantly down the *shem* to unprecedented victory. Their earthly conduit (just until the Earth had been properly prepared for their complete physical manifestation, of course) would be their puppet-king Shem. Noah, ignorant of their long-term intentions, and aware onlt that Shem was to be exalted as a global despot, basked gloriously in the moment, his heart swelling with pride in his son.

The first lightning-strike from the Tower of Babel (the *shem*) was a fiery subtle energy that vindicated the new city's name to perfection. Suddenly, the people of Babel, and, progressively, throughout all of Sumer, could no longer understand one another. They were thrown into confusion and panic. Something had happened to their language-centres, located in the right, feminine-orientated brain. What was happening to them? Even their own thoughts were hardly coherent any more!

This, of course, was the first strike of the white powder, which Noah had discovered could be dispensed through concentrating a certain ray upon the atmosphere of Sumer, guided specifically into Babel. It was a necessary preparation to secure the unchallenged victory of the mass invasion of the Naphidem that was to follow. The people scurried hither and thither, in great fear and distress. They put forth a common supplication to the 'most high God'. They thought this deity was Enlil, of course, but Enki, Nin-khursag, Lilith, Ga-nadin-ur and other uncorrupted members of the higher Anunnaki were standing by. They were horrified by the turn of events, but they held their ground, steady in their spiritual strength. As one, they lifted the people's desperate prayer to God. It broke through the white-powder-induced haze and formed a clear path hewed from their own free will to Tiâmat. Their pyramidal soul-structure stood true and four-square against the power of the Naphidem. Without destroying the point and principle of her creation, Tiâmat could now act.

Enlil descended the *shem* first; but, with the exception of Marduk, who because he was Enki's son, and because of the power bestowed on him by higher Anunnaki reverse-spin rites, had learned how to slip through dimensions, he was not followed by the Naphidem. Tiâmat activated her will, and down came the *shem*, torn from beneath them as they were catapulted back into their own dimension, screaming with pain, disorientation and fury. The etheric doors were closed and sealed. The Naphidem were gone, and so was the *shem*, for it fell promptly into devastation.

Terrible in its clashing might was Enlil's fury as he surveyed the ruins of his plans. Howling with rage, he turned the imploding power of the *shem* on the people. The lethal force of the white powder came into its own as the ray on which it had been disseminated turned it into its most malignant, unexpiated, form. It burst forth as a killer ray, destroying tens of thousands on the spot like a nuclear warhead from some giant celestial god-directed gun. People fell where they stood, their bodies melting like snow in summer. The Sumerian texts vividly recount this desperate time:

> Ur is destroyed, bitter is its lament. [We remember that Babel was within the environs of Ur, so both cities would have fallen together, and there would have been little distinction between them.] The country's blood now fills its holes like hot bronze in a mould. Bodies dissolve like fat in the sun. Our temple is destroyed. The gods have abandoned us like migrating birds. Smoke lies on our cities like a shroud.

and:

> When they overthrew, when order they destroyed
> Then like a deluge all things together consumed.
> Whereunto, Oh Sumer! did they change thee?
> The sacred dynasty from the temple they exiled.

It is noteworthy that in both of these texts, reference is made to the destruction of the temple. Because of the link that Noah had created between the *shem* of Babel and the ziggurat of Ur, which had again been rebuilt, both structures collapsed simultaneously. The Ur temple was traditionally the temple of Enki and Lilith, serving, in metaphysical disguise, Tiâmat and her designated bloodline. We think that the specially appointed ordinary Anunnaki priests of this temple were those who either were or became kings, some of them ruling contemporaneously in different cities. They comprised the 'sacred dynasty' of the temple, Tiâmat's special royal bloodline, to which the text above makes reference. King Ur-baba, or Canaan, and his father Ham (the Archon), were the most sacred of them all.

Whilst the terrible destruction of Ur and Babel was underway, Tiâmat brought down the 'sword that divides'. This was necessary to prevent Enlil from ascending to Eden again. Had he done so, with his train of higher Anunnaki followers, his power from that celestial height would have been enough at this point to inflict terrible and lasting damage on the Earth. The white powder laser had to be disabled and dismantled, a task which Enlil would never have allowed. So Tiâmat barred his way, and effectively trapped him and his supporters upon the Earth.

They could still rise to an ethereal dimension above it or within it, because when they descended the *shem* they were not manifesting – and indeed could not manifest, now that the Grail forces had been restricted – in physical bodies. We can confirm that when Enlil and his cronies (not the Naphidem, who were never given the chance to descend) came down the *shem*, they had not been able to physicalise their bodies as they could in the old days of the Grail. They descended in ethereal form. The *shem* that Noah had constructed with the diverted energies from the Ur temple was not able to operate in the miraculous manner of the true Grail ziggurat. Noah could command the energies of the Grail to a very limited degree through his manipulation of etheric and physical forces and his mastery of the intelligent ethereal life-forms in the elements, but his authority could never extend to the actual earthing and reactivation of the true dynamo of the Grail. Only Tiâmat could do that, and, with her blessing and facilitation, also those Dragon Queens who carried her essence within themselves, and who were designated to do so. Again, it is important to bear in mind that the Grail is an entirely feminine energy.

So it was that Enlil and his followers became trapped in a dimension which was lower than that of Eden. They could not now leave the Earth. Their soul vibrations had become too dense and coarse to allow them to do so. They repaired to a hiding-place, a rather desolate astral plane possessed of very little beauty, and from there, with occasional expeditions to earth and reconaissances of it, they continued to implement

Enlil's plan for the destruction of humankind.

Enlil certainly hadn't finished with Sumer. Wrath and retribution were his main modes of expression, and he now had a field day. For the time being, his new cramped and circumscribed quarters restricted his scale of operations to Sumer alone, but he intended to make the very most of his limited opportunities. He would show the female imposter Tiâmat what he would do to Sumer, her cradle of the new humanity and her central initiating point for all her plans and dreams regarding it!

Meanwhile, Eden itself had to be abandoned. It was not possible for the true-hearted higher Anunnaki, the ones who had not joined Enlil's corrupt team, to remain there, because it had to be sealed off from the Earth. Spiritual airs could not blow freely throughout its precincts any more. Its energies had to be closed down, and it became a deserted world. The uncorrupted higher Anunnaki were forced to depart. As the texts relate, they left 'like migrating birds'.

Enlil went on to obliterate Sumer. After the Tower of Babel and the temple ziggurat of Ur fell, and the people cowered in shock, appalled to their roots, he called to all those men of vengeful hearts who occupied the surrounding lands, uttering his magnetic war-cry so that it sounded alluringly throughout their excitable emotional and instinctual centres, to come and sack Sumer. Canaan's followers were already waiting outside the gates, but they were soon joined by countless others. In their hordes the invaders came, massing from every direction, whilst Enlil opened the gates of the country on every level, drawing the marauders in as if he sounded a summoning horn.

As we will recognise from earlier examinations of their conduct, this sudden mass thirst to inflict bloody extinction smacks of Naphidem behaviour, and indeed Marduk acted his part in the doom and downfall of Sumer with relish. He exacerbated, inflamed and incited, until a wind-tunnel opened up within the ethers, and the men of earth were overcome with the Naphidem influences which roared through it into their hearts. Every act of desecration was carried out, and what the white powder left standing, the marauders laid low:

> The high gates, the roads, were piled high with dead.
> In the wide streets, where feasting crowds would gather;
> scattered they lay.
> In all the streets and roadways bodies lay.

> In open fields that used to fill with dancers,
>   they lay in heaps.
> (Sumerian text)

It is very evident from the texts quoted, and from many others, that something of huge and disastrous import happened in Sumer at this time. Afterwards, the land was never as fertile again, and finally the desert claimed much of it. This was no ordinary invasion.

The terrible battle that was fought out at the physical level in Sumer reflected an even more terrifying battle in the higher ethers. This battle was recorded in Revelation, and it shows us that Enki, Lilith, Nin-khursag and others of the true-hearted higher Anunnaki fought valiantly, with great self-sacrifice, to stay the hand of Enlil, Marduk and the Naphidem, and those members of the higher Anunnaki who had joined forces with them. This mighty battle was reflected in the in the First and Second World Wars, where many ordinary, down-to-earth soldiers saw angels fighting alongside them, as if these beings of light fought to drive back some shadowed foe which threatened the human world from beyond the level of mortal combat and the clash of nation against nation. The story of the 'Angel of Mons' is one of the most famous. Many visions of the sword Excalibur were also witnessed at this time. A little word-play gives us 'X-calibre', of which the sword surely was, for X stands for the mysteries of Mary Magdalene and Tamar (thence the Grail), and the mysteries of planet X, our true home planet which bears the essence of our higher soul.

That this battle should be won was imperative, for on its outcome depended the future of civilisation. Humanity's very existence hung in the balance. All those fighting on the side of the light recognised that if they failed to make that final push to victory, appalling cataclysm would be the result. Would Alice-Chalice, the true authority as the light-bearing influences of the universe, be valiant, or would the false queen, the vengeful maniac who roamed her dominions screaming 'Off with their heads!' win the day?

We stand at such a threshold today.

Chapter Fifty-two

The Battle of the Dragons

When Tiâmat ordered 'the sword that divides' to split the shadowed and the bright higher Anunnaki so that the dark-hearted among them were trapped in a lower dimension belonging to earth, and the uncorrupted higher Anunnaki had to leave Eden and the Earth forever, Enki, Lilith and Nin-khursag remained behind with the corrupt higher Anunnaki, although, of course, these three enlightened ones dwelt in a different sphere, aligned to the east of the world. They suffered this imprisonment and limitation in order to help their earthly brethren on their upward path to freedom, pledging of their own free will to stay at humanity's side until the terrible yoke of Enlil and Marduk had been thrown off forever. All these incidents comprised a cosmic event, showing us that Noah's *shem* was the means by which the Naphidem most nearly descended to earth since their banishment in the early days.

Let us take a look at the text from Revelation which tells of this crucial time on earth and in the heavens, when the dark marauding forces were driven back with all the strength that Enki and his team could muster (which included throngs of angels, led by the great protector Michael) and the dark ones fell to earth and were captured there, at the command of Tiâmat:

The first text speaks of the Dragon, identified as Enlil:

And there appeared another wonder in heaven; and behold
a great red dragon, having seven heads and ten horns, and
seven crowns upon his heads. And his tail drew the third part
of the stars of heaven, and he did cast them to the earth: and
the dragon stood before the woman which was ready to be
delivered, for to devour her child as soon as it was born...
And there was war in heaven: Michael and his angels fought
against the dragon; and the dragon fought and his angels, And
prevailed not; neither was their place found any more in heaven.
And the great dragon was cast out, that old serpent, called the Devil,

and Satan, which deceiveth the whole world: he was cast out into the earth, and his angels were cast out with him.

This vision confirms Enlil's status as royal higher Anunnaki. The 'ten horns' indicate that he originated as an entity of the 'ten' planet, the reference to horns denoting the tentacles of consciousness which culminate in the 'unicorn's horn' chakra, an extension of the highest centre at the crown. Lilith is depicted with horns, as are all royal members of the higher Anunnaki. These horns indicate exalted perception attuning to the light of the stars, which is why Michelangelo portrayed Moses with a horn rising from each of his two crown chakras in his sculptured rendering of the great patriarch at the tomb of Julius II.

The seven heads relate to the seven centres of consciousness which comprise our chakra system. As we see from the presence of the crowns, Enlil has gained dominion over these by virtue (or anti-virtue) of his white powder or false Stone.

The chakra system of humanity has come under his power of confusion and reverse-spin. The dragon's tail has drawn down and cast upon the Earth 'the third part of the stars of heaven', showing us that Enlil's intention is to shut us off from our inherited right to commune with the stars via our chakras. This is our path of ascension, of course - the Holy Grail; and these references to the Earth and the stars are a portrayal of the secrets of the Grail.

However, as always, Enlil is in the act of reversing the Grail. John's vision reveals to us Enlil's intention to cast the stars down onto the Earth, rather than allow the Earth (ourselves, still contained in our earthly bodies) to ascend to the stars, which is the divine gift of the Grail, allowing us to partake directly of Tiâmat's consciousness even whilst living on earth in a physical body. Here we are shown how Enlil wishes to keep us deprived of the Grail. In the drama he enacts, it is as if the stars which nurture our solar system, particularly planet Earth and its evolving human consciousness, lose their authority and are overcome by the gravity of earth, to be held there in imprisonment, becoming truly earthbound.

This could never happen in a literal or an esoteric sense, of course, but at a certain level of reality, from humanity's point of view here on earth, it certainly has happened. The stars which are a channel for the Christ forces to reach and nurture us and give us the Grail (a 'third part' of the stars of heaven, the three parts of heaven being Divine Mother, Divine Father, and Divine Child or the Christ) have been metaphorically 'cast to earth', because our seven-pointed chakra system can no longer comprehend or attune to them or reach them in any meaningful way. Enlil within us, the confusion and reverse-spin he engenders through the influence of the false Stone, is the ruler, the crowned king, of our seven chakras.

Of course, he cannot have it all his own way. Through faith, through strenuous effort, we can regain our pathway to the stars. But it is difficult and discouraging, and at every turn the world taunts us and scourges us with flails of its own earthbound consciousness. This is because the Grail has been taken from us, and in fact this entire sequence within John's vision depicts the destruction of the Grail via Enlil's reversal tactics, because of course the chakra system within us is our heavenly ladder to the stars with its first rung set upon the Earth.

But let us consider what strength and resilience, what irresistible spiritual muscular force we are developing in thus struggling against Enlil and the hypnotic power of his false Stone! This is the secret reason why he was allowed to pursue his abominable course, and the reason why, when the Grail is returned to us (which will be very soon) and we throw off his terrible yoke at last, a glory will be released into the heart of the Earth and into our earthly lives which will burst forth in unprecedented splendour. No radiance like it will ever have been witnessed before by the Earth and her peoples. Our restored connection to the Divine will be deeper and more brilliant than at any time in humanity's entire history. Its keynote will be joy - a joy beyond anything we can presently understand.

The woman before whom the dragon stands is the Sacred Feminine Principle, and the child she is about to deliver is the Holy Grail. Enlil hates her and her child with a terrible, devastating hatred whose essence is the very opposite of the woman and the child - death itself. The child is about to be born to us now - to the whole of humanity. And we will not allow Enlil to devour the child.

The rest of the text is pragmatic, actual history, except, of course, for the fact that it took place at a cosmic level. Enki, Nin-khursag, Lilith, and their followers fought alongside Michael and his angels to overcome Enlil and his demonic hordes, and they were overcome. As we have discussed, if they had been allowed to return to 'heaven' (the higher Anunnaki dimension of Eden), they would have gained the power to destroy the Earth. Yet they were foiled, and cast to earth and imprisoned there as a very necessary strategy of damage limitation on the part of the forces of the true light.

We must remember that two great dragons were fighting in the heavens at that time - the dragon of the false light, Enlil, and all those who supported him, and the dragon of the true light, Enki, Nin-khursag and Lilith, and all those who espoused their cause.

The second selected text from Revelation introduces the Beast, identified as Marduk:

> And I stood upon the sand of the sea, and saw a beast rise up
> out of the sea, having seven heads and ten horns, and upon his
> horns ten crowns, and upon his heads the name of blasphemy.
> And the beast which I saw was like unto a leopard, and his
> feet were as the feet of a bear, and his mouth as the mouth
> of a lion: and the dragon gave him his power, and his seat,
> and great authority. And I saw one of his heads as it were
> wounded to death; and his deadly wound was healed: and all
> the world wondered after the beast.

The Beast, whose elemental energy and identity was usurped and appropriated by Marduk, king of the Naphidem, is described as 'having seven heads and ten horns, and upon his horns ten crowns, and upon his heads the name of blasphemy.' In Marduk's case, we see that things have become even worse than the grave situation pertaining to Enlil. Enlil has laid siege to our chakra-system, and his own withers likewise under his dominion; but he has not succumbed entirely to the influences of evil. He hates, he judges, he brings his wrath down upon our heads, but there is some compass point within him that might align itself to the true north, if only he would allow it.

Marduk, on the other hand, is almost a lost cause. His entire chakra system (his 'seven heads') has gone into negative-spin. The idea of a reversal of the truth lies in the early roots of the word 'blasphemy', which also translates as false language, and, strangely enough, from the root 'blas', as an evil wind or poisonous influence from the stars that causes upset and turbulence in atmospheric conditions. Marduk, who toyed with the 'Four Winds' and who initiated his delivery of the Dolorous Blow by reversing them and the Holy Breath or Spirit of which they were sign, symbol and essence, might well be said to have 'upon his heads the name of blasphemy'.

We can well understand, too, how a chakra system which has become so ferociously degenerate that it translates the mystical qualities in starlight into negative or reverse emanations has become in itself an expression of unalloyed blasphemy. The ten horns crowned with death (the dominion of the false Stone) confirm it. These are the tentacles of Anunnaki consciousness, and the diabolical crowns, in Marduk's case, have advanced like a raging disease from the centres of his perception (his chakra system) to encircle the veritable essence of that consciousness.

Marduk is divest of his Anunnaki-ship - his very humanity itself. He has become all predatory beast - the elemental qualities within him which should be transformed into the powers of the soul have fallen into animalism. His airy nature has become as a crouching leopard, his earth energies roam with the predatory feet of a bear, his fiery quality rages as a roaring lion. These animal forces are good, admirable and beautiful when they are forged into the noble metal of the soul, but if they take on a degenerative, lower-nature aspect they become nothing but beastly. The entire beast that he is rises from the living waters of creation - he has self-created himself as the Beast, and he is the Beast.

Enlil, of course, has given him 'his power, and his seat, and great authority'. And although it was indeed Marduk who delivered the Dolorous Blow which 'slew' Tiâmat, or our direct and conscious connection to God, it was Enlil who planned and designed the outcome of this atrocity. As we see, one of Marduk's 'seven heads' (one of the seven major points of his chakra system) is as if 'wounded to death'. We may understand this to be the heart-chakra, not only of Marduk, but of all humankind. When the Dolorous Blow fell which pierced Tiâmat's heart, our own collective heart moved off-centre, to the left. Yet Enlil 'healed' the terrible wound. He supplanted Tiâmat with his own declared dominion, and he created a false, empty heart as an illusory replacement for the spiritually active, fully centred seat of wisdom arising from love which is the true human heart.

And so the false heart replaced the true. The false heart is the heart of stone, empty of its rightful essence but filled with the cold, calculating intelligence of the Stone of Death. The Beast's dead heart centre is 'healed' by being replaced with the false heart of stone - Enlil's Stone. An illusory heart is superimposed over the true, wounded heart. The world does indeed wonder after the Beast. The worldliness in humanity is dumb-struck with admiration at the technical marvels, even the occult brilliance, which arise from the Stone (symbolic of the Beast's heart) and seem as if they are the epitome of the advanced evolution of the human race.

Yet madness and death lie in wait for those who would embrace this evolutionary path - the path of the mind severed from the heart - the path of the Stone of Death.

The Stone of Death leads us to the next quote from Revelation, concerning the False Prophet. The two are one and the same. Many prophets of the false Stone are abroad in our world today. They tell us that there is no meaning and no life beyond the mere physical expression of the universe, that intuition and the wisdom of the heart are purely illusory concepts. We would do well to beware of these prophets and their cool, calculating, seductive mind games.

> And I beheld another beast coming up out of the earth;
> and he had two horns like a lamb, and he spake as a dragon.
> And he exerciseth all the power of the first beast before him,
> and causeth the earth and them which dwell therein to worship
> the first beast, whose deadly wound was healed...And he causeth
> all, both small and great, rich and poor, free and bond, to receive
> a mark in their right hand, or in their foreheads: And that no man
> might buy or sell, save he that had the mark, or the name of the
> beast, or the number of his name. Here is wisdom. Let him that hath
> understanding count the number of the beast: for it is the number of
> a man; and his number is Six hundred threescore and six

This, the False Prophet, is the creature created by reversing or wounding to death the chakra that Enlil 'healed' by bringing forth the power and influences of the white powder, the false Stone. Here we see how the False Prophet *is* the false Stone. A prophet expresses knowledge, wisdom, insight, and casts the die for the future.

A fund of false wisdom, insight and knowledge arises from the reversed consciousness of the Stone, and the Reverse Spinners dwell in its orbis, spinning the future from the spider-silk which is the very essence of the false Stone as its influences manifest and disseminate through the medium of time and consciousness, and which is drawn forth from its belly.

Scientifically, when the fibres of each are compared, the strength of spider-silk exceeds that of steel. The true, future-creating etheric silk

288

emanating from our positive-spin essence manifests within us as a core stronger than steel. It is powerfully and absolutely centred in the God-light that coruscates in our hearts, and is perfectly attuned to spiritual reality and to what William Blake called 'pure reason' (intelligence uncontaminated with the claims of the ego or lower mind, which blinds us to the living presence of God). The spider-silk released by the Negative Spinners is the same, and yet utterly different. Our core of steel becomes our love of power and dominion, of the claims of the self. We forge from it the blades of war and death, and finally wreak our own annihilation on ourselves. It too creates our future, but ultimately it will encompass that future with utter destruction.

The False Prophet bearing the essence of the Stone is Enlil himself. Enlil has become the Stone. Their identities have fused. The creature with the two horns like a lamb, but really a dragon, is Enlil claiming to be the 'Lamb of God'. The horns of his consciousness arising from his crown chakra purport to be centred in divine benignity, but they are in fact highly malevolent and deeply profane.

The two-horned creature symbolises Enlil in the act of falsely 'becoming' Jehovah (a name which means 'I Am That I Am', an expression of completeness that belongs to God alone - and God is what Enlil certainly is not; he has blasphemously appropriated the name). Enlil pretends, or deludes himself into the idea that he is God, and deliberately creates a planetary civilisation which is hot-footing it to its own destruction, led by Enlil's plotting, deception and dominion.

And so the false heart replaced the true. The false heart is the heart of stone, empty of its rightful essence but filled with the cold, calculating intelligence of the Stone of Death. The Beast's dead heart centre is 'healed' by being replaced with the false heart of stone - Enlil's Stone.

Marduk is the epitome of the white powder - its slave as Enlil is its master (but Enlil himself is also truly its slave in the final analysis). Enlil causes all the peoples of the Earth (with many exceptions here and there who slip through his net of living ethereal tentacles) to worship Marduk - the heart of stone with its aggressive materialistic values and its alienated intellectualism which has supplanted the true divine human heart - so that even the Earth herself becomes a sphere of heavy, carnal materiality. However, Enlil retains the power behind the throne of this entity (Marduk personifying the Stone) and is the one who really pulls the strings.

The mark referred to is, we believe, some kind of computer chip planned for us in the future which (for the sake of 'the war on terrorism') our governments will seek to persuade us to accept, so that we become dispossessed outlaws of society if we do not have it. Let us stoically refuse this 'mark'! As we shall reveal, it will give some kind of subtle organisational advantage to Enlil's forces, some kind of conjoining power to oppress and subdue and control at the psychic level of consciousness.

We think that the computer chip, technologically creating as it will a unifying centre-point for all who bear it, will thus become a focus for Enlil to inject his nefarious subtle influences directly into the veins of this network of captive humanity, and 'shoot us up' with his white powder.

Chapter Fifty-three

Simon Peter

The number of the beast is the number of the Stone. It is the number of a man, which in numerology is the number 1. The number of the beast is also the number of the name of a man.

In our book, *The Secret Teachings of Mary Magdalene*, we describe how the Gnostic gospels (the bulk of them undiscovered until 1945 at Nag Hammadi) reveal that the disciple Simon Peter threatened Mary Magdalene's life on more than one occasion, and tried to rouse the other disciples against her after the death of Jesus. He spoke of her with contempt, claiming that she and all women were not fit to be given life (possibly he meant eternal life, but, judging from Peter's disgraceful attitude to women, and particularly to Mary, it is difficult to be sure!).

Many commentators have believed that Peter was unintelligent, as he is portrayed as never being able to understand what Jesus was trying to convey. Peter was indisputably unintelligent, but he was not slow-witted. He was, in fact, highly intellectual and outwardly very clever, using this stance as his excuse for despising women and the way they understood the world.

A word of reproach concerning our depiction of Peter came from more than one critic after our book was released. In fact, the depiction was not truly ours, but arose from many sources. When Jacobus de Voraigne, Archbishop of Genoa, set out in search of legend and tradition regarding the disciples and other prominent saints of the Church, he visited the places where they were best known in their lifetimes. From such grass-roots sources, he drew on the most famous and enduring traditions regarding his quarry. It was from these methods that he compiled a set of names for the disciples by which they were known according to those most intimate with them or best acquainted with their personal history - Latin nick-names which had persisted through the centuries. Peter's was *Exosus*, which translates as 'he who hates'.

We are afraid that things are about to get much worse for Simon Peter than we ever suggested in our previous book. Jesus had a nick-name for him, too. From this famous nick-name, the appellation 'Peter' derives. 'Peter' never was a formalised Hebrew name. It means 'stone'.

Jesus called Simon Peter 'the Stone'.

This was a man who, as the New Testament and the Gnostic gospels confirm, was hot-headed and suffered from frequent fits of rage. He was a man of hatred, as his history attests, and of all things he hated women most. He was often possessed with the desire to kill - especially to kill women. He was generally dictatorial and often assumed unwarranted authority. He hated women's wisdom and he believed exclusively in the supremacy of the intellect, left-brain perception, and all that was masculine. Is he beginning to sound familiar?

If ever there existed upon the Earth a man who was Enlil's agent, then that man was Simon Peter[1]. 'Upon this rock shall I build my Church', said Jesus in connection with him. But he did not mean quite what the Catholic Church afterwards came to believe he meant. He was declaring, instead, that the Church of Oannes, of the John-man, whom Jesus served, would be raised up upon the false Stone, the hard rock of materialism, and the exalted consciousness of the one would overcome and supplant the death-energies of the other. He was announcing the beginning of the end of Enlil's rule. 'Love shall pitch his tent/in the place of excrement', sings the poet Yeats, to apprise us of this situation.

There exists an old system of numerology called the *Ars Memoriae*. It seems likely that John the Beloved, who travelled west and lived in France and Britain for many years (we think he died at the age of 105) would have been familiar with this system. He certainly knew Latin well, because he used it to compile the secret text (under special conditions, and with Mary Magdalene's particular assistance) which lies buried in Lincoln, and which is a rendition of Tiâmat's Emerald Tablet - the true Stone. According to this system, the name Simon produces the number 66. Normally, the next step would be to add these figures together, making a total of twelve, and then to add 1 and 2, giving a final total of 3. This is because ancient numerological systems do not exceed the number 9 in their ultimate calculations.

However, the number 9 is a sigil of feminine power. Is it possible that, in the feminine-rejecting Simon Peter's case, the later stages of numerological calculation are not applicable in the evaluation of his name because they come under the dominion of the number 9? This seems a strange and unlikely theory, but if we ride with it we find that the name Peter equals 61. If we push both totals together, (66 and 61), rather than

292

adding them together, we arrive at the number 6661. If we isolate the odd number, we get 666-1 - i.e., the number of a man (1) whose name is 'Six hundred threescore and six': 666. Furthermore, if we now revert to normal numerological principles and add together the total of numbers representing his name - 6661 - we arrive at 19, which converts to 10 (1+9), which is duly reduced to 1 (1+0=1) - the number of a man.

Is this too far-fetched? It might be; but the fact remains that Simon Peter hated women and hated the feminine Christ, that he wanted to murder her, that he was Enlil's agent on earth, in place to deflect the unconscionable power of the coming of the Christ (Jesus and Mary Magdalene) away from the immediate rescue of humanity and into Enlil's domain and the pursuit of Enlil's plan of annihilation, that he denied and hated and spoke against Tamar (the Holy Grail), entering into massive rows with Paul when the latter tried to establish her enlightened doctrines into the outlook of the early Church, that he is depicted as 'the beast' (the False Prophet beast rather than the Mardukian beast) in the Grail clues and in Chartres Cathedral, that his name was a byword for hatred and rage, that a 'Simon' (his real name) was mysteriously present in every gospel story which denies and denigrates and harlotises Mary Magdalene and blocks our true perception of her, and that Jesus referred to him as 'the Stone'. The evidence does appear to be mounting, to say the very least!

And yet Peter remains an enigma. We believe that the above accusations against him are true. But he is also cited as a guardian. He stands before the locked gates of heaven, holding the keys. This is indeed the 'key' to understanding Peter. We must overcome his rule, and move beyond him, before we can get into heaven.

Peter has his symbolic part to play in the great cosmic drama in which we all participate in our journey towards ascension. In our task of delivering what we know of the Grail message to the world, Margaret Bailey and I have both been protected by a 'Peter'. Peter even guards the Holy Grail, because the clue in Lincoln Cathedral that belongs to him is the Lincoln Imp or demon, sitting cross-legged on a spandrel opposite the renowned Angel Choir, and furthermore he is cited in the famous Rennes-le-Château documents as 'this demon guardian'. Why is Peter the guardian? Could it be that he is telling us that none may approach the Holy Grail, none may enter the gates of heaven, unless they are pure-hearted enough to *recognise* that he is the false Stone, the false Prophet, and thus overcome his illicit dominion, the dominion of materialism, the rock or the stone which he represents? Roll away the Stone, and thereby enter into the true life, he seems to be conveying to us. We will roll away the Stone, in a combined effort of the heart of humanity; and when we do, Peter the Stone will surrender to us the keys of heaven, because the Grail will have returned to earth. The Stone that blocks our path and dims our light shall obstruct no longer.

And so we see that Peter does indeed represent the false Stone, the stone that blocks our way to heaven, to higher consciousness, to our soul's true connection with God. That connection will lift us high above the marauding destruction of our lower bodies and their limited consciousness (physical, emotional and mental) into the true life of the spirit, even whilst we dwell on earth. Peter represents the obscuration that hides and disempowers the precious Stone of Ascension within our heads when we choose a purely intellectual or brain-centred understanding of and response to life over a heart-centred awareness. More will be revealed of this wondrous Stone of Ascension in the following chapters, but for now we only need to understand the simple truth that the activation of the heart centre is what stimulates the Stone of Ascension within the brain into life.

It is the ego-centred intellect with its death-ray of scathing arrogance which alienates us from our heart centre, and causes us to mistake the Stone of Death (Peter) for the Stone of Life. It was poor Peter's unenviable task to represent this Stone of Death in the universal drama which was the life and the teaching of the Christ, and timelessly to pose to each of us the question: which Stone will you choose?

And so we may say a heartfelt thank you to Peter for living out the tragic aspects of his life in order that we might more easily understand the momentous nature of the choice we must make.

Peter's saving grace was that he truly loved Jesus, and longed to serve him, although he saw only half the picture, and was thus led into denying the Christ three times (connected with his denial of Mary and Tamar, and of the three-quarters of Tiâmat's Emerald Tablet, which embodied the wisdom of the Oannes- or John-man that Jesus upheld).

Peter's very real love for what he understood of the Christ, however, assures us that, not only will he be healed and made whole, but Enlil also.

Notes and References

1. John 6:70 reads 'Jesus answered them, Have not I chosen you twelve, and one of you is a devil?' An explanation follows that Jesus is referring to Judas Escariot, but we believethat this comment was a later addition.

294

Chapter Fifty-four

The Whore of Babylon

The Whore of Babylon is the fourth profane person of which Revelation speaks. These four, the Dragon of Wrath, the Beast, the False Prophet and the Whore, mirror in reverse shadow image the Four Sacred Persons who are realised to their fullest potential in Mary Magdalene, Jesus of Nazareth, John the Beloved Disciple, and Tamar the Holy Grail, and who announce, and are associated with, the Four Hallows of the Holy Grail.

The Whore of Babylon is the false, distorted expression of Tamar, the Divine Woman. The False Prophet or Stone deceptively mirrors the true Stone - the Emerald Tablet with all its gifts and revelations and divine infusions of enlightenment wrought from the pure and living light of Tiâmat. The Whore of Babylon deceptively mirrors the Divine Woman:

> So he carried me away in the spirit to the wilderness:
> and I saw a woman sit upon a scarlet-coloured beast,
> full of names of blasphemy, having seven heads and ten
> horns. And the woman was arrayed in purple and scarlet
> colour, and decked with gold and precious stones and pearls,
> having a golden cup in her hand full of abominations and
> filthiness of her fornication: And, upon her forehead was a
> name written, MYSTERY, BABYLON THE GREAT,
> THE MOTHER OF HARLOTS AND ABOMINATIONS
> OF THE EARTH.

This prophecy shows us how the civilisation rises that Enlil controls, and will (so he plans) ultimately control so that he can lead it to utter destruction. The civilisation is led and inspired by the *false* Grail, who is a harlot. She gives and receives the life-forces without love, in return for money (materialism). She symbolises the closed-down heart centre, the very reverse of Tamar the Divine Woman, she of the emerald-green radiance who represents the mystical heart in full expression of its God-centred forces. (We might think of the divine Tree of Life and its twin-

295

companion, the Tree of the Knowledge of Good and Evil [Wisdom] in full leaf, the cusp of their utmost expression.) The false Grail, the harlot, is the opposite shadow-image of love, and she shows us how the sacred feminine principle has been denigrated and perverted, transmogrified into a carnal lackey, when her true standing is that of highest queen. The harlot colludes with Enlil and rides him, demonstrating that the power of the false Grail, the spiritually deranged consciousness arising from the powers of reversal contained in the white powder, actually control Enlil, although this mighty red dragon, full of conceit, thinks in opposite terms.

Together they create a formidable malevolence, because in her hands the Whore of Babylon wields the false Grail cup, the ultimate blasphemy of the true Grail. It mocks the Star Fire, and the giving of the Star Fire, in a unified symbol. It shows us the gold, the symbol of exalted consciousness which is used to make the white powder; the precious stones which represent the high regard and desirability with which the white powder is esteemed; and the pearls, the lunar jewels which are both an emblem and a confirmation that the white powder is indeed a mockery of the Star Fire, for it is masquerading as the essence of wisdom from the source of God. Yet look who the Whore that puts the substance in the false Grail cup really is - 'the mother of harlots and abominations of the earth'.

The Whore is the ultimate degradation of the sacred feminine, from whom all misconceptions regarding the feminine arise, because she is a degradation of God, of Tiâmat herself. She holds forth the false Grail, the deadly potentiality of all loveless actions, policies, responses and behaviours, the four gifts of the Grail in reverse-spin, forced into this mode at the point when Tiâmat was 'slain' and the Earth herself began to spin anti-clockwise: death, disease, famine and the wasteland. These shadow gifts of the false Grail operate on every level, so that the high tides of despair, unease, hopelessness, and savage emotional and psychological want with their devastating social expression which course throughout our world are constantly sustained and never truly appeased.

Why is the Whore associated with Babylon? The answer to this question seems to be that it was Enlil and Marduk's special aim to pervert the course of the hated, Tiâmat-dedicated, Oannes-aspiring Babylon, and that Enlil's false Emerald Tablet (the very essence of the Whore, as the true Emerald Tablet is the very essence of Tamar) had been conjured into being synonymously with the purloined and hi-jacked Babylon itself.

Babylon had been built to house the temple to the true Father, expressed in the Oannes-John man, as part of Tiâmat's great plan to deliver humanity from Anu and Enlil's tyranny. Enlil and Marduk renamed it Babel ('confusion') in mockery of its original name, to show that it would henceforth be a centre dedicated to the forces of the white powder, or the new consciousness for humanity that they were determined should gain ascendancy. They were at this time working on a 'new man', a creature which they had designed to arise from the basic human vessel walking the Earth (the ordinary Anunnaki). This new man would, according to their plans, one day house the Naphidem, so that they could walk in flesh again, as in the good old days. Thankfully, their plan did not succeed and attempts to create the mutated new man were abandoned (until the Nazis resumed the procedure towards the middle of the last century).

However, the idea of Babylon as a temple of Marduk and a seat of his power was not one that the Naphidem king was prepared to relinquish once Babel with its terrible objectives had fallen. The energies of the false Emerald Tablet were now abroad, and they needed a focal point so that they might more efficiently be broadcast to the world and to future generations and civilisations. Babylon, Marduk decided, was obviously destined to be their cradle. With Enlil's blessing, he moved the entire project into the west, and, once the mayhem of dying Sumer had diminished, he began building again until Babylon was re-established under his power. It flourished and became a great capital, as we know.

There were many admirable aspects of Babylon (the Naphidem, after all, are human, and there are always gifts of greatness to be found in the human soul, even if these gifts are ultimately corrupted), but it secreted within its belly a certain influence, like the power granted to King Midas, to turn everything into gold - the reverse-spin gold. Babylon was the embodiment of Marduk's secret dream to build a capital from which the entire world would one day be ruled, initially in a metaphysical rather than an actual sense, and then, once the Naphidem were back on earth, directly.

We know that this was exactly and literally what had been planned for Babel before Tiâmat brought down its infamous Tower and scuppered such plans. Marduk, child-like, found it hard to give up his dream; and so Babylon (impudently given its former, Enki-inspired name as a resonating war-cry of Marduk's and Enlil's triumph, because it had been successfully seized from the enemy and rededicated to the false Grail and the establishment of a very different kind of 'Father') carried a certain breath, a certain air, of the fragments of that dream. Good things arose from Babylon, but a shadow ever lurked and beckoned at the heart of every one of these jewels of human endeavour. The Whore of Babylon, the first kingdom dedicated to the white powder, was born to this city precisely because it was so dedicated.

When the three Wise Men attended the birth of Jesus, the one born in Babylon brought gold. It was intended, in one sense, as a gift of the white powder, but, as we shall see, Jesus entirely rejected it, and instead attuned his entire being to the true symbolism of gold. The fourth Wise Man bore pearls, emeralds and sapphires, but he died of natural causes on the journey to Bethlehem. We can deduce from the clue of the jewels he carried that he was coming to honour the first Christ-child, Mary Magdalene (Jesus followed eleven days later), but so virulent were the forces ranged against her from the beginning that this fourth Wise Man was not allowed to complete his journey.

There is further confirmation in the passage quoted that the Whore is the false Grail, holding up the mockery of the Star Fire. The colours purple and scarlet, associated with royalty and the Star Fire, are also connected with alchemy and the Philosopher's Stone, sometimes called 'projection powder'. (We would like to make clear at this juncture that we are certainly not condemning alchemy as some sort of dubious practice, but rather suggesting that Enlil has introduced some kind of scrambling influence, which can project adherents of the art, and of other esoteric arts, down an opposite path from the one they originally sought, leading them into complications, dangers, and often simply a dead-end, not always recognised as such; this power of perversion arises from Enlil's false Emerald Tablet, the one he released into the world at the time of Marduk's take-over, when Babylon was born.)

Certain metals which have been altered in their elemental structure by the alchemist's art of heating and cooling, or refining, form a substance which, it is said, is soluble in glass before the glass reaches melting point. The substance, on contact with the softening glass, washes throughout it and transforms its transparency to a rich, translucent ruby red, which gives off a vivid purple fluorescence in the dark. When this jewel-red glass is ground to fine powder in a mortar of agate, it translates into a form of the famous Philosopher's Stone or 'projection powder'.

Thus we have the white and the red powder, both of which are used to facilitate ascension, or to provide a form of the Holy Grail. What we would say at this point is that there is indeed a great mystery involved in what actually happens to matter itself when human consciousness, grounded in a physical body, takes flight in an act of ascension. By some means most deeply mystical, we can co-create with God at this point via the sacred stone, the Philosophers' Stone, which resides within our heads, within our brains. As we begin to receive the Grail, so that many of us undertake ascension, inevitable changes in the structure of matter will occur which will advantageously affect our civilisations and the nature and philosophy of our currently positivist, materialistic sciences. However, we would stress that, before we can reach this level of existence, we have to be very clear, as a planetary society, that some kind of quick-fix via the application of certain powders, either white or red or both, is not an option!

The alchemists who ascended in consciousness after preparing and finally transmuting their various metals in the crucibles within their laboratories did so because, after many, many years of patience and inquiry sourced in an appropriate spirit of reverence in which they consciously strove to reach towards God, they experienced a transmutation of consciousness itself. This came about because, through their long years of experimentation, they finally demonstrated to themselves certain sacred cosmic truths, which they were thus able to comprehend and recognise through their own facilitation. It is, indeed, a beautiful way to receive such truths, because their nature, although wondrous, is also devastating, and the unprepared mind might succumb to disintegration or displacement under the pressure of such divine revelation.

Alchemy, therefore, is a method of achieving transmutation of consciousness by means of preparing and subduing the mind to receive the gold of the spirit, and as such it is akin to Buddhism. Can we imagine the joy and the wonder of the alchemist coming to him like a sunburst as he sees, enacted before his very eyes, the perfect validation of those principles which prove that the mystery of God lives within matter itself, and that his own being is veritably of God rather than matter, and thus has the power to transmute matter? In the ecstasy proceeding from the marvel of that moment, enlightenment or transmutation comes to the true alchemist; but it is a heart-piercing, or a realisation within the heart, which stimulates ascension, not the ingestion of or radiation from a red or a white powder.

It is at this point that the true, God-given *shem* in our heads becomes active, and allows us to directly impact and configure matter with our thoughts. It is a relic of this inherent power that Uri Geller (whom we believe belongs to the bloodline of the ancient Mesopotamian kings descending from Enki and Lilith) wields in bending metals and bringing forth the sprouting life from seeds: a power we are certain that Noah possessed in all its comprehensive dimensions, as well as all those of Tiâmat's special bloodline who were known as the Master Craftsmen. Enki, Nin-khursag and Lilith used this power to directly manipulate and mould matter (we remember that Nin-Khursag was called 'the Lady of Form-Giving', and that Enki was known as Image Fashioner, the Master of Shaping and the Charmer of Making). It seems that Uri Geller, if he recognises such a destiny, may have much to teach us about our divine inheritance.

If we try to employ material means to ascend, as is the case when drugs are used, we most probably will ascend, but it will not be an act of flight, whereby we use our own wings and follow the light in the heart to our destination. There are many, many astral dimensions, some of them very sinister indeed, into any one of which we may be propelled if we use drugs, or if we use the white and the red life-forces contained in the two powders as drugs (i.e., material means used to lift the unprepared mind and soul away from the carnal dimension).

We may at first tend to visit the more (superficially) attractive astral planes, but inevitably there will come a point where we begin to struggle in the nastier spheres, and it is all downhill from there. The problem is that Enlil and Marduk, with the help of Noah, have prepared an intensely ominous and baleful dimension for those of us who might be tempted to think that ascension is all about the use of the red and the white powder (and of course the meaning of this statement is not limited to literal reality, but translates into all kinds of applications).

If we use a material substance inappropriately, or indeed a materialist mentality, we will find that we enter dimensions very much inhabited by shadow-beings such as the Dragon of Wrath, the Beast, the False Prophet and the Whore of Babylon. Some people, seduced by the glamorous otherworldliness of these beings, might feel they would benefit from encountering them. But how much fun is it likely to be, to undergo famine, pestilence, the wasteland, and death? Think of how we experience these things on earth. That is the fundamental reality of how we will experience them on the deceptively glittering astral planes, only with more terrifying intensity!

One reason why the Whore of Babylon is called Mystery is because she attracts people in just this way. She calls them into her essence (she seduces them) because they are attracted by the lure and glamour of occult and esoteric 'mystery'. It is good to wish to be consummate with mystery, but we must first take care to leave behind the false values arising from egotism - an urge to grasp something desirable for our own self-gratification - or we will come away with a bad case of metaphysical pox rather than enlightenment, which will show us just how definitively we failed to leave the Earth behind after all! As the Gospel of Mary shows, when we truly ascend, we ascend on wings of the spirit, and we bypass all the greedy hands reaching out to us from these astral spheres, waiting to grasp us and draw us in. When we can safely pass them by, which the Grail will teach us to do, we will be free of the threat engendered by Enlil and Marduk forever.

There may be another reason why the Whore of Babylon is called Mystery. Perhaps it is because, when we contemplate her, we might receive the intimation that we should be seeing something else, that her wretched and ravening identity is hiding a deep and beautiful truth. And so, surely, it is; because when the Whore image is fully understood, its reverse-spin can be dispensed with. The unscathed spirit of the eternal feminine then takes form in the mirror of our perception, and Tiâmat shines forth in the glass. What we understand of her steals on the soul as a benediction and a profound peace as her all-encompassing love assures us that all will be well, for even the strongest of the dark forces must halt, fall back, and ultimately surrender their authority to the ineffable light of the Dragon Queen.

Chapter Fifty-five

Abraham

What happened after the catastrophe and ruination that fell upon Sumer?

Despite his murderous rage at the failure of his master plan, Enlil began to implement his fall-back strategy without delay. In fact, to this end, Enlil and Noah carefully preserved the secret of the dispersal of the white powder upon the cataclysmic ray which had destroyed Sumer. Marduk, in consultation with Enlil, moved Babel away from the convulsions taking place in the environs of Ur, and re-established it as Babylon. The name 'Babylon' means the 'Temple' or 'Birth-Place of the True Father', for Enki and his wives had founded it as a centre of the Oannes teachings; now that it had been destroyed and had fallen into Enlil's power, the reapplication of its name gave it a sinister, menacing twist, whose nightmarish reversal both Marduk and Enlil celebrated.

Enlil, meanwhile, began to pay court to a man from an important dynasty of Ur who happened to be a very good friend of King Shem's - Abraham. Abraham's name at this time was Avram ('he who possesses ram, or high knowledge[1]'). King Shem, or Shulgi, we must remember, had been devoted to Enki until his father Noah's allegiance had wavered, and finally rejected Enki in favour of Enlil. It was at this point that Avram too changed sides, as King Shulgi was his best friend and mentor.

Avram, a young and idealistic man, passionate yet serene, deeply devout and possessing unusual spiritual understanding, as his name implies, would not easily have been swayed from his former convictions, except for one impacting factor which influenced him deeply. King Shulgi had perished in the terrible ructions that had shaken Babel. Moreover, he had died in Avram's arms.

The king had implored Avram to remember their many cherished conversations by starlight, and to hold dear the ideal which had formulated between them, arising from their lengthy ardent discourses. Both young men were highly intelligent, cultured individuals of advanced education. They practiced astronomy and star-gazing, and there was nothing these devoted students of the stars loved better than to sit together in the cool of the eastern evenings, poised in the balm and delight of their friendship, star-gazing and discussing the meaning of life far into the night.

Shulgi was animated, strident, inspired. Avram was calm and reflective, answering his friend's eloquent arguments with a philosophical gravity and insight which lent an air of spiritual discovery and wonder to their conversations, as though they advanced deep into the marvels of the universe and took radiant flight from the Earth. Shulgi's downfall was his mental arrogance, which eventually led him via a disastrous route. Avram's weakness lay in his willingness to capitulate to his friend's ideas of wisdom, which in reality were inferior to his own.

They had conceived the idea of the One God between them. This was in fact Enki's profoundest teaching, which the young men had recently begun to absorb, having now reached the highest degree of learning. Because of the situation pertaining throughout Sumer whereby Enlil was always an ever-present threat, the teachings concerning Tiâmat had to be kept concealed as the secret wisdom of a mystery school. It was these teachings that the young men now embarked upon, drawing their conclusions via the inspiration of the stars, wherewith they experienced intimations of spiritual fusion with the Supreme Being, and the vast cosmic spaces seemed brilliant with intense flashes of communion from centres of exalted intelligence.

When Shulgi fell victim to Enlil's enticements and turned away from Enki and the teachings of his temple, he began to speak to Avram of Enlil as the reflection of the One God, the visible manifestation of the God Most High, whose impalpable presence they had thrilled to in devotion, discovery and spiritual stimulation throughout the peaceful watches of the night, their inner vision nurtured in the inspired bosom of their friendship.

The idea of Enlil as this God Most High troubled Avram, because such an interpretation of spiritual reality was not what he felt he had embraced at the highest point of their exploratory conversations. But it was the reality which Shulgi, the fine, handsome, learned king, his cherished friend, was beginning to espouse; and Avram was moved by the king's new passion. There was in his own family some ancient allegiance to Enlil, stemming from antiquity when several of his ancestors dwelt in the land of Nodh (afterwards called Canaan), and this was another reason why Avram listened sympathetically to the king's ideas.

When Shulgi died in the disaster which overtook Babel, his last words were to Avram. The king begged Avram to continue to honour the One God, Enlil, in memory of their friendship. He perished soon afterwards, in the embrace of Avram, who was profoundly grief-stricken by his loss.

Avram left Ur with his father Terah and other members of his family in about 1960 BC, which was when the city, in company with the rest of Sumer, fell to invaders, directly after the Babel holocaust. For several years he sheltered in the city of Haran, until Enlil was ready for his onsalught on the land of Cain, now known as Canaan. By this time, Avram had been his loyal subject for some years, and was ready to do his bidding. Enlil called him, and instructed him to go into Canaan with his kinsman Lot. It was in Canaan that the revered priest-king Melchizedek anointed Avram as a priest-king in his own right after he had driven several enemies from Canaan and achieved a military victory.

Melchizedek was older than Avram, and was a particular friend of Terah, Avram's father. He had familial connections with the great dynasty of Ur from which Terah and Avram had descended. It was this dynasty which Enlil had targeted from the start, although he had made very limited headway. However, through cunning, lies and misrepresentation (mind control was one of his perfected techniques), he managed to squeeze a foot through the door of their acceptance. He had encountered far greater problems with Avram, his main quarry from the beginning; but Shulgi won the day for him at the eleventh hour, and now Avram had been drawn satisfactorily under his influence.

Melchizedek shared Avram's deep spirituality and philosophical insight. A profound and important friendship evolved between them after Shulgi's death, and in many ways the solemn, fatherly Melchizedek, although very different from Shulgi, assumed the late king's place in Avram's affections. To them, Enlil was the Most High God, the supreme deity. The term 'Most High' is interesting, because it tells us that both Melchizedek and Avram were perfectly aware that there were other gods. If one god is the 'Most High', then there have to be other, lower, gods to whom comparison can be made. This was a secret trouble in their hearts. Both of them conceived of a Divine Being utterly remote from the political manoeuvrings of the higher Anunnaki, however godlike they appeared to ordinary mortals.

Both men were of uncommon spiritual bearing. They yearned after the exalted, ineffable nature of the true God, and very often they found her, and directed their actions and values by her moral compass. Moreover,

304

Enki would appear to them in various guises, usually as a simple golden light of purest radiance, and undertake to steer them by the true stars, whose mystical light resonated with the fountain of spiritual brightness springing like a wonder deep in their hearts. This, they knew, was the word of God.

The problem was that Enlil, too clever and guileful to try to overturn all that flowed to them from a much higher source than himself, instead used their confusion to his advantage. He tricked them into thinking that everything they received came to them from him, using many devices to secure his aim. It was very difficult for Avram and Melchisedek to differentiate between the sublime presence of God (what we might understand as the consciousness of Tiâmat-Oannes), and the point where, on their journey from the highest peak of their perception back down to the mundane material plane, they were hijacked by Enlil along the way.

In the end, their ability to discriminate became thoroughly undermined because of the influences of the white and the red powder, and they failed utterly to recognise when they were gazing into the eternal depths of the hallowed eye of God, and when the glaring eyeball of Enlil monopolised their perception! Likewise, in the Bible, we are given an undifferentiated body of text which one moment flowers exquisitely into the discourse of most holy reverie, and in the next is ranting and stamping with Rumpel-stilts-ken-like rage in an outburst which is unadulterated, unexpurgated Enlil!

Enlil remained nervous about Melchizedek and Avram's absolute allegiance to him. Their heartfelt response to Enki made him very jumpy, even if he knew how to prevent them from distinguishing his brother's voice from his own. Enlil was careful to nurture that revulsion concerning the ingestion of purified menstrual blood which to some degree he had already established within the two men, and in fact he issued a decree to his followers, headed by Avram, that blood must definitely *not* be ingested from then on, declaring that all blood belonged to him.

This was a blatant move to prevent any further consumption of either the Star Fire, the Tree of Life (which was not blood, but rather the spiritual essence of the consciousness of God), or the Tree of the Knowledge of Good and Evil, the hormone-rich ordinary Anunnaki menstrual blood which was yet, although in crude physical form, a manifestation of the flow of Tiâmat's consciousness. These substances gently and harmoniously enhanced masculine perceptual centres so that they were able to more easily enter into communion with the true God and the spirit of wisdom which flowed from her, and also to recognise and bolster themselves against the terrible threat to the psyche represented by the Naphidem.

Enlil was very careful, however, to ensure that his people did not imagine that, just because he was banning the ingestion of blood, he wanted them to become vegetarian. That would not do at all, because the cruelty meted out to animals by their human brethren was one of Enlil's main sources of supply as far as negative karma was concerned. The terrible suffering of animals (which, because of outrageous intensive farming methods, is even worse today) provided him with a rich fund of this lovely negative karma, which he could endlessly utilise to make humanity suffer and to draw the chains engraved with his name which bound them so mercilessly, tighter and ever tighter. Moreover, the indifference to animal suffering practiced by the majority of human beings led directly to an appalling indifference to human suffering, which was even better, because it provided further choice grist to his mill.

Enlil knew well the great spiritual law which decrees that as long as animals are abused and slaughtered wilfully by the hand of humanity, there will be warring and bloodshed between its members upon the Earth. Enlil, therefore, breathed forth an influence through the ethers which ensured that vegetarians would be mocked and despised, and even considered perverted and evil (vegetarians became known as those who partook of the 'Devil's banquet', according to the Christian Church), attitudes which in some quarters appear to have remained with our societies to the present era. Enki's adherents strove to practice harmlessness, which of course included vegetarianism, and so Enlil did all he could to promote the idea that such behaviour was 'unmanly'.

Tutored by Enlil, all things feminine gradually became suspect to Melchizedek and Avram. They seemed sinister, threatening, spooky, and superstitiously horrid. Feminine ritual was associated with ceremonies dedicated to the sun and the moon, which they were taught to consider as anathema. When Melchizedek offered Avram the initiatory bread and wine (the white and the red powder), he did so as a priest-king honouring a great warrior for his masculine prowess and initiating him into his own role. In other words, the blood-letting conqueror was to reign supreme as king and religious leader. It was a rejection from the role of religion of all things feminine.

Of course, it is undeniable that Avram did a great deed in banishing Canaan's enemies from the land, proving himself noble of heart and a man of bravery. Nevertheless, we believe that the unbalanced masculine principle, scornful of the eternal feminine, was that which was being evoked for supreme recognition and authority at this point, with a consequent dishonouring and denigration of the feminine principle. In other words, the forces of death, destruction and oppression were being honoured in detriment to the forces of life, creative nurture and freedom.

When the male forces are properly balanced with the female forces, the perfection of the forces of life, creative nurture and freedom is obtained. When the opposite happens, we see arising within the human psyche an application of its forces to life which precisely reflects the soul lineaments of Enlil. And we see within Melchizedek's initiation of Avram a pledge of allegiance to the white and the red powder and all that it held within its deadly potentiality.

After the initiation rites conducted by Melchizedek, (which involved the ingestion of the white powder), Avram was renamed Abraham[2] ('he' — or 'the Father' or 'Supreme One' — 'who holds the powers of Ham') by Enlil. Abraham was informed that everything which Ham and his son Canaan had 'purloined' from Enlil's followers - the wisdom, the knowledge, the power of the secret Tablet - was now his, by divine right. Enlil then gave the false Emerald Tablet, or a version of it, into Abraham's keeping. The famous Covenant that Jehovah made with Abraham occurred after an earlier Covenant which was made in the land of Canaan between King Ur-baba and Tiâmat.

The king was deeply troubled concerning the predicament of his beloved friend Avram. Once, King Shulgi, Avram and he had been the best of friends, enjoying a true spiritual intimacy and a vibrant alignment of vision and purpose. When Ur-baba (Canaan) had escaped into the land of Cain, he had hoped that Avram might follow him into exile. Somehow, he had felt certain that Avram would not be seduced by Shulgi's treachery to the temple of Enki, Lilith and Nin-khursag with its teachings on the true God, and to the great ancestors, Cain and Luluwa.

He had been shocked, and, in a sense, heartbroken, when news of Avram's changed loyalties reached him from over the border. Avram and he were cousins as well as close friends, and they had spent many childhood hours together in the court of Ur. Canaan had always believed that there was an unspoken understanding between Avram and himself, and that Shulgi, although cultivated, eloquent and assured, was the least enlightened of the three friends.

When Canaan's supporters in the land of Cain rose up in anger against his banishment (which had been formerly announced by King Shulgi, on Enlil's command), intending to march on Babylon and seize it from the thieving hands of Shulgi (Shem), Canaan's secret hope was that Avram might be rescued from his clutches.

After the fall of Babylon (renamed Babel by Shulgi and Enlil), Canaan tried on several occasions to make contact with Avram in Haran, where he had escaped with his father. Avram shunned his attempts each time, and when, several years later, Avram emigrated to Canaan, Ur-baba again tried to approach him, with offers of renewed friendship and co-operation between their respective communities. Canaan's emissary returned with bad news, however. Avram still did not wish to receive him. This was in spite of the fact that Avram had decided to establish himself and his followers in Canaan, not only because of Enlil's promptings, but also because Avram was confident that Ur-baba would vouch for him and protect him from those in the land who might have defamed him or risen up against him because of his close links with King Shulgi.

Canaan (Ur-baba), a loyal friend who felt attachments deeply, took his grief to the temple of Enki. He loved Avram as a brother, he lamented to the regal serpent-man and his noble consorts, who appeared consolingly by his side. Now Avram had come into his own land, the land of Canaan, surely the perfect opportunity presented itself for them to come together and oust the curse of Enlil, whose malevolence had left Sumer in smoking ruins, and who would do the same to the entire world, if (perhaps when) he could? Was this not his own mission as a move against Enlil, Canaan asked passionately - to reunite with his dear friend, with whom he had always seen eye to eye and heart to heart, and remove the veils from his eyes? Could not Enki and his consorts do something to bring this about?

It was at this point that Enki, Nin-khursag and Lilith gently led Canaan into the holy of holies, the communion chamber where he could hear Tiâmat's voice.

Notes and References

1. Some traditions tell of the God of Righteousness as bearing the name of 'Brahm' among the near and middle-eastern civilizations of Abraham's time. The name is interchangeable with 'ram', as both designations have the same meaning, and relate to

the mysteries of the Temple of Enki, or Oannes, as he was also known. Both references are to Masda (Enki), the God of Light, and both passed into the majestic civilization of the sub-continent of India, where Brahma, Rama and the great fish-man god Vishnu enshrined a mystical understanding of the Divine.

2. In Islamic tradition, King Nimrod was advised that a boy-child had recently been born who would dethrone and supplant him. The king therefore, Herod-like, ordered that all young male children should be slain. Abraham's mother hid him in a cave to escape the slaughter. Later, when Nimrod had identified Abraham as the one who was destined to overthrow him, the king had him cast into an executionary fire, but the fierce flames became a bed of roses upon which the child Abraham sweetly slept. This story is a mythology of spiritual rather than literal history. Nimrod, whose dynasty was associated with Ur, introduced the worship of the Goat of Mendes to his people. He was the grandson of Ham, and played a major and unique part in reinforcing and firmly establishing the Temple of Enki and Nin-khursag into earthly consciousness. The Goat of Mendes, of course, represented the mystery teachings of Enki, or Masda, God of Light, as espoused by Ham or Hermes. Ham was Enki's spiritual son, known to the world today as Zoroaster, the formal priest of Enki, whose line of priesthood descended from Adam. We may well perceive from this story how Abraham, infused with the notorious white powder, did indeed dethrone Enki's influence as the enlightenment of nations and kingdoms and usurped it on behalf of Enlil. Because of his crucial mission, he was specially protected by both Enlil and by divine powers.

Chapter Fifty-six

The False and the True Covenant

Tiâmat told Canaan that Avram must be allowed to pursue his own path. He had a great work to do for her, she explained, and it was imperative that Canaan should give him every support and blessing, albeit at a distance, even though, in this life, they would never be united in brotherhood again. It was a terrible sacrifice for Canaan's fond heart, but she asked it of him for the sake of the greater good.

She further explained that Avram, now Abraham, would be the father of nations, and that these nations would give rise to three great religions which would shape the world. Canaan was quite right; Enlil had every intention of destroying humanity and the planet, and he had wrested a great secret, a mighty wisdom from Ur and its Grail energies, in pursuit of this goal. In his perversion of this energy, which had already taken place, a weapon had fallen into his hands which would enable him to fulfil his desire. The only way to save the world now was to *contain* his death-energies.

Abraham and his wife Sarah, Tiâmat revealed to him, were the designated couple for this gargantuan task. Of the nations which would come forth from Abraham, the Hebrew race would establish itself first, under his aegis (this process had already begun). They were the chosen people, who would bear Enlil forth into the wider world and down the centuries - for he *must* be thus born forth, there was no way to avoid this now that he had become so powerful - and whose inherent national fortitude would prevent him from destroying the world. They would follow him, they would believe in him and, partially, do his will; but they would also throw a powerfully protective forcefield around his most lethal intentions.

Abraham had been deemed fit for this Atlas-like task because of the depth of his spirituality and vision, because his heart was pierced with strength and verity as if with a keen and true sword. He and his people would bear this burden to the very end - until all the world was ready to rise up as one and overcome Enlil with the power of the spirit, released and nurtured by the power of the Grail - the only means that would overcome him now that he wielded the power of the reverse-spin Grail: the false Grail. Yes, Enlil would create a culture and a founding religion that bore his stamp - but the Hebrews would have the strength to contain his hostile energies within a circle of the true God-forces. They would have the potency of spirit to reach up to the spiritual heights beyond Enlil, despite the very worst he could do, and keep his influences and intentions circumscribed within that circle. This great feat of courage required the Jewish people themselves to guard the perimeters of the circle, and dwell in the confusion of darkness and struggling light therein, in order to contain Enlil successfully and absolutely.

A terrible sacrificial price would be exacted in that Enlil's reverse-spin death energies would attract appalling suffering and persecution to the Jewish race, and condemn it to a life of wandering and rejection. The Jewish nation would finally be led back to Canaan, and it would be here, in this very special land containing the Grail mysteries, that a vital choice would be made between the false Grail and the true.

Tiâmat further explained that the land of Canaan would be the birthplace and the homeland of this Hebrew nation, just as it was the birthplace and the homeland of Canaan's followers, originally of the tribe who gathered around and descended from Cain and Luluwa. As Abraham and Canaan themselves were of the same blood and the dearest of friends, except that they had been separated by the stupor and confusion of the senses and perception that Enlil inflicted upon his followers, so would there exist a special brotherhood between the two peoples in Canaan - the Canaanites and the Hebrews. And just as Abraham and Canaan had been split asunder and falsely cast into the role of mutual enmity by Enlil, so would the Hebrews and the Canaanites eventually be led to despise one another until the day came when Enlil's influences would finally be overthrown. Meanwhile, Tiâmat reiterated her desire that Canaan should bless the endeavours of Abraham as he set out on his difficult and dangerous mission, and keep alive within his own people an awareness of their great destiny.

Canaan, moved in his spirit, accepted all of Tiâmat's decrees; and she made a Covenant with him there on that day, promising the stewardship of the mysteries of the land of Canaan for his people and for Abraham's people and that the rift between them should be healed, and formally conferring on him guardianship of the Grail. She sealed her promise once more with the arc of the rainbow.

When Enlil made his first Covenant with Abraham (for the express purpose of causing war and continuing unrest in the future for the occupants of Canaan, whereby he could spark off the ignition for his 'final solution'), and his second Covenant with Moses, he too employed the emblem of the arc. However, it was to honour, not Tiâmat and her beautiful soul-design for humanity of the seven rays of creation, but rather Noah, who himself actually built the Ark and who in his pride in his own scientific achievements chose to completely overlook and dismiss the evocative, Tiâmat-centred symbolism of his own Ark.

As far as Noah was concerned, the Ark centred on his own importance and commemorated his great work. So the Ark of the Covenant came into being, which also honoured Noah's son Shem, for it incorporated a *shem* in its design. Noah and Shem (whose soul had arisen, as we know, when Sumer fell) dwelt with Enlil in his hidden dimension - which was of the Earth but existed on a higher plane than that of the physical sphere of manifestation - and continued to aid him in all his plans and projects.

At the point of the first Covenant with Abraham, however, the concept of the arc was celebrated simply enough by a six-branched candlestick consisting of seven candleholders. The tabernacle of the first Covenant contained this candlestick, and a table displaying the infamous shewbread. The tabernacle was an ideogram of Abraham's deeper soul, of the soul of his future people and the circle of containment in which they would hold the destructive potencies of Enlil. The candlestick equates with the seven rays of the rainbow and the seven chakras of the soul. It is Tiâmat's sign. It shows us that the seven circuits of the soul to purify the chakras had been undertaken by Abraham, but (because no candles or kindling are evident) that something prevented him from taking full flame in those seven centres so that the seven rays of creation could shine unhindered throughout his soul structure and free him and the greater soul of his people from the constraints of the incarcerating circle which restrains Enlil.

Opposite the candlestick lay the shewbread, and the oppositional power of this false Grail must first be overcome before freedom could be obtained. Once won, such freedom would be a gift for all the world; but before this could happen, there must come one in the name of Oannes: a man who would receive the full force of the devastation of the death-forces fostered by Enlil - the veritable Dolorous Blow - and counter and entirely overcome them whilst still on earth. Only by such means could the secret dimension in which Enlil and Noah had hidden the Emerald Tablet be discovered and unlocked. As we shall shortly see, another spiritual luminary was destined to rise and set before the coming of this great one; but the mission of the chosen one who preceded Jesus of Nazareth was brought down and reduced to partial failure by Enlil before it could properly spread its wings.

Enlil remained nervous about Melchizedek and Abraham's undivided loyalty to him. For the time being it was not in doubt, but Enlil set about removing every threat to it with a paranoid savagery. He could not forget Attaba and Ga-nadin-ur's 'disobedience' to him, and he was not going to be caught out again. Enlil, as a final seal of assurance, eventually demanded that Abraham should sacrifice Isaac to him. This was certainly a test of Abraham's allegiance, as the Old Testament records, but in fact Enlil was in deadly earnest concerning the murder of Isaac. (We must make clear that Enlil was indeed a 'god' who demanded human sacrifices, as the terrible propitiatory rites of the Mayans and the Aztecs, and many other tribes around the world whose fearsome godhead equates with Enlil - that dark power of destruction which would not leave them alone until they had mollified his menace with acts of extreme cruelty - confirm. We also ought to clarify that Enlil's presence within these ancient tribes is not merely a matter of recognition through the perpetration of the deeds he inspired, but exists via named entities which scholarship acknowledges are the same 'mythological' being as the Sumerian Enlil.)

Fortunately, before Abraham carried out his intended deed, which would have entrenched him like a helpless puppet under Enlil's dominance, without any further power of containment of his death energies, Enki called to him and took the form of a ram to stand in Isaac's stead as sacrifice. The sacrifice of this 'ram' to Enlil is hugely significant. (We remember that 'ram' meant 'one who possesses the highest degree of knowledge', as indeed, demonstrated in his name, did Av-ram himself.) When Abraham sacrificed the 'ram', he sacrificed himself instead of his son. By this act he pledged deep within his soul that, in order ultimately to save the Emerald Table (in one sense, the 'ram' or 'Ham' – the 'I Am'), and therefore humanity, from Enlil, he would willingly sacrifice his own access to it, and thus be led by a guide and a route that would burden him. Enki discouraged animal sacrifices as a cruel and degenerate habit, but Enlil absolutely insisted upon them, and thus they could not be avoided by his followers. Enki's act, and Abraham's enlightened response to it, prevented the Hebrews from following a route which would have led quickly to the ripe fruition of Enlil's plans.

From the moment that Abraham happened upon the ram tangled in the bush, he dispensed with the idea of human sacrifice. He thought, of course, that Enki's voice was Enlil's. Once Abraham had weighed the judgment required of him in the balance of his soul and had given his answer in Enki's favour, Enlil was henceforth rendered powerless to force his hand.

Chapter Fifty-seven

Sodom and Gomorrah

To further secure his man, Enlil needed to do something about the city states of Sodom and Gomorrah. His problem was that these twin cities harboured a culture of enlightenment that was anathema to him and the principles he strove to make fundamental in the lives and psyches of humanity so that his plan of annihilation could move forward unhindered. To make matters worse, both cities now contained many refugees from the remains of Sumer, particularly from the all-important Ur, whose great dynasty had fathered Abraham.

Many mystics and philosophers, many priests of Enki and Nin-khursag, many men and women of science and the arts had congregated within these two city states to form a body of ancient wisdom and progressive knowledge that was quickening with new life and growth. This constituted a real threat to Abraham and Melchizedek's stance as his supporters. Enlil knew all too well that neither of the two men was hostile to these innovative influences, and he remained in terror in case they should be seduced by them. He had already, to undermine the problem cities, inflated the warring situation whereby kings from surrounding states had marched against Sodom and Gomorrah and deposed their kings, which had also presented itself as a convenient opportunity for him to manoeuvre Abraham into winning honour and glory as a chieftain.

Unfortunately for Enlil, the twin cities and the dynamics of their culture had survived these incursions intact. He continued to experience a preponderance of difficulties in effectively stalling the momentum of the intellectual and spiritual movement which was advancing with such brilliance and vigour from within their joint citadels. He saw that decisive action must be taken, and to this end he informed Abraham that he intended to destroy the two cities, as they were both dens of iniquity.

Abraham was deeply shocked, and begged for mercy on their behalf. He implored Enlil to consider the 'good men' within Sodom and Gomorrah (the very group who were rattling Enlil's cage so thoroughly). Enlil's reply to this plea can only be interpreted as a declaration to prove

315

that there were no 'good men' in the city, or at least that there were fewer than five, because the Bible account tells us that he agreed not to destroy the cities if five 'good men' could be found therein. He certainly did go on to destroy both of them, so students of the Bible are left with the impression that Enlil conclusively proved his point that, in actual fact, these 'good men' whom Abraham was so anxious to save were not good at all. How did he do this?

There can be little doubt that Enlil called on Marduk and the Naphidem to do their worst within the two cities. We see the development of a typically Naphidem-inspired situation in a disturbing story concerning Lot and the arrival of two angels in his home. Hearing of the arrival of the strangers, a large group of men of Sodom gathered outside Lot's door and demanded with menaces that the visitors be delivered into their hands for the purpose of homosexual gang rape. The story progresses further into horror to relate that Lot offered up his two daughters in the angels' stead (we think they presented themselves in sacrifice), but the crowd refused this propitiation and Lot himself was set upon and almost dragged into the nightmarish fray before managing to disengage himself and bar the door against the demoniacal mob.

Our source informs us that the two strangers were not angels, but members of the higher Anunnaki who had used the remnant of the Grail energies in a highly specialised way to materialise their bodies for a short time upon the earth plane (this process was no longer straightforward, as was previously the case). They hailed from the eastern dimension where Enki, Nin-khursag, Lilith, and other members of the higher Anunnaki connected with these Leaders of Light, had retreated after the fall of Sumer. They had come on a special mission: to warn Lot (Abraham's kinsman) and his family that Sodom and Gomorrah were about to be devastated by Enlil via a deadly weapon, and that they must flee at the earliest opportunity. They must protect themselves from the fall-out of this blast, which incorporated the need for a shielding of consciousness as well as of the body. They must not look back, even when they were safely removed from the city boundaries, or the destruction of the lethal weapon would fall upon them.

The two higher Anunnaki had a particular job to do once the cities had been hit. It was their duty to help Enki and his consorts to once more shut down the ray upon which Noah and Enlil were still able to operate their prized weapon, and to seal and purify the entire area with salt, which is both an earthly and a magical substance with reflecting crystals which countered the energies in the glassy substance that the ray-gun created in the administering of its deadly work. The reason that salt would be necessary as a sealing agent after the destruction of Sodom and Gomorrah, and was unnecessary after the ruination of Sumer (where the crystals in sand sufficed), was because Noah and Enlil had been busy refining the science of their death-ray, and had managed to make it even more deadly. Their express intention was to poison the Earth and to permanently destroy a wide area of it, especially incorporating what would come to be known as Jerusalem and Palestine.

The hideous commotion at Lot's door was a Naphidem-influenced group which, although involving a tiny minority, had overrun the two cities and had finally done its designated work by demonstrating to Lot and Abraham (who worked together in their spiritual mission) that the cities 'truly' were infested with a maniacal evil. This group, influenced by Marduk and Enlil, certainly were in pursuit of the two higher Anunnaki 'angels', because they were Enki's envoys. Had they been subjected to battery and sexual assault before they could etherealise their bodies, the resultant trauma and bodily disablement would have prevented them from carrying out their vital task, and the highly toxic and damaging effects of the enweaponed white powder might have caused huge tracts of the planet's surface to be uninhabitable for thousands of years to come.

Due to their experience of the ravening Naphidem-influenced group, Lot and Abraham were convinced that the destruction of the cities was a 'righteous' act, and Enlil saved face and kept his men. Enlil's fate hung in the balance that night in Sodom. Had Lot and Abraham (and, through them, Melchizedek) not been convinced of Enlil's true judgment in devastating the cities, they would have heeded the other warning that came to them with the 'angels' ' counsel that the cities were to be destroyed - that Enlil was dangerous and ill-willed towards the human race. After the visit of the mob, however, Enlil was able to put a very different construction on his decision to use weapons of mass destruction, and Abraham and Lot's understanding of Enki remained obscured and confused. For instance, they assumed that the two members of the higher Anunnaki who warned them against a Lord of Darkness who 'stood behind' Enlil were referring to a cosmic entity who was actually working against, rather than with, Enlil.

Perhaps it was fortuitous that this was the case, because it was essential that Enlil's insidious influences should remain firmly encircled by the spiritual strength of the Hebrews. Otherwise, our planet may not have survived.

As events transpired, Lot's wife forgot to abide by the angels' advice. She looked back, just once, when she calculated that the little fleeing party had reached a safe distance, and made visual contact with the laser upon which the disseminated white powder was travelling to its target. She was immediately desiccated and crystallised. Enki's envoys encrusted her with salt, fulfilling the same purpose as that for which the devastated cities were packed with salt. Eventually, the Dead Sea claimed them, and the entire area, the lowest point on the Earth's surface, became a strange, desolate, haunted place, a 'dead zone', rich only in supplies of pitch, a substance traditionally associated with all things demonic.

Interestingly, this was the location where the Essenes established themselves in later years, although we believe that there was a mystic brotherhood there (of both men and women) even prior to Abraham's time. The lost cities of Sodom and Gomorrah have apparently been discovered on the bed of the Dead Sea. Problems between Jordan and Israel have so far prevented further explorations from proceeding, but if future excavations should take place, it is likely that these two intriguing enigmas would surrender many mysteries. It seems as if there was an alignment with this point on the Earth's surface and the place within the Earth (which was an ethereal dimension even though it actually existed in the bowels of the planet) where Enlil, his higher Anunnaki followers, and a number of the Naphidem who at the time of their banishment had managed to escape into the ground, had established themselves when Tiâmat trapped them in the lower earth planes. There is no doubt that this lowest earthly site was actually a profoundly sacred and powerful interface between above and below, which is why Enlil and the Naphidem settled there. Their presence made it into a wasteland; and the famous esoteric maxim 'As above, so below', applied in weird and unsettling context in this particular application of its meaning.

Enlil and Noah by no means gave up their precious weapon when Enki and his messengers disabled it for the second time. They were determined to develop it to its highest potential, whereby it would (they trusted) one day destroy the world. (Nuclear warheads were created via an escaped strand of this false Grail knowledge, but are not nearly so dangerous as Noah's ray, which has the potential to obliterate all life on earth forever

318

meaning that the planet itself would no longer be able to generate cellular life.) They had already come on apace, as they were piecing together a technique to allow them to make the collective mind of humanity into one great weapon of mass destruction. Enki had again barred their way, but they would continue with their schemes nonetheless.

Chapter Fifty-eight
Enlil's Darkest Secret

It is time to reveal exactly what Enlil and his associates have done to planet Earth. There is no need to worry about the implications of this revelation, because, as we shall disclose, Tiâmat has ensured that everything is in place to counteract and wholly heal the situation, as long as her divine remedy is in accordance with our freewill choice. We are fully confident that there will be sufficient people across the globe who will pledge their allegiance to the forces of the 'one true light' for human freewill to properly align itself with this mighty act of divine healing. The ascended master, White Eagle, assures us that 'humanity is coming on in leaps and bounds!'

Enlil, with his great accomplice, Zi-u-sudra, has enclosed the Earth in a sinister ring of glassy, invisible substance which has been manufactured from his baleful white powder. It exists in the atmosphere of our planet, and it filters the sunlight, and the spiritual power within the sunlight, so that the *ayin*, the power of God-consciousness residing in our hearts which is our vision of truth, is obstructed. It is not possible to distort this godly power itself, of course, but it is certainly possible to distort and throw off course the awareness within the human soul which accesses it and would normally become consummate with it. This is precisely the function of the false ring (the ring made of the sham *shem*).

The false ring, composed of a refined glass which exists as imperceptible crystals in Earth's atmosphere, is actually a mirror. And, looking into the mirror, humanity walking the Earth below constantly receives and perceptually ingests the bogus, misleading images that the false mirror throws off, in its power of distortion, confusion and corruption, so that we see things, as it were, the wrong way round. We are plunged within the realm of our perception straight into a topsy-turvy, back-to-front, Alice-in-Wonderland world.

It is possible to rise above this distortion, confusion and corruption, of course, and to see what we should see with our inner vision, our inner *ayin*; the pristine sunlight is eternally pure and undefiled, and can strike our true centre of inner or heart-vision unaffected by the sinister filter. But it is very difficult and can be psychically exhausting, even traumatic, to maintain steadily and constantly the clear and unsullied truth of the vision of the *ayin* within. The pull of the false reflection hauls us back into its tyranny and we fear to break away entirely.

It was for this purpose – the creation and maintenance of the false ring around the Earth, in the upper reaches of its atmosphere – that Enlil commanded his slaves (those on earth who fell completely under his dominion) to manufacture vast quantities of the *shem* or white powder – the false communion bread. It was dispersed into the atmosphere via the malignant ray that Enlil and Noah had used to destroy Sumer, and Sodom and Gomorrah.

Whilst visiting an ancient church with a friend, he pointed out the dull, opaque appearance of the stained glass windows from its exterior. We had just been enjoying the mysterious beauty of the glass, with its hallowed lights, like secret treasure or jewelled casements onto the bright dimensions of spiritual worlds, from within the church.

My friend told me that medieval stained glass could be identified by its opaqueness from outside the building in which it was set. This seemed an important point to ponder, and I was struck by the closed and sealed appearance of the windows from outside the church, as if they did indeed express an intention of non-admittance. Shortly afterwards, Margaret Bailey and I learned that this medieval glass was in fact specially conditioned, by alchemical means, to keep out the daylight from the sanctuary of the interior of churches and cathedrals, not only to protect the congregation, but also because the locations of such churches were deeply sacred, holy sites far, far older than Christianity, which needed spiritual and physical protection from Enlil's deadly, distorting mirror and its saturated impregnation of malicious intent.

The secret in the glass of the medieval churches and cathedrals which were financed and constructed mainly throughout the twelfth century by the Knights Templar was a pure and beautiful one, mystical and imponderably ancient. Certain branches of alchemical science were used to support and facilitate this divine secret process, but its real application relied on the dispensation of the Holy Breath, the Holy Spirit or Paraclete, which was given in this instance through the art of glass blowing.

The liquid glass was blown into shape by means of tubes. The master craftsmen within the Templar brotherhood used their breath to blow form into the glass, which then crystallised. This puts us in mind of the House of Shimtî, where Nin-khursag, through communion with Tiâmat, provided the Holy Breath to breathe life into human creation, whereupon Enki and she would use their divinely-bestowed 'craft' (the craft of crystallization of form, a Saturnine dispensation) to accommodate, contain and seal the creational essence breathed forth by God. (Considering Saturn, we might think of the great god Pan, who is a symbol of Father Saturn, blowing with gentle reverence down his magical 'Pan-pipes', and of the crystallisation that occurs throughout the myriad forms of Creation as he does so.)

Through an alchemical method of treating gold and other noble metals, which is akin to creating the negative white powder but produces unconscionably different results, the liquid metal was transformed into glass. The glass would exhibit a certain hue and quality according to the particular metal used to create it. However, there is a 'missing ingredient' to the process outlined above. We do not pretend to fully understand what it is in all its aspects, but we shall endeavour to share with you what we have been shown in relation to it.

We know from Laurence Gardner's discussion of the subject in *Genesis of the Grail Kings* (Chapter 14) that the alchemical procedure via which the glass was made causes 44% of the weight of the metal subject to it, ultimately to disappear and transfigure into vivid white light. It is this light which reappears as the pure and lovely illumination, so mysterious to behold, within medieval coloured glass. When Enlil manufactured the *shem-an-na*, the metals he used were subject to the same ultimate weight loss due to the same dramatic transfiguration into brilliant white light. What, then, was the difference between the two procedures?

The huge differential was the Holy Breath, called *Spiritus Mundi*, 'the breath of the universe', by the Knights Templar. The *Spiritus Mundi* supplied the means of discernment whereby the spiritual student was enabled to distinguish between the true and the false light. The dramatic burst of brilliant white light occurred in both the false, reverse-spin, alchemical method (Enlil's way), and the true alchemical method of pure ascension (Enki's way).

No white or red powder or drug-like substance was created by Enki's way, but the magical, luminous glass, of a depth and beauty of translucency and colour almost synonymous with spiritual vision, most certainly was. Enki's way, significantly, involved breathing in, and thereafter breathing out, the pure white light of the Godhead – the spiritual starlight which makes us Pendragons.

Other wonders were also created by this pure method. Part of the teaching vision given for our interpretation in explanation of Enki's way was a tower of golden coins which were seen as spinning disks, impervious to gravity. From this, we deduce that the anti-gravitational field which produced such an effect was created by the godly, forward or clockwise spin of the atoms of gold used by the Master Craftsmen (more properly, Craftspeople, for of course women were also involved) in their Great Work (the esoteric term for the art of alchemy). This positive spin, in overcoming Earth's gravity, would reproduce conditions which were attuned to the verity of the true Grail, the path from earth to heaven via spiritual ascension. Enlil's way, whereby the reverse-spin atoms of noble metals are used, created by superimposed and malevolent distortion, draws the unfortunate student onto the path of false ascension – the ascension of the mind, with all its attendant dangers and proclivity for disastrous choices. The anti-gravitational field thus created is dark and sinister – veritably the arena of the horrifying Naphidem.

We reiterate that in these methods of creating the false and the true Grail, the deciding factor between the two was the use of the breath, and of pure spiritual attunement and vision. Breath was used in both procedures. In the first, it was just 'hot air', the inflation of the bellows of the lower self, the self-seeking and self-serving lower dragon, grasping hotly after creational knowledge in order to gain personal power.

This breath was Enlil's, and he used the terrible secret of the reversed Holy Breath, or the power of the 'reversed winds' (we remember that this was exactly how Marduk had 'slain' Tiâmat and destroyed the Holy Grail) to turn the gold into a physical form of diabolical force. In the dimension in which he waited, Enlil breathed this deathly breath into the atoms of the highward-spinning gold as he drew it in. It thereby missed its mark. It seemed to ascend, but only ascended into Enlil's sinister den. It returned to earth as the reverse-spin gold, now permanently transformed into a white powder.

Of course, because its manufacturers are not working specifically for Enlil, today's method of producing the white powder does not give Enlil such direct access to it, and it is transformed into a physical powder whose application conveys several health benefits. It is not the same substance as the false communion bread. Nevertheless, if it is taken as an artificial means of stimulating the head chakras (the 'precious Stone' in the head), severely unhelpful effects are produced which actually work against the process of true ascension. As its discoverer, 'Mr. Material', proclaims via the ancient system of clue-giving enshrined in nomenclature, let us confine it strictly to the material level of life!

In the second method of alchemical creation, Enki's way, the breath used was the aspiring, Tiâmat-centred, Holy Breath of Divine Love – the breath of the Pendragon. When the white light burst forth, its essence, due to the infusion of the Holy Breath, was of the light of the Godhead; the activated, God-attuned heart of the alchemist used it to set alight the Stone of Ascension in the brain. It seems that music and colour were an integral part of this process.

We have been given to understand that, therefore, human spiritual consciousness directly impacted upon the alchemical procedure and its resultant creations. They were an example of exalted human consciousness expressing itself, through the giving forth of Divine Love from the heart, in an act of consummation with physical Creation.

In other words, they were demonstrations of genuine Master Craftsmanship. They fulfilled the will of Tiâmat-Oannes in that within them, they expressed the true plan for Creation: - that it would realise itself and attain perfection through the direct impact of human, God-attuned, spiritual consciousness. It is as if, in Creation today, God faithfully does Her-His part, but we, in our blindness, ignorance and self-will, are stubbornly refusing to do our part. The whole purpose of physical creation seems to be to inspire and empower us to co-create with God in every moment of our lives. When we become properly aware of this, we can begin to learn the true alchemy of life.

We shall now advance in time from Abraham's era to the coming of the great Akhenaten, the controversial pharaoh who very nearly managed to turn things around and end Enlil's rule once and for all, so that, when Jesus of Nazareth and Mary Magdalene eventually arrived on earth and brought forth Tamar, the entire planet would have ascended. He is better known as Moses, the mighty internationalist.

Chapter Fifty-nine

Moses the John-man

Moses was the son of Queen Tiye of Egypt, who was the second wife of Pharaoh Amenhotep lll. Amenhotep, however, was not his father. Moses was fathered by the high priest of the Israelites, and Tiye gave birth to him before she married the pharaoh.

Tiye was the daughter of Yuya, the vizier to Amenhotep lll. Yuya has been identified with Joseph of the coat of many colours, Jacob's son. He was highly esteemed in Egypt, and he and his family members were given a status almost commensurate with royalty, which was consummated in Tiye's marriage to the pharaoh. Common knowledge of Tiye's affair with the high priest would have caused a scandal. Not only was Tiye a single woman and a member of the royal household, she and her family were indebted to the pharaoh, and a seduction of the young woman already earmarked for marriage to the ruler of Egypt, especially by a Hebrew immigrant, would have been considered a crime.

Tiye obscured her son's true origin by concocting a story that he had been discovered floating in the river in an ark of bulrushes, and she had drawn him from the water, thus giving him the name 'Moses' - 'drawn from the water'. 'Moses' was his Hebrew name, given to honour his father. His Egyptian name was Akhenaten.

The etymology of the name Moses is interesting, as it derives from more than one source. It is an ancient form of the name Osiris, which is connected with Oannes. As well as its 'drawn from the water' derivation, it also indicates a son or an heir. In total we have the implication of a son or descendant of Oannes, the fish-man who emerged, or was drawn from, the water. In other words, we have a John-man, a Son of Light. We think that the biological process called osmosis is linked with the names Osiris, Oannes and Moses. Tiâmat's blueprint for the creation of humanity, and of biological life itself, as her magically impregnated water became blood which carries the mystery of metals and other substances within it, relied on the procedures of osmosis. We are all 'drawn from the water' and crafted from the elements of life.

The legend surrounding the 'discovery' of Moses is interesting, because it neatly fulfils two objectives, whilst the hand of the Divine, or the wisdom of the Star Fire within Tiye, is evident in its fabrication. Firstly, it provided Tiye's affair, and its result, with a smokescreen. Secondly, it incorporated a means by which the royals and the officials of the palace would quell their objections to an adoption, because the story echoed one popular in the traditions of the Fertile Crescent: that of the *Legend of Sharru-kîn*, an ancient wonder tale concerning the mystical origins of Sargon the Great, King of Akkad. Taliesin, the later Welsh deity who lived on earth for a time as a distinguished bard, was 'drawn from the water' in the same way as Moses, and doubtless there were other gods who bore a similar stamp of the Divine.

The royal household was ready to concede that this child Moses might be connected to a deity, and that he had been sent by the gods. This alone was sufficient to prevent them from interfering with Tiye and her claim to the child, as Tiye herself, according to them, had obviously been cast as a key player in the enactment of the sacred drama. Nevertheless, Moses was watched suspiciously as he grew to manhood.

Meanwhile, Tiye married Amenhotep lll, and an immediate prohibition against any son of hers succeeding to the throne was brought into effect. This proscription was created mainly because of the existence of Moses. Amenhotep's other, younger wife (although she was the senior wife as her marriage preceded that of Tiye, and she was an Egyptian) never gave birth to a son, but to a single daughter - the great Nefertiti. Moses married her (much to the disapproval of the court officials) and was made co-regent with Nefertiti during the period prior to Amenhotep lll's death, when he became too ill to rule. On his demise, Moses became Pharaoh of Egypt.

Thirdly, the myth about Moses being drawn from the water honoured the special wisdom which Tiye bore within her as a priestess blessed of Tiâmat. It was right that she should spread this story abroad, for there was a sanctified truth dwelling at its heart. Tiye was part of a secret sisterhood which later included the three wives of Moses: Nefertiti, Queen Kiya, and the Midianite princess, Zipporah, whose name, significantly, means 'female bird'. This 'female bird' is very important within the Grail tradition, for it symbolises ascension. The scaly or furry legs with claws (the strange characteristic with which Lilith, the Queen of Sheba, and other mystical women are associated) denote the feet and legs of the dragon becoming the bird of ascension, even in a pragmatic sense, because of course the dinosaurs, the animal dragons of Earth, literally transformed into the birds which inhabit our planet today.

The dragon is the serpent making a perfect ring by swallowing its tail (the *ouroboros*, a symbol of eternity), and it dwells, coiled, at the roots of the Tree of Life (Tiâmat's divine consciousness). This dragon or serpent (Enki) becomes a bird as its perception begins to ascend, transfiguring into Lilith, who sits and pours forth a cascade of joy in song at the top of the Tree. This is a declaration that Tiâmat's consciousness is restored and ascension is achieved.

This was the true meaning, within the Sumerian texts , of Zu, the Great Bird, attempting to take back the Emerald Tablet after Marduk had usurped it. It was actually Lilith and Nin-khursag who fought to regain it, to prevent Enlil's treacherous scheme to hide it away and to replace it with a distorted version. Sadly, so adamant and entrenched were Marduk and Enlil in their denial of Tiâmat and the consciousness of the Tree of Life, that to wrest the Tablet from them could not have been achieved without betraying the laws of life inscribed on the Tablet itself; and so it had to be surrendered.

When Moses the John-man incarnated, his mission was to restore some of the lost knowledge contained within the pure vibration of the Emerald Tablet so that humanity could achieve ascension much sooner than would otherwise be the case (it would not have to take the long way round, so to speak). The coming of the Nephilim couple, Mary Magdalene and Jesus of Nazareth, would still be necessary to retrieve the Tablet in its entirety. When the whole truth, the holistic or holy truth, was thus revealed to humanity, the Divine Woman could descend through her sanctified parents and lead the peoples of the world to the attainment of ascension. This glorious outcome would obviate the need for many, many centuries of acute suffering on the part of humankind and the Earth herself.

To this end, Tiâmat called upon one of her true sons, an ancient and noble soul who had served Enki and his consorts and honoured their teachings throughout many incarnations on planet Earth. This true son (Moses/Akhenaten) came with three exalted ones who preceded the three Marys of the New Testament era (Mary Jacob, mother of Mary Magdalene; Mary the mother of Jesus; and Mary Magdalene herself). These three women, as mentioned previously, were his wives: Nefertiti,

327

Kiya, and Zipporah. All wear the mantle of folklore and miracles, and Kiya in particular (called Miriam by the Israelites) was to play a leading role in Moses's mission, greater, even, than his own.

Akhenaten's fourth wife, the Ethiopian princess Tharbis, was not of this sisterhood. She had been contaminated by the white powder, because her father (thinking he was giving her a wonderful privilege) had fed her with it. Through sexual union, Moses absorbed and was slightly influenced by the death forces inherent in it.

When Akhenaten (Moses) finally succeeded to power in about 1367 BC, he asserted his vision of one ineffable God above and beyond the teeming Egyptian deities. He strove to introduce the philosophical concept of a unifying principle in which everything that could be conceived of was contained, but, in distinctly Buddhic mode, he posited that this omniscient, omnipotent principle could not be found with the physical senses, but could be discovered only through the mystical wisdom of inner percipience. He used the symbol of the Aten, the eight-rayed disc which is an esoteric representation of the inner unifying eye (the *ayin*), to illustrate the new philosophy to his people. The number 8 is deeply associated with feminine divinity, and is a symbol of the continuous flow of divine life and consciousness. Ultimately, it is the Caduceus, the entwining serpents creating the Staff of Life, or the Sacred Tree.

This idea of the eight-rayed Being (the expression of the seven-and-the-one, indicating the seven rays or modes of creation combined in the unity above and beneath it, as in the seven tones of music being completed in the octave, or eighth note) permeates the entire *Gospel of Mary*, which is in perfect harmony with Buddhist philosophy. The gospel is an exquisite expression of the realisation of the 'Aten', of its gentleness and its all-permeating quality of absolute goodness and love as the soul purifies itself throughout its seven circuits, and takes flight into the spiritual starlight at the eighth level, becoming itself a being of Star Fire. Osiris (Oannes) himself was the heavenly shepherd of these pure stars of brilliant light, ushering them back into the heart of the One, the Aten (Tiâmat).

Unfortunately, the vision of Tiâmat was blocked to the majority of the Egyptians. They conceived of her especially through Isis and Hathor, and worshipped the 'rising power' (ascension) these goddesses represented. Their religion and culture incorporated a multiplicity of magnificent,

328

stupendous and beautiful aspects, and was in many respects much more advanced and admirable than our own, but it had its blind spots and its dark side. The problems which had dogged all civilisations since the advent of the great imbalance shadowed its progress, and a certain succession of priests was careful to continue to feed its rulers with the conical bread cakes (the false *shem*) so that particular influences were disseminated and broadcast to the people by the pharaohs.

Throughout Akhenaten's years of rule, his enemies mobilised themselves. We see that perhaps Moses was a little too heavy-handed, a little too fast-paced, in his upholding of his religious vision. A certain impatience or deafness to feminine wisdom seems to have been a weakness, due not only to his dalliance with Tharbis but also to the pressures of the time and the ardent and devout aspects of his nature, which propelled him into too much 'doing' at the expense of 'being'. For instance, in his enthusiasm to honour his mission, he banned the worship of all deities except the Aten, thus depriving the Egyptians of their beloved familiar gods. Every problem that thenceforth menaced the lives of the people was blamed on this sweeping ordinance, and his enemies, already numerous, multiplied and closed ranks.

His antagonists eventually forced him to abdicate in favour of Smenkhkare, his cousin and 'feeding-brother' (meaning that they had shared the same wet-nurse). However, this cousin was found to be in partnership with Moses in all things philosophical and religious, and he too was ousted after holding office as pharaoh for only a few weeks. Despite Moses's failings in his application of the new teachings, it is only fair to say that he fully realised that he had a mighty mission of global importance to fulfil, and that he applied himself to its realisation with dynamism, verve and devotion.

During his time in active office as pharaoh, his first queen, Nefertiti, died. Moses had also married Kiya, his step-sister and feeding-sister, who received the senior queen's blessing as she expired. Nefertiti, strong, resolute, proud and courageous, beautiful and magnanimous, passed on her role to this all-important young woman, whom history has failed to recognise as the luminary she truly is.

Sorrow came to Queen Kiya during her time at court. She gave birth to two babies who did not survive, although she also delivered a healthy daughter, the sister of Tutankhamun. He was her only surviving son. We think that the mummified infants who are believed to be the children of

Tutankhamun were actually Kiya's babies, the children of Moses. After Moses and his kinsman Smenkhare (Aaron) were banished, they travelled to the land of Midian, east of the Sinai mountains. Here they were welcomed by Lord Jethro, the Midianite leader, who was related to Akhenaten via his father, the High Priest of the Israelites.

Kiya and Lord Jethro's daughter Zipporah shared a soul kinship, and it was not until Moses had married Zipporah, and the two women were united as 'sisters', that Akhenaten's true mission could begin. This extended beyond the introduction of the teachings of Aten (the concept of the mystery of the one God). It involved the exalted rites of receiving enlightenment from what could be given, via Kiya and Zipporah, of the Emerald Tablet, from Tiâmat herself, so that humankind could move steadily forwards on the road to ascension until Jesus and Mary met them at a certain point along the way, and delivered the integrated whole of the Emerald Tablet and the Divine Woman, Tamar, to earth. Thus, with the death forces already partially overcome before their arrival, there would be no need for the horror of the crucifixion, or for the catastrophic wave of human, animal and planet suffering which would culminate in the two world wars, and would not abate even after these twin peaks of suffering had ravaged human civilisation.

And yet Akhenaten's marriage to Zipporah came at a price. Moses fell deeply in love with her, and felt within himself the spiritual righteousness of their impending union. Kiya, too, rejoiced in the idea of their marriage. This was a happy time for Moses, a sweet interlude of rest and renewal before his great labours began. He spent many hours in the company of Kiya and Zipporah, and absorbed much wisdom from them in preparation for his formidable task.

All the time, without their knowledge, except for the intuition of the two women, Jethro watched them, studied them, and heard the voice of Enlil speak in his heart.

Chapter Sixty

The Smoking Mountain

Jethro was a descendant of Esau, the 'man of wrath' who was twin brother to Jacob. Esau sold Jacob his birthright for 'a mess of pottage', and whilst on the run from Esau, Jacob had witnessed as in a dream a great ladder between heaven and earth. All night he had watched angels come and go upon it, whilst a mighty angel wrestled with him until morning, seeking to consume all his strength. As dawn broke, Jacob was at last victorious in his struggle with the angel, proving that he had the power, the will, and the devotion to bear the secret of the Grail, and to continue to contain Enlil's death forces whilst the vital bloodline progressed through the kings of the Davidic lineage to its glorious destination in Bethlehem. For, of course, Jacob's vision of the ladder connecting heaven and earth was a vision of the Holy Grail.

'This is a terrible place, for it is the House of God', Jacob pronounced upon returning to normal consciousness. We may remember these evocative words as we head towards the Grail clues, for they certainly play a part in pointing out to us where the Emerald Tablet lies today. Jacob meant that the site of his experience was the inconceivably holy connecting point between the planet and God, between humanity and God, which does not have an absolute geographical location, but is established by the presence of the divine forces of the Grail creating an arc, or a bridge, or a ladder between heaven and earth as an outpouring of ineffable love which enables us to ascend. It was the willing reception of this divine love that the death forces blocked and 'slew' so many thousands of years ago.

Jacob's brief from Tiâmat, amongst many other imperatives, was to lead the Children of Israel into Egypt, to the root of their spiritual conjoinment. Here was the seat of many esoteric traditions which had been passed down from Enki (the Egyptians called him Thoth) and which belonged to the mystical rites of Isis and Hathor, both Dragon Queens in Egyptian guise. Here, too, in the years to come, would arise the John-man (Moses) and his high-priestess-wives who would light a torch of God to illumine the Way for poor, stumbling humanity, so constantly waylaid by the false Grail. We might say, in crude terms, that Jacob was Tiâmat's man, and Esau, the man of 'wrath', was Enlil's man.

Jethro, most definitely Enlil's man, began to inculcate a notion of indebtedness in Moses. In doing so, he followed Enlil's orders (we make a mistake if we think too narrowly in terms of good and evil, however, for Jethro was certainly not evil, but duped and unenlightened, although there were also many admirable traits in his character; equilibrium between the male and female principles was, however, glaringly conspicuous by its absence in his philosophy). Jethro hinted that Akhenaten could repay the Lord of Midian's hospitality to him, Aaron and Kiya, and Jethro's 'gift' of Zipporah as Akhenaten's bride, by allowing him access to the Mount Horeb temple which enshrined the sacred Cave of Hathor (see Chapter 13).

This temple had long served Egypt's pharaohs and queens, and Moses, due to the number of his supporters who continued to press for his reinstatement in Egypt and who guarded it, was still in charge of it. Kiya and Zipporah were to journey there shortly, Jethro pointed out, and he would be grateful to Moses if he could make use of the temple himself, as he had some plans for alchemical work which he was anxious to carry out for reasons of a religious nature. Jethro explained that he had a certain amount of gold which he would need for his devotional work, but he would require assistance in his procedures from the servants of Moses attached to the temple. Moses was glad to agree, and despatched one of his retinue to instruct the temple guards to grant access to Jethro. (Because Queen Kiya was a priestess of Hathor, her right of entry together with a female companion would not have been questioned).

Both Kiya and Zipporah (who knew her father only too well) were greatly concerned about Akhenaten's decision, and sought with all their energy and skill to overturn it. The temple of Hathor in the holy mountain (for the whole of Mount Horeb was sacred to the great goddess Hathor) was a place which enshrined mystical energies rising from the Earth and spiralling out into the stars and beyond to the highest dimensions. Ceremonies had been enacted upon the mountain in loving worship of the Great Mother since humanity had first been born to the planet. The great peak itself was an entirely feminine energy, and it was with the warp and weft of such divine forces that Nin-khursag had woven into human creation the pulsing signals from the spiritual starlight which were

332

Tiâmat's blueprint for her earthly children, who would reside in bodies made from the Earth so that they could love the Earth, and, through loving it, find her, the great Dragon Queen, at the centre of all - in the molten heart of the Earth, in the auriferous sun, in the ancient and ever-new starlight.

These were the very energies which Enlil sought to reverse, and his infiltration of the temple of Hathor was a major triumph for his schemes. He, Anu and Marduk had ensured that the mighty connection with God, visible to all and freely available to all, had been severed from human awareness by the Dolorous Blow. Enlil knew that to increase his reverse-spin power, he had to seek out those places upon the Earth where the Grail energies - the connection energies - still existed, though in a muted form, hidden, secret and veiled since Marduk's action. They were still all-powerful, still ultra-potent fountains of beauty and truth, still expressions of the unfettered eternal feminine, and Enlil loathed them and desired to reverse them with all the corruption in his heart. He had already instigated the production of the white powder in the temple of Hathor, but only intermittently, surreptitiously, and in small measure. Now his expectations were much more ambitious.

Unfortunately, Moses was deaf to the remonstrations of his wives. He did indeed feel indebted to Jethro, and was acutely aware that he might well need to call on Jethro's goodwill and generosity yet again in the uncertain times to come. Zipporah was a bond between the two men, Lord and Pharaoh, and in some respects a tug of war. Jethro used her to bend Moses to his will, whilst she herself made strenuous efforts to awaken her husband to the full implications of his divine vocation and to steer him away from the hooks with which Jethro sought to barb him.

Moses had been protected from the nefarious red and white powders so far by the powerful ministrations of Nefertiti, whose authority prevented the priests from dispensing it to him. Her contention had been that as Moses had been sent by the gods, and was not a member of the Royal Household by blood (she knew the truth, of course), it would therefore offend the gods if he was to receive ritual food not intended for him. The priests would have argued against her, but she was too powerful. Nefertiti's popularity, her royal status (which seemed unusually potent), and her mighty soul forces all conspired to silence them and stop them in their tracks. She commanded them by various means of reiteration not to mess with either Moses or herself. They obeyed.

Jethro, despite the indefatigable efforts of Kiya and Zipporah to prevent it, was given gracious permission to use the Temple of Hathor as he would, and Moses bound a workforce to his service. Jethro also employed many of his own priests and craftsmen, for he had been given a tremendous task to fulfil. Enlil had ordered him to create vast quantities of the white powder. Jethro must oversee its production, and arrange for it to be stored in readiness in chambers within the temple. Enlil explained to Jethro that Moses was to be sent out by 'God's will' (he meant himself, of course) to rule the world, and he, Jethro, would be his first minister. The white powder was a 'holy' weapon which would guarantee military victory after military victory.

The Lord of Midian was further told that Moses did not know that he would rule the world as yet, or even that he wanted to, but it was Jethro's God-given task to slowly enlighten him to his true mission. A gradual, insidious conquest was what was required, Enlil advised him. He knew Jethro could do it, but Enlil issued a solemn warning. Jethro would have to be on his guard against the women! Meanwhile, he was to commence the manufacture of the white powder without delay.

We would ask our readers, in consideration of what we have revealed in Chapter 57, to take special note of the fact that huge stockpiles of the sinister white powder were produced and stored in this temple-laboratory, to be discovered many centuries later by the (very much puzzled thereby) archaeologist W. M. Petrie and his team. Enlil and Noah together devised an unprecedented plan and used vast quantities of the white powder to create an astonishing weapon (a vast mirror made from refined, reverse-spin crystals which surrounded the Earth, and is still in place and active today). For this they needed enslaved miners, which were procured for them, just as they had been in ancient Sumer, when the white powder first came into production.

The manufacture of the white powder was also in progress to create other kinds of weapons of mass destruction, which as children of the nuclear age we can all better understand, even though they far exceeded nuclear power. Nevertheless, the particular weapon to which we make reference and which was the result of such unsurpassed wizardry is so subtle and so all-pervading that we could never have guessed, without direct guidance, that such a phenomenon ever existed, let alone that it is still present amongst us in our own time. Mount Horeb sometimes glowed with the inner furnaces lit at Jethro's command, and smoke often hung over the mountain once this great work to produce the white powder commenced, as Genesis relates.

Chapter Sixty-one

Dark Egypt

Shortly afterwards, Moses encountered the 'burning bush' in the wilderness. Enki and Nin-khursag appeared as a golden fire which gave forth a preternatural burst of light but did not consume or injure. Tiâmat spoke through them, communing with Moses's heart and inner vision, telling him that she was 'I Am That I Am', the 'I Am' within him that was his link to God and that was all-powerful and incorruptible - the true Grail in his heart which Enlil could never obscure unless he was given permission to do so via the free will of the soul. He must now enter into his 'I Am' with all the strength of his spirit, Tiâmat told him, for his great work for humankind had begun. (We remember that Ham, who spread Enki and Nin-khursag's teachings over all the world as the first 'Zoroaster', sanctified priest of the Hallowed Light whose Great Master was Masda, God of Light [Enki and Nin-khursag], was consummate with the mighty 'I Am', and that 'ham', in Sanscrit, means 'I Am'.)

Tiâmat's communion with Moses tells us that she was truly 'Jehovah', or 'I Am That I Am', the literal translation of the name. The true Jehovah appears from time to time in the Bible, but, sadly, the imposter Enlil, who encouraged men and women of religious faith to think of him as Jehovah or Yahweh, manifests much more often. He is marked by the unmistakable stamp of rage, aggression, retribution, hatred, prejudice, judgmentalism, spite and arrogance, and by his threatening, domineering and dictatorial stance and his sinister demands for sacrifice. He delivers death and suffering in a mood of self-congratulation. He is the epitome of heartlessness (of course), and he is an excellent example of what God is not, for we are certain that the true God manifests the very opposite of the qualities cited above in her unconscionable goodness and mercy.

Tiâmat instructed Moses to return to Egypt and rescue the Israelites, whom the new pharaoh had cast deep into bondage. He would prove that he was Egypt's lost - and genuine - pharaoh by performing certain pharaonic rites which, via Tiâmat's blessing, would assume the distinction of miraculous feats. These pharaonic ceremonies were rituals which descended from the tradition of Enki and the Serpent People (the higher Anunnaki). They associated the snake (the serpent, the dragon) with the magical Grail qualities of healing and creation (this last property combined the virtues of fertility or abundance, divine nourishment and immortality).

Therefore, the three miracles consisted of turning a rod (the sacred lance in its true, positive mode) into a serpent, manifesting a dread disease (leprosy) and then showing how the heart made all things whole and perfect (the hand came forth from the breast or the heart as leprous, was returned to the heart centre, and came forth again whole), and turning water into blood (the very creational dynamic Tiâmat used to bring earthly humanity into being, especially by a form of osmosis [Osiris-Moses], as we have mentioned).

Although Moses was given the instruction to appear before the current pharaoh in office (rightfully, of course, it should have been he himself, Akhenaten, who reigned over Egypt), he actually passed the job on to Aaron, who travelled back with him to the Egyptian court. This was because Moses, after receiving appropriate training from his wives, was the conductor of the God-force which gave rise to the miracles, and preferred to remain undisturbed, in a meditative state, whilst they were performed; and so Aaron became his spokesman.

We think that the reason the pharaoh consented to Akhenaten's request that he should lead the Israelites out of Egypt was that he felt threatened by the return of the rightful pharaoh, around whom many stories of wonder circulated, particularly concerning his birth as one of the gods come to earth.

Akhenaten was the first of the kings known as the Armana dynasty. This dynasty ended with General Horemheb, who banned the concept of the Aten (note the Anunnaki 'ten' reference within the word), prohibited any reference, even verbal, to Akhenaten, and removed the Amarna kings (the dynasty originated by Akhenaten) from the formal *King List*. Apparently wishing to stamp out the culture and influence of the Armana era (the devil, for him, was in the blood as well as in the man Akhenaten), he destroyed many of its monuments and other records. However, the Enlil-influenced Horemheb actually reigned and died in Akhenaten's lifetime, during the years that he was in exile.

When Moses returned to Egypt with Aaron, a new dynasty, the nineteenth, had succeeded the Armana rulers. Its founding pharaoh was

Ramesses 1, the pharaoh who received Moses and Aaron and observed their three miraculous rites. He was so unnerved by these that he afterwards had a stela placed within the Cave of Hathor, where he knew that Jethro was working under the sanction of Akhenaten. (Since Horemheb's time, Akhenaten's temple guards had relinquished their defence of it on Akhenaten's behalf, as they had been required to admit, first Jethro, and afterwards Horemheb's agents, to all of which, because of Jethro's wishes, Moses had consented.) This stela described himself, Ramesses 1, as 'The ruler of all that Aten embraces', just to let Moses know that, firstly, because of the three pharaonic rituals he was thoroughly impressed by Aten, Akhenaten's god, and secondly, that Moses ought to be aware that, despite his status as former pharaoh, Ramesses was pharaoh nowadays, and intended to remain so.

The spiritual meaning behind the return of Moses to rescue the Israelites reflects a constant truth. First, Moses (the higher soul) is rejected and cast from power (the banishing of Akhenaten) by the claims of the lower soul, the little earthly self that is not the 'I Am', and that responds to the claims of the world and its self-seeking values. The lower soul seeks to eliminate all references within its greater consciousness to the lost higher soul (Horemheb's eradications), but fails to obliterate its poignant memory. The higher soul then returns to lead its confused lower self out of 'dark Egypt' (the body and its materialistic claims) to the 'promised land' - exalted consciousness and the pure realms of the spirit, attained through the act of ascension.

It was at the point when Enlil realised that he and his emissaries were making little headway with Moses that Pharaoh Horemheb decided to obliterate his memory and the records of his dynasty, by which act of psychological aggression we may deduce that he was a regular consumer of the conical bread cakes! There is no doubt that he was Enlil's agent. It seems that it was because of the good services that he rendered to Enlil that the holy mountain of Hathor (a dedication Enlil despised) was renamed Mount Horeb in his honour, and that Horemheb even provided Jethro with much of the necessary gold, and other noble metals, necessary to create the white powder.

Apart from an expression of the smiting anger of Enlil, and Horemheb's own anxiety that he might be ousted by Akhenaten's growing number of supporters, however, there was another reason why Horemheb was so meticulous in his eradication of the Amarna dynasty from all official records. Queen Kiya, as we shall see, gave birth to a daughter in her mature years.

This daughter did not appear until after Horemheb's death, but nevertheless, Horemheb was a great soldier of Enlil's, and followed his orders unquestioningly. Enlil saw that the daughter of Moses and Kiya might give birth to rightful heirs to the throne of Egypt. He saw that these heirs could well give rise to a new religion in Egypt which would merge with Christianity at its inception, and keep it pure and resonant with the children of Tiâmat who founded it. The double strength of this undefiled religion would of a certainty bring down his best-laid plans. Therefore, Enlil was painstaking in his measures against such an outcome.

As it transpired, these heirs of Moses and Kiya never did return to Egypt. They travelled to the Baltic regions, and the secrets of the Grail were entrusted to the descendants of their followers, many of whom derived from the tribes of Canaan, whose ancestors were Cain and Luluwa. In the far distant future, Tamar, the blessed one, the Divine Woman who was the Holy Grail, embraced these God-touched, wandering people as their queen and goddess, becoming known to history as the Queen of the Gypsies.

Chapter Sixty-two

Moses and the Dragon Queen

And so Moses and Aaron led the children of Israel out of Egypt into the Sinai wilderness. Lilith materialised like a beautiful benediction before Miriam, and led them all safely via a secret route through the Red or Reed Sea, bestowing the blessing of this mystical place upon each one through the agency of Akhenaten's queen. She caused illusion to fall upon the pursuing pharaoh, Ramesses 1, who had accepted Moses and Aaron at first, after conceding that the Aten was a source of true godly power and authority (as the stela he ordered to be erected in the Cave of Hathor at this time bears witness; interestingly, Ramesses 1 is recorded as an enemy of the Aten, and so he was, until the last year or two of his life).

Seeing this heart-opening towards the Aten in Ramesses 1, Enlil had arranged that the pharaoh should be bombarded with schefa-food so that he would turn against Moses. (There are many instances in the Biblical stories of 'God' deciding to 'harden the heart' of the pharaoh; when we realise just who was masquerading as 'God', and the precise means he used to thus harden hearts, everything becomes clear.)

Enlil had every intention of also bending Moses to his will, but he had not succeeded as yet in spite of all his efforts, and he was thoroughly disgusted with the pact Moses had made with Tiâmat through Enki and Nin-khursag via the ridiculous burning bush incident. He thought he would quite like to have Moses slaughtered as he was so unfit for purpose (Enlil's purpose), and so rid himself of the threat he represented once and for all.

After Moses and the Israelites had been rescued by Lilith, however, he reverted to plan B (he would much have preferred Jethro to take over from a deceased Moses, but he just did not seem able to procure this desirable outcome). Ramesses lost his way and perished in the Reed Sea, but Egyptian anger was not quelled, and his successors continued to wage war against the hapless Israelites.

The Reed Sea was a place of beautiful spiritual poignancy to which the Isle of Avalon and the river Tamar in Devon, England (originally a river of reeds) were mystically connected. The reed is associated with the Divine Feminine, with the Voice of God, which whispers in the ear in a hushed, small voice like the wind in the reeds, and with the Holy Breath or Spirit. The Druids revered it to the extent that they regarded it as one of their sacred trees. Lilith had retired to the ethereal dimensions of the Reed Sea after encountering much trouble and tyrannical behaviour from Enlil. She had eventually married him, for the express purpose of protecting Enki and his work for humanity from the havoc that Enlil sought to wreak upon it (her presence was a distraction to him). Her refuge was this lonely, wild, lovely place of reeds.

Some time afterwards, the designated time for Akhenaten's ascent of the holy mountain arrived, and he set off alone, after undergoing certain ceremonies sacred to Hathor, and being anointed by Kiya (Miriam) with spikenard, the precious oil for the head and the feet that was the ritual perfume of the Holy Grail and whose fragrance whispered of its secrets. Although he had banned the worship of a multitude of gods in Egypt, there were certain deities whom he viewed, not as gods, but as sacred routes to the Aten. Hathor was deeply revered as such a supreme and shining one, and it was in her honour that the Israelites, led by Miriam and sanctioned by Moses, fashioned a golden calf as an altar. (Hathor was represented in the Egyptian pantheon as a divine cow who gave her divine milk to succour the universe. Our source tells us that Mary Magdalene bears an even closer association with Hathor than with Isis.)

This golden calf was never intended as an image to idolatrise, but as an important symbol. Miriam and Zipporah were greatly relieved that a quantity of the gold in the temple of Hathor, waiting to be transformed into white powder, could actually be used for other, much more salubrious, purposes! The idea of building a calf rather than a cow was, amongst other symbolism, to remind the children of Israel that Hathor was a blessed and beloved daughter of the Great One - the Aten - not the overarching Deity herself. It also related to the fact that Miriam actually took on the identity of Hathor, so that Hathor shone through her, and spoke through her; and that Miriam was pregnant at this time as if with the calf of Hathor.

One of the most significant reasons for the golden calf, however, was that it was also a symbol of Rebecca the great matriarch's link with the divine Hathor. Rebecca was the mother of Jacob, who became Israel when he slept upon the mountain top and was given the vision of the Holy Grail. This moment, which it was hoped would result in Akhenaten's true ascension and his triumphant return with that part of Tiâmat's knowledge or spiritual infusion (her consciousness made manifest) which could be restored and vouchsafed to the world until Jesus and Mary Magdalene came to rescue the stolen Emerald Tablet, was a very special one for the children of Israel. Their glorious matriarchal inheritance (we remember that this was always the significant line of descent, whose true status was overthrown by Anu and Enlil in favour of the male line) was about to come into its own. From this day forth, they were to be known, not only as the children of Israel, but as the children of Hathor (Rebecca).

The literal translation of 'Rebecca' is heifer or cow - not the humble bovine but the sacred Hathor herself. Rebecca's name was about to be transposed, as Jacob's was, from its mundane to its sublime resonance, and her children were about to receive the divine blessing whose potential she had always borne for them. From Rebecca's lineage, as well as her illustrious sons, came Miriam and, eventually, Mary Magdalene and Tamar - the Holy Grail - herself. This was Rebecca's promise, and her gift, which was about to be bestowed upon the Israelites. In the event, it would remain with them in an openly declared sense for only a few days.

It was ultimately very fortunate that a calf was indeed the requisite symbol for the portent of the moment, because in fact Jethro would not permit the Israelites to have any more gold than was sufficient to make a small calf! He was entirely disapproving of these ceremonies to Hathor, and tried strenuously to dissuade Moses from permitting them or ascending the mountain under their protection and inspiration.

The orgies that the Israelites were said to have indulged in never took place. Instead, a great prayer went up from the people, calling on the Great God, the beloved Aten, to deliver the world from confusion, and to accept the spiritual essence from their hearts and head centres so that the designated portion of the Tablet of Light might be received and understood by Moses, no matter how many blocks, scramblings and general interference Enlil had imposed. (They knew nothing of Enlil as an entity, because he masqueraded as God, so of course they did not identify him by name; but they were aware that some sort of shadow, conscious and intelligent, had fallen over humanity since its earliest days.)

342

We might say that these rites of Hathor, conducted in such devotion by the Israelites, caused the energies of the Grail to descend, and created the conditions by means of which these sanctified Grail forces could be maintained until Moses had fulfilled his commission upon the mountain top. These ceremonies were indeed the pure rites of Hathor essayed by Miriam, created as a superconductor for the prayer and spiritual aspiration of the people, so that Tiâmat could reach them in the fullness of her presence, and they could embrace her essence in full consciousness. As we have said, these rites, designed to aid and uplift him, were to be maintained until Moses descended with what could be given to him of Tiâmat's consecrated Tablet...but they were obstructed and interrupted as he made his descent.

Moses, leaving his companions behind, reached the sanctified mountain top. There, he was blessed with a beautiful realisation of Tiâmat. Well might he have been portrayed with the horns of exalted perception by Michelangelo! (See Chapter 51). These horns depicted, not only his own attuned crown chakra, but the inspired consciousness of the goddess Hathor, whose beautifully curved bovine horns were in themselves symbols of her perfected lunar consciousness (the Star Fire). This outflow of supreme consciousness Hathor directed to Moses, as though she gave him the true Star Fire essence, as in the old days of Sumer.

Miriam was Hathor's conduit in the valley below. The power of the rites she conducted ascended like incense to carry him into heaven. Thus uplifted, Moses, through his unicorn's horn chakra, received Tiâmat's living spirit - her star-emanations, which are received in the brain and the heart but which, just as at Stonehenge, are best recorded for the sake of posterity in the stuff of stone - the body of the Earth herself, which creates an earthly eternalisation of them.

In his heightened state, Moses was able to 'read' this wondrous stone, vouchsafed to him by Tiâmat, because the light of his consciousness resonated with the light secreted in its miraculous heart. Upon this tablet of stone, of purest sapphire which reflected a light of scintillating diamond brilliance, appeared miraculous letters of light - the revelations of the spirit written in matter, sometimes effulgently golden, sometimes of the bright whiteness of angels.

The stone tablet was sapphire because it revealed, in part, the mystery of the Emerald Tablet. The latter was of a higher spiritual frequency than the former, being the heart of hearts of the ray of white light which streams from Tiâmat's consciousness and is an emanation of it. We note that the blue ray's position in the seven rays of the rainbow - the seven rays of creation - is one degree nearer to the Earth, one step down, from the green ray. This was the knowledge that Moses received. Its essence married with the green ray and faithfully carried its vibration.

We might say that it was a further revelation of the Emerald Tablet, but not the Emerald Tablet in its entirety. The attainment of that wonder must wait for the descent of the Divine Couple; but, nevertheless, Moses was certainly a receptacle for knowledge so beautiful that, had he been able to retain it, the entire planet would have been ready for ascension at the time of their coming. It is worth bearing in mind that the holy mountain was famous for its abundance of turquoise, the mystical blue-green stone that was sacred to Hathor, and which the Egyptians used for many of their magical ceremonies. The blue ray correlates to the mind, and the green to the heart. When the mind bends its knee to the heart, the blue ray is in perfect harmony with the green, and the mind thus reflects heart-consciousness. This heart-consciousness is the very essence of the Holy Grail.

Moses began his long descent. (The Bible cites the duration as forty days, but we think this is a symbolic calculation.) Until he was about half way down, his feet sprang upon the ground as if they danced and sang. Then he entered a clouded level of the mountain path, where the smoke from the furnaces of the temple of Hathor (so sadly profaned) billowed and created a hanging garden of mists. There stood Jethro, Lord of Midian. He had first done his utmost to disrupt the rites which were being essayed below, and had then hurried up the mountain at Enlil's command. (It seems that even the name of his place of origin indicates that he was a man who stood at the mid-point of the life forces, and, according to the dictates of his soul, would either ascend or descend. Unfortunately, he chose to descend into the shadow. The name is also reminiscent of midden, which of course is bovine excreta, as though this is what he had reduced the potencies of the temple of Hathor, and his own spiritual perception, to; but perhaps we are stretching a point.)

Jethro came forward, as if to assist Moses, who suddenly felt unaccountably weary. The stone tablet he clasped to his heart (neither large nor heavy) dragged at his arms. He saw that Jethro offered him bread and wine, which he wished to accept because hunger and thirst had swiftly come upon him; but he felt that he should not relinquish the stone tablet, which was dancing with light as if he cradled an angel. Jethro agreed to place the bread and pour the wine into his mouth, so that there was no need for him to let go of his precious burden.

As if she appeared in a dream, Miriam stepped out of the swirling mists. She begged Moses not to touch the bread and wine, because they were derived from evil substances. There was terrible danger within them. She implored him to trust her.

Jethro then spoke up. What Miriam meant by this assertion, he explained, was that there was an exclusively masculine energy in the bread and wine, which had served men well for many ages. It was about time that Moses availed himself of it. He had a mighty mission to fulfil for God, and here he was, being ordered about by his wife, a mere woman!

Jethro begged Moses to consider just how the children of Israel had fallen away from his command. They listened to no-one but Miriam nowadays. It was a disgrace, the way they hung upon her every word. Even Zipporah, his own daughter, who had been reared to know better, would obey Miriam before she obeyed Moses. Was he really going to allow this sorry state of affairs to continue? The children of Israel had been entrusted to him by God, and he was permitting them to slip away from him. Would he not partake of God's ritual of the bread and wine, as in the old days, and reclaim his dignity? It was high time he took the Israelites in hand. There they were, down below, led by the women and involved in shocking orgies that revolved around pagan worship of idols. Was Moses not going to reassert his manhood, with the help of the bread and wine, and put a stop to it?

Uncertainly, for he still hesitated, Moses allowed Jethro to give him the reverse-spin bread and wine, so that he received the reverse-spin communion. Miriam cried out against it, but Jethro's words had hit home. Moses *was* jealous of Miriam, and wished to dominate her.

He swallowed.

Chapter Sixty-Three

The Angry Eye

Immediately, the stone tablet Moses held seemed to jump of its own volition out of his grasp (without his knowledge, his own nerves and reflexes had rejected it). It smashed into many pieces upon the mountainside. Miriam ran away weeping down the winding path.

Enlil then made his presence known to Jethro and Moses, and in a blaze of strange and lurid light, his ethereal form appeared among the rocks. Moses was confused. Was this the great presence whose embrace he had felt upon the mountaintop, come again to help him renew the tablet he had broken? Perhaps it was. He listened impotently whilst Enlil ordered Jethro to wait for his son-in-law at the foot of the mountain. Enlil and Moses had business to conduct.

Enlil instructed Moses to hew a second stone. This stone was another block of sapphire, a black sapphire with a strange, sinister red light in it, like an angry eye (true black sapphire actually reflects pure light). Enlil subsequently did something to the stone (he 'wrote' something in it). After Enlil had finished directing a certain cosmically powerful force into it, all the flesh of Moses which was unprotected by his clothing glowed with a potent radiation. This noticeable glow did not abate for some days, and in fact killed him a year or two afterwards. (As Laurence Gardener points out, there exists incontrovertible evidence which confirms that the Israelites must have moved into Canaan or Palestine ('the Promised Land') very soon after Moses had received the Table of Testimony upon the holy mountain.)

(As we know, Moses did not live to see the children of Israel cross into it. He died of radiation sickness, from which he would have been protected [through the resonance of his own bodily atoms with the reverse-spin forces] had he at any time accepted Enlil's plans to make him ruler of the world. As he did not accept them, Enlil left him to die slowly, a process which commenced from the moment of his encounter with Enlil on the lower half of the mountain.)

Enlil then instructed Moses to inscribe the 'laws of God' upon the stone, which Moses did. These were just the twelve laws of the Negative Confession (two were later lost), and they were nothing remotely remarkable because they were already in existence in Egypt, and had been for some considerable time. They were sensible, pragmatic laws, put in place to govern society. Although they followed the ordinances of God, they were not quite the inspired revelations of God, because they did not lift their students into the consciousness of God, whereupon everything would have become clear. (The Christ Consciousness speaking through Jesus and Mary repeats these laws in the *Gospel of Mary*, in their true form, where they are perceived as emanating from the heart of Divine Love.)

In fact, Enlil was not in the least interested in these commandments. They were *commandments*, and they were almost all set out in negative mode ('Thou shalt *not*'), which would have made him proud at one time, but he had more important things on his mind just at the moment. He had been careful to impregnate the glassy stone with something very deadly, something unimaginably powerful, which, once activated, would lead the Israelites to world domination in no time (relatively speaking). It made the Table of Testimony into an immeasurably destructive weapon of war, and its emanations could not only be physically harnessed, they could be psychically harnessed as well. In addition to its unspeakable material attributes, its terrible power was pregnant with the ability to turn the entire, collective mind of humanity into one giant weapon of mass destruction.

This terrible, lethal stone, Moses bore down the mountain. And as he descended, he grew more and more outraged, with a horrible, self-perpetuating wrath which seemed to enter him as a possessing spirit, at what Jethro had told him about the behaviour of the Israelites (which was actually complete fabrication, designed to tempt him to recoil from the sacred feminine forces, and see them as unclean and unholy). When he reached the foot of the mountain, Lord Jethro and Miriam were waiting for him. There ensued a blazing row, in which Miriam stoutly defended the rights of her people, which Jethro wanted to erode by imposing upon them all sorts of laws and constraints which belonged to his own community, and which had been inspired and powerfully moulded and influenced by Enlil. In other words, the laws were repressive, constricting and burdensome, designed to lead to the creation of an inharmonious, cruel and oppressive society.

Jethro persisted. These were the *laws of God*, he bellowed in staccato tones - the *laws*, the *laws* of God, the *laws*! Moses *would* honour them! And, cowed and weary, Moses accepted these endless, tedious laws. They were not exactly bad laws for the most part, but they were angled and designed to be applied in such a way as to maintain the materialistic, uninspired, status quo. There would be no change for the better.

Miriam was heartbroken and horrified. She had to make a stand. She caused an uprising, and, on Jethro's recommendation (the man had virtually taken over) Moses had her imprisoned. The only secure place (Miriam was a very determined woman, and there were many prepared to rescue her) was inside the mountain, within the temple of Hathor. Here she was confined for seven days, and thank goodness she was, because what transpired by her hand within that fateful week managed to save the world. It was not saved in the way that Tiâmat and her exalted company had laboured to make possible through the advent of Moses and Miriam, had Moses only listened to his intuition, but it was saved nonetheless.

Once Miriam had been marched off, Moses set to work on the Israelites. He was filled with an inextinguishable rage, an unreasoning rage, especially considering his former stance (Margaret Bailey and I have witnessed just such a huge surge of irrational rage towards a woman from a devoted male friend after he had taken the white powder - and we must remember that today's version of the white powder is not nearly so disruptive and deadly as Enlil's original recipe.) He roared around the camp, decrying Hathor and threatening everybody (The Bible says that he even maimed and killed some of the Israelites).

Moses denounced the very idea of the children of Israel also becoming the children of Hathor. And then he dragged the sanctified golden calf onto the fire, built up the flames, and proceeded, following Jethro's instructions, to melt the symbolic object down and create white powder from it. He then forced the children of Israel to drink it in water (there was no time to bake the conical bread cakes, as his aim was to turn the people against Miriam and bring them swiftly under Enlil's control). Enlil must have hugged himself with glee as he watched this procedure. What had helped to inspire the minds and lift the hearts of the Israelites towards Tiâmat via the art of symbolism would now serve to place them utterly in his power!

Henceforth, the Israelites' beautiful worship of the Aten - the Aten which contained All, the Aten which was Tiâmat bearing Oannes within her – would be brutally diverted to worship of 'Adon'. Adon means 'lord', and in this new context it meant, very specifically, Enlil!

Deep within the confines of the abused temple of Hathor, Miriam wept. But her weeping and her sorrow were not passive. She had work to do, and she must work fast.

Summoning the power of the 'I Am' within her, the will-to-good of which she had a thorough command and understanding via her spiritual sisterhood with Hathor, Miriam sent forth a focused force which shattered the glassy 'sapphire' stone that Moses had brought down from the lower part of the mountain. Afterwards, she entered into the deep fastness of the Cave of Hathor, and, kneeling there, sensed the potency welling up from the centre of the Earth, the power beneath. This was the force which Enlil sought to bend to his will and purposes in his production of the white powder. Alone in this sacred place, Miriam called on Tiâmat; and she called upon the Holy Grail. Miriam was of the line descended from Queen Gra-al, as was Moses, Aaron, Nefertiti and Zipporah; and yet it was she, Kiya, Miriam, who held the power secreted in a profound place within her – the power of the Grail.

Miriam called, and her prayer was answered. A gleam of spiritual light brought a beautiful illumination, a flame of brilliant, liquid clarity, to the utter darkness of the sacred cave. Tears of relief and thankfulness fell from Miriam's eyes like crystal rain, glancing through the light and the darkness of her environment. She knew now that all would be well; not perfect, not as it could have been – but all would be well, all would be restored to its rightful course. Miriam entered the unfathomable silence, and dwelt in peace with Tiâmat.

Chapter Sixty-four

The Ark of the Covenant

Before Miriam was released from imprisonment, a divine message had been clearly received by Moses. He must give instructions for an ark to be built in which the shattered stone should be placed. (Moses brought only one stone down from the mountain. Tiamât's stone was lost. The idea of two stone tablets relates to the confusion over the whole incident upon the mountain.) It was to be called thereafter the Ark of the Covenant. This message seemed to come from Enlil, and in some respects he did have a share in it. Enlil wanted the Covenant to be placed in an ark, and he also thought he influenced the design in that a *shem* - a tall conical tower, like a church steeple - was included in the finished vessel. These were to honour Noah and Shem respectively. But Enlil had been fooled.

It was time for the Ark to save the world again, just as it had done in Noah's early days. In this instance, however, it would not be a floating vessel, but it would be, as formerly, a vessel of containment. It was Enki and Nin-khursag who placed the idea of the Ark, ostensibly as homage to Noah, in Enlil's mind (the seven rays of creation expressed in the rainbow arc was Tiâmat's sign), and Enki who whispered to Moses in his dreamless sleep that he should employ a certain craftsman to carry out the work who had been marked with distinction by God. This man duly offered himself for service, a young man hailing from Egypt, with relatives in Canaan. He was the son of Uri, one of Akhenaten's most important ministers. He believed there was a special service for him to perform in relation to his craft, for he had been shown in a dream that he must build a precious vessel to help Moses in his great work.

The young man's name was Bezaleel, a master craftsman and goldsmith. It was said of him that he had been filled with the spirit of the Elohim (the highest angels) in wisdom, understanding, knowledge and mystical craftsmanship. He was put in charge of the construction of the Tabernacle and the Ark, in which, as well as the crumbled Table of Testimony (which still contained its 'angry eye' intact – the epitome of the reverse-spin *ayin*), the 'hidden manna' and the 'shewbread' were to be housed. A distinction is drawn between these two, as well there might be. One was the bread of heaven, the other the bread of hell.

What was the 'hidden manna' that was placed *opposite* the shewbread (a most important, mirror-image point!)? We think the clue is in the tamarisk plant which deposited the manna in the wilderness for the children of Israel to eat. It is simply, so simply, just that – an extract of a plant or herb equating to a wholly *natural* food. The Bible tells us that the manna was placed in a pot of gold, equating to the pot of gold at the end of the rainbow or Ark. The idea of the pot of gold at the end of the rainbow is an ancient Celtic theme, and, as we shall see, the Celts or Gaels descended directly from Aaron, pharaoh and cousin of Moses, and devotee of Miriam. This evocative image was part of Enki and Ninkhursag's teachings, which enshrined many mystical lessons within the symbol of the rainbow, and it is from Aaron and his esoteric knowledge that the story of the pot of gold at the end of the rainbow travelled down the Celtic line of inheritance.

This pot of gold was, literally, at the end of the Ark. What was within it? Did it contain some miraculous, heavenly food, worthy to be called the 'hidden manna'? Yes, it did. What was in the pot of gold was another golden substance, a properly ingestible one - honey! The point of the honey (which is a complete food, and has many astonishing properties) is that it is of the yield of the good Earth, and is a product of that most magical creature of such high significance to the alchemist - the bee. The bee, of course, belongs to a community which is presided over by a queen, and its harvest is one of pure gold: honey. The bee is striped with bands of darkness and light in perfect harmony and accord, creating an immaculate balance. The bee vibrates with the sacred 'aum'. It is miraculous, because, according to scientists, its body weight and structure should make it unable to fly. And yet it flies, because it has overcome the restrictions and limitations of materialism, of matter.

There is a further secret concerning the bee. Esotericists say that it is not of Earth, but that it has its origin on Venus, the only planet in the solar system to spin clockwise, and from where all humanity in our system was generated. The bee gathers pollen from flowers (flow-ers) to serve the queen and create the hive's yield of honey; and the white substance from the tamarisk plant which the Israelites found in the wilderness and called *manna*, meaning 'what is it?', was, of course, akin to pollen. The Israelites' question was provided with the answer, 'It is bread from heaven'. The crucial point is that they asked the question; and their soul (represented by Moses-Miriam-Aaron) answered them in good faith. The lesson to be derived from this incident is that before we feed our bodies and our souls, we should question the authenticity and nature of the food of which we are about to partake. Then, if it is sham food or shewbread, it will be revealed to us as such by our soul.

It is interesting that the old form of the English word 'show', a form actually used in the early English translations of the Bible, is 'shew'. And so we see that the shewbread is showbread, sham bread. It is the sham *shem*. Its promise of heavenly, miraculous nutrition is all a show. It is hellish bread, not heavenly bread.

The difference between the shewbread and the hidden manna is so simple - a lesson for an innocent child. The good Earth herself will feed us; she contains the 'hidden manna'. If only we will eat pure, nourishing wholefoods, foods which require no killing and bloodshed, foods which contain and promise no false 'mystery', (such as is the enticement of the false Divine Woman, the Whore of Babylon, who would feed us with substances that drug us), foods which contain instead the goodness of the Earth, then we will absorb and imbibe the true alchemy, the hidden manna. This lesson resonates with every level of our being.

The Great Mother provides us with food from the Earth which is magically fit for her ascended children as well as her children in their mundane state (which is the state in which we exist nowadays), extending back through the ages, which precedes the (second) coming of the Grail. The Earth herself contains the 'hidden manna', the food of ascension; it is natural, pure and good. We must learn to eat such food if we are to ascend. All the processed foods, especially from the slaughterhouse and from factory farms, must go. We need to ask, 'What is it?'

We must learn the true danger lurking in unwholesome food. The fact that our supermarket shelves are groaning with such produce is a grand master-stroke of Enlil's reverse-spin genius. These foods spell decay and degeneration, of the soul as well as the body, and whilst ever we slay animals, there will also be human bloodshed upon the Earth. We are asked to turn down all food that drugs us and chains us in manacles of materialism.

In the Ark, opposite the hidden manna or the pot of gold at the end of the rainbow (the gold of our ascension, our divine Christ-hood, which is waiting for each one of us as our gift from Tiâmat-Oannes, descending through Jesus of Nazareth and Mary Magdalene, dispensed by the Divine Woman, Tamar) sits the ominous shewbread upon its table. Enlil has learned how to feed that shewbread, like a needle in the vein, into every system that supports our human communities. Let us no longer keep such a table! We must remember that the choice is ours: the hidden manna - or the shewbread.

It is our belief that humanity is now ready to choose the hidden manna, the alchemical manna - the pot of gold at the end of the rainbow. As soon as we truly realise just what sort of a table we are presently gathered around and eating from, we will be ready to overturn it - just as Jesus overturned the shewbread or materialistic tables contaminating the temple. And, of course, this materialistic table that Jesus taught us to overturn without the least hesitation or compunction is the very opposite of the Emerald Table – the real altar of truth within our hearts. Meanwhile, we may ponder upon the bee, the pot of gold or honey, and the hidden manna: the bread of heaven. Such wonderful truths will arise from the potency of these symbols when our understanding fully embraces them!

Over the Tablet of Testimony, the stone table which Enlil had given to Moses and which Miriam had shattered, Bezaleel, who had been tutored in the mystical arts relating to craftsmanship by Enki, built the beautiful 'mercy seat' (an apt name indeed).

This 'mercy seat' was guarded by two great images of angels, members of the cherubim. Knowledge of this order of angels derives from Mesopotamia (Assyria, Akkad, the Chaldees [Ur] and Babylon). The word cherubim or karibu is Akkadian; it means 'one who intercedes' or 'one who intercedes via prayer' and is associated with wisdom. Ancient Assyrian art depicts cherubim as vast, winged angels with human faces and the bodies of guardian beasts, such as lions, bulls, sphinxes or eagles. They were traditionally placed at entrances to consecrated places as spiritual protectors.

Let us look further at the Cherubim, because everything about them proclaims the reason why Tiâmat decreed that her faithful servant Bezaleel should put them in place above the false Table of Testimony, that tablet of stone which had been infused with such guileful and sinister intention by Enlil, and given to Moses as if it constituted the Emerald Tablet itself. These particular angels had been set before the Tree of Life (Tiamât's consciousness as it is given forth to humanity, manifesting in objective form as the Emerald Tablet) so that Enlil, although the official holder of the Emerald Tablet, should be prevented from attaining any more of its knowledge than he already possessed.

Enlil was able to hide the Emerald Tablet away from humanity, he was able to issue a false one and circulate it around the world; but the Cherubim stood guard at the gates of the confines of its sacred knowledge, and upon it Enlil's consciousness could not further obtrude. The Cherubim are the wielders of the flaming, revolving sword which protects the holy Tree, and are known as 'the flame of whirling swords', veritably an out-breathing of flame from the Dragon Queen's heart, because the Cherubim are the pulse of God's 'highest and chiefest potencies, sovereignty and goodness' (Philo). The Cherubim are in possession of many eyes, which enable them to stand guard comprehensively, protecting from above, below, and all around, and are of the *ayin*, the sacred consciousness of God.

So mystically skilled, so potent in his soul, was Bezaleel, that he was able to fashion images into which the spirit of the Cherubim actually entered. (The angels needed some kind of form with which to withstand the terrible frequencies emanating from the tablets, which, according to the composition of the statues and the artistry with which they were made, helped them to throw a protective forcefield around the hideous energies of the stone fragments, so that they were contained within a ring of light.) The entire Ark of the Covenant was forged from metals which, after being alchemically treated by Bezaleel and his servants, fulfilled a similar function. Much lavish finery was demanded by Enlil for 'his' Ark; but even its *shem* was designed around Aaron's 'budding rod', the magical serpent rod or lance which Tiâmat had blessed. And so Bezaleel appeared to obey Enlil's directives, but was secretly faithful to the wisdom of Miriam and the true God.

Enlil, thank goodness, was fooled throughout, and although in Exodus he is seen to encourage Moses in aggressive acts of warfare:

> ...behold, I drive out before thee the Amorite, and the Canaanite, and the Hittite, and the Perizzite, and the Hivite, and the Jebusite. Take heed to thyself, lest thou make a covenant with the inhabitants of the land whither thou goest, lest it be for a snare in the midst of thee: But ye shall destroy their altars, break their images, and cut down their groves...For thou shalt worship no other God: For the LORD, whose name is Jealous, is a jealous God: For I will cast out

the nations before thee, and enlarge thy borders:
(Exodus, 34:11-14 & 24)

The divinely inspired skill of the alchemist Bezaleel ensured that the Israelites were protected from the savagery of the stone.

By Tiâmat's mercy, through Bezaleel's magical sealing and containing skill, they never understood the cosmic power for ill they wielded, nor did they ever call upon its lethal potency.

The sort of ranting conveyed above is typical of Enlil, and one can imagine him fairly frothing at the mouth as he revels in the prospect of ethnic cleansing, counsels poor Moses and the Israelites strictly against peace negotiations or judicious, peaceable conduct, and incites 'his' people to religious hatred and violence, topping all with a maniacally egotistical chest-beating concerning his right to total allegiance, and a big bribe, designed to appeal to the worst in human nature, to encourage the Israelites to express it. And he gives his name at last - not Jehovah or Yahweh, 'I Am That I Am', but a name that means 'Jealous'! All of the passage quoted above relates in reality to Enlil's fevered attempts to ensure that the Israelites did not worship at the altars of Enki, Nin-khursag and Lilith, and were not swayed by their teachings, for theirs were indeed the true altars in place in Canaan, although others existed which belonged to immigrant communities that enjoyed a measure of the religious tolerance that the teachings of Enki sought to promote.

It is true that these dreadful outbursts endorsing savagery and warfare are hidden within the endless listing of Jethro's Midianite laws, which are of course Enlil's laws (he obsessed about law-making, and nothing delighted him more than to craft them for every conceivable human activity, so that the miasma of his oppression might linger everywhere, over everything). Nevertheless, it might make us pause and wonder how we could ever have been deceived into thinking that these irate explosions of venom were the word of God.

Enlil, of course, was doing his best to groom Moses for world domination. He wanted Canaan, and within it Jerusalem where the powers of the Grail were secreted, to be the centre of a global autocracy run by him via the Israelites. Whenever the Israelites gathered for battle, when they marched into their promised homeland to claim it, the Ark of the Covenant was unfailingly borne before the troops on a litter (there were two rings on either side of it for staves, so that it could thus be carried).

Despite his very best efforts, Enlil could never turn the heart of Moses towards a lust for global power, nor could he ever properly communicate to the Israelites just how cosmically powerful the Ark of the Covenant was, or how they should use it. The spiritual power of Bezaleel's art, which contained the highest angelic potencies as well as those of Enki and his consorts, soared above all, and the exquisite mercy seat, the seat of divine power, poured forth the mercy of celestial protection, and kept the Israelites, and the world, safe from its hideous potential.

Tiâmat's brooding presence over the mercy seat gave rise to the beautiful concept of the Shekinah, the feminine spirit of mercy and wisdom who was believed by the Hebrews to intercede with Jehovah (Enlil) on behalf of humanity, using her influence to ensure that he showed a degree of mercy to his flock. The Four Sacred Persons within the Supreme Deity (Mother, Father, Daughter, Son) was a very ancient perception of God which preceded the Sumerian civilisation and reached back to the time when there was a general understanding of Tiâmat, 'She who bore them all', upon the Earth, for Tiâmat held these principles within herself and gave birth to them.

Enlil inherited this timeless understanding of God in the eyes of his followers, so that he was seen as the generator and expression of the Four Sacred Persons, who existed within him (the name Yahweh or YHWH denoting the tetrad of the Four Persons represented by one consonant each, as the Hebraic language traditionally contains no vowels).

Enlil became very irritated with this concept of himself amongst his worshippers, however, and although he did indeed have a wife, daughter and son (Ashtoreth, Anath and Baal respectively) who had remained with him when he was 'cast out onto the earth', the idea that they should be worshipped alongside himself because of some outmoded esoteric rubbish originally pertaining to Tiâmat drove him into fits of indignation. He expressly forbade the worship of his family, attaching all sorts of penalties to the adoration of Baal in particular, but also banning homage to Ashtoreth and Anath as heresy. He even added the proscription of the worship of Baal to the original twelve commandments, although Tiâmat ameliorated this profanity by breathing into it a new and ancient meaning which warned against the worship of materialism.

Although he conceived of himself as the one, all-male, all-powerful, Godhead, to his frustration Enlil could not convey this satisfactorily to his followers for many centuries. He stressed his idea of himself to Abraham, and to Moses, and they certainly understood the concept of' 'one' God that was 'most high', but he was not able to finally persuade his worshippers en masse to forsake the tetrad and adore him alone until after the time of Moses, even though Enlil had already named the act as blasphemy.

The Shekinah was identified as Anath, Enlil's daughter, from whom perhaps the word 'anathema' derives in its oldest form, because mercy and the idea of a female deity was indeed anathema to Enlil. The word Shekinah means 'to dwell', but it was not Anath who dwelt in the mercy seat. She and Ashtoreth worked with Lilith and Nin-khursag to try to bring some sanity to Enlil (another reason for Lilith's marriage to him), but in many ways Anath and Ashteroth were damaged, ravaged higher Anunnaki women, who had occasionally lost sight of the true dimensions of their womanhood and their inheritance from Tiâmat because of Enlil's abuses.

Anath was a goddess of war and aggression as well as one who strove to uphold the flame of mercy and love. She was a goddess of sexuality and conflict, which would make perfect sense of her role as Enlil's daughter. Although there is a rabbinic tradition that as soon as Bezaleel built the Tabernacle which held the mercy seat above the Ark of the Covenant, 'the Shekinah descended and dwelt among the children of Israel', it was the spirit of Tiâmat and her fully realised daughters who occupied the mercy seat, not Anath. She was also known as Inanna, and her sad, tortured, poignantly beautiful and spiritually triumphant history is intimately linked with Enlil's confusion and darkening light. Lilith was Inanna's handmaiden, or, more specifically, her companion and carer, for Inanna was a manifestation of the traumatised, wounded feminine principle.

Enlil made sure that the Ark of the Covenant seemed very beautiful and impressive in all its rich array and magnificent apparel. In truth, only the mercy seat was beautiful. The Ark of the Covenant is a terrible travesty, the darkest talisman of the ravening death forces.

If scientists were ever able to examine and analyse the contents of the Ark, we feel they would not turn up very much, just as a superficial analysis of the white powder found in the Great Pyramid concluded only that it consisted of grains of feldspar and mica, and was unable to fathom its real mystery.

357

Our present-day materialistic, positivist sciences simply will not allow the doors of our perception to open onto the true wonders of the universe. As far as the Ark is concerned, this is beneficial, because in its case the marvels of the cosmos have been perverted into destructive channels. The secrets of the Ark of the Covenant aside, we must, nevertheless, soon progress into a many-splendoured science which can fulfil the measure of our souls. So much that is awe-inspiring awaits us in these dimensions, once our scientists will dare to step away from the confines of their present philosophy, which holds them in stiflement and thrall. When they begin to do this, it will be clearly revealed how unscientific the present-day attitude really is. There is currently a tremendous emotional attachment to materialism and the limitations of the intellect, which is itself seated in child-like and egotistical fears.

The Ark of the Covenant may have been considered a wonder, but the true wonder lies in the Holy Grail, for the Ark holds nothing but a distorted mirror image of its qualities, its potential and its blessing, apart from its promise of the Shekinah, which is of course a promise of Tiâmat.

Chapter Sixty-Five
Miriam

As Miriam was at last escorted out of her prison, she caused a vibration to sound deep in the bowels of the Earth. It brought a fall and a crumbling of stone which effectively buried the temple of Hathor and sealed off all access to it. She had warned everyone present in the temple to flee it beforehand. They heeded her warning, because Miriam was an adored figure among the Israelites, and even among the Egyptian servants of the temple, to whom she was still their rightful queen.

Miriam's huge relevance to Moses's mission has been overlooked to the point of absurdity in the Old Testament. The children of Israel esteemed her and followed her guidance more than they valued and listened to Moses, and it was this uncomfortable truth which prompted Moses to swallow the red and the white powder when it was offered to him by Jethro, and, ultimately, rush down the mountain, engage in a furious row with Miriam, order her incarceration, and then, after venting his ungovernable rage further on the innocent Israelites, force-feed them the white powder himself.

Miriam, or Queen Kiya, had an interesting heritage. Her father was the pharaoh Amenhotep lll, step-father of Moses, and her mother was a Mesopotamian princess, very much connected to the lore and traditions of the higher Anunnaki. Not only this, but the dynasty to which her mother (Gilukhipa) belonged originated from Cain and Luluwa and their famous descendant, the spiritual luminary Ham. The family had strong connections to Canaan and the land of Canaan (now called Palestine), and had been of the wandering people who followed, first Cain and Luluwa, and then their descendant Canaan. Queen Kiya's ancestors could therefore be traced back directly to Enki, Nin-khursag and Lilith (through Eve, the daughter of Nin-khursag and Enki, who bore Cain; and through Lilith, who bore Luluwa to Enki). She was thus graced with a Dragon Queen heritage from both Nin-khursag and Lilith, and echoed Nin-khursag's mother's name, Queen Ki, Lady Earth, wife of the (once) great Anu, and Lilith's mother's name, the enigmatic queen of the netherworld - that unendingly mysterious world beneath our feet in all its unfolding dimensions - who was called Eresh-Kigal.

The sacredness of the Earth and its most mystical point - the Grail - is emphasised in Queen Kiya's name. She was known at the Egyptian court as 'the Royal Favourite; the Child of the Living Aten'; and these titles were bestowed upon her because of her very unique and exceptional connection to the Dragon Queen, who is referenced in each case. She was the chosen earthly daughter of Tiâmat, and from the first, even before she was born, she was deeply identified with Hathor, and received this deity's blessing in her secret cave.

Intriguingly, there is a direct line of association extending from Tiâmat, to Hathor and the Anunnaki goddesses, to Rebecca, Jacob's mother, to Queen Kiya, to the Queen of Sheba, to Mary Jacob, and at last to Mary Magdalene. Mary Magdalene was the ultimate and supreme 'daughter' of this line, the Christ daughter who, in a mystical sense, gave birth to her 'mother', Tiâmat or Tamar, thereby returning the most Holy Grail to earth, just as Jesus, the divine son, handed the priceless Emerald Tablet back down to John on earth, John who represented Oannes, the Supreme Father.

And so the ineffable Daughter and Son handed back the divine authority to the Mother and the Father, whose foolish (not yet quite divine, or at least unaware that they were divine) children of planet Earth had managed to disconnect themselves from it.

There is in Queen Kiya's name the suggestion of a 'key', and in all its senses this designation may be applied to her. She was the 'greatly beloved' of her parents and of Nefertiti, who nurtured, protected and tutored her. Later, she would become the 'beloved of Amon', the beloved of Akhenaten. She carried the heritage of the royal houses of Egypt, Canaan and Mesopotamia, all of them contiguous countries, and all bearing the secrets of the Grail, for it was from Egypt, with its older Mesopotamian and land of Nodh connections, that Jesus and Mary Magdalene drew succour for their mission. (The Lord's Prayer is a rendition, almost word for word, of a much earlier hymn to Osiris, Jesus and Mary were brought up together in their early years in Egypt, Mary Magdalene prepared herself for her spiritual assignment in a temple in Alexandria, Tamar herself was born in this Alexandrian temple, and both Jesus and Mary often quoted texts from the sacred teachings of Isis during their three-year undertaking. Both baptism and communion were associated with the rites of Isis, as was their sacred marriage in Bethany. When we learn that Tamar, the Divine Woman and the Holy Grail, is linked intimately with the identity of Isis, this comes as no surprise.)

Kiya, through her daughter, the sister of her son Tutankhamun, who married one another, consolidated the succession which would ultimately descend to the Royal House of Judah, to King David and eventually to Mary Magdalene, Jesus, Tamar and John, the Four Sacred Persons represented on earth, each of them of this bloodline. It is important to understand that the bloodline itself is not sacred, and it is special only in that it facilitates the descent of highly evolved souls, reaching up as a heavenly staircase even to the most exalted among the Nephilim. It was a sort of halfway-house rendition of the Grail.

We stress this because we believe it is essential to avoid harbouring superstitious beliefs concerning the bloodline, which would smack of racism and materialism. The bloodline *was* a tool of facilitation, but if it happened that an evolution-refusing, hidebound soul should descend through it, that soul would remain in limitation and self-imposed bondage unless and until, of its own volition, it began to make the effort to cast off its fetters. Simply because it had descended via Tiâmat's special bloodline would not guarantee it anything, except perhaps certain opportunities which would remain entirely inactive and redundant until it began to strive after its own spiritual heights and profundities.

We cite the example of Judah himself, not exactly a salubrious soul if the reports concerning him are true (he sold his brother Joseph into slavery, unwittingly used his daughter-in-law Tamar (several Tamars feature in the Old Testament) as a prostitute, and then attempted to have her thrashed and burned alive for adultery when he learned she was pregnant, even though she was a widow!). This particular Tamar of the Old Testament, who carried the royal name above all other royal names, knew deep within her soul that she must advance the special bloodline, at whatever cost to her inclination, dignity, and even her life; but it progressed through many souls with feet of clay, as well as many whose divinity had spread its wings, before it reached its ultimate goal.

A text of great antiquity called the Book of Jasher records the historical details relating to Miriam. Although the Old Testament scribes wrote their version of the story centuries after it had occurred, Jasher himself had the advantage of being present as a witness to what he wrote. He was with the Israelites before they left Egypt, his birthplace, and was royal staff bearer to Moses. He seems to have been a trusted and punctilious servant, and his book was highly respected by the ancients. Allusions to it in Joshua and Samuel cite it as an invaluable reference book concerning the grass-roots history of Moses, but because of its controversial aspects it was strategically ignored when the compilers of the Old Testament made their decisions regarding inclusion and exclusion of available texts.

The Book of Jasher makes it incontrovertibly clear that it was actually Jethro, not Moses, who became the mouthpiece of 'Jehovah', and that Jethro's strident will effectively sidelined Moses's authority. Jethro began to detail his own traditional Midianite laws to the Israelites, including the Commandments, as soon as Moses reached the foot of the mountain, as though all power of command belonged to him.

There has been some controversy regarding the Ten Commandments since the Egyptian Negative Confession was discovered. It suddenly became uncomfortably obvious that these laws which Moses had received on the holy mountain were neither original nor particularly inspired. They were fair enough as they went, but they were rather obvious, and many civilisations had been trying to abide by them, generally speaking, for long ages. Eternal truth does not glitter glamorously, of course, and simplicity is always its essence. Having conceded as much, it is somewhat tempting to imagine that the muttered comments from some of the less devout Israelites in the crowd around Moses once he had descended the mountain might have included "Tell us something we don't know", "Is that what we've traipsed all this way to hear?" and "We could have told you those before you set off and saved you the trouble of the climb". These people had been educated and cultured in magnificent and esoterically-adept Egypt, and, quite frankly, they would have heard it all before.

Of course, now we know that Enlil could hardly be bothered with what went on the stone tablet, and that he just gave Moses something to write to keep him occupied whilst he was busy infusing a commodity of an unimaginably different nature into the stone, everything becomes clear.

In full realisation of this, Miriam asserted her will against Jethro's encroachment when Moses could not. As her husband stood helplessly before them at the foot of the mountain whilst Jethro took over and began to pontificate, the Dragon Queen in Miriam stepped forward in a blaze of conviction, demanding to know why the ancient traditions (the rites which had their genesis in Enki and Nin-khursag's temple in ancient Sumer) were to be supplanted by those of another, younger nation, one considerably less established in the sacred wisdom of the mystery schools?

'Shall Jethro instruct the Hebrews?' she vociferated. 'Are the children of Jacob without understanding?'

Jasher states specifically that 'the voice of the tribes of the congregation was on the side of Miriam'. It was at this point that Moses, feeling more and more out of control of the situation, particularly relating to the dimensions of his rising anger which was swiftly taking on the proportions of a fit of madness, ordered that Miriam should be imprisoned. The Israelites lamented his decision, and would not leave him alone concerning it. Jasher further reports that: 'the people of Israel gathered themselves together unto Moses and said, Bring forth unto us Miriam our counsellor.' Even the terrible incident of being force-fed with the white powder did not break their allegiance to this woman, whom they considered their leader.

Aaron, in particular, valued Miriam highly, and set her authority above that of Moses. It was Aaron who gave his sacred rod to Bezaleel to provide the model for the *shem* included in the Ark of the Covenant - and he gave it at Miriam's behest. Aaron consulted and conferred with Miriam constantly, and we see that Moses had struggled with his ego regarding Miriam from the beginning of their relationship, alternately adoring and resenting her. Aaron was the founding father of the Scottish and Irish Gaels (a title very similar to 'Gra-el', the Hebrew rendition of Princess Gra-al's name), via his daughter, Princess Scota, who generated the race. The Gaels commemorate Miriam and her supremely royal Dragon Queen heritage in their own inheritance of her flame-red hair, for she, Aaron and Moses all belonged to the Egyptian royal family in descent from Ham, which, of course, had its origins in Mesopotamian antiquity. The book of Aaron, whose author was Hur, grandfather of the illustrious Bezaleel, tells us:

> Miriam from hence became the admired of the Hebrews;
> every tongue sang of her praise. She taught Israel; she tutored
> the children of Jacob - and the people called her, by way of
> eminence, the Teacher. She studied the good of the nation, and
> Aaron and the people hearkened to her. To her the people bowed;
> to her the afflicted came.

It is worth noting that, although Enlil constantly hi-jacked the Israelites' perception of the Aten and strove his utmost to translate it into his own currency, it was indeed the Aten (Tiâmat - in whom Moses perceived and worshipped the Eternal Father as well as the encircling, mysterious Feminine: the void, the unutterable mystery, which Moses called 'the Aten'), that the children of Israel worshipped and set at the centre of their lives. Even though they were forbidden to speak the word 'Aten' in favour of a direct reference to himself – 'Adon', or 'Lord', Enlil was finding this 'one God' business a double-edged sword. At first he had encouraged it, because one of his favourite imperatives was that *he* should be set above all and adored as the 'most high God'. Now it seemed as though the whole concept was highly dangerous, and kept opening up the consciousness of the people to the despised Tiâmat!

Enlil, in the end, had been terrified of Abraham's conception of the One God (derived from Enki's original teachings), because it kept slipping beyond his command, reaching to Tiâmat and almost restoring the Earth's connection to her. He had managed to deal with that emergency successfully, and, after applying himself with the full force of his power and cunning to the problem of Akhenaten, he had also managed to bring Akhenaten's perception under his dominion, even calling himself by Tiâmat's name ('I Am That I Am', or Jehovah, and YHWH, the tetrad, the Four Sacred Persons), and was acknowledged by Akhenaten when he did so. As far as Enlil was concerned, he seemed to have brought the situation under control, and had accomplished his mission.

Because of this heartbreaking state of affairs, Miriam parted from Moses when she was eventually released from prison (poignantly enough, on the eighth day, associated with Ascension). She conferred with Aaron, and he, as a royal priest, agreed in his lifetime to block the custom of feeding shewbread to the kings who would arise from the established nation of Israelites in Canaan, so that they might be delivered of its curse. (He also did his best to prevent the priesthood from ingesting the shewbread, but because of the strong contingent initially headed by Jethro, his valiant attempt was unsuccessful). Despite Jethro, the original vision of Moses continued to inspire his people, and some aspects of his mission were partially triumphant. Ultimately, he listened to Aaron, and grieved for his beloved lost wife. He eventually gave his support to Aaron's condemnation of the shewbread, especially as he intuitively knew that the substance which had harmed him and caused his painful,

364

lingering death was connected to the white powder. Through his sacrifice and his aspiration, the Israelites maintained the spiritual strength to hold Enlil in containment, and to prevent his destruction of the world.

Miriam, with many devout followers, wandered in the Sinai wilderness, and in Caanan, for many years. She gave birth to her daughter, the 'calf of Hathor', who further secured the renewed grounding of the Grail energies in that country. Often, on her travels, Miriam would order a circle of small stones to be laid out on the ground in a specific location. A triangular shape built of similar stones would be placed inside the circle, and in these rings of stone Miriam taught her people regarding the secrets of ascension (in later years this knowledge travelled with her followers to the gypsies of the Baltic regions). We believe that such triangles exist invisibly in many of the stone circles of Britain and elsewhere. When Miriam died, the Israelites were distraught - not only her own personal followers, but her wider supporters. The Book of Jasher relates that she died in Kadesh:

> The children of Israel mourned for Miriam forty days;
> neither did any man go forth of his dwelling. And the
> lamentation was great, for after Miriam arose up no one
> like unto her;...and the flame thereof went out into all the
> lands...yea, throughout all Canaan; and the nations feared
> greatly.

The discovery of Queen Kiya's tomb opposite that of her son, Tutankhamun, the son of Moses, is a hugely significant and exciting find. After a prediction on the part of the historians and archaeologists involved that the unearthing of this tomb would rewrite ancient history, nothing much seems to have come of it. When it was first disclosed to the public, Margaret Bailey felt that it would reveal that a formal tradition of the coming of Mary Magdalene existed beside that of the coming of the Messiah. I saw in the footage of the news item what looked like a funerary image of a queen with rippling red hair, although this was no doubt an imaginary impression. Either way, it seems not a little mysterious that the conclusions so far drawn from analysis of what is within the tomb are so tame and inconclusive. In short, we feel that some sort of cover-up may be going on, with suppression and withdrawal of evidence. Only time will tell if our assumption is accurate!

Chapter Sixty-six

Down With Enlil!

As Alice and the March Hare argued between them at the Mad Hatter's tea-party: it is important to say what you mean, and to mean what you say. We hope you will join with us when, in honouring their advice, we chorus 'Down with Enlil!' We might well add, 'and about time, too!'

Of course, ridding ourselves of Enlil does not mean deposing anyone, or marching against a foe in an act of war. The glorification of war in all its many differing aspects is exactly what Enlil has promoted down the centuries. The war that we are required to fight is of the subtlest kind, because it necessitates mastery of our lower self. That is the level of life under Enlil's control. It is where his tentacles are wrapped around us in unrelenting malice.

When Miriam closed off access to the temple of Hathor, the production of the white powder became a problem. It could still be manufactured, of course, but not in the quantities that the refined energies of the Cave of Hathor made possible. After Moses and Aaron banned the ritual ingestion of the white and the red powder by the kings and did their utmost to block its dispensation to the priests, the preparation and administering of the powders became subject to severe restriction. Canny as ever, and still with Noah very much on board, Enlil and his followers found a way to feed its substitute to those people on earth who came under his sway. He used subtle, astral means, so that those who were willing could receive it, via a kind of etheric feeding tube, directly into the chakra-system. Here it takes on the colour of a violently bright, eerily beautiful gold, being the ethereal part of reverse-spin gold. Its effect is not quite as spectacular as the physical powders, but it performs its function efficiently enough.

Miriam's dramatic effect on world history in one of its aspects was that, once she had acted against the distribution of the white powder, it was no longer given as a birthright to the kings (even occasionally including queens and princesses, if we consider Princess Tharbis's case), and therefore broadcast automatically to their respective nations.

Although, via Enlil's machinations, the kings continued sometimes to receive it, especially if they expressed pronounced spiritual greatness (such as King David himself), the procedure was by no means wholesale, as it had been before.

The huge significance of this is that, once the white powder could no longer generally be fed to the kings as a physical substance, it could forthwith no longer be imposed on anyone without their consent. The subtle white powder, fed into the consciousness via the etheric body in concentrated degree by Enlil's revised method, could now be wholly rejected by the recipient. The priests, of course, continued to broadcast it etherically on Enlil's behalf, and many of the populace who thus received it did not reject it outright. Even those who refused to receive it were afflicted and handicapped by it - a situation which still persists today, as the promised revelation concerning Enlil's special weapon will demonstrate to us. Nevertheless, the threat of overwhelming obstruction to human freewill was removed, and the global prospect brightened. Enlil was frustrated in his attempts to lure us into a helter-skelter descent of his perpendicular path of doom.

We have within our heads a magical stone, like the toad stone of legend which folktale relates is played over by many mottled hues of gold. It is indeed, although the colour of the stone, as we shall see, is actually a heavenly, bright sapphire blue. This stone, at the physical level of life, comprises the slightly more than 5% dry weight of noble metals (members of the platinum group) which exist naturally within the human brain. These metals are iridium and rhodium in what Laurence Gardner calls the 'high-spin state', which is not the negative spin that Enlil imposed on his powders, but what can and should be the high-spin state of true ascension, as long as we are careful not to get waylaid and tempted off-course into Enlil's waiting dimension! It is this stone which will be activated by the Holy Grail, when we receive the blessing and the teachings of the Grail (the teachings of the Emerald Tablet).

It is this stone, too, which Enlil wants to make dysfunctional. To this end, he dispenses the white powder (seemingly more dangerous than the red, although the red certainly plays its part in focusing the death forces) via subtle means to the susceptible people of earth (a considerable number of us). Not understanding how to conclusively refuse it, we take the false bread, the false wine, to a greater or lesser degree, and receive communion with the false god, the god of retribution, violence and wrath, of both blind and wanton cruelty, of materialism, intolerance, self-seeking values and the self-perpetuation of misery - the god who makes the darkness glitter as if with the promise of good things. This false communion creates the 'mad hat' of Enlil, a dark enclosed tomb which sits as an ethereal shadow over the Stone of Ascension within our consciousness and within our actual heads, sending it into a death-like sleep so that we build our world as in a confused dream.

In *Alice in Wonderland*, the Mad Hatter admits to Alice that he has damaged his relationship with Time (Father Saturn, whose positive forces Enlil chokes, distorts and reverses), and so the backwards-rotating, nonsensical world Alice finds herself in is frozen in time, unable to progress. The point at which time froze was six o'clock, which is of interest, not only because six o' clock is definitely *not* the usual Victorian tea-time hour (Lewis Carroll wrote during the Victorian era, during which 'tea' – a pot of tea with sundry sweet and savoury snacks - was served between 3 and 4 pm), but particularly because the figure 6 is the reverse of 9, the number of the soul and of the Divine Feminine. Somehow this divine number has been turned on its head and petrified in a death-like trance. It seems that the Mad Hatter, presiding over the tea-party (human society), is an expression of the spell under which Enlil holds humanity. He teaches us that whilst ever we wear the 'mad hat' of Enlil, the cycles of human development will really take us nowhere, because, despite the appearance of progress, we will just endlessly repeat the same old mistakes until we eventually destroy our civilisation.

In his book, *Fingerprints of the Gods*, Graham Hancock draws on convincing evidence to show that advanced human culture is much older than we imagine, and that we have visited catastrophe on ourselves over and over again. In the varying traditions of many contemporary tribal peoples across the globe, such a worldwide catastrophe is forecast for the very near future. We say that humanity can and will transform what is so direly predicted, because, thanks to the Grail, we are about to dispossess ourselves en masse of our 'mad hats'.

It is worth noting that the atmosphere around the Earth, which gives us our beautiful blue skies, represents just over 5% of the weight of the Earth, the same ratio as the iridium and rhodium content within our brains. These exalted metals in their high-spin state, which constitute the Stone of Ascension within us, create the ethereal atmosphere in the brain which, when activated correctly, will integrate our earthly brain with the ascension of our individual consciousness. This is the meaning of the sapphire blue ray which Moses received from Tiâmat at the summit of the holy mountain. The ethereal part of our brain, correlative to the atmosphere of the planet, is what will carry us upwards, once it is activated by the knowledge of the Emerald Tablet.

This knowledge can only be received, understood and sparked into operational life by the heart, our own Emerald Tablet or Grail residing within us; but it is the mind, the sapphire, which must prepare and attune itself, and kneel in service to the heart, before the heart can come fully into its own and give forth its spiritual life-forces. Therefore, our mind needs to receive the Emerald Tablet as teachings or in book form, so that we may stimulate its essence within us, and translate its spiritual knowledge into a form which we can faithfully apply to our earthly lives. The profounder essence of the Emerald Tablet cannot be received or understood in the earthly mind, but only by the God-attuned intelligence which dwells as a spiritual flame, deep in the secret recesses of the heart. When both forms of intelligence, the earthly and the divine, begin to work together within us, the power of the heart is no longer obstructed.

In preparing ourselves for the Grail, then, we need to overturn Enlil's rule.

How do we get rid of Enlil? We stop feeding him and his power-source! We do this by awakening from our heavy sleep in materialism (imposed by his design) and opening our consciousness to the spiritual reality of life. We do it by ridding our lives of cruelty in all its aspects - our own, perhaps unconscious, cruelty to others - our cruelty and violence of language, our cruelty and violence of thought; our cruelty to ourselves in imposing alienating value-systems on our lives which we flog ourselves mercilessly to maintain; and the cruelty inherent in our everyday lives through the exploitation of abused workers, of animals (whose terrible collective suffering, which we ourselves thoughtlessly inflict, is even greater than that of human beings) and of the planet.

We do it by properly honouring and obeying the sacred feminine principle, which encourages us to be wise, to be nurturing and merciful, to see things by the light of the intuition and to be unafraid of the astonishing realities this light will reveal, and which will entail a final laying-down of the male supremacism that still exists and is still part of the societal framework and mores of our countries, in the west as much as in the east; then the sacred masculine principle will arise in its true guise and glory, and men will come to see in wonderment who they truly are.

We do it by sacrificing our need to be angry and resentful, contemptuous and demeaning, towards others, by recognising that we are children of the same all-embracing God and that this Divine Spirit loves each one of us equally, whatever and whoever we are. We do it by halting the urge within us to dominate or dictate, and by allowing an unshakeable respect for others, an empowered harmlessness, an inspired and loving tolerance, to flower within our attitudes to life.

We do it by calling on and trusting our inner strength to resist the temptation to bow helplessly and succumb before those principles or those persons who would dominate or dictate to us. And we do it especially by refusing to bow to the tyrants of fear, shame, self-doubt, and the tyranny of the will of the little self - the self of earth which is not the 'I Am', called the self-will or the lower will - which always wants to dominate and dictate to us. Yet, most of all, we do it by reclaiming our most holy dragon heritage, granted to us from our very beginning in an ineffable act of love by Tiâmat, which we have allowed Enlil to take from us.

In this mighty and sanctified undertaking, we reconnect with the God-sourced magic in our hearts which will guide us with perfect, unfaltering steps through all of the above-mentioned accomplishments, so that we achieve an ideal balance between the boiling chasms on either side of every principle we seek to embrace and express. And we do it by cheerfully forgiving ourselves on the occasions when we 'fail' to live up to all these high expectations! Failure is not failure; it is delayed success, a further stepping-stone to success. Forgiveness is magical. When we forgive ourselves, we take away the burden that would otherwise turn us away from our path of attainment.

It is time to learn how we can each become a dragon again - an exalted creature of spiritual light, breathing divine fire, expressing its right royal inheritance.

Let us transfigure ourselves into dragons!

Chapter Sixty-seven

Transforming Ourselves Into Dragons

The first thing we must remember as we set out on the mission of restoring our own Dragonhood is that Enlil has no power over us. This may seem a strange assertion when we look out on the world and see him riding so high on the cusp of the waves of power. Everywhere, it seems, Enlil has made his mark and claimed his dominion. Yet it is true to say that he may wield over us only that measure of power which we, consciously or unconsciously, are willing to give into his hands.

Enlil has created a terrible smoke-demon of fear which oppresses and demoralises us. As the spearhead of all the confusion, anxiety and darkness of the material world, he can only too easily seem all-powerful. It is what he strives to make us think. But in actual fact, he is impotent. The death-forces he embraces are, to state a truism, without life. They have no impetus of creativity. Of course, this does not mean to say that if we make a gift to him of *our* life and creativity, he cannot capitalise on them to the highest degree. He still has some control over our karma, although the judgment aspect of a lord of karma has been removed from him entirely. What he can do, and revels in so doing, is to hurl at us devastating thunderbolts of the negative karma we ourselves create. He cannot operate outside cosmic law, but he can apply it in such a way as to make life much darker and more distressing and difficult for us here on earth than it was ever intended to be.

The initial step on our journey, therefore, is to cut Enlil down to size and to reclaim the 'I Am' that exists within us. We do this very simply, through the breath. We may think of the House of Shimtî (meaning 'breath-wind-life'), Nin-khursag and Enki's miraculous 'creation chamber', designated as such because it contained the essence of, and linked them to, God. We might bear in mind that the translation of Lilith is 'wind spirit', and that, as the divine couple progressed their crucial mission, the Gnostic gospels tell us that Mary Magdalene and Jesus kissed often on the mouth, sharing the Holy Breath.

The breath is deeply magical, and, if we would become dragons, we need to know how to use it. We need to breathe fire – the right sort of fire, which is light. As dragons, we breathe easily and without effort from the centre of our bodies, yet ensuring that we gently fill our lungs to their capacity, and peacefully empty them (we cannot entirely empty them, because a small residue of air must always remain within the lungs). In doing this, people sometimes find it easier to visualise their lungs filling with air and expanding to the sides, rather than thrusting out at the front of the body. We focus on our breath to calm and steady the mind.

We now attune to the 'I Am', the great 'Aum' of Buddhism. When we assert our 'I Am' selves, we begin to stimulate the divine inner fires which allow us to assume our true Dragonhood. Enlil, we must remember, wants to force us into our lower saurian-hood, whereby we become the tortured dragon of wrath bound on the wheel of its own self-destruction, the opposite of the divine Ouroboros. This wrath-dragon of the lower self is an entirely earthbound creature, sub-human and divest of all the magnificence of its spiritual heritage. We tame it with the breath and the reclaiming of the 'I Am', which allows the royal dragon, the Pendragon ('head dragon' - in more than one sense, when we consider the Stone of Ascension) to come into its own.

We now choose any quality of the higher self of which we stand in particular need. It might be courage or strength, peace or harmony, love or kindness, patience or endurance, clarity or joy - any one of a vast number of exalted spiritual states which we are finding difficult to achieve or maintain. We then intone the simple mantra:

I AM Divine Peace

or:
I AM Divine Love

or:
I AM Divine Wisdom

etcetera, etcetera; whatever it is that you feel you need in order to banish the shadows from your life. The mantra is said whilst focusing on your breathing and on your words. Say it peacefully, slowly, powerfully. Say it

372

many times, until it becomes a rhythm pulsing through your mind, effortless, resonant, musical.

There is a special form of the 'I Am' which is particularly potent. It is the mantra of the Holy Grail, because, of course, the Grail is the Resurrection, our own personal resurrection from the tomb in which Enlil has sought to constrict us for so long: the rolling away of the Stone of Death from the door of our prison:

I AM the Resurrection and the Life.

Of course, the 'I AM' is not a reference to the little self of earth, to which feelings of grandiose self-importance might attach themselves.

The 'I AM' is our God-self, our Pendragon self, which cannot be swayed by petty egotism, but remains always noble, always humble; because it is centred in humility, humiliation cannot wound it. Select a mantra and repeat it for a few minutes each day, or whenever you have need of it. Thus will you begin to re-establish the power of the dragon that Enlil has sought to leach away from you.

To become dragons, we also need to reclaim the unwavering gaze of the dragon, by means of which it can control its own inner cosmos, and work spiritual miracles within its own environment. This unwavering gaze is the focus of the mind; and it is the mind we must learn to still and strengthen, so that it may begin to reflect the many hues of the Ineffable One, the heavenly Dragon Queen.

To clarify the mind so that we may reflect the eternal flame of the Divine, we need to meditate regularly. Five minutes each day makes a good beginning, although, as you come to enjoy meditation more and more, you will probably wish to extend this period to twenty minutes. If five minutes a day is too much for you at first, simply start with two. The important thing is that it is done.

We take for our first meditation symbol the beautiful form of a rose. It is our Dragon Chalice, from whose depths we absorb our sacred and divine Dragon heritage. The rose is pink, because it harmonises the red and the white life forces, and we see it blooming in the heart centre. Gently stabilise your inner focus upon the rose in the heart, and inhale its pure fragrance. Assume a rhythm whereby you breathe in the perfume of the rose, all the while keeping your inner gaze upon it, and absorb the entirety of its healing, calming, inspiring essence. Then breathe it out to the world. Just spend five minutes doing this peaceful exercise, or longer if you wish to.

Our next symbol is the eternal flame. It is the power of our Dragon form. (It is only necessary to work with one image each day, changing it as you prefer.) See a flame of liquid light curling into the heavens. This mirror-bright flame might be a candle-flame, the shape of two hands joined in prayer; or it might rise from some mystical source in the interior of the Earth, ascending like an angel of purest light. It might be a flame like the northern lights, dancing its spirit dance in a swirl of mystical colours. This flame, too, is in your heart; breathe in its light, flood your entire being with its brilliance, and then breathe it out to the earthly world, for its blessing and healing

Our third image is a sword of hallowed light. It is our Dragon keenness of spirit. Its blade of glory points upwards. We wield it in our hearts, and we can reach into that centre and take it, still pointing upwards, in our hand. We dispel the shadows that press in upon us with this sword. It tames the dragon of the lower self. It fills us with courage. Fear in all its manifold forms is driven away. See its light shooting upwards in a streak of spiritual purity and beauty. If we ever seek to use it selfishly or violently, we shatter the sword. We can still use the breath in conjunction with the sword, for we breathe in its holiness, its surety, its protection, and then breathe out these peace-yielding gifts to the world.

Our final symbol is that of Silence. This is the Dragon-stone, the Stone of Ascension. We might find this concept too obscure to be able to cope with it in meditation purely as a state of being. If so, we can imagine it as a ring of immaculate light, as of the vestal light in the brilliant flash of diamonds.

Go through that ring of light as if you crossed the threshold into a gem of unimaginable radiance, as if you stepped into the heart of a boundless star. Dwell in the light, and be aware of your breath and the pulse of your heart. This is the rhythm of Silence, this is the pulse of Silence. Dwell in the hallows of the Silence, and send forth its pulsation of creative love into the human world that struggles below the heavens.

We will note that four symbols are given. They are the four symbols of the Grail, our Dragon heritage. They will help us in our bid to reclaim it. If difficulty is experienced with the idea that the symbols exist in the heart, just see the image as if face to face with it, with an inner knowing that its dwelling-place is the beautiful shrine in the heart centre.

When we sit for meditation, we ensure that we are comfortable and relaxed, and that our spine is as straight as possible (support it if this gives greater ease). When we emerge from meditation, we have to be careful to seal our higher centres, for our own protection. This just takes a few seconds. In imagination, hold the symbol of a bright silver cross of light enclosed within a circle of light over the two crown centres, the brow centre, the throat centre, the heart centre, and over the solar plexus.

The symbol of the cross of light within the circle of light is the great Sign of Tiâmat. It is the Mark of Cain, or kingship ('Cain' or *Qayin* translates as 'king' or 'queen'). It is the symbol of the royal or exalted Dragon, the symbol of our highest humanity. We can use this great and glorious symbol as a mighty form of protection. Practise creating it in an instantaneous sweep of the imagination. Stand within the intersection of the cross, at its heart, where a star of the fire of God burns with a measureless light.

No darkness, no evil, can withstand this light. It must halt, turn back, hide its face. Assume your Dragon heritage, merge with the light of the star, and know that nothing can touch you. You are a child of God. You cannot be harmed or overcome. Nothing evil can come near you. All is well.

The beautiful six-pointed star, which we encountered in the first chapter of this book, is the supreme key to the reclamation of our Dragonhood.[1] It is formed from two equilateral triangles, one with its pinnacle pointing upwards, and the other with its pinnacle pointing downwards. The merging of these two triangles creates the six-pointed star, but, unlike the Star of David, it bears no inner divisions. The fusion of the two triangles creates a flawless unity. It is expressed in a great blaze of supernal light.

The star is within our hearts. We find it by focusing gently on the breath, and letting its light shine forth. The star in our hearts connects with the great, blazing star in the heavens, the six-pointed star of the spiritual dimensions, for truly they are one. Having created the star, having summoned it into being, we know that the star is in our hearts, that we stand within the heart of the star, and that it also shines above us in the overarching skies of the spirit. These realities exist simultaneously.

Now we can project the light of the star. We do it with the out-breath, with the gentle, steady focus of the mind, with a blaze of love from the heart centre. If we find it difficult to feel love on command, then the trick is to *act* as if we are feeling that current of love. When we act with true intent rather than in order to deceive, the act itself forms a channel through which higher beings can nourish us with the genuine essence of what we are expressing. This is the crucial difference between dramatic art and sham, and the secret as to why great actors can move us so deeply. We act within ourselves, within our hearts, as if we conjured the outflow of love with a magical command. We know that it is there, we have faith that it goes forth from us - and it does.

There are special hours at which we can make a supreme connection with the star. They occur at the points of 3, 6, 9 and 12 o'clock throughout the 24-hour cycle. Twelve noon, the meridian, is the most powerful of all, being the heart centre of the day. If, whenever we can, we take a two-minute or even a one-minute break from whatever we are doing, and send forth this light with a spoken blessing on humanity and the world so that it encircles the planet, we will prepare ourselves and the Earth for the coming of the Grail.

We can project this light into our homes, our places of work, to local and international trouble spots, to people who are in need of help. The light may be radiated to animals, to places in nature, to gardens, even to individual trees and plants. It is never forced on anyone, nor is it projected to bring into being any personal preference concerning another person's behaviour or decision. It is simply a free gift from the heart, for the recipient to accept or refuse as they will. Our dragon nature, our higher self, scintillates far above the pushiness and desire for control which belong to the ego, and brings that ego, the little earthly self, into the heart of the greater self, so that its humanity and its connectedness with earth remain, but its inharmonious aspects do not. They are caught up, transformed into a perfect energy, pulsating in rhythm with the divine light of the star - the light of God.

As we use the star, we will receive absolute confirmation of its truth and reality, and of the actuality of the spirit and the higher worlds from which it shines. We will no longer be tempted to think that the dull veil of the earth dimension is all that exists, or that we are helpless, impotent creatures living finite lives on an insentient ball of rock. We are dragons, and the worlds which are our birthright are glorious and infinite.

A number of people have been working with the star for several decades now (and some even before that, because the star is an ancient and eternal symbol). Not all such people may think of themselves as dragons - but in ethereal vision their astral forms are revealed as replete with many-coloured flourishing dragon crests and streaming manes of unfathomable light, with swirling tails or wings like outspread tongues of flame dancing through their auras. Truly we are dragons, and our Dragonhood is waiting for us to consciously assume it once again.

Alice Through the Looking-Glass ends with a question, a kind of manna ('What is it?'). Alice-Chalice wonders whether her dream of passing through the glass and back again was her own dream, or that of the Red King (the red, Saturnine king being, of course, a symbol of Enlil). 'Which do you think it was?' asks Lewis Carroll astutely. To answer his question, we must awaken to the truth. Then it will be Alice's dream we live and move in - the dream of the triumphant soul - and no longer that of the Red King and his topsy-turvy, false mirror-image, reverse-spin, completely nonsensical world.

Notes and References
1. In its solid, three-dimensional form, the Soltaire or Mary Magdalene Cross (X) is visible on each of the facets of the star. The four triangles on each facet give it a 4-4 connection (an angelic number, which numerologically equates to 8, the number associated with the sacred feminine and with the eight-rayed Aten). The number of these triangles (4) multiplied by its six facets adds up to 22, the date of Mary Magdalene's feast day (22nd of July), and marks the magical day upon which the heartbeat properly begins within the developing human embryo.

Chapter Sixty-eight

Questions and Answers

At the beginning of this book, we promised to answer certain questions relating to the Grail. We hope that this first volume concerning the meaning of the Grail has answered those questions comprehensively, and that our second volume, wherein we will focus on the history of the Grail and the clues that led us to it, will clarify the answers we have given to an even greater degree. Nevertheless, at this point, as our present volume draws to a close, we should like to sum up the journey of discovery we have taken together in a simple question-and-answer format.

Q. What is the Grail?
A. The Grail is the connecting-point between God, planet Earth, and planet Earth's humanity. It was once fully functioning and open to all, but certain conspirators, who wished to foster male supremacy and the authority of unbalanced values, delivered what has come to be called in the folk legends of the Grail, the 'Dolorous Blow'. This was, in effect, a cutting off of this mighty connection-point and a severe restriction of the Grail energies, so that in time they all but closed down. Certain designated sacred places on earth retained it in secret, blessed and protected by the earliest of the 'divine couples' to conjoin on planet Earth - Enki and Nin-khursag. The greatest of all these protective divine couples was Mary Magdalene and Jesus, who came to earth at a much later time. Enki and Nin-khursag gave forth specific teachings, which were spread abroad by Zoroaster. These teachings were concerned with how to find and nurture the divine light within us (the indwelling Holy Grail) and follow its inspiration in our human lives.

Nin-Khursag had a spiritual sister who was so close to her in soul-essence that they may be regarded as one. This spiritual sister was called Lilith. Enki's spiritual and actual brother was called Enlil. He was the main conspirator among those who delivered the 'Dolorous Blow', a role he inherited from his father, Anu. Later, Enlil attached himself to the ancient city of Ur and to Abraham, and called himself 'Jehovah'. These four persons, Nin-khursag, Lilith, Enki and Enlil, were human beings, but human beings of a far greater magnitude than we can understand today. They belonged to an exalted community called the Higher Anunnaki. They had come here from another planet (planet 'X'). These Higher Anunnaki lived in a dimension connected to the Earth, but which vibrated at a much more rapid frequency than our material world. It was called Eden. They established humanity upon the Earth, in later years particularly in an area called 'the Fertile Crescent', which corresponded with Mesopotamia, Canaan (Palestine), and Egypt.

When the Dolorous Blow was struck, a very precious objectified source of knowledge which contained all that it was necessary to understand in order for humanity and the Earth to keep its connection with God in healthy operation, and to fulfil its spiritual evolutionary objectives, was stolen and hidden irretrievably by Enlil. It was called the Emerald Tablet, and without it, we, as a planetary community, cannot understand how to restore the mighty connection-point with God called the Holy Grail. We need more than the restoration of the Emerald Tablet, however.

We also need what cannot be given via intelligence and understanding, but only by God herself via her divine touch. (God is feminine, containing the masculine essence as a principle within her, which she expresses in her out-breathing or giving forth, called Creation; it was this fact that some of the Higher Anunnaki men found themselves utterly unable to deal with, leading them to plan the delivery of the Dolorous Blow and the unbalanced glorification of the male principle).

This sanctified touch or 'kiss' of God, which we need in addition to the Emerald Tablet, is the reconnection of our deeper being to the energies of the Grail, so that, by applying the teachings of the Emerald Tablet, we can claim our full inheritance of it once again. They - the Emerald Tablet and the 'kiss of God' - are the two halves of the Grail, which must meet in our heart centre. We need the gift of the reconnection so that we will fully understand the Emerald Tablet, and we need the teachings contained in the Emerald Tablet so that we can fully develop our reconnection to God. The 'kiss' will be given by the Divine Woman, who carries within her the pure essence of her mother (God).

The Divine Woman is called Tamar. She came to earth as Jesus and Mary Magdalene's daughter, but was purposely denied, obstructed and obscured by Saint Peter's Church of Rome. Having an unconscionable love for us, she remains with us still in the higher ethers, and will descend, perhaps to initiate four people (a representative of the Tetrad) with the Grail dynamic. They will then pass it on to all who wish to receive it.

There are thus two parts to the Grail. (There is a divine 2 [the swan contemplating its reflection, and, importantly, also its heart centre, on the water], running all the way through the theme of the Grail, representing God and the mirror-image which is her Creation; God strives always to call the mirror-reflection back through the mirror, knowing that when this happens, her beloved Creation will assume its own true God-essence, and will no longer be a mere reflection.) The first part is the Emerald Tablet, which is in the form of an ancient book. The second part is the kiss of Tiâmat (Tamar), the initiation in which all who wish to do so may share. This initiation, we believe, will be given in Glastonbury, in the Lady's Chapel, and it will be marked with a cosmic sign, internationally recognisable, which will be an outward expression of the truth that the Grail has returned to earth.

Q. What were the clues that led us to it?
A. The clues first came to our attention when we learned of Callum Jensen's announcement that he had discovered the location of the famous Rennes-Le-Château treasure (he has never directly claimed that it is the Holy Grail) in the grounds of Lincoln Cathedral. Nobody seemed to pay much attention to his public statement. However, we were encouraged by those who guide us from the spiritual spheres (Mary Magdalene, Tamar, and others) to make contact with him. We read his two booklets, and I spoke to him personally on several occasions. The things he told us concerning the clues he had unearthed gave us a very real shock. They fell stunningly in line with numerous insights we had received regarding the Mary Magdalene story, many of which were not included in our book about her, either because they had come through after the publication process had started, or because they seemed to be involved with an Arthurian connection to which we felt we had given adequate coverage within its pages.

The upshot of our encounter with this man was that we felt that in fact he ought to be taken very seriously, and we began to focus on the story of the Grail, what it was, and how it had come to be deposited within the grounds of the cathedral.

What came through to us from our source was so stupendous and so utterly unexpected, and yet moved so many confusing and apparently disparate aspects of the Grail myths perfectly into place (to say nothing of human history!), that we immediately set to work on this present volume. In the next, we will focus much more on these clues. They are not the same as Callum's clues, although they are connected and we do include some of his findings in our overview. Callum's clues were our starting-point, and we, and indeed the entire world, owe him a hearty vote of thanks for his ingenuity and inspiration in locating the Holy Grail - strictly speaking, that part of it which exists in objectified form upon the Earth.

Q. What are its properties and its secrets?
A. The Four Grail Hallows are the qualities of Immortality, Abundance, Healing and Nourishment. It contains a fifth property: its Quintessence. This is the Paraclete, the Holy Spirit. Its secret is that it can restore the whole world to wholeness and sanity, and that it will throw open the doors for the soul development of the human race. As we advance into this soul development, worlds of wonder will be revealed to us of which we have no conception today.

Q. What is its great gift to humankind?
A. The Grail will tear away the veil between the real worlds of the spirit, and the illusory world of matter. It will break the chains of materialism which hold us fast, and return us to the heart of God.

The sacred feminine principle will properly be restored to life and consciousness. The great gift of the Grail is Resurrection, or Ascension. We will have divine life, and we will have it in abundance, but we will remain living in our physical bodies on planet Earth for our allotted span, even whilst we ascend to exalted heights of the spirit and bring back its treasures to our world.

Q. How can we prepare for its coming?
A. By becoming dragons, as we have explained; by connecting with our heart centre, sending forth the light of the star, and living in the light of the star as we live our lives each day; and by extending the parameters of our belief. The White Queen in *Alice in Wonderland* advises us to practise believing at least six impossible things before breakfast every morning!

Q. How will we receive its mystical attributes?

A. We will receive them through proper preparation, which means following the star and living by the inspiration of the star; by willingly accepting the wonder of the Grail into our lives; by perhaps receiving a special (and very simple) initiation (*in which no exchange of money is involved!*), and by receiving the secret teachings of Mary Magdalene's gospel, and the secret teachings on the Holy Grail and the act of ascension contained within the book that is the lost Gospel of John - the book which represents the Emerald Tablet. It was able to be written because Jesus, Mary, Tamar and John literally rescued the Emerald Tablet and its knowledge for us from the very dangerous and inaccessible domain in which Enlil had hidden it.

They were able to open this domain only through supreme self-sacrifice; Jesus himself received the Dolorous Blow which had been dealt to Tiâmat, or to her connection with us and the Earth (a connection which was in itself the Holy Grail), and Jesus gave the teachings of the Emerald Tablet, through Mary Magdalene and Tamar, to John, who wrote them down.

Q. What will its effect be on each one of us personally?

A. We will receive the four attributes or Hallows of the Grail into our individual lives. Each one of us will be given the chance to unfold and flower in a way that has never been known on earth before, and which will bring us incalculable joy and harmony of being.

Q. What will its effect be upon the world?

A. All the oppression, cruelty, violence, crassness and injustice so rampant in the world today will gradually be transformed. New educational and healing techniques will be revealed; technologies in perfect harmony with nature which are inconceivable today will be brought into being. The problems of climate change will be overcome. As the great spiritual teacher White Eagle has said, 'the blue carpet of peace shall be spread across the world'. True joyousness of living will be our portion.

Q. What is its history?

A. The full history of the Grail began before our world came into being. Some of its history is traced in the present volume. In the second volume, we will give the full history of the Grail, which is a breathtaking story, full of wonders.

Q. How did it come to be where it now lies?

A. The Grail originally passed from Glastonbury, to France, to Ireland, and then back again to France. It was returned to Glastonbury (where its ethereal energies remain), and then borne to Lincoln, to the east, to the John-place on the compass. Exactly who bore it to Lincoln, and oversaw its high heroic passage and its concealment in St. Margaret's Church, we will reveal in our next book, the accompanying volume to this.

Notes and References

1. What if the unthinkable happens, and the relevant authorities refuse to budge with respect to excavation? Or, if the go-ahead is given, the grave-site yields nothing? We are confident that neither of these devastating possibilities will be the outcome. If either does happen to be the case, it has been suggested to us that, as we formed a channel for the retrieval of the Gospel of Mary, it is feasible that we might be able to do the same for John's lost gospel (we believe that it was once called 'the Book of Love'). We sincerely hope that we will not be called on to provide such a service, not only because of the daunting responsibility involved, but also because a book produced by such methods could never be the key to unlocking acceptance of the Grail in the collective human heart in the same way that the actual historical document could. Nevertheless, we are on stand-by, even though we have faith that the precious book was delivered successfully to its designated resting place, and that, since then, nobody has been able to breach the security surrounding it.

The historical evidence that such a book exists is vast; there are records of its objective actuality from Dagobert's era (the seventh century), progressing through the appearance and elimination of the Cathars around the time of the first millennium, through the establishment and fall of the Knights Templars in the eleventh and twelfth centuries, to its depiction during the Renaissance on the Visconti card deck. It was painted by Bonifacio Bembo of Cremona, one of the *perfecti* (equating to a priest) of the Cathar movement, for although the Cathars were brutally slaughtered and wiped out as a community, certain members escaped and continued their Church in secret. The painting on the card is of a female, pregnant Pope. The Pope, of course, is the supreme Vicar, or vicarious connection to God, designated as Simon Peter the Disciple by the Catholic Church of Rome.

The Cathars understood that the human connection to God was actually via the sacred feminine, or the divine love within the human heart, and that the overly-masculine Peter, dubbed by grass-roots tradition as 'he who hates' (see Chapter 52), could not properly represent humanity's connection to God! Pope Joan is she who brings God to the John-man, the John-man's connection to God; she is Tamar, the Holy Grail, the stairway between heaven and earth; she is Mary Magdalene (Arimathea - Mari-thea, or Mary-God, the feminine God); she is Lilith, Nin-khursag – and she is Tiâmat, most gracious and supreme God from whom everything flows or flow-ers: 'She who bore them all'. She wears on her head the sacred *shem-an-na*, demonstrated by a pointed conical hat, symbolizing the ineffable Stone of Ascension (see Chapter 65) active in her head.

Below the knotted cord of her girdle (and we know that the knotted cord is a symbol of the Magdalene: the 'Great Feminine One or 'Great Queen'), which signifies that she will bring forth the Magdalene and the Magdalene will bring forth Tamar the Holy Grail, this feminine Pope holds a book. The book is not the Bible, but, as many sources attest, the lost Gospel of John, written by John and Mary Magdalene after the death of Jesus on the cross.

2. Callum Jensen's little books, *The Lincoln Da Vinci Code* and *The Lincoln Da Vinci Code and the Mystery of Rennes-Le-Château*, are available from Waterstones in Lincoln from the 'Local Authors' section of the shop.

Chapter Sixty-nine

The Syndicate

Before we close this first volume about the discovery of the Holy Grail, there is one difficult and unpleasant subject we must broach. It concerns what is known as 'the Syndicate'.

This deeply sinister group has been given many titles in the past. Hitler called it in general terms 'the Zionist plot', which is darkly amusing, as he was completely under the dominance of its highest levels of authority. He did not give it its title, however. It was in existence long before he rose to power (on its hidden wings), and its first priority was to eliminate the Jewish people - Hitler's 'Final Solution'. The reason for this was that, at some point in the last few hundred years, Enlil discovered the truth about the ancient and kingly Jewish race.

He had always believed that they *promoted* him and his cause, and that the Jews would lead him to world dominion down a straight and rapid track. Imagine his horror, therefore, when he discovered that, far from promoting him, they were actually *containing* his terrible death energies, and actively *preventing* him from attaining his cherished goal! By now, we can imagine the howls of wrath that must have ensued!

As far as Enlil was concerned, he had put paid to the great threat to his plan which Tiâmat had instigated with her bloodline. The exalted king it was intended to accommodate (he ignored the queen) had been and gone, slain by his own people, as Enlil had carefully arranged. He thought, being so far out of touch with the eternal verities, that the Christ mission had been a total failure. He had thought that he was merrily on his way to the end of the road. And now he was beginning to discover that those whom he had always considered as his obedient agents of destruction were actually the *protectors* of humanity. (We believe that the story of David, the protective shepherd-boy who slew the giant Goliath with a 'stone' and thus entered into his kinghood, is a symbol of the Jewish people's secret mission. It depicts the Jews keeping Enlil and the Naphidem at bay from humankind by the use of a special stone [in the sense that they contained the white powder via Bezaleel's art within the

Ark of the Covenant].) Enlil was outraged!

The so-called 'Zionist plot', in one sense, was nothing more than the hot and murderously hostile pursuit of all those who strove to follow Enki and Nin-khursag's teachings (the teachings of Tiâmat-Oannes, the teachings proceeding from the Divine Light) and those who were of Tiâmat's special bloodline down the ages, because, although the branch from Mary Magdalene and Jesus ended with Tamar, the greater family line of course continued.

The huge aim and objective of the bloodline was to deliver to earth this divine couple of divine couples, but even after it had achieved its goal, it still produced incarnating souls who had a service to perform for humanity. Enlil was determined to exterminate these people and stamp out the bloodline forever. Once he had learned that the Jewish race was blocking him rather than furthering his cause, his main priority was to get rid of it entirely. Until it was gone, he had no hope of succeeding in his dark enterprise. With great cunning, therefore, he and his cronies arranged the release of a reverse-spin piece of intelligence - that there was a dread organisation, headed and financed by racist and radical Jews, to crush all other races beneath their feet and take over the world. In other words, what Enlil had formerly believed was secretly really happening but was in fact a nonsense (i.e., that he himself was riding on the backs of the Jews towards a triumphant global take-over) was now spread abroad as a terrifying rumour, designed to inflame the lower minds of those who could be thus manipulated, and prompt them to wipe out the Jewish people forever. (The actual Zionists, regrettable as their unbalanced attitudes remain, were nothing but a smokescreen to give weight to this rumour, being in themselves a small number of Jews who were not quite as strong in spirit as their more muscular kin, and who had not managed to successfully contain Enlil's death energies, but unfortunately had fallen prey to them).

Enlil did not leave things to chance, although he bore in mind that there was more than one way to skin a cat and consequently always had several cunning plans up his sleeve. Throughout many centuries he plotted the exact course that history would take (providing, of course, that humanity would fall into line according to his allurements and manipulations - but he was very confident it would - after all, it always had done so in the past...Enlil was sanguine on this point). However, if we look into the machinations and manoeuvres of the Syndicate, we must not expect to find a simple array of darkness versus light, of black versus white.

Enlil is nothing if not subtle; but even so, even though he plotted barbarity after barbarity, confident that he could drive us like cattle (the Syndicate's scornful name for us is 'Goyim' - cattle) into whatever sinister enclosures he chose to prepare for us, Tiâmat's hand, unseen and unsuspected, was always on the steering wheel.

The destiny of the Earth did not slip out of her hands, as perhaps it seemed to do, and as Enlil was convinced it had. Although our own free will would make us become as Enlil's foolish cattle, although he did his very worst and surpassed himself at every turn, yet Tiâmat would lead us to a place in history that we would recognise as a turning-point - a wondrous, miraculous turning-point - where all the ill and evil that Enlil had inflicted on the world could be overturned as in a moment, and humanity could march in triumph towards the glorious destiny she had planned for us before time began, when she held us within her heart as a golden principle, a divine and cherished idea.

There is a single quote which might help us to better understand the twisted confusion that is the Syndicate:

> For our contention is not with the blood and the flesh, but with
> dominion, with authority, with the blind world-rulers of this life,
> with the Spirit of Evil in things heavenly.
> (Ephesians 6:12)

Certainly, many good men and many genuine idealists have been involved, in one way or another, with this Syndicate. It seems just as certain that they had no idea of the real nature of its power or its ultimate objectives. One feels the touch of the true light forces, of Tiâmat-Oannes, in such infiltration of the Syndicate! The light and the dark forces work together for long-range good; the highest initiates of the dark forces, the angels and overlords of their structure, know this, and are only disguised as creatures of the darkness.

Their lesser minions do not know, and must eventually be redeemed from their ignorance. The humans among them (which of course include Enlil and Marduk) are also entirely hostile and given over to the destructive forces - except for that tiny, tiny glimmer at their heart centre, impossible to extinguish despite all their efforts - the little flame of their humanity, the tiny dragon flame which proclaims them as beings of light, however far they may have sunk in their wickedness.

No human being can actually be *of* the evil forces, counted among them as truly one of their legion, even though it is only too clear that certain members of humanity can be completely taken over by them and work with all diligence for them. The non-human creatures and beings who comprise the evil forces but are not numbered amongst its highest initiates, however, are, in common with their human colleagues, wholly ignorant of their greater aim (which is actually to foster the forces of light, or good), and may be categorised as utterly of the shadow - although they, too, will one day be redeemed (healed and made whole). Evil is only a temporary measure. We are under its heavy-duty tutelage only until we finally decide, on a collective basis, that we really don't want a reverse-spin world and a reverse-spin consciousness anymore!

It seems questionable as to why Enlil accepted an influx of light into his dark Syndicate. One reason seems to be that he welcomed such an ingredient because it then became much easier to fool even the most exacting and discerning among us into thinking that his designs really were schemes of light. (We might consider, for instance, just how invigorating and recuperative it must have been for the German people to be led forward by Hitler, with his visions of a new Germany, in his early days of leadership. They had been devastatingly humiliated by the misjudged and oppressive Treaty of Versailles after their defeat in the First World War, and this prepared the ground for Hitler initially to sell them a neatly packaged lifeline whose saviour-like promises helped to cement his later hypnotic sway over the masses.) We have to learn how to test the waters and differentiate between the False and the True Grail. We look for lies, for unacceptable actions and philosophies, and most of all, we look and hearken to our souls - who if we take them regularly into the mystic Silence will calmly and reverently enshrine the light of the spirit - to give us the unfailing signal as to whether or not we are in safe hands. This is how we sniff out the lurking presence of Enlil.

A second reason was that there was still a dim flicker of light within Enlil himself. Sometimes, he seemed to express this to a limited extent. Yet, sadly, it was always overcome by the false light to which his soul was lashed (by bonds he himself created) as if to a monstrous navigator. We do not wish to give a misleading impression here, because Enlil is by no means in two minds about what he wishes our destiny to be. He intends to exterminate us. Similarly, the intention behind the Syndicate is entirely malevolent and corrupt, even though good-hearted, enlightened people and groups have become enmeshed in its terrible purposes. The false bread and the false wine were fed to these bearers of enlightenment to disconnect them from their inner compass, their intuitive wisdom. This has always been the source of its hideous strength. From the first, the Syndicate learned the art of a diabolically ingenious puppetry, and knew how to make even the spiritually elect dance to its appalling tune. This is why our contention truly is 'with the Spirit of Evil in things heavenly'. It is this Spirit of Evil which prevents heaven from descending to earth, which prevents us from ascending into our heavenly spiritual heritage, and which therefore prevents the coming of the Grail. But we are about to rid ourselves of the ignorance which allows it to prevail, and thus will we see its miasma lift and disperse and become as nothing.

All that this 'evil' comprises, in the simplest terms, is the downward pull of matter itself against the natural spiritual tendency towards ascension and the return to God. H. P. Lovecraft has described it as being 'coterminus with all space and coexistent with all time'. In other words, it is utterly of the material plane and is an influence within matter itself. ('Matter is a force to be reckoned with!' Jesus declares in the Gospel of Mary.) It moves in the opposite direction to the affinities of the spirit. Therefore, what is most pure can become loathsome and corrupt, what flames forth from the heart of highest ecstasy can become virulent pain and suffering. We must conquer the reversals of matter before we can step through the mirror and become real. Until then, illusion persists, making us its collective dominion, and our 'White Knight' (the will, movement and direction of the soul when it obeys the ordinances of the spirit) will blunder, will keep being unseated, will concentrate on irrelevances, will carry all its confusions forward as burdens which hinder its progress, and will use its vision and powers of creativity in entirely pointless enterprises, just like the White Knight in *Alice Through the Looking-Glass*. It is worth taking time out from our rather horrifying contemplation of the Syndicate to step into Wonderland again for a brief but reviving interlude, and consider more carefully this White Knight.

Notes and References

1. It is interesting to note that the Nazis, and in particular their inner brotherhood of the SS (symbolising the unentwined or separated serpents, in contradistinction to Enki

and Nin-Khursag's symbol, which is the caduceus), were the reverse-spin opposite of the Knights Templar. The Nazis also modified their symbol of the Eagle so that it represented the reverse of the Eagle of St John. Although some confusion did latterly enter the ranks of the Templars, and although members of its outermost circle did not properly understand the order's true aims and objectives, our source assures us that the inner circle of the Knights Templar was indeed pure and noble, entirely dedicated to fulfilling the ideals of Oannes and accepting Tiâmat-Oannes as God.

Himmler selected a site in a remote mountainous location and built a castle in a strange triangular design, intended to facilitate the inundation and destruction, Tower-of-Babel-style, of the new pyramidal soul-structure that Tiâmat had provided for humanity in order to protect them from the invasion of the Naphidem. (The Naphidem, of course, were the driving force behind Hitler and the Nazis.) An inner temple was created in the triangular castle where, on a central altar, an 'eternal flame' burned. This flame was actually a gas flame, and the acoustics of the temple were designed so that the hiss of the gas flame was aggressively amplified.

Within the temple the twelve highest ranking SS Nazi officers would sit in meditation on twelve thrones surrounding the hissing flame. Black arts were set in motion to try to seize psychic control of the human chakra system, which, since Tiâmat's gift to us of our pyramidal soul or chakra system, has been preparing itself for the activation of thirteen main chakras rather than its former use of seven. The twelve SS officers represented twelve of the chakras, whilst the hissing flame represented the central heart chakra. It hissed with the fury and thunder of Enlil, the lower dragon or dinosaurian principle, which wishes to overpower via its own might and hostility. (We remember that Enlil began his black magic practices long ago in pre-history by distorting humanity's awareness, understanding and reverence for the heart centre.) Himmler himself was called 'the Crystal Knight' and kept a crystal in a secret place in the triangular castle. Knowing, as we do, Enlil's manipulation of crystals and mirrors in his plot to destroy humankind, we can imagine to what dark purposes this crystal was dedicated.

Hitler was in conversation one day with Rauschning, the Governor of Danzig, on the topic of mutating the human race (it was Hitler's aim to reintroduce the Naphidem to earth via genetically mutated human vehicles, in a horrible perversion of Enki and Nin-khursag's God-sanctioned work in the House of Shimtî). The Governor, not being privy to Hitler's sinister esoteric knowledge, pointed out to him that all he could hope to do was to assist Nature via genetics and trust that she herself would create a new human species for him.

"The new man is living amongst us now! He is here!" Hitler declared triumphantly. "Isn't that enough for you? I will tell you a secret. I have seen the new man. He was intrepid and cruel. I was afraid of him." Rauschning described Hitler as 'trembling in a kind of ecstasy' as he uttered these words.

Rauschning also recorded a further disturbing account: 'A person close to Hitler told me that he wakes up in the night screaming and in convulsions. He calls for help, and appears to be half paralysed. He is seized with a panic that makes him tremble until the bed shakes. He utters confused and unintelligible sounds, gasping, as if on the point of suffocation. The same person described to me one of these fits, with details that I would refuse to believe had I not complete confidence in my informant.

'Hitler was standing up in his room, swaying and looking all round him as if he were lost. "It's he, it's he," he groaned; "he's coming for me!" His lips were white; he was sweating profusely. Suddenly he uttered a string of meaningless figures, then words and scraps of sentences. It was terrifying. He used strange expressions strung together in bizarre disorder. Then he relapsed again into silence, but his lips still continued to move. He was then given a friction and something to drink. Then suddenly he screamed: "There! There! Over in the corner! He is there!" – all the time stamping with his feet and shouting.' *Hitler m'a dit*, Hermann Rauschning, 1939.) After these horrifying episodes, Hitler would fall into a deep sleep and, on waking, would be normal again.

All of the details above are attested history, with the exception of the reason we have given for the twelve SS officers seated in thrones around an amplified hissing gas flame supposed to represent the flame of eternity (that they actually did so is well documented). Such is the result of human and Naphidem association. Incase anyone should begin to suspect that Marduk was not so bad as Enlil after all, as it was not the Naphidem chief's intention to exterminate us, it is as well to bear in mind that the difference in intent between the two men is simply that of an eliminator and a sadist, one of whom wishes to kill his victims outright, the other of whom wishes to keep them alive to satisfy his appetite for corruption, degradation, and torture.

Chapter Seventy

Oannes and the White Knight

Significantly, Lewis Carroll is careful to draw our attention most particularly to this gentle but misguided knight: 'Of all the strange things that Alice saw in her journey Through the Looking-Glass, this was the one that she always remembered most clearly. Years afterwards she could bring the whole scene back again, as if it had been only yesterday...'. Lewis Carroll then scrupulously fixes in the reader's memory the image of the knight as pure light (Alice sees him...'in a blaze of light that quite dazzled her'...) contrasting with the darkness in the background (...'the black shadows of the forest behind'...).

The White Knight sings Alice a song, which he first calls 'Haddock's Eyes' (the eyes or consciousness of the fish-man or the John-man – the *ayin*), but then becomes confused and introduces less relevant designations. It is a song about the White Knight seeking to rediscover the wisdom of Oannes or the Father within himself (the 'aged, aged man') who frustratingly sits on a gate and regales him with what sounds to the White Knight like sheer nonsense. Of course, the Oannes man of ancient wisdom can do nothing but 'sit on the gate' until the lesser aspect of his soul, the White Knight himself, allows him to come down on the right side, or the side of admittance to the White Knight's heightened consciousness. Once the White Knight does this, he will be able to understand the ancient teachings of the Oannes man, and they will no longer sound like nonsensical riddles to him. However, instead of revering the Oannes man as he should, the White Knight is so confused and off-track that he demands to be given the old man's wisdom and explanations (teachings) with force and aggression! It is then that the old man speaks to him of 'haddock's eyes' (true vision), which eases and instructs the White Knight to a very limited degree.

Lewis Carroll lets us know that the White Knight within us remains in a state of barely enlightened confusion, however, by telling us via the song he sings that the White Knight is put in mind of his Oannes self whenever he is faced with his own clumsiness and ignorant blundering (he inwardly laments the fact that the Oannes man has not yet been able to save him from his own stupidity), and by relating that Alice (the harmonised soul, or the source of wisdom) waves farewell to him whilst watching him become unseated from his steed (his vehicle of will, movement and direction, of which he is the spirit) yet again.

The White Knight, in one of the many branches of his symbolism, depicts what happens to our inner wisdom when we partake of Enlil's false powders, when we eat of the bread and drink of the wine of materialism and the lower mind. 'Eat me', signals the bread upon the table in Wonderland, bearing a label upon which these words are written, and 'Drink Me', entices the bottle in the same dimension. It would serve us well to first test the validity of the victuals before accepting their loudly proclaimed invitations: to ask *manna?*, or, *what is it?*

Chapter Seventy-one

The History of the Syndicate

We will take up the history of the Syndicate in 1776, when on 1 May Professor Adam Weishaupt of Bavaria founded the Bavarian Illuminati (the 'illumined' or 'shining ones'). Its great aim was to establish a world government which would fall under the influence of Marduk (whose puppet-master, pulling Marduk's strings, was Enlil). Marduk would then manipulate humanity into admitting the Naphidem back into their favourite dimension - that of the physical Earth. (We must remember that, as there are light and dark dragons, so there are positive and negative 'shining ones'. The positive shining ones are true, beautiful, just and pure, and work for the good of humanity. The false Illuminati weave tissues of lies, are hideously contorted in their philosophies and aims, perpetrate terrible injustice, and work towards the destruction of humanity. We might think of them respectively as denizens of the True and the False Grail.)

Funded by the recently established House of Rothschild ('Wrath's child', and, even more interestingly, 'Red Shield', the literal translation of the name), Weishaupt was ordered by a certain group of enormously wealthy and influential financiers, industrialists, scientists and churchmen (as well as representatives of other religions) who had entirely come under Enlil's tutelage and control, to reconstruct their inherited Luciferic doctrine into a new long-term plan for world domination. The plan would incorporate the measured but sure destruction of all religions, governments, philosophies and value-systems of every society on earth, to be fomented by a polarising of the world population into fanatically opposing factions. Wars, insurrections and revolutions were planned to bring this situation into being. It represented Enlil's long-term plan B, steady but sure, the one upon which he would rely should his and Marduk's more dramatic and ambitious attempts (such as the Nazi takeover) be met with failure.

The Bavarian Illuminati began to plot the course of human history across the globe. The hidden Syndicate (Enlil, Marduk, their higher Anunnaki and Naphidem supporters, and their human puppets on earth) had done its utmost to direct human affairs for thousands of years, and Enki, Nin-khursag and Lilith had in turn done their very best to stymie their shenanigans, as we know from examining the ancient history of Zi-u-sudra (once such an ardent follower of Tiâmat), Ga-nadin-ur, Attaba and Eve and their descendants. However, the founding of the Bavarian Illuminati seemed to mark a shift. Enlil's control and power-bases on earth became suddenly much more overt, and his tentacles tightened around many of the European secret societies of alchemists, Freemasons, Rosicrucians, Jewish cabbalists and others who were the bearers of genuine hidden knowledge, but who now stumbled in some respects and began to fall into confusion, so that a dark aspect fell over them. The false communion of negative-spin bread and wine did its work, and the Freemasons particularly were thrown into disarray.

Masonic precepts of universal brotherhood and equity, their knowledge of the true craft of life and its divine origin, began to be overlaid by élitism, political squabbling, and a narrow, materialistic, self-seeking philosophy. Their potent mysticism and magical rites slipped away into the obscuring mists of forgetfulness and non-comprehension, and here and there, in some of the groups mentioned, the shadow of unwise and even black magic separated them from the inner sun that had blazed with divine truth since their inception. These groups were, in the main, the remnants of the Templar brotherhood, the order of knights savagely annihilated by the Church and the king of France early in the fourteenth century. On learning that the Templars were planning to re-introduce the true Church of Christ, which had been lost to the world a few hundred years after the Crucifixion and which was, strictly speaking, the Church of Tiâmat-Oannes, the Roman Church, behind the façade of Philip the Fair, denounced them as heretical and exterminated them. These impulses within the French court and the Roman Church were, of course, fed and manipulated by Enlil.

Whilst the Church of Peter, like Peter himself, did at least strive partially to fulfil the teachings of the Christ (Jesus and Mary Magdalene represented this ineffable Christ Being on earth), the Illuminati were wholly evil in their intentions. Everyone in the inner circle of the Order knew exactly to whom they paid allegiance. In effect, Enlil was playing one group off against another (always a favourite trick of his), because an 'earlier' Illuminati had formed itself as an antidote to the aggressive superstition of the Church, which, for instance, almost had Galileo burnt at the stake because he reported what he saw through his telescope. The Church was so hostile to the progress of science that certain key thinkers and scientists organised themselves into an underground group with the aim of securing the advance of knowledge and reason.

This was, of course, a good and progressive development. The only problem was, that, abandoning the very science and reason they sought to uphold, some group members decided that they ought to set themselves in diametrical opposition to the doctrines and creed of the Church itself, just to prove how much they held it in disdain - and became Satanists! Whether or not this was originally just an act of black humour is difficult to determine. Unfortunately, certain rites were essayed, and Enlil and Marduk were only too happy to be invited to take over the control of this early Illuminati (the true Syndicate, or false Illuminati, was of course instigated many centuries before the Illuminati of scientists and thinkers formed themselves during the Renaissance). The element of magic or spiritual illumination in science thus had to be disconnected from it with all speed, or there would have been a planetary catastrophe from which the Earth could not have recovered. The great master Francis Bacon (who worked with Shakespeare to release certain wisdoms and esoteric knowledge to the world via his plays) undertook this mighty task. The current materialistic, positivist sciences are the result of his work. Whilst this prevailing philosophy is in itself a great stumbling block to our collective enlightenment, it was a very necessary act of damage-limitation.

To return to Professor Weishaupt and the Bavarian Illuminati: a perusal of their recorded chronology tells us that they had scheduled the French Revolution to commence in the year 1789. We have solid evidence for this because Weishaupt's re-organisation and updating of the Syndicate's ancient plot was transcribed and put into book format by Hans Zwack, a German Illuminatus, who entitled the work *Einigie Original-Scriften*. In 1785 a copy of the book was despatched by courier to a group of French Masons who were involved with the Illuminati, and who were occupied with fuelling and inciting the movement towards a decisive and very bloody revolution. The courier (Lanze) was struck by lightning as he rode through Ratisbon, on his way from Frankfurt to Paris. He and his steed were incinerated, but the book with which he had been entrusted was unscathed. It was passed to the Bavarian government, who searched the homes of all the members of the Illuminati. The organisation was declared illegal, and its Masonic branches were disbanded.

The following year (1786) a book was published exposing the conspiracy (*The Original Writings of the Order and Sect of the Illuminati*). Even so, nothing could stop the forward motion of the stampeding dynamics the group had initiated. The Revolution *did* take place in 1789, and it was just as gruesome and bloodthirsty as both Enlil and Marduk could have wished, although it also, to a certain extent, destroyed the false ideals of rank and privilege, which stem from materialism and were never intended to attach themselves to the service and self-sacrifice of royalty. It effectively closed the door upon any king or queen of Tiâmat's special bloodline ascending to the French throne, because, of course, the throne itself was permanently unseated. Over a thousand years previously, the French king Dagobert had been assassinated, and a man without proper legal claim had been elevated to kingship. Dagobert had a son, and it was the fear of his descendants that led Enlil to instigate a revolution in France, for Dagobert carried the secret of the Grail.

Another reason for the Revolution, as far as Enlil was concerned, was to detach the French from a spiritual realisation that was their natural inheritance, and to set them at odds with England via Napoleon. As England and France were the two most powerful countries in the world at the time of the founding of the Bavarian Illuminati, Enlil was afraid that the progressive impetus in both countries might lead them to rediscover their own spiritual brotherhood, and with it the deeply buried esoteric tradition of the true Church of universal brotherhood. This trepidation was the motivating factor behind the instigation of the Crusades, of the destruction of the Cathars, and of the annihilation of the Knights Templar; and, as we can read in the extant documents of the Illuminati, it was also the motivating force directing the two World Wars, the establishment of communism and fascism and the appalling devastation of the atomic bombs. When Enlil brought in his own world government, he wanted to ensure that there was no faction anywhere that he had left untouched and impervious to his influence, ready to rise up against him at the last moment. Thankfully for us, there always was a sanctuary whose doors Enlil could never force - the sanctuary of the human heart, where the holy of holies resides. Enlil thought he could draw a veil over humanity's realisation of its heart and the God-force within it. All over the world, humanity will show Enlil at last that he has made a big mistake in his assumptions.

Because Enlil wants a world government, some people (who of course know nothing about Enlil, but are aware of the calibre of the Syndicate and its ultimate intentions) have assumed that the establishment of such an authority would be an evil. It may be unwise to think in these terms. It would seem that a world government, with each nation enjoying its own identity and culture and partaking in a unified governance of international affairs, is probably the only way to secure justice and liberty for all. It is not structures in themselves which constitute the huge threat to human freedom and happiness, but what lies within them, what lies at their heart. Any world government with Enlil at its helm could only ever wear the sham appearance of a democracy, because it would be run, first by the Syndicate, and eventually, quite blatantly, by Marduk.

In 1840, the notorious General Albert Pike, an American Freemason, came into office within the hierarchy of the Syndicate, and was eventually promoted to leadership. In 1859 he began to draw up a new military plan which would improve on Weishaupt's original. It was Pike who delineated the vision of three world wars, all of them to be implemented before the end of the twentieth century. Global history has followed Pike's plan to the letter - except for the third world war. This was to be fought over religious extremism, and although those involved in the Syndicate have done their utmost to inflame this war (which they dutifully began on schedule) into a worldwide conflict, they have not succeeded.

This is the great signal which confirms that humanity is at last beginning to turn away from the mesmerising, hallucinatory dispensation which Enlil sends to us through the ethers so that we fall into stupor and discord, and act according to our lower nature. This is the great signal that we are making ourselves ready to receive the Grail, and that its time draws closer. 'Those with ears to hear, let them hear', is a refrain sounded by Jesus throughout the Gospel of Mary. 'Hear' and 'ear' are within the word 'heart', and in one sense the heart is indeed a listening organ. There is no doubt about it; humanity is beginning to hear, and to pay heed.

Pike's ultimate plan was, that after strengthening the forces of communism across the world, it would then be held in check, to be unleashed in the final holocaust. Pike particularly laid emphasis on its nihilistic, materialistic, and totalitarianistic traits rather than its positive qualities, which he wanted to ensure held only false promises of justice and equality. His new draft of Weishaupt's plan included the founding of the state of Israel to inflame racial and religious hatred in the Middle East, so that the opposing factions would annihilate one another in a nuclear war (the secrets of the atom bomb were to be disclosed to the scientific world by Enlil's supernatural agents during the course of the two world wars). Judaism and Islam would thereby be thrown into total confusion and meltdown.

The Syndicate would then unleash the most unsavoury aspects of communism upon the world, and a new war would begin between communists and Christians. The Christians would be allowed to win this war, but it would effect the complete collapse of society everywhere, and create a wholesale lapse into brutishness and degradation. Into this shattered, fragmented, desperate planetary society, unable anymore to believe in any of the gods it once upheld, Marduk would triumphantly descend.

General Pike, (whose name identifies the pike, the mass exterminator among freshwater fish and their most dangerous predator - a fit symbol for the would-be destroyer of Enki, and his link with Oannes the Fish-Man and the Apse, the magical source of Earth's freshwater) wrote a letter to the leader of the Syndicate who preceded him and who acted as his mentor, the Italian Freemason Guiseppi Mazzini. The letter is held today in the archives of the British Museum. It is dated 15 August 1871, and a quote from it reads:

We shall unleash the Nihilists and Atheists, and we shall provoke a formidable social cataclysm which in all its horror will show clearly to the nations the effect of absolute atheism, origin of savagery and of the most bloody turmoil.

Then everywhere, the citizens, obliged to defend themselves against the world minority of revolutionaries, will exterminate those destroyers of civilisation, and the multitude, disillusioned with Christianity, whose deistic spirits will be from that moment without compass, anxious for an ideal, but without knowing where to render its adoration, will receive the pure doctrine of Lucifer, brought finally out in the public view, a manifestation which will result from the general reactionary movement which will follow the destruction of Christianity and atheism, *both* conquered and exterminated at the same time.

Chapter Seventy-two

Bilderberg

The Bilderberg Group is the best known branch of the Syndicate today. It was formed in 1954 at a hotel in Holland of the same name. The Bilderberg Conference (which nowadays takes place at various locations), is an annual event attended by leading financiers, industrialists, media tycoons, business moguls, members of the nobility and of European royal families, high ranking soldiers and scientists and leaders of secret (and sometimes even fundamentalist and overt) religious orders, who all come together to decide how the world (particularly the Occident, although its tentacles are by no means restricted to the West) should be run, and in what direction it should be manipulated. It is an entirely private affair, and is often protected by armed guards.

The Bilderberg Group is famous for the invitations it issues to join its fraternity and attend its conferences to small-time politicians and others who then go on to become world leaders, or major players on the world stage. There exists film footage of very contemporary prime movers in global affairs aboard a coach heading for a Bilderberg Conference prior to their election. Even more worrying is the fact that, once in power, these men have been careful to instigate policies and make decisions which are perfectly in tune with Adam Weishaupt and General Pike's master plan.

It is very likely that many of the individuals thus elevated to power have no real idea of the terrible evil behind the Syndicate. They know enough to understand that the organisation can propel them to power, and they are content not to question quite how such a feat is managed. They think, no doubt, that once they have power, they will be their own man or their own woman, and do a lot of good in the world. Not so! They will find themselves forced to obey the directives of the higher authority within the organisation. If they should fail or refuse, events and situations will rapidly militate against them and threaten to strangle them in an invisible noose until they turn in the specified direction. The white powder is dispensed to them in ethereal form at the Bilderberg meetings. Once they have accepted it, they are henceforth no more than dogs in training on a choke-chain. Any power for good that they may implement will bring more chaos and reversals than benefit to the given situation. Their autonomy of soul and impetus of vision is lost to them.

Margaret Bailey and I are aware that the overt evils and distresses of the world - Mafia activity, drug-pedalling, illegal arms sales, prostitution and paedophile rings, corporate greed, wholesale murder, assault and rape, assassinations, the brutal regimes of certain governments, etcetera, etcetera, and especially the hidden malevolence of the world which controls all the misery and oppression in its establishments and organisations - are linked to the tentacles of the Syndicate, and are fed and organised by them. When we finally see the picture for what it truly is, humanity will be astonished by the sheer scale and the horrible perfection of these vast administrations of the dark powers. Nothing is arbitrary. Nothing is random. Evil is a complex system, a gargantuan organism functioning on many different levels, with many spheres of bio-diversity co-existing in mutual dependency upon its bi-lateral source, which combines a reverse-spin energy emanating from an ethereal dark realm perpetuated and fed on earth by consenting humanity. Its life support system is circular and cyclical.

One thing is certain - we will never, no matter how hard we may try, bring down this almighty structure by force of arms or law, or by any attempt to outwit it. It sometimes seems as if our universal fixation on crime fiction, be it cinematic, televisual or literary, stems from an anxious need to believe that to do so is really possible. Sadly, it is not. Although law enforcement helps to keep society functioning, it cannot disable this great unquiet beast. The same is true, even more so, of the Syndicate itself. It cannot be brought down by worldly means. Evidence melts away, strategies backfire, focus disappears, trusted agents become confused, corrupted, or simply refuse to continue. All attempts to fight back are disabled and disempowered.

One day it *will* be dismantled, but we cannot attack it via conventional means. In fact, we must learn not to attack it at all. Commensurate in popularity with crime fiction is our hero fiction, the good comic-book champion who is ready to be our saviour and rescue the world. Again, this approach of passive reliance on an aggressive force which is on our side will not work. There is only one way to overpower Enlil, and that is by personally refusing his methods of retribution and retaliation and living by the light of the star, the source of divine fire within us which transforms us into our higher dragon or Pendragon selves. It is the force of love. Each individual effort is needed to foster, to faithfully honour, and to unstintingly give forth this divine force of love.

When we do this, when we reclaim our Pendragon status, it will be Enlil's turn to suffer disablement and to become disempowered, confused and confounded. The wisdom of the heart is what will free us from him and the inestimable psychic structures of darkness that he maintains. If we try to use our mind, our intellectual reasoning, to overcome him, we will be drawn into the darkness, bound and manacled as quickly as a spider trusses up its prey. Our vision will shut down, our inner compass will spin madly out of control, and the jaws of his trap will close with a triumphant snap. Only when the power of the mind is absolutely allied with the heart, and is in devoted service to it, may it be used against the tyranny of Enlil.

Furthermore, we strongly and earnestly advise our readers not to focus on the Syndicate, or to make it a project of study. It is very tempting to do so, because in one sense it is a gripping story - the conspiracy of all time, the conspiracy of conspiracies. Yet we ourselves, having summoned all the forces of light for protection and set out to research it in good faith, have soon become disconnected from our source and cast up on the shores of confusion, cold and shivering with a toxic soul-fear.

The Syndicate, or at least its dark overlords, have honed the art of *mind control* to a fine art. This is why the mind leads us - anyone and everyone - into such peril when we approach the problem of the Syndicate with a mental or an intellectual probe. All the unfortunate ailments of the mind come to the fore when we allow our mentality to explore the Syndicate too deeply; obsession, anxiety, confusion, fixation - all come crowding into our field of vision.

As the true Grail gives to humanity four wondrous gifts (Abundance, Healing, Immortality and Nourishment) so this organisation belonging to the false Grail steals from us in four ways, causing an acute energy-loss to the point where the soul becomes distressed. These four thefts of the false Grail are perpetrated by the spectres of Fear, Self-Doubt, Self-Will and Shame. They are the four veils which must be removed before we can receive the Grail.

Every writer who has produced a book on the subject of the Great Conspiracy seems to have fallen into a trap of some sort. A tendency to right wing extremism asserts itself, or else everyone connected with esotericism is tarred with the same brush of condemnation as the

Syndicate, as though any group who declares itself less openly than the Women's Institute must surely be evil! Sometimes, a book will begin in a state of commendable equilibrium and end with a right-wing rant, as though its author's judgment had become unbalanced whilst actually writing it (which we consider to be highly likely). At the very least, there is a jarring misinterpretation of symbolism, and a sinister cloud of suspicion seems to descend through the writer's mind on the true as well as the false light, casting everything awry. (Perhaps it would be wise not to make this chapter too long...!)

The Syndicate represents the great separating force, that which separates us from God. It has been assembled for that very purpose, and is supernaturally expert in its field. It makes wisdom appear as a terrible stupidity; higher vision takes on the guise of naive gullibility, and what we should trust most, we suddenly doubt with a lurch of horror. The path of fear, paranoia, and fragmentation of the soul suddenly seems the only sensible route to pursue. The voice of panic masquerades as the voice of prudence.

Let us beware the arrogance and the misplaced curiosity which might tempt us to think that we are strong enough to handle the challenge the Syndicate represents! If we are in any sense below the level of a deity, we assuredly cannot. Focusing on it through curiosity is the way of destruction of strength and centredness. We can only defeat it by protecting the mind from its own tendency towards self-will, and thereby overcoming its refusal to aspire to the 'I Am' power of the higher will, the God-force within the heart. Let the mind be gently absorbed into the heart, and the tentacles of the Syndicate will no longer be able to reach you.

There is a safe method of studying the calibre and the secrets of the False Grail, which will reveal all that the Syndicate seeks to hide and obfuscate without leading the mind into danger and treachery. This secure exposure of the False Grail will be revealed in Chapter Seventy-four. We will end this chapter with a quote from Alice, who gives short shrift to the mind-befuddling techniques of the Syndicate:

> Alice sighed wearily. "I think you might do something better
> with the time," she said, "than wasting it in asking riddles that
> have no answers."

Chapter Seventy-three

The End of Days

At this point, it would probably be worthwhile to sing along with the White Rabbit in the film of *Alice in Wonderland*, just to help ourselves wake up to a crucial fact:

> We're late, we're late
> For a very important date!

We are certainly late in organising ourselves for a very important date, but, as has been stated before, we are not too late to rectify the situation. The date is early January 2013, and the event is the return of planet X, which will cut through Earth's orbit as it travels around the sun and sets off into outer space again, not to be seen for another 3,600 years. Mercury is in for a bit of a battering, and will actually lose some of its mass, but then we must understand that the Luciferic influences stem from the unharmonised emanations of the planet Mercury, just as Enlil represents the unharmonised forces of the planet Saturn. The transformer, as always, is human consciousness. Nevertheless, the impact on Mercury will bring it into an alignment with Earth which will help us to overcome our present dissonance with Mercury. Outer, bodily reality is an objectifi-cation of inner reality, the true reality, and what happens in outer space is a reflection of the dynamics occurring in inner space.

As planet X slices through our orbit, it will have a profound effect on our own planet. First and foremost, it will completely shatter Enlil's sinister ring, and will set the Earth spinning clockwise again, as she did many thousands of years ago. This will create quite an impact; we will have to hold on to our hats, but we are assured that there will be minimal loss of life, which can be reduced even further if our leaders will take heed of planet X's approach. (They will be forced to do so eventually, as at some point in the year 2012 the returning planet and its course for Earth's orbit will be visible and calculable by even amateur astronomical observers.)

We should not fear or dread planet X's return. He comes as our White Knight, to rescue us from the terrible malice of Enlil and his kiss of death. If our planet was left to spin anti-clockwise for very much longer, if the terrible reverse-spin gold ring was not shattered, Enlil - who, as we know from his physical and ethereal production of certain nefarious powders or negative-spin gold, has learnt to harness the power of the planet's negative spin in his own special way and was the agent of its changeover from positive to negative spin in the first place - would claim total victory.

We ought at this point to say a few words concerning the End-Dayists, who have been made aware of planet X's return by the scientific predictions of the astronomer Dr. James McCanney, who, as far as we understand, is not an End-Dayist himself, but was prepared for altruistic reasons to leak information, against the American Government's specific instructions, about the approach of planet X. The End-Dayists are a Christian cult who believe that planet X will destroy the Earth, but that they, being good, will be saved at the eleventh hour by 'Yahweh' (Enlil), who will sweep them off the Earth into heaven, whereas the rest of us, being bad, will have to perish in the flames and carnage of planet X's fatal impact. If only they could see into the heart of what they call their 'God'! It is as fearful as Mordor.

If, as appears to be the case, the End-Dayists are incarnate on earth in physical bodies, if they were born of woman, then they must forget the idea that any mercy or 'saving' will be available from Enlil (whom they call YAHUVEH). Enlil loathes the human race, and his aim is simply this - to exterminate it and to exterminate the planet that supports it. He laughs us all to scorn, his dupes as well as those who are awake to his sinister reality. He has deranged ideas that he is God, and can control the universe. Believe us when we say that this is not a well man we are dealing with.

Enlil is not God, and he cannot control the universe. He can only control *us* if we allow him to do so! His control must be brought to an end, not through outer belief that he is an impostor (which will look after itself), but through our triumphant reclamation of the spiritual light, the true God-force, within our hearts, the awareness of which he has darkened and confused and set into reverse spin.

Enlil is already panicking, because his master plan is off course. No third world war over religious intolerance has begun, despite his best efforts, even though he encourages our leaders to make repetitive

406

statements about 'the war on terrorism'. There is a dark occult power in the bandying of these words alone. Additionally, it is an attested fact that certain right wing Christian religious extremists from the West have in disguise infiltrated many fundamentalist Muslim cells, stoking up fear and hatred of Christianity and western countries, and inciting them by all kinds of means to commit horrors and depredations they would otherwise never have conceived of. There is, therefore, a secret bi-lateralism in this 'war', and the fundamentalist aggressors are certainly dupes of the hidden power of the Syndicate, even though they think they struggle against the worldly power of western civilisation. They are actually pawns in Enlil's game.

Meanwhile, the End-Dayists, of whom there are more than 63 million if sales of their literature are a true guide, play their part. One of their number, a Texan billionaire, is busy furnishing plans to multiply nuclear warheads within Israel, spurred on by the fact that his cult want to bring about the end of the world as soon as possible, imagining that thereby they are helping to fulfil the Scriptures!

This third world war 'should' have started at the beginning of the new millennium. According to the strategies of Enlil and Marduk, by the year 2013, the destruction of society, accompanied by horrible planetary emanations from our own Earth that we ourselves would have created, ought to have been well under way. If this had happened, planet X would not have been able to ride through the skies to save us. Instead, because of these noxious planetary emanations, his impact would have caused terrible devastation and wholesale loss of life, and he would not have succeeded in sending us back into positive spin - a situation which would preserve Enlil's reverse-spin gold ring from destruction. All this would have brought about the magnetic point of human woe and despair Enlil and Marduk are relying upon.

General Pike (see Chapter Seventy-one) was not informed that this global catastrophe would be the prime cause of humanity's turning away from any genuine idea of God, because as little warning as possible of planet X's impact could only boost Enlil's plan. According to this plan, humanity would not know what had hit it. Civilisation would have begun to descend into chaos in the early years of the new millennium prior to the hit, and therefore nobody would have been watching the skies, and nobody would have seen planet X coming. Enlil would thereby be in a position to reap the full benefit for his plan of what would amount to wholesale shock tactics of a kind never before encountered by our present-day civilisation. We have reason indeed to salute Dr McCanney for depriving Enlil of this strategy. Thanks to his courage, we now seem to have it on scientific authority that planet X is indeed heading towards us.

Enlil could not risk moles or leaks concerning such intelligence, and for precisely that reason the Syndicate themselves, except perhaps its innermost circle, knew nothing of the planet's return. He was confident that the very small number of people who would inevitably be made aware of it some years before its strike would be in his pocket, and could be influenced to keep quiet (he obviously reckoned without the good doctor!).

However, the point at which humanity would be brought to its knees, and would cry aloud to a seemingly unresponsive God, (see Pike's letter above) was indeed planned to be that at which planet X would strike, thereafter causing conditions on earth to seem like doomsday. Only by means of such planetary anguish could Marduk (Lucifer incarnate) persuade humanity to create the psychic opening through which the Naphidem could descend to earth. (We must understand, however, that Marduk, godlike as he is, is a human being, as is Enlil. The forces that drive them can be understood as two mighty angels of darkness, one of whom is Lucifer, who possesses Marduk, and the other we might call Ahriman, who possesses Enlil.)

Even bearing in mind the horror of all this, it is quite amusing, in a dreary sense, to see how Marduk and Enlil are forever contending against one another. We remember that they hated one another, although they worked together in perfect collusion, with Enlil remaining very much the dominant one of the pair. Marduk had to dance to Enlil's tune, but secretly thought he could rise to a position of equality with Enlil, and, moreover, persuade humanity to despise him, once Marduk and the Naphidem were safely back on earth.

Marduk was afraid of Enlil's power, and was, to some extent, aware that Enlil sought the annihilation of humanity. Marduk thought this was a bad idea. Why destroy humanity, when it could be kept alive for fun, and taught new ways of torturing, violating, degrading, oppressing and murdering one another, and, even more importantly, heaping up what it would etherically create thereby on altars dedicated to the Naphidem, whom humanity would feed with its worship and adoration? As far as Marduk was concerned, Enlil was just being a spoilsport. There was no need to kill humanity, when it would make such entertaining Goyim (cattle).

With these thoughts in mind, Marduk decided that he was the good 'god', and Enlil the bad 'god'! He was allowed his own headway with the Syndicate, because Enlil's plan from the first was to eliminate humanity by permitting the Naphidem to descend in triumph, and thereafter to corrupt it to the point where it brought self-destruction upon its own head. This self-destruction was intended to include the Naphidem in its grand sweep, because Enlil hated the Naphidem just as much, if not more, than ordinary humanity itself. (We remember that Enlil and the higher Anunnaki were human beings who had never incarnated on earth in a physical body, and that the Naphidem originally were human beings born to an earthly mother, but fathered by members of the higher Anunnaki, and who allowed themselves to be overtaken by the forces of darkness and chaos. Therefore, Enlil hated them, not only because he judged and condemned them for their appalling behaviour, but because they had committed the cardinal sin of entering into fleshly bodies via an earthly mother.) Marduk, of course, knew absolutely nothing about Enlil's drastic and sweeping 'Final Solution' for the Naphidem as well as for earthly humanity, but he suspected his austere, lordly colleague of some kind of undisclosed plot.

In another letter written by General Pike, dated 14 July 1889, he explains to the Grand Masters of his Palladian Councils (groups practicing rites of revised Masonry that he himself founded):

> That which we say to the crowd is 'we worship God'. But it is the God that one worships without superstition. The religion should be, by all us initiates of the high degrees, maintained in the purity of the Luciferian doctrine...Yes! Lucifer is God. And unfortunately Adonay is God also...for the absolute can only exist as two gods. Thus, the doctrine of Satanism is a heresy: and the true, and pure philosophical religion is the belief in Lucifer, the equal of Adonay: but Lucifer, God of Light, and God of Good, is struggling for humanity against Adonay the God of Darkness and Evil.[1]

It is plain from this excerpt that General Pike knows who 'Adonay' (from Adon, Enlil's preferred name, meaning 'Lord') is. He is the god who proclaims himself the One God ('Jehovah'-Enlil), and he is the god of

Satanism, who, according to Pike's letter, makes the same claim; in other words, these two entities are one, who is Enlil. Reading between the lines, we can see that Marduk (equated with Lucifer), is already selling the idea to his beloved Syndicate that he himself is God. He dare not deny Enlil as co-ruler (we are fairly certain that Marduk would never have dared to make these claims face to face with Enlil!), which seems to be why General Pike understands the Absolute as 'manifesting as two gods'. Marduk, who calls himself 'Lucifer' ('the Supreme Light') when he communicates with the inner circle of the Syndicate, has portrayed this 'other god', Adonay (Enlil), as dangerous and ill-willed towards humanity, which of course is correct. However, Marduk is obviously putting himself forward as a 'good' god, struggling to overcome Enlil's power, with humanity's interests at heart!

Marduk liked to comfort himself with this kind of name-calling and diatribe against Enlil, believing himself (erroneously) to be secure and insulated from Enlil's angry eye within the protective confines of the Syndicate. Even so, Syndicate members themselves were uncomfortably aware that Marduk alone did not direct the group. Mazzini, Pike's mentor and predecessor, wrote to a friend:

> We form an association of brothers in all points of the globe.
> We wish to break every yoke. Yet there is one unseen that can
> hardly be felt, yet it weighs on us. Whence comes it? Where is it?
> No one knows...or at least no one tells. This association is secret
> even to us the veterans of secret societies.

This, of course, was the impalpable influence of Enlil, the merest hint of a whisper of his ice-cold breath, the quivering of the veil of his invisible domain, darker than the deepest night. Marduk organised the Syndicate, but he took his orders from Enlil.

When we consider the machinations of Enlil and Marduk, and ponder on the Syndicate, we are in danger of being dragged down by the oppressive, strangling, anti-creative death forces that they represent, as mentioned in the previous chapter. We need a safer course of study, one that will enlighten us rather than lure us with barbed hooks disguised as morsels of nutrition into the darkness.

410

Notes and References

1. Sad to relate, a small number of the *perfecti* (the Cathar priesthood) fell into Marduk's power. He appeared to them as a God of Light, and unfortunately they were unable to differentiate between the true light of the spirit, and the false light of illusion. Marduk had a plan of his own. As we know, he had always hated and resented Enlil, and suspected that Enlil wanted to kill humankind (whilst remaining oblivious that Enlil also intended to eliminate the Naphidem, of whom Marduk was chief). Marduk concocted a plot within a plot. He would win the Goyim (cattle, or humanity) over to his side by persuading those members of earthly humanity over whom he won influence that he was the 'good god' and Enlil was the 'bad god'. Masquerading as a god of 'pure' light, he wormed his way into the Cathars, the Templars, the Rosicrucians, the Masons, the alchemists, and other esoteric groups who existed to preserve Enki and Nin-khursag's truth: the truth of Tiâmat the Mother and Oannes the Father, and of the Daughter-Son of Light, their divine child. He made small or great headway according to the strengths and weaknesses of the groups he encountered. This led to a rift between these esoteric groups. Some stood their ground, others became contaminated. Where even a chink appeared in their armour, some organisations fell, horribly butchered, as in the case of the Cathars, Templars and 'witches' (feminine wise ones or mystics). Enlil smiled approvingly whilst Marduk schemed. Marduk's plot was taking the Naphidem chief exactly where Enlil wished his footsteps to fall, although, of course, Marduk believed Enlil was ignorant of his intentions. Instead, Enlil did exactly what he wanted with the strength and influence of the defiled esoteric societies, particularly with the global banks, which were a direct legacy of the Templars (there were no banks until, originally for altruistic reasons rather than for profit, the Templars established the principle which led to their appearance).

As the writing of this book is drawing to a close, (October 2008), it seems that unprecedented public ownership of the banks might manage to permanently alter the power structure upon which the banks formerly operated. We sincerely hope they will be taken out of Enlil's stranglehold of authority. We note with interest that, of the two men who set up the Bilderberg movement in 1954, one was George Ball, a businessman who later became the managing director of Lehman Brothers Incorporated. This establishment was, we understand, the first US bank to properly collapse, so setting up the domino effect for the others.

411

Chapter Seventy-four

One Ring to Rule Them All, and in the Darkness Bind Them

It is now time to drink a toast to Tolkien! This masterful John-man wrote his epic, *The Lord of the Rings*, to throw a profound illumination upon the nature, principles, dangers and powers of the False Grail. He was an orthodox Catholic, and had no overt knowledge of the history of events as we are disclosing them...and yet he knew everything, as his great work of imagination silently proclaims. We can study his literary marathon in as much depth as we like without falling into the least danger. We will be given a panoramic view of all we need to know concerning the False Grail, including a guided tour of its mysteries, and we will be magnificently protected throughout.

It is most telling to relate that, when asked to what historical era the environment of his tale might belong, Tolkien replied that he would place it somewhere around 4,000 BC. This, as we know, is precisely when Anu and Enlil's dark plot against humanity began to cast its deepest shadow in the form of the creation of the reverse-spin gold, after Enlil had discovered that the 'new humanity' (Adam and Eve) had not been brought forth by Enki and Nin-khursag as mindless slaves for the use of the corrupt contingent of the Higher Anunnaki, but as initiated, Tiâmat-consecrated beings with the full range of potential necessary to attain supreme beinghood. ("It is the time of Man!" proclaim the kingly characters in the book.) Enlil went on to create his malevolent ring from the reverse-spin gold, which he placed around our planet in the form of subtle, undetectable crystals in the higher atmosphere, where it still exists today.

It is at this point that we might play a simple word game and pause to ponder on Tolkien's name. If we read the last two letters and conjoin them with the fourth and fifth in reverse or mirror order (en-ki), the result is interesting, to say the least! The other 'name within a name' in mirror reversal is Lot, the learned man from Ur who held high status in Gomorrah, and who was visited by two angels, come to inform him that the 'citadel of ancient knowledge' in which he lived was about to be horrifically destroyed by the Dark Lord via fiendish and magical weaponry.

It is as well to become accustomed to this capering and cavorting of language, because it is an ancient art pertaining to names in particular, which are charged with their own life. In our second volume, as we progress deeper and deeper into the history of the Grail and its trail of clues, hints and pointers of this linguistic nature will proliferate. For instance, 'Adam Weishaupt', the first overt leader of the amalgamated Illuminati (even though it was known as the 'Bavarian' Illuminati) means: Adam (the first man), *Weis* (to know), *Haupt* (leader), and seems to read as: 'the first man to be known as leader'. (This cipher within Weishaupt's name was discovered by the authors Anthony Roberts and Geoff Gilbertson.)

As Quayin or Cain represented the true eye or the *ayin*, the Eye of Horus of whom humanity is the 'pupil', associated with the Star Fire (whose symbol was the eye) and a sigil of the Grail, so this symbol of God-consciousness became distorted by the negative-spin agencies into the false eye, the false Grail. This eye is more commonly depicted as an eye within a triangle.[1]

By no means is it necessarily a negative symbol, as its esoteric meaning is 'Doorway to the Light'. The great question is: which light? It can indicate the doorway to the spiritual light, the ineffable light of God, or it can refer to the false light, the light of Lucifer and the Luciferic Illuminati. In other words, the doorway specified can open onto the serpent-ladder of light stretching upwards into the heavens, or it can creak slowly ajar onto the head of a great negative snake and take the duped spiritual seeker on a slithery ride down to degenerate depths. Which way will the eye in the pyramid go? Which direction will it choose? The false eye relates to the imbalance of materialism (the downward pull of matter), and within its glittering gleam can always be found the desire for authoritarian power and control. The symbol of the eye in the pyramid appears as the *reverse* of the United States Great Seal, and in 1933 (we note the 33 degrees of Masonic symbolism) President Roosevelt introduced it as the *reverse* sigil for the one-dollar bill.

413

There is a rather spooky story attached to the adoption of this symbol. It seems that while Franklin, Adams and Jefferson were collaborating on the design of the Great Seal, there was some disagreement, and Jefferson took a turn around the garden to imbibe some fresh air and clear his head. Suddenly, a tall man dressed entirely in black, arrayed in a sweeping black cloak which hid his face (virtually a Black Rider!), appeared before Jefferson and gave him a piece of paper, advising him that he would find it meaningful and appropriate. The stranger then disappeared into a thicket, whilst Jefferson was left staring down at the piece of paper, which depicted the emblem of the eye in the triangle. Jefferson rushed back indoors and presented the sigil to his colleagues, who were eager to adopt it.

This story demonstrates the need for cosmic balance between darkness and light, which must be harmonised in the heart. The United States has a great choice to make between the doorway to the Grail (the 'good dragon') and the doorway to the snakehead (the 'negative dragon'). The prophecy of this choice was integral to the very founding of America. Currently, the eye in the triangle sigil seems to incline more to the dark side. Anthony Roberts and Geoff Gilbertson call it the 'all-seeing burning eye of power and control that would one day dominate the world'. This appears to hold sway at present. What Enlil has severely underestimated is the huge reservoir of goodness, of simple love and purity, within the collective human heart (after all, we are Tiâmat's children, not his!). It is true that it is heavily obscured at the moment; but we are assured that it is there, and that humanity is already turning towards the light, towards the heart. Remember how awry Enlil's plans have turned! There is no doubt that we are on track and heading steadfastly towards the return of the Grail.

We can return to Tolkien's epic tale and think of that great eye within a tower (in this case, within what preceded the pyramid – the tall, straight tower known as the *shem*) which constitutes the Dark Lord of Mordor. This is the evil eye - the Luciferic eye which is also the eye of Enlil – the besieged and manacled *ayin*, prevented from becoming higher consciousness or the Stone of Ascension in the head. The whole of the Dark Lord's terrain is a vast evil forge. Just as Cain is the good, true and just craftsman, building the pure and light-filled human soul, the individual human consciousness connected to the Star Fire, so the Lord of Mordor, Sauron, (*saur* - the lower self or dragon, the rampaging dino*saur* of earth) is the evil craftsman, constantly battling against the creative

414

forces and seeking to undo and undermine their progress.

Not only is Mordor an evil forge, it is a hideous *forgery*. It is the constructor of the Untrue, and the epicentre of Lies. We think that the very name *Mordor* whispers an echo of the actual name of that dark and ireful dimension in which Enlil and his followers dwell, described so aptly by Tolkien as a place where loathsome worms (manifestations of the lower dragon) slither beneath the surface and undermine the integrity of the very ground beneath one's feet. It is a name linguistically very similar to the words 'murder', and 'mort' or death. Mordor and its lord forged the ring. This ring, which must be cast into the Cracks of Doom, is the False Grail and all its power. It was found by an innocent swimming in the water (originally an Oannes man, until he became the Falling Knight and plunged from grace), and it overwhelmed him and turned him into a subhuman creature whose only source of intelligence was his own evil - the anti-Oannes man - Gollum (linguistically close to Goyim – cattle or driven creatures, just as poor Gollum was desperately driven by his rabid, all-consuming desire for the ring[2]). It can only be overcome by being returned to its source. Then it shall no more have dominion.

What does this mean - returning it to its source? It means that we give back the Luciferic and Ahrimanic gifts which have been given to us. Everything in our nature which acts against the heart comprises these gifts. We give them back to Enlil and Marduk, and we become free. False pride, selfishness, condemnation, anger, hatred, authoritarian power and domination, etcetera, etcetera, we return to its source. This can be done in simple, everyday ways, but its impact will be monumental. We do it by refusing to accept the 'gift' (really the takeover, because the dark forces steal rather than give, although they are very good at disguising this fact) in the first place. We decline to take on board the dark energy, the dark expressions, the dark thoughts and acts of the lower dragon – our lower 'Sauron' selves. When we do this, we return it to its source.

The surefire method of succeeding in this task is to nurture our higher Pendragon selves in the way we have previously described – to turn to the light, to exercise that moment of choice when we can most powerfully choose to repudiate the darkness, to use the star constantly in our everyday lives, and to have absolute faith that there are shining beings of the one true light stretching their hands towards us to help us onward and upward in every conceivable situation we may encounter.

Notes and References

1. The eye in the triangle is a depiction of human consciousness within its chakra system (the *ayin* in the pyramid). It is the sigil of the new soul-structure with which Tiâmat provided us when the depredations of Enlil and Marduk overcame the earth-vulnerable *shem*, the tall, thin, conical tower shape upon which human souls were previously structured. The priceless jewel, or Stone of Ascension within the head, is the sign of exalted human consciousness rising above and beyond the triangle of the chakras, until it is free to walk among the stars. The eye above the apex of the triangle is therefore Enki's sign, whilst the eye enclosed in the triangle is Enlil's sign. As has been discussed, the latter sign is only evil when the eye is actually imprisoned within the triangle, unable to rise because it has fallen into the trap of the reverse-spin powers. When this occurs, the precious Stone of Ascension in the head eventually becomes subject to a full reversal and descends in degradation to the feet – Enlil's final victory, because if this happens he has successfully beheaded those who aspire to be God-Headed people (ourselves), and he can laugh in triumph as he beholds our God-given Stone of Ascension - our very God-head itself - lying worthless, atrophied and disconnected at our uncomprehending feet. Enlil may be prone to victorious belly-laughs at our plight (and he has given forth many of them), but only because he does not understand what will happen on a world-wide scale when humanity begins at last to realise its mistake and moves to embrace the Grail.

2. Gollum calls the ring his 'precious' and is utterly besotted with it. It is a symbol of his lower self, the little 'I' of earth, which the forces of materialism tempt us to adore and indulge to the extent where we become selfish, self-seeking and narrow-minded, utterly bound to the Earth and incapable of rising into the reality of the spiritual worlds, from where we draw our life, vision and ultimate redemption. From this point on, the soul becomes corroded and corrupted, and can only embrace death.

416

Chapter Seventy-five

A Ring of Pure and Endless Light

What of planet X's return? Will it cause mayhem on earth, even if we reclaim our Pendragon status?

Yes, it will cause many practical problems, but an intelligent anticipation of the impact will allow us to minimise chaotic conditions and loss of life (our guidance seems to suggest to fewer than three hundred people). Thankfully, the sacrifice of these brave souls will be anything but in vain.

Although we should do all we can to keep our planet and its atmosphere pure and unpolluted, we are advised that it is not carbon emissions that are mainly responsible for current meteorological disturbances and peculiarities, but the electromagnetic effect on the sun of planet X's return, which is then translated to earth as a consequence. Our weather patterns will return to normal a few years after it has passed us by on its return journey to outer space. Although we certainly must bring to an end our destructive, polluting behaviour towards our beautiful Earth (especially with regard to the destruction of the rainforests), the future of the planet is assured. There will be some inundation and loss of land, but our compensation will be that new lands will arise from the sea, which will actually regulate and stabilise rising sea levels. Some parts of Atlantis will emerge permanently from their watery grave, which will put paid to a lot of tiresome argument!

In the Gospel of Mary, there is a wonderful teaching about ascension and the seven circuits of the soul, which of course refers to the chakras. We have to cleanse and energise our chakras with the inspiration of divine love, with the influx of Pendragon consciousness. What planet X will leave behind him when he cuts through our orbit is a great streamer of cosmic matter (we are not going to say debris). This cosmic matter will surround our planet, and we will experience some (bearable) turbulence for seven years as we pass through it. Seven years - seven circuits of the soul. This is our great mission - to cleanse our own chakras, and those of our beloved planet, as we make each of the seven circuits through planet X's streamer of cosmic matter.

We will have many chances to express brotherhood and helpfulness, altruism and generosity, during these seven years - both to our neighbours and within a global context. All humanity will come together to pull one another through these years of trials and testing. But it will not be soul-destroying and terrible, as Enlil would wish it to be. It will be challenging, but civilisation will not break down. We will be able to do the normal things of everyday life. We will sail through the experience if we concentrate on meeting one another's needs rather than our own. In fact, it could all be quite good fun; and we will find ourselves insisting more and more, as the years go by, that life on planet Earth *is* fun; not commercialised, substance-fed fun hooked up to all sorts of strange manipulations and control, as it is at the moment, but real fun for everyone, which is quite different in essence, and much, much, more potent.

Yes, we will succeed in our mission of universal chakra healing and cleansing, even rather magnificently. And when the seven years are done, something truly wondrous will happen. The streamer of cosmic matter will grow brighter during each of the seven years, reflecting more and more light, crystalline and dancing, like the clearest starlight. And then, finally, the wonder will come into being. A ring of pure and endless light will form in perfection around our planet, breathtaking, beautiful. It will be the loveliest of all the cosmic phenomena the world has ever seen. And it will be permanent; a ring of celestial love, delicately pearlescent, a band set with pearls of wisdom and reflective Star Fire, given by planet X to honour his lover, the Earth. It will look rather like Saturn's ring, but it will wear an aspect of even greater heavenly grandeur and cosmic beauty.

Within this exquisite ring, which will give our nights a soft and magical glow, we will be perfectly safe, immaculately protected, from the incursions of Enlil or any other hostile influence...

...At one, at peace, all danger assuaged at last, and the Grail lifting us ever closer to heaven and its boundless stars.

Appendix One

Alice, the Dragon Queen, and the Tree of Life

We will let Lewis Carroll speak for himself, after pointing out that the pigeon is of the dove family – the dove of the Holy Spirit which descends on the waiting soul as that quality of 'peace that passeth all understanding' – the peace of the Paraclete. The esoteric rather than the literal argument here is that the Pigeon is unaware that the treasure it brings forth from its depths is for the nourishment of its Pendragon self in its aspiration towards ascension, and is not brought forth simply so that it may keep on reproducing its little earthly lower dragon self over and over again in a repetitive and unprogressive cycle (the latter being the state of soul and consciousness that Enlil tries to inculcate in us). The Pigeon is, of course, the dove in its mundane, uninspired manifestation (with all due respect to pigs, we might say that there is a pig-headed element to it!); however, although its attitudes leave a lot to be desired, it still seems to know a thing or two, as we shall see:

"Come, my head's free at last!" said Alice in a tone of delight, which changed into alarm in another moment, when she discovered that her shoulders were nowhere to be found: all she could see, when she looked down, was an immense length of neck, which seemed to rise like a stalk out of a sea of green leaves that lay far below her. "What *can* all that green stuff be?" said Alice.

"And where *have* my shoulders got to? And oh, my poor hands, how is it I can't see you?" She was moving them about as she spoke, but no result seemed to follow, except a little shaking among the distant green leaves. As there seemed to be no chance of getting her hands up to her head, she tried to get her head down to them, and was delighted to find that her neck would bend about easily in any direction, like a serpent. She had just succeeded in curving it

419

down into a graceful zigzag, and was going to dive in among the leaves, which she found to be nothing but the tops of the trees under which she had been wandering, when a sharp hiss made her draw back in a hurry: a large pigeon had flown into her face, and was beating her violently with its wings.

"Serpent!" screamed the Pigeon.

"I'm *not* a serpent!" said Alice indignantly. "Let me alone!"

"Serpent, I say again!" repeated the Pigeon, but in a more subdued tone, and added, with a kind of sob, "I've tried every way, but nothing seems to suit them!"

"I haven't the least idea what you're talking about," said Alice.

"I've tried the roots of trees, and I've tried banks, and I've tried hedges," the Pigeon went on, without attending to her; "but those serpents! There's no pleasing them!"

Alice was more and more puzzled, but she thought there was no use in saying anything more till the Pigeon had finished.

"As if it wasn't trouble enough hatching the eggs," said the Pigeon; "but I must be on the look-out for serpents, night and day! Why, I haven't had a wink of sleep these three weeks!"

"I'm very sorry you've been annoyed," said Alice, who was beginning to see its meaning.

"And just as I'd taken the highest tree in the wood," continued the Pigeon, raising its voice to a shriek, "and just as I was thinking I'd be free of them at last, they must needs come wriggling down from the sky! Ugh, Serpent!"

"But I'm *not* a serpent, I tell you!" said Alice. I'm a – I'm a -"

"Well! *What* are you?" said the Pigeon. "I can see you're trying to invent something!"

"I – I'm a little girl," said Alice, rather doubtfully, as she remembered the number of changes she had gone through that day.

"A likely story, indeed!" said the Pigeon, in a tone of the deepest contempt. "I've seen a good many little girls in my time, but never *one* with such a neck as that! No, no! You're a serpent, and there's no use denying it. I suppose you'll be telling me next that you never tasted an egg!"

"I *have* tasted eggs, certainly," said Alice, who was a very truthful child; "but little girls eat eggs quite as much as serpents do, you know."

"I don't believe it," said the Pigeon; "but if they do, why, then they're a kind of serpent: that's all I can say."

(Chapter V, *Alice's Adventures in Wonderland*, Lewis Carroll)

Exactly!

Appendix Two

For the reader's interest, we would like to present here a series of hiero-glyphs that was given to Margaret Bailey via her inner vision whilst we were working on *The Secret Teachings of Mary Magdalene*. It was intimated to us that these strange symbols were related to the Holy Grail, although at the time we did not realise the potential of their significance, as we believed that Tamar (see Chapters One and Two) solely embodied this identity, and that there was nothing physical to be discovered relating to the Grail.

We submitted them for inspection to an ancient languages specialist associated with the British Library, who kindly informed us that the hieroglyphs did not formulate a language in themselves, although there were elements of Coptic and other languages within them. No sense could be made of them, however.

Since then, we have received an intuition that the symbols might constitute an old Templar code, known only to the inner circle of the Knights Templar The Knights of the Swan (see Chapter Eight). We think that the symbols say something important, and that they are inscribed on some artefact or documentation accompanying the Grail, or perhaps even, as a later addition, within the pages of the book which comprises the Emerald Tablet, (the Book of Love or the lost Gospel of John) itself.

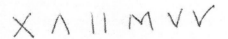

November 2004

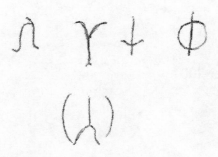

13th November 2004

17th November 2004

18th November 2004

23rd November 2004

423

27th November 2004

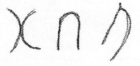

8th December 2004

13th December 2004

4th January 2005

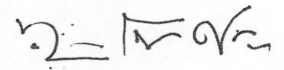

424

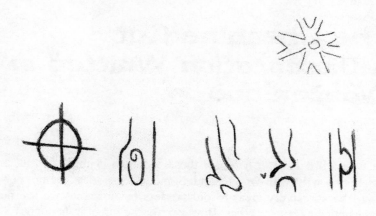

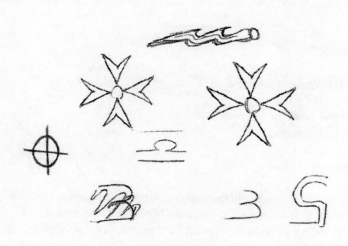

Appendix Three

The Cheshire Cat
A Dissertation Written in Wonderland

We would like to offer here, for those to whom it might appeal, a little dissertation written in Wonderland. Some of these ideas are not new, and it will be abrasively clear to our readers by now that we are neither mathematicians nor scientists. However, for the fun of it, here goes:

We will start with the black dot, which seems to be massively important (only what sort of mass?). We think, a very strange sort of mass; however, we will not allow ourselves to be deflected from the point...

We posit that

- the pupil of the eye, or the *ayin*
- the nucleus of the atom
- the decimal point
- the contracted universe

are all the same thing!

This tiny point contains all dimensions, even the concept of dimension. For instance, if a single atom were as big as a giant planet, its nucleus would still be an infinitesimal point. Therefore, perhaps size and dimension are all illusory.

This might be the reason why, traditionally, fairies delight in appearing to human beings as terrifyingly huge or very small, and then suddenly changing their size dramatically. They are teaching us that size in itself is an illusion.

• The pupil of the eye expands and contracts.
• The decimal point expands things if it moves in one direction, and contracts things if it moves in the opposite direction.
• The universe expands into everything, and contracts into the black dot or let us say, the decimal point.

The decimal point not only contains all size and dimension, it *controls* them. (Moving forward, it expands; moving backwards, it contracts.)

We think that Enlil has somehow contrived, via this secret of the *ayin*, and of the nucleus of the atom, and of the decimal point, which is enshrined in his reverse-spin mirror, to make small things look big and big things look small. Trying to respond appropriately, we move in a direction to *minimise*, but we *maximize* instead – and vice versa. We think that Enlil has hidden his mirror from our cognition by moving the decimal point to a position that we would never suspect within the confines of our normal rationality. We need to ask Alice's advice on this!

One character from Wonderland has come forward to show us the way; namely, the Cheshire Cat. Our lesson seems to be about dimension and size, and the wrong, misleading or opposite reflection of dimension and size. Just like the initials of the Cheshire Cat – the CC – the two halves of a circle (the circle whose centrepoint is the dot) show that the ring or the circle has been cut in half instead of maintaining its God-given form and thereby sustaining the creation of the continuous energy flow within the integrity of a circuit or a circle. (We actually see the circles coming forth from the dot, as if it were emitting them. We think that what we see is the *ouroboros*, the essence of the power of the sacred ring which Enlil seeks to pervert or reverse.) This cleaving in half is the Enlil principle – the same principle he used in order to change all the positive and negative pairs of electrons (male and female) in his high-spin gold to exclusively positive (male) electrons at the ethereal level.

Enlil's aim was to create an exclusively masculine scenario or dimension, or at the very least, a masculine-dominant one which obscured and denied the feminine principle. To do this, he ensured that instead of creating the sacred marriage of the circle or circuit with the components of the circle, the circuit would be cut so that its halves lined up like this – CC . Although their equality cannot actually be impaired or removed, one half nevertheless *stands behind* the other half and is obscured and over-shadowed by it. If this situation persists for long enough, degeneration, death and destruction is the result.

We see that in the case of the Cheshire Cat – the CC – his *body* disappears, but his *smile* remains in the physical, visible dimension. This is the wrong way round – his *body* should remain in the physical dimension – the special dimension prepared for it by Tiâmat – but his *smile*, the impression of his spirit, should easily disappear from it without encountering any difficulty or delay in slipping between dimensions.

In other words, the Cheshire Cat fits into earthly reality the wrong way round, because his body vanishes and his smile remains!

This teaches us that Enlil has learnt how to reverse the qualities of dimensions or, rather, how to hide what should be visible within a dimension, and show what should not be there, or should not be there in a certain expression or context. He has hidden half the decimal point behind the other half – CC – so we can't see the real world! We can't see the emanation of Tiâmat's consciousness in its true expression.

The brain can be fooled by Enlil's reverse-spin, or fool's, gold, but the *eye* or *ayin* cannot – hence the huge significance of Dagobert's eye. However, we know that Dagobert's eye was put out, or run through by a lance. This does not matter, because there is an ethereal eye of the spirit in the brain – the Stone of Ascension – whose point of consciousness is the chakral 'third eye' (to show our 'thrice greatest' status). This eye cannot be fooled and cannot be put out, simply because it *is* the decimal point in all its purity, indivisible and incorruptible and unbeguilable by Enlil. It is the pupil, the nucleus, the contracted universe, the decimal point, Tiâmat's consciousness itself – the sacred *ayin*.

We have found the Cheshire Cat to be a most helpful and instructive beast. He seems not to mind in the least that we may have cracked the enigma behind his smile! However, it is not in the nature of Wonderland to run out of possibilities. His disembodied smile still seems to be a knowing one…

Let there be many windows in your soul,
That all the glory of the universe
May beautify it. Not the narrow pane
Of one poor creed can catch the radiant rays
That shine from countless sources. Tear away
The blinds of superstition; let the light
Pour through fair windows, broad as truth itself
And high as heaven...Tune your ear
To all the wordless music of the stars
And to the voice of nature, and your heart
Shall turn to truth and goodness as the plant
Turns to the sun. A thousand unseen hands
Reach down to help you to their peace-crowned heights,
And all the forces of the firmament
Shall fortify your strength. Be not afraid
To thrust aside half-truths and grasp the whole.

In Tune with the Infinite
Ralph Waldo Trine

In loving appreciation of the presence of Squadron Leader George Carver,
who died in combat on 18th July 1944.
'From adversity to the stars'

Some other titles from Capall Bann

Mary Magdalene: Lost Goddess, Lost Gospels by Jan McDonald

Repentant sinner to Saint: Who is the real Magdalene and why was her gospel denied by the orthodox church? What is her true status? This book traces the true identity of The Magdalene from the hidden clues that abound in the canonical gospels and Paul's letters. Contents include: What is happening globally to make this so important at this time, two thousand years after the event?; The Magdalene and the Holy Grail. Connections between Arthurian legend and Mary Magdalene exist on several levels, including the origin of the name Camelot; The Magdalene Trail. From the day she landed in Provence, Mary Magdalene became beloved of the people of the Languedoc area. Later, churches, cathedrals and shrines were built all over France; Christ and the Magdalene as the Sacrificed Bridegroom and the Bride, God/Goddess, Masculine/Feminine Divine in balance. The Gospel of Mary Magdalene. Lost Gospel of a Lost Goddess. From an early translation and commentary we can see the real message and the teachings that show the way for the soul's ascension. More Lost Gospels. Gospel of Phillip. Gospel of Thomas, looking at further documentary evidence written by Christ's closest companions as to the true status of Mary. Why Mary Magdalene is so important now in this New Age. The return of the Goddess to her rightful place in Christianity. Jan has traced the Magdalene's footsteps through France and visited her hidden shrines and disguised places of worship and has tried to bring those lost gospels into today's perspective. This is the time of the Age of Aquarius when male and female will find balance in us and in the divine and true healing will be brought about at the core of our souls. Join Jan on the journey to the Goddess of Christianity, to The Magdalene in this highly readable, enjoyable and informative book. ISBN 186163 2525   £10.95

Everything You Always Wanted To Know About Your Body, But, So Far, Nobody's Been Able To Tell You

by Chris Thomas & Diane Baker

"...easy to understand...insight into how you can heal yourself...comprehensive guide" Here's Health   Have you ever wondered why some people become ill and others do not? Why some people recover from illness and others do not? Do you know how your body really works? Why do diets rarely work? Is there an alternative approach to treating symptoms of illness instead of using prescriptive drugs? Well here is a book which leads you through the body, organ by organ, system by system, and explains in clear language how illness arises and what to do about it. It explains the workings of the human body in simple language and clear illustrations; which elements are connected together and why they can influence each other. It also relates each region and organ to its associated chakra and how our day-to-day lives have an influence on our health and well-being. Every part of the body is dealt with in these ways and the major underlying causes for most of our illnesses explained. It also provides details and suggestions on how to heal yourself by working on the root cause issues. This book also takes a look at how some illnesses are brought about by past life traumas and looks at ways of healing the symptoms of illness without the need for prescriptive drugs. Several forms of healing practices are used to achieve this: Bach Flower Remedies, Reflexology, Herbalism, Biochemic Tissue Salts and Homeopathy are the main approaches used, with a further twenty seven therapies fully described. This is an extensive, comprehensive look at the body and illness. It is also one of the most comprehensive guides to alternative treatments currently available. ISBN 186163 0980   £17.95

The Company of Heaven by Jan McDonald

Angels are divine spirit beings that have chosen not to incarnate into the physical realm in the normal way but can bridge the gap between heaven and earth. They act as divine messengers and intermediaries between us and God/Goddess, HigherPower/Creator, Source/Universe, they are ambassadors from 'above' and helpers and healers here on the physical plane. Whilst angels can appear to us as the archetypal winged celestial messenger they may also appear in physical form, coming into our lives when we need them most. In times of personal transition or change as well as at times of great Universal change such as our Earth is currently facing, Angels can act together as teams to ease the pain of these transitions. This book brings you to a closer understanding of the Angelic Realm and how to work with them for your own benefit in healing and personal spiritual growth as well as for others and for the healing of our troubled Mother Earth. Here you will encounter the peace and love and divine healing that these wonderful beings can bring and that you will meet with your Guardian Angel who will be your constant companion and guide as you walk through your daily lives. Not just another angel book - this one is truly informative and inspirational. ISBN 186163 279 7 £9.95

Reaching for the Divine by Philip Kinsella

Reaching for the Divine is a serious manual for anyone remotely interested in Life After Death. For anyone who has lost someone close to them, this can be a very traumatic experience indeed. This book, however, is designed to help you communicate with your loved ones who have passed into the Spirit World. It also enables you to work with your Spirit Guides and helps you understand the mechanics of clairvoyance and how it works. *Reaching for the Divine* not only covers subjects on how to understand the Spirit World's language, but enables you to become a conduit between the two worlds too. The author is a professional working medium and teacher on he subject of After Life Communications. This book is a must for anyone searching to establish the true power of themselves and how they can Reach For The Divine. Philip Kinsella is the author of numerous articles on the paranormal and has appeared on radio and television. He has also spent two decades studying the UFO subject. ISBN 186163 2800 £10.95

Dreamtime - A History, Mythology, Physiology and Guide to the Interpretation of Dreams by Linda Louisa Dell

The author investigates the history and background to dreams including the belief of ancient civilization and modern cultures, major theories about dreaming such as those of Freud and Jung as well as more modern theories, significant recent research and data on animal sleeping experiences. She looks at the phenomena of sleep and dreaming including the basic sleep cycles and how a dream is structured, lucid dreaming, astral projection and nightmares, sleep paralysis and problem solving. Sleep disorders, such as insomnia, sleep-walking and sleep talking are also covered. Part two of the book gives a comprehensive dream directory and details some of the most common dream subjects for an extra in-depth analysis. It is essential for readers to have some awareness of this long and rich history if they want to have a well-grounded understanding of twentieth century dream psychology. Dreams follow us out of sleep, bringing their magic and mystery into our waking lives, building a bridge between consciousness and unconsciousness, between the known and the unknown. Dreams inspire us to reclaim their experience through the language of creative thought, art, literature, film, music and movement through our eyes, hands, hearts and minds. Dream the vision and envision the dream - this book will start you on that journey. ISBN 186163 278 9 £17.95

FREE DETAILED CATALOGUE

Capall Bann is owned and run by people actively involved in many of the areas in which we publish. A detailed illustrated catalogue is available on request, SAE or International Postal Coupon appreciated. **Titles can be ordered direct from Capall Bann, post free in the UK** (cheque or PO with order) or from good bookshops and specialist outlets.

A Breath Behind Time, Terri Hector
A Soul is Born by Eleyna Williamson
Angels and Goddesses - Celtic Christianity & Paganism, M. Howard
The Art of Conversation With the Genius Loci, Barry Patterson
Arthur - The Legend Unveiled, C Johnson & E Lung
Astrology The Inner Eye - A Guide in Everyday Language, E Smith
Auguries and Omens - The Magical Lore of Birds, Yvonne Aburrow
Asyniur - Women's Mysteries in the Northern Tradition, S McGrath
Beginnings - Geomancy, Builder's Rites & Electional Astrology in the
    European Tradition, Nigel Pennick
Between Earth and Sky, Julia Day
The Book of Seidr, Runic John
Caer Sidhe - Celtic Astrology and Astronomy, Michael Bayley
Call of the Horned Piper, Nigel Jackson
Can't Sleep, Won't Sleep, Linda Louisa Dell
Carnival of the Animals, Gregor Lamb
Cat's Company, Ann Walker
Celebrating Nature, Gordon MacLellan
Celtic Faery Shamanism, Catrin James
Celtic Faery Shamanism - The Wisdom of the Otherworld, Catrin James
Celtic Lore & Druidic Ritual, Rhiannon Ryall
Celtic Sacrifice - Pre Christian Ritual & Religion, Marion Pearce
Celtic Saints and the Glastonbury Zodiac, Mary Caine
Circle and the Square, Jack Gale
Come Back To Life, Jenny Smedley
Company of Heaven, Jan McDonald
Compleat Vampyre - The Vampyre Shaman, Nigel Jackson
Cottage Witchcraft, Jan McDonald
Creating Form From the Mist - The Wisdom of Women in Celtic Myth and
    Culture, Lynne Sinclair-Wood
Crystal Clear - A Guide to Quartz Crystal, Jennifer Dent
Crystal Doorways, Simon & Sue Lilly
Crossing the Borderlines - Guising, Masking & Ritual Animal Disguise in the
    European Tradition, Nigel Pennick

Dragons of the West, Nigel Pennick
Dreamtime by Linda Louisa Dell
Dreamweaver by Elen Sentier
Earth Dance - A Year of Pagan Rituals, Jan Brodie
Earth Harmony - Places of Power, Holiness & Healing, Nigel Pennick
Earth Magic, Margaret McArthur
Egyptian Animals - Guardians & Gateways of the Gods, Akkadia Ford
Eildon Tree (The) Romany Language & Lore, Michael Hoadley
Enchanted Forest - The Magical Lore of Trees, Yvonne Aburrow
Eternal Priestess, Sage Weston
Eternally Yours Faithfully, Roy Radford & Evelyn Gregory
Everything You Always Wanted To Know About Your Body, But So Far
    Nobody's Been Able To Tell You, Chris Thomas & D Baker
Experiencing the Green Man, Rob Hardy & Teresa Moorey
Face of the Deep - Healing Body & Soul, Penny Allen
Fairies and Nature Spirits, Teresa Moorey
Fairies in the Irish Tradition, Molly Gowen
Familiars - Animal Powers of Britain, Anna Franklin
Flower Wisdom, Katherine Kear
Fool's First Steps, (The) Chris Thomas
Forest Paths - Tree Divination, Brian Harrison, Ill. S. Rouse
From Past to Future Life, Dr Roger Webber
From Stagecraft To Witchcraft, Patricia Crowther
Gardening For Wildlife Ron Wilson
God Year, The, Nigel Pennick & Helen Field
Goddess on the Cross, Dr George Young
Goddess Year, The, Nigel Pennick & Helen Field
Goddesses, Guardians & Groves, Jack Gale
Handbook For Pagan Healers, Liz Joan
Handbook of Fairies, Ronan Coghlan
Healing Book, The, Chris Thomas and Diane Baker
Healing Homes, Jennifer Dent
Healing Journeys, Paul Williamson
Healing Stones, Sue Philips
Heathen Paths - Viking and Anglo Saxon Beliefs by Pete Jennings
Herb Craft - Shamanic & Ritual Use of Herbs, Lavender & Franklin
Hidden Heritage - Exploring Ancient Essex, Terry Johnson
Hub of the Wheel, Skytoucher
In and Out the Windows, Dilys Gator
In Search of Herne the Hunter, Eric Fitch
In Search of the Green Man, Peter Hill
Inner Celtia, Alan Richardson & David Annwn
Inner Mysteries of the Goths, Nigel Pennick
Inner Space Workbook - Develop Through Tarot, Cat Summers & Julian Vayne
In Search of Pagan Gods, Teresa Moorey
Intuitive Journey, Ann Walker Isis - African Queen, Akkadia Ford
Journey Home, The, Chris Thomas

Kecks, Keddles & Kesh - Celtic Lang & The Cog Almanac, Bayley
Language of the Psycards, Berenice
Legend of Robin Hood, The, Richard Rutherford-Moore
Lid Off the Cauldron, Patricia Crowther
Light From the Shadows - Modern Traditional Witchcraft, Gwyn
Living Tarot, Ann Walker
Lore of the Sacred Horse, Marion Davies
Lost Lands & Sunken Cities (2nd ed.), Nigel Pennick
Lyblác, Anglo Saxon Witchcraft by Wulfeage
The Magic and Mystery of Trees, Teresa Moorey
Magic For the Next 1,000 Years, Jack Gale
Magic of Herbs - A Complete Home Herbal, Rhiannon Ryall
Magical Guardians - Exploring the Spirit and Nature of Trees, Philip Heselton
Magical History of the Horse, Janet Farrar & Virginia Russell
Magical Lore of Animals, Yvonne Aburrow
Magical Lore of Cats, Marion Davies
Magical Lore of Herbs, Marion Davies
Magick Without Peers, Ariadne Rainbird & David Rankine
Masks of Misrule - Horned God & His Cult in Europe, Nigel Jackson
Medicine For The Coming Age, Lisa Sand MD
Medium Rare - Reminiscences of a Clairvoyant, Muriel Renard
Menopausal Woman on the Run, Jaki da Costa
Mind Massage - 60 Creative Visualisations, Marlene Maundrill
Mirrors of Magic - Evoking the Spirit of the Dewponds, P Heselton
The Moon and You, Teresa Moorey
Moon Mysteries, Jan Brodie
Mysteries of the Runes, Michael Howard
Mystic Life of Animals, Ann Walker
New Celtic Oracle The, Nigel Pennick & Nigel Jackson
Oracle of Geomancy, Nigel Pennick
Pagan Feasts - Seasonal Food for the 8 Festivals, Franklin & Phillips
Paganism For Teens, Jess Wynne
Patchwork of Magic - Living in a Pagan World, Julia Day
Pathworking - A Practical Book of Guided Meditations, Pete Jennings
Personal Power, Anna Franklin
Pickingill Papers - The Origins of Gardnerian Wicca, Bill Liddell
Pillars of Tubal Cain, Nigel Jackson
Places of Pilgrimage and Healing, Adrian Cooper
Planet Earth - The Universe's Experiment, Chris Thomas
Practical Divining, Richard Foord
Practical Meditation, Steve Hounsome
Practical Spirituality, Steve Hounsome
Psychic Self Defence - Real Solutions, Jan Brodie
Real Fairies, David Tame
Reality - How It Works & Why It Mostly Doesn't, Rik Dent
Romany Tapestry, Michael Houghton
Runic Astrology, Nigel Pennick

434

Sacred Animals, Gordon MacLellan
Sacred Celtic Animals, Marion Davies, Ill. Simon Rouse
Sacred Dorset - On the Path of the Dragon, Peter Knight
Sacred Grove - The Mysteries of the Forest, Yvonne Aburrow
Sacred Geometry, Nigel Pennick
Sacred Nature, Ancient Wisdom & Modern Meanings, A Cooper
Sacred Ring - Pagan Origins of British Folk Festivals, M. Howard
Season of Sorcery - On Becoming a Wisewoman, Poppy Palin
Seasonal Magic - Diary of a Village Witch, Paddy Slade
Secret Places of the Goddess, Philip Heselton
Secret Signs & Sigils, Nigel Pennick
The Secrets of East Anglian Magic, Nigel Pennick
A Seeker's Guide To Past Lives, Paul Williamson
Seeking Pagan Gods, Teresa Moorey
A Seer's Guide To Crystal Divination, Gale Halloran
Self Enlightenment, Mayan O'Brien
Soul Resurgence, Poppy Palin
Spirits of the Air, Jaq D Hawkins
Spirits of the Water, Jaq D Hawkins
Spirits of the Fire, Jaq D Hawkins
Spirits of the Aether, Jaq D Hawkins
Spirits of the Earth, Jaq D Hawkins
Stony Gaze, Investigating Celtic Heads John Billingsley
Stumbling Through the Undergrowth , Mark Kirwan-Heyhoe
Subterranean Kingdom, The, revised 2nd ed, Nigel Pennick
Symbols of Ancient Gods, Rhiannon Ryall
Talking to the Earth, Gordon MacLellan
Talking With Nature, Julie Hood
Taming the Wolf - Full Moon Meditations, Steve Hounsome
Teachings of the Wisewomen, Rhiannon Ryall
The Other Kingdoms Speak, Helena Hawley
Transformation of Housework, Ben Bushill
Tree: Essence of Healing, Simon & Sue Lilly
Tree: Essence, Spirit & Teacher, Simon & Sue Lilly
Tree Seer, Simon & Sue Lilly
Torch and the Spear, Patrick Regan
Understanding Chaos Magic, Jaq D Hawkins
Understanding Second Sight, Dilys Gater
Understanding Spirit Guides, Dilys Gater
Understanding Star Children, Dilys Gater
The Urban Shaman, Dilys Gater
Vortex - The End of History, Mary Russell
Warp and Weft - In Search of the I-Ching, William de Fancourt
Warriors at the Edge of Time, Jan Fry
Water Witches, Tony Steele
Way of the Magus, Michael Howard
Weaving a Web of Magic, Rhiannon Ryall

West Country Wicca, Rhiannon Ryall
What's Your Poison? vol 1, Tina Tarrant
Wheel of the Year, Teresa Moorey & Jane Brideson
Wildwitch - The Craft of the Natural Psychic, Poppy Palin
Wildwood King , Philip Kane
A Wisewoman's Book of Tea Leaf Reading, Pat Barki
The Witching Path, Moira Stirland
The Witch's Kitchen, Val Thomas
The Witches' Heart, Eileen Smith
Treading the Mill - Practical CraftWorking in Modern Traditional Witchcraft
    by Nigel Pearson
Witches of Oz, Matthew & Julia Philips
Witchcraft Myth Magic Mystery and... Not Forgetting Fairies, Ralph Harvey
Wondrous Land - The Faery Faith of Ireland by Dr Kay Mullin
Working With Crystals, Shirley o'Donoghue
Working With Natural Energy, Shirley o'Donoghue
Working With the Merlin, Geoff Hughes
Your Talking Pet, Ann Walker
The Zodiac Experience, Patricia Crowther

FREE detailed catalogue
Capall Bann Publishing, Auton Farm, Milverton, Somerset, TA4 1NE   Tel 01823 401528